International Women's Year

International Women's Year

The Greatest Consciousness-Raising Event in History

JOCELYN OLCOTT

OXFORD
UNIVERSITY PRESS

OXFORD
UNIVERSITY PRESS

Oxford University Press is a department of the University of Oxford. It furthers
the University's objective of excellence in research, scholarship, and education
by publishing worldwide. Oxford is a registered trade mark of Oxford University
Press in the UK and certain other countries.

Published in the United States of America by Oxford University Press
198 Madison Avenue, New York, NY 10016, United States of America.

Library of Congress Cataloging-in-Publication Data
Names: Olcott, Jocelyn, 1970– author.
Title: International Women's Year : the greatest consciousness-raising
event in history / Jocelyn Olcott.
Description: New York, NY : Oxford University Press, [2017] |
Includes bibliographical references and index.
Identifiers: LCCN 2017000714 (print) | LCCN 2017011786 (ebook) |
ISBN 9780199716647 (Updf) | ISBN 9780190649982 (Epub) |
ISBN 9780195327687 (hardcover : alk. paper)
Subjects: LCSH: International Women's Year, 1975. | Women's rights—History—20th century. |
Feminism—International cooperation—History—20th century. |
Women—International cooperation—History—20th century.
Classification: LCC HQ1154 (ebook) | LCC HQ1154 .O39558 2017 (print) |
DDC 305.42—dc23
LC record available at https://lccn.loc.gov/2017000714

1 3 5 7 9 8 6 4 2
Printed by Sheridan Books, Inc., United States of America

To Phoebe

CONTENTS

ACT III   LEGACIES

ACKNOWLEDGMENTS

When I first started on this project, I imagined it as a sliver of a chapter of a completely different book. As I was coming up for my tenure review, I figured I would crank out a quickie article on the IWY conference. After all, how long could it take to write about a conference that only lasted two weeks?

Over the past eight years, this project has mushroomed from a modest, one-off article into a wide-ranging reconsideration of a critical moment in 1970s feminism. At every turn, I have been inspired and humbled by the material, intellectual, and emotional support I've received. Fellowships and research support have allowed me to explore the nooks and crannies where my curiosity led me, and questions and comments from readers and patient listeners have launched new explorations.

Duke University has incubated this book in every conceivable way. Duke's support for research and scholarly inquiry extend well beyond the standard sabbaticals and research accounts (although those are hardly to be sneezed at) and funding from an Arts and Sciences Council Faculty Research Grant. It includes a deep commitment to fostering interdisciplinary conversations and investigations. The year I arrived, I participated in a seminar titled "Feminism, Transnationalism, and the International," convened through the John Hope Franklin Center for Interdisciplinary and International Studies by Robyn Wiegman, Ranji Khanna, and Tina Campt. Women's Studies (now Gender, Sexuality, and Feminist Studies) has hosted talks and working groups and pre-publication seminars that cultivate a vibrant intellectual community. Laura Micham and Kelly Wooten continue to build an astonishing resource for studying contemporary feminism at the Sallie Bingham Center for Women's History and Culture in the Rubenstein Library. The Franklin Humanities Institute and Mellon Humanities Writ Large program (both the brainchildren of the inimitable Srinivas Aravamudan) sponsored a manuscript workshop that allowed me to invite two formidable historians (Dan Rodgers and Joanne Meyerowitz), one exacting editor (Susan Ferber), and a dozen local colleagues to offer critical feedback on a complete draft.

NYU's Tamiment Library and the Center for the US and the Cold War, under the leadership of Michael Nash and Marilyn Young, supported the earliest stages of research on this project. The Tamiment is a treasure trove for historians of social movements, and the Cold War seminar offered a perfect launch pad for this project.

Two years later, Dan Rodgers invited me to join the fellows at the Shelby Cullom Davis Center at Princeton University. Under his leadership and with the ultra-competent and always friendly assistance of Jennifer Houle Goldman, fellows benefited from not only the famously engaged Davis Seminar but also more informal but equally generative weekly lunch conversations. I think it's safe to say that presenting my work to the Davis Seminar with the renowned gender historian Joan Scott as my commentator was among the most terrifying and stimulating moments of my intellectual life to date.

The National Humanities Center in North Carolina offered an idyllic setting in which to write the bulk of this book. The setting alone is enough to calm anyone's nerves, and it was not lost on me that I had time to read and write about domestic labor because the NHC staff took care of everything else—including cooking our meals and washing our coffee mugs. The librarians made good on their promise to meet every bibliographic challenge, and Brooke Andrade used her smarts and charms to obtain sources that substantially transformed my understanding of the IWY events.

None of these fellowships would be possible if not for the generous support of colleagues and mentors who wrote recommendations, often several years in a row. Many thanks to Nancy Cott, Sally Deutsch, Greg Grandin, John French, Temma Kaplan, Dan Rodgers, and Heidi Tinsman.

This project has taken me to different parts of the world for research and heightened my already considerable admiration and appreciation for the archivists and librarians who make research feasible. Their professionalism and deep knowledge of their holdings allowed me to trace connections that otherwise would have remained invisible to me. Scholars of US women's history are particularly fortunate to have the remarkable collections at the Sophia Smith Collection (Smith College), the Schlesinger Library (Radcliffe Institute for Advanced Studies), and the Sallie Bingham Center (Rubenstein Library, Duke University). The Sophia Smith Collection also supported this research with a travel grant. Beth Harris at Hollins University allowed me to work in Mildred Persinger's papers when she was still in the process of cataloguing them. Australian National University has done a magnificent job archiving the personal papers of Elizabeth Reid. Idelle Nissila-Stone went an extra mile in helping me to locate materials in the Ford Foundation Archive, which has now relocated to the beautiful (and beautifully run) Rockefeller Archive Center. Katharine French-Fuller, Damien Huffer, Taylor Jardno, and Jessica Malitoris all provided research assistance.

This book is in many ways a product of the Internet age, which has allowed researchers to track down people and organizations and to discern otherwise imperceptible patterns. Digital technologies also allow researchers to share more readily materials from their own research. Ileana Gómez, Lucy Grinnell, Ana Lau, Lisa Levenstein, Bryan Pitts, Brad Simpson, and Debbie Wright all sent me valuable documents. Mathieu Caulier gave me digital access to the many hours of interviews he had done with feminists and activists in Mexico City. Valerie Pettis, who designed the ubiquitous IWY logo and has allowed its use free of charge around the world, has shared wonderful images of its reproduction on all manner of material artifacts.

As I've worked on this book, I have been astonished by my friends' and colleagues' intellectual generosity. Literally dozens of already overcommitted people have taken time and energy away from their own worthy pursuits to read and offer feedback on all or part of this project. Among those who tried their best to help me improve the final book (but in no way should be held responsible for its failings) are Sonia Alvarez, Gabriela Cano, Dirk Bonker, Emily Burrill, Julie Byrne, Ellen Chesler, Francisca de Haan, Sally Deutsch, Kathleen DuVal, Laura Edwards, Jan French, John French, Elisabeth Jay Friedman, Jim Green, Frances Hasso, Laura Helper-Ferris, Reeve Huston, Liz Hutchison, Temma Kaplan, Shelagh Kenney, Ranji Khanna, Tom Klubock, Anna Krylova, Alice Kessler-Harris, Tom Lekan, Lisa Levenstein, Nancy MacLean, Joanne Meyerowitz, Negar Mottahedeh, Verónica Oikión, Gunther Peck, Lara Putnam, Sumathi Ramaswamy, Cara Robertson, Dan Rodgers, David Sartorius, Joan Scott, Swati Shah, Bill Sharman, Jenni Siegel, Pete Sigal, Brad Simpson, Marjorie Spruill, Rebecca Stein, Kim Stern, Phil Stern, Vanessa Taylor, Kathi Weeks, Barbara Weinstein, Ara Wilson, and several anonymous reviewers for OUP.

The project benefited tremendously from questions and comments I received from audiences at conferences and invited lectures at the American Historical Association, the Berkshires Conference on Women's History, the Latin American Studies Association, and the Organization of American Historians, as well as at Boston University, Center for the US and the Cold War (NYU/Columbia), El Colegio de Michoacán, CUNY Graduate Center, Ford Foundation, Harvard University, London School of Economics, National Humanities Center, New York City Latin American History Workshop, Newberry Library, Program in Latin American Studies at Princeton, Rutgers University, the Tepoztlán Institute for Transnational History, the University of New Mexico, University of Newcastle, Université Paris 13, the University of South Carolina, University of Texas, University of Vermont, Washington University, and Yale University.

Susan Ferber at Oxford University Press has a well-deserved reputation as the hardest-working woman in the publishing business. She saw the promise in this project when it was barely a twinkle in my eye and has offered careful, critical feedback over its many iterations. While countless historians owe Susan a tremendous debt of gratitude, our readers owe her even more. She has a peerless talent for rooting out jargon, keeping narrators on task, and weeding out overgrown prose. Susan handed the manuscript off to Maya Bringe, who expertly shepherded it through the production process.

My family has always formed a vocal and enthusiastic cheerleading squad. Neil Olcott and Nancy Dickmeyer have celebrate important milestones. Cory Olcott and Allison Mnookin and their children Hailey and Eli are always ready with encouraging words and difficult questions.

Russell Lacy has patiently talked through all the issues that arose as I researched this book and humored me as the characters became household names. He has averted his gaze when my retreats into the writing cave led to some regrettably anti-social behaviors, and he reminds me occasionally to step away from the computer screen. Most of all, he just makes everything better and every day joyful.

This book is dedicated to Phoebe, although it's really her fault that it was so long in coming. I had written a handful of carefully crafted thematic chapters, all in the analytical style that befits an academic historian, but Phoebe offered constant reminders that a good story should never go to waste. (In my defense, I have remained faithful to the historical record, which she would have found inconvenient.) Countless colleagues and mentors have helped me grapple with methodologies and analytical frameworks, but Phoebe always reminded me about characters and pacing and humor. Sadly, she did not live to see this book completed, but I'm sure she is raising a glass from a reef rock somewhere and enjoying a good yarn.

GLOSSARY OF ACRONYMS

AAAS	American Association for the Advancement of Science
AAUW	American Association of University Women
CEDAW	Convention on the Elimination of All Forms of Discrimination against Women
CERDS	Charter on the Economic Rights and Duties of States
CESI	Centre for Economic and Social Information (a UN center)
CIA	Central Intelligence Agency (United States)
CONGO	Conference of NGOs in Consultative Status with ECOSOC
CORE	Congress of Racial Equality
COYOTE	Call Off Your Old Tired Ethics (a San Francisco-based prostitutes' rights organization)
CSW	Commission on the Status of Women (a subcommittee of ECOSOC)
DAWN	Development Alternatives with Women for a New Era
DEDAW	Declaration on the Elimination of Discrimination against Women
ECOSOC	Economic and Social Council of the United Nations
ERA	Equal Rights Amendment (to the United States Constitution)
FAO	Food and Agriculture Organization (UN specialized agency)
G-77	Group of 77 (bloc of UN member states)
GA	General Assembly
GAD	Gender and Development
IAW	International Association of Women
ICW	International Council of Women
IFBPW	International Federation of Business and Professional Women
ILO	International Labor Organization (UN specialized agency)
INGO	International Non-Governmental Organization
IPPF	International Planned Parenthood Federation
IWY	International Women's Year
LDC	less-developed country (term used mostly in the US State Department)

MAS	Mujeres en Acción Solidaria (Women in Solidarity Action—Mexico)
MLM	Movimiento de Liberación de la Mujer (Women's Liberation Movement—Mexico)
MNM	Movimiento Nacional de Mujeres (National Women's Movement—Mexico)
NAC	National Advisory Committee (Australia)
NAM	Non-Aligned Movement
NGO	Non-Governmental Organization
NCNW	National Council of Negro Women
NIEO	New International Economic Order
NOW	National Organization for Women (United States)
NWICO	New World Information and Communication Order
OPEC	Organization of Petroleum Exporting Countries
PAN	Partido de Acción Nacional (National Action Party—Mexico)
PLO	Palestinian Liberation Organization
PRI	Partido Revolucionario Institucional (Institutional Revolutionary Party Mexico)
UNA	United Nations Association
UNAA	United Nations Association, Australia
UNCTAD	United Nations Conference on Trade and Development
UNDP	United Nations Development Programme
UNEC	United Nations Economic Committee (inter-agency committee of the executive branch of the US government)
UNESCO	United Nations Educational, Scientific, and Cultural Organization
UNFPA	United Nations Fund for Population Activities
UNGA	United Nations General Assembly
UNMM	Unión Nacional de Mujeres Mexicanas (National Union of Mexican Women)
USAID	United States Agency for International Development
USIA	United States Information Agency
UU	Unitarian Universalist Church
WCIWY	World Conference for IWY
WEL	Women's Electoral Lobby (Australia)
WEO	Western European and Others (bloc of UN member states)
WFUNA	World Federation of United Nations Associations
WHO	World Health Organization (UN specialized agency)
WID	Women in Development
WIDF	Women's International Democratic Federation
WILPF	Women's International League for Peace and Freedom
WIN	Women's International Network
WINGO	Women's International NGO
WOI	Women's Organization of Iran
WYWCA	World Young Women's Christian Association

DRAMATIS PERSONAE

Shahnaz Alami—WIDF leader who originally proposed International Women's Year and shepherded it through the CSW in 1972

Elinor Barber—Ford Foundation program officer

Domitila Barrios de Chungara—leader of the Housewives' Committee of the Siglo XX Tin Miners' Union (Bolivia)

Laurie Bebbington—leader of Australian Student Union

Marcia-Ximena Bravo—executive director of the IWY NGO tribune in Mexico City

Esperanza Brito de Martí—leader of the Movimiento Nacional de Mujeres (National Women's Movement—Mexico)

Margaret Bruce—Deputy-Secretary-General to Helvi Sipilä

Nancy Cárdenas—Mexican dramaturg and leading activist for gay and lesbian rights

Julie Dahlitz—leader of the UNAA

Luis Echeverría—President of Mexico

Betty Friedan—leading US feminist; founder of NOW

Adrienne Germain—Ford Foundation program officer

Aída González Martínez—Deputy Director, International Organizations Division, Mexican Ministry of Foreign Relations

Rosalind Harris—President of CONGO

Snowden Herrick—Deputy Director, CESI who organized the journalists' encounter

Esther Hymer—chair of CONGO subcommittee on women and development that became the IWY committee; representative of the International Federation of Business and Professional Women

Devaki Jain—Indian development economist

Annie Jiagge—Guinean Supreme Court justice

John Jova—US ambassador to Mexico

Susan Jane Kedgley—staffer in UN Secretariat

Mildred Marcy—US Information Agency officer working in State Department on IWY

Pedro Ojeda Paullada—Mexican Attorney General, coordinator of Mexico's IWY Program

Ashraf Pahlavi (Princess Ashraf)—twin sister of Shah of Iran; principal IWY sponsor

Marjorie Paxson—editor of *Xilonen*

Mildred Persinger—chair of IWY NGO tribune organizing committee, a subset of Hymer's committee

Elizabeth Reid—advisor on women's issues to Australian Prime Minister Gough Whitlam

John Scali—US ambassador to the United Nations

Mary Craig Schuller-McGeachy—former president of the ICW

Helvi Sipilä—first woman named as UN Assistant Secretary-General; Secretary-General of IWY as well as the IWY conference

Zohreh (ZuZu) Tabatabai—staffer at Iranian mission to the UN

International Women's Year

Introduction

Two images linger from the first United Nations (UN) world conference of women—one visual and one textual. Both of them tell lies. Both of them also tell truths.

The first comes from a moment ten days into the two-week conference. The Associated Press wire service sent around the world a photograph of two women in hand-to-hand combat over a microphone, creating the regrettable image of a "global catfight" just as feminists labored to demonstrate that women could rally around a shared political program.[1] The episode occurred on a Friday; the image accompanied any media coverage of the conference all weekend. Cropped to heighten the sense of conflict and captioned to imply that it represented official delegates at the government conference rather than activists at the accompanying non-governmental organization (NGO) tribune, the photo was the most widely circulated image of the 1975 International Women's Year (IWY) gatherings in Mexico City, perhaps because it captured the fracas that many reporters had anticipated even before the conference opened.

Organizers scrambled to counter the photo's impact, arranging a press conference for the following Monday that they dubbed the "unity panel," the moment that generated the second and even more enduring image of the IWY events. Activists and journalists crowded into the smaller of the two auditoriums in Mexico City's Centro Médico for what the session's organizers hoped would demonstrate to the press corps—and, through them, to the world—that women could overcome whatever differences might divide them to join together and fight to improve women's conditions around the world. Countless studies had shown, after all, that no matter what their circumstances, women were worse off than their male counterparts: they had poorer diets, labored more hours and in greater drudgery, enjoyed fewer rights, earned less income, had fewer educational and career opportunities, had lower literacy rates, and possessed less social and cultural freedom. Surely, the press conference organizers believed, women could agree on a basic set of priorities to improve their lot in life. Almost immediately, however, the unity panel exploded into what one journalist described as

Figure I.1   AP photo as cropped for *New York Times,* June 29, 1975, and captioned, "Two delegates from Latin America fighting over the microphone at International Women's Year conference in Mexico City on Friday. The dispute was part of a protest by Latin women, who felt their views had been overlooked."

a "verbal brawl" that would become IWY's most frequently recalled image. Amid chants of "Domitila, Domitila, Domitila!," Domitila Barrios de Chungara—stocky, humbly dressed, and nearly toothless from a beating she had taken during a recent arrest—leaned into the microphone and asked, "How can we speak of equality among women? . . . We can't speak of equality between games of canasta. Women cannot be equals any more than poor and rich countries."[2]

Domitila, as everyone called the Bolivian tin miner's wife, had first drawn attention in Mexico City five days earlier during a marathon tribune session titled "Women against Imperialism," where activists from Chile, Puerto Rico, Guatemala, the American Indian Movement, and the Palestinian Liberation Organization lambasted US policies and decried multinational corporations' power to dominate Third World economies.[3] By the time conflicts erupted again two days later over who might represent the NGO tribune to the UN's intergovernmental conference, Domitila had emerged as the standard-bearer of a dissident faction.

Figure I.2 Adriana Puiggrós and Antonieta Rascón compete for the microphone at the NGO tribune of the International Women's Year conference. Courtesy of Associated Press.

On the esplanade outside the NGO tribune where the unity panel took place, amid musicians and dancing, Ukrainian dissidents staged a hunger strike to protest Soviet detentions of political prisoners while tribune-goers milled, concocting plans for the coming days and the coming months. Across town at the Ministry of Foreign Relations, official government delegates to the UN conference considered seventy different resolutions that morning on issues ranging from prostitution to pensions to Palestine. The unity panel's organizers hoped to put aside policy debates and focus on what they considered properly in the domain of women's issues—or at least to demonstrate that for the duration of one press conference a diverse group of women could show solidarity. Domitila stepped up to the microphone to remind them that solidarity and unity required drawing boundaries that left some people on the outside looking in. She described women on her Housewives' Committee worrying over how to feed their children, watching their husbands cough up blood after contracting silicosis, and fretting over where they would live if their husbands got any sicker or died, leaving them ninety days to vacate drafty, company-supplied shacks. "What can you possibly understand about all that?" she recalled asking the well-heeled crowd of several thousand. "For you, the solution is fighting with men. And that's it. But for us it isn't that way, that isn't the basic solution."[4]

Scholars and activists widely allow this episode to stand in for the entire IWY conference and portray it as a showdown between US feminist Betty

Friedan—representing First World, liberal, white feminism—and Domitila Barrios de Chungara—symbolizing Third World, militant, non-white Marxism.[5] *Let Me Speak!*, Domitila's testimonial memoir of life in a Bolivian tin-mining community—of labor protests amid military dictatorship, of being beaten in prison while eight months pregnant, of debating and cajoling her husband to allow her to join the deceptively domestic-sounding Housewives' Committee, all framed by her alienation in Mexico City—became a canonical account of the challenges of forging solidarity among women across lines of class, color, and ideology.[6] Narrating her experience at the NGO tribune, Domitila briefly described a "discussion" with Friedan but then related at length the real clash that appeared in the pages of Mexico City newspapers and the secret police accounts: her confrontation at the unity panel with Mexican feminist Esperanza Brito de Martí.

So, why is Domitila's tirade remembered as being directed at Betty Friedan, and Esperanza Brito is nowhere to be seen? The substitution reflects, in part, the power of reiteration: the encounter has been retold so many times that it is now presumed to be true.[7] Perhaps the story simply changed as it passed from one person to another. But the part that stuck was this image of a fictional showdown.

In many ways, the substitution makes sense. Particularly for an Anglophone audience, the mere mention of Friedan's name allows readers to conjure a caricature of the brash National Organization for Women (NOW) leader presuming to speak for global feminism. She arguably was the US analogue for Brito, a magazine writer who had helped to organize the Movimiento Nacional de Mujeres (MNM, National Women's Movement), a reformist organization similar to NOW with detractors on both the left and the right. Like NOW, Brito's MNM made abortion rights and reproductive freedom more generally—"voluntary motherhood," as the placards and T-shirts demanded—a top priority. In many ways, however, Friedan was closer to Domitila on many issues than she was to Brito. Like Domitila, Friedan had come from a labor-union background and named as one of her chief complaints the onerous, unpaid, disrespected grind of keeping households running from day to day.[8]

This retrospective reimagining of Domitila's confrontation at the NGO tribune reveals less about the conference itself than about shared aspirations for social justice that might be fulfilled by a critical assessment of the past. Perhaps the most striking mischaracterization of the Mexico City conference was that it ignored issues of racial discrimination, economic marginality, and geopolitical inequalities. To the contrary, IWY showcased the intense debates under way about how best to combat these ills. Taking place amid cresting waves of decolonization and a wholesale reexamination of prevailing development models, the IWY events—including the UN's intergovernmental conference of member states and the parallel NGO tribune as well as a pre-conference seminar on development and an "encounter" for Third World journalists—closely attended to these concerns. Further, the meetings fostered some of the most important and enduring UN programs, moving women from the periphery to the center of development projects, establishing research centers and credit programs, and fostering activist networks that would expand exponentially over the next two decades.

The most disconcerting piece of received wisdom about the 1975 Mexico City conference is the idea—captured in the AP photo and in the oft-repeated apocrypha about Domitila Barrios de Chungara and Betty Friedan—that although IWY marked a critical turning point, it failed in its objectives because it ended in disunity and because First World women failed to listen to Third World women or because Third World participants ambushed First World participants. Most accounts compare Mexico City unfavorably to the subsequent UN women's conferences, particularly Nairobi (1985) and Beijing (1995).

The evidence from Mexico City demonstrates that disunity was, in fact, an achievement of IWY and that it was accomplished precisely because First World women finally did listen closely to Third World women. They mostly listened to cosmopolitan women like the Ghanaian Supreme Court justice Annie Jiagge and the Indian economist Devaki Jain and the Colombian senator turned UNESCO consultant Esmeralda Arboleda de Cuevas rather than to more unworldly women like Domitila, but these exchanges still left an indelible imprint. The gatherings in Mexico City—from the opening meeting of the development seminar to the NGO tribune to the closing session of the post-conference journalism workshop—had been designed precisely to encourage First World participants to listen to Third World participants. Indeed, forcing these encounters had been the highest priority for everyone involved in organizing these events, and participants consistently reported encounters across divides of ideology, experience, and geopolitics as the most significant aspect of the IWY gatherings.

This book considers how an event that might have been a parade of bureaucrats, talking heads, and garden parties instead became the launch pad for an array of global feminisms. The answer lies to a great extent in this cultivation of disunity, which came about because key players took the risk of inviting chaos and conflict. Throughout the planning and execution of IWY events, an inverse correlation became evident: the less controlled, managed, and scripted a gathering, the more likely it was to become memorable and generative—of new friendships and networks, of new policies and practices, and of new institutions and structures. The UN and its affiliated NGOs provided indispensable structure and resources to enable these encounters, but their success depended upon relinquishing control once they had started.

In mid-June 1975, thousands of reporters, diplomats, policy wonks, social reformers, grassroots activists, and curious onlookers converged on Mexico City for what organizers and journalists alike billed as the "greatest consciousness-raising event in history," the UN's International Women's Year conference.[9] Although women from the popular classes were badly underrepresented, the gathering drew an all-star cast of prominent women intellectuals, activists, and political leaders from around the world—Friedan and Australian feminist Germaine Greer; international icons such as the Soviet cosmonaut Valentina Tereshkova and the Iranian Shah's twin sister, Princess Ashraf Pahlavi; first ladies, including Egypt's Jehan Sadat and her Israeli counterpart Leah Rabin; and prominent stateswomen, including Sri Lankan Prime Minister Sirimavo Bandaranaike and US Congresswoman Bella Abzug. As the Juan de la Barrera Gymnasium filled for the inaugural ceremony, reporters and participants marveled at the visual novelty of the sea of women in saris, kaftans, huipiles, and European-style suits—an image that signaled both the unprecedented diversity of attendees and the unusual focus on women's status.

By 1975, women's organizations and movements around the world had begun to gather in large and small groups around a wide variety of issues. Some joined larger struggles against discrimination or colonial domination, others fought for reproductive autonomy or educational opportunities, still others tried to gain access to health clinics and potable water or to contain the effects of wars and ethnic conflicts. These groups resembled one another in important ways: they were overwhelmingly headquartered in urban areas and both led and populated by educated, cosmopolitan women who had encountered women's activism—often in the form of women's liberation movements—during studies or travel abroad. Still, ideas picked up in New York or London or Paris, for example, took on new meanings as they made their way to Delhi or Accra or São Paulo. Reproductive rights, for example, carried different implications among women who campaigned for access to contraception and abortion than among those who resisted UN- and US-sponsored population-control policies.

This proliferating diversity of women's concerns fueled the impetus to consolidate them under the umbrella of "women's issues" but unsettled celebrations of "global sisterhood," "herstory," and essentialist ideas about a universal female subject. The decision to hold a world conference on "women's issues" raised the question of what those issues entailed and the extent to which they could be extricated from the larger tangle of social, economic, and political concerns. While the proclamation of IWY as a UN theme year fostered a host of local and regional conferences, often with a particular focus such as prostitution or handicrafts production or media representation, a global conference called for a unified agenda that would weave together diverse and even competing concerns.

Women's movements were not the only entities in flux in 1975. In the space of a generation, seemingly everything had changed. Former colonies had become new nations. Vietnam had become a quagmire, then an icon of US militarism, and then an exemplar of successful anti-imperialist struggle. Liberation movements of all kinds—racial, ethnic, and national—had fragmented and proliferated. Watergate and countless revelations of official abuse of power around the world had badly eroded public confidence in governments. The 1973 oil embargo highlighted the vulnerability of commodities markets to geopolitical conflicts. At every scale, from the individual to the global, the world seemed on the brink of radical transformation as decolonization came to refer not only to national self-rule but also to personal emancipation. The IWY conference brought together activists who saw the personal as political with UN leaders who organized the world into national interests and regional blocs.

These ongoing transformations were dramatically showcased at the UN General Assembly (GA), whose membership had ballooned with the addition of scores of recently decolonized countries. Two decades after the 1955 Bandung Conference had brought together a group of Asian and African countries pledging to remain neutral amid the Cold War, the Non-Aligned Movement (NAM) countries had taken control of the GA.[10] The formation of the NAM was always closely linked to the UN's ideals; the first principle of membership was to uphold the UN Charter. In 1964, three years after the NAM was formally established, the Group of 77 (G-77) formed during the founding meeting of the United Nations Conference on Trade and Development, fashioning itself as a UN bloc that mapped closely to the Third World countries that comprised the NAM. The G-77 and NAM remained distinct entities but generally acted in concert.[11]

The combination of Cold War rivalries—including not only the US-Soviet enmity but also the Sino-Soviet clash and the G-77's growing antagonism toward industrialized nations—created an opening for mid-level powers that lacked the resources to make a comprehensive diplomatic effort and often selected issues on which to focus their attention. The International Women's Year offered such an opportunity for three important mid-level powers in 1975: Australia, Mexico, and Iran. Diplomats from these three countries took leading roles in the promotion of women's rights as a means to elevate their countries' geopolitical status and to create openings for further negotiation on other issues. That the issue of women's rights offered that opportunity reflects the strength of those countries' women's movements.

Beginning in 1968, the GA focused its energies on a series of thematic conferences on what were generally deemed "soft" issues related principally to economic and social justice rather than security and peacekeeping.[12] In 1972, Stockholm had hosted a conference on the environment, and 1974 brought two major conferences: one in Bucharest on population and another in Rome on food. Marking the rise of civil-society organizations during this period, these conferences had held parallel NGO gatherings that would serve as models for the IWY tribune in Mexico City.[13] These thematic conferences highlighted the ways in which the UN and its agencies serve as sites of knowledge production, dividing the world into regions to collect and analyze data according to those regions and to categories the UN itself sanctions. By the early 1970s, the very concepts of knowledge and expertise were under fire—not least from feminists who saw claims to expertise as efforts to exclude women by discounting local and experiential knowledge.[14] In Mexico City, the NGO tribune highlighted professionals from a broad range of fields but also explicitly honored lived experience as a form of expertise. The questions that dominated the GA sessions—apartheid, Palestine, economic justice—all drew considerable notice in Mexico City but competed for attention with discussions of domestic labor, sex work, and health care.

The IWY conference's structure and agenda also reflected the changing nature and understanding of civil society as UN conferences grew from technical meetings of specialists into more action-oriented meetings intended to draw media attention and galvanize policymakers.[15] Taking place amid the UN-declared Second Decade for Development, IWY attracted strong participation from civil-society groups, ranging broadly from white-glove voluntarist organizations to radical liberation movements. This expanded participation raised the question of who could stand in for the interests of a given group and what groups might be considered worthy of representation. After all, participants understood representation in a wide variety of ways, whether through religion, class, generation, political party, or demographic designations such as race or ethnicity; salient categories depended principally on the social and political contexts in their home communities.

As at all UN gatherings, delegations represented member states, generally assumed to share something imagined as a national interest—a claim that many participants challenged. Particularly for participants from recently decolonized states, hard-won national identifications were worn with pride. These national identifications elide the fact that many of them came from the ranks of postcolonial cosmopolitans—women and men from relatively privileged backgrounds who attended Western universities and may have spent little time as adults in their native countries before going to work in the diplomatic corps or a branch of the UN.[16] Some ended up in Mexico City because of particular experience or expertise; many went because they were members of a ruling family or political party. At the NGO tribune, which operated on an even skimpier budget than the government conference, longtime residents of the United States were asked to offer perspectives of their home countries in Africa or South Asia or Latin America. Many participants had come of age in Cold War hotspots such as Guatemala, Angola, and Vietnam that became bloody proxy sites for the US-Soviet conflict; they carried these experiences with them as well.[17]

The perception that Third World women were ignored or—as one participant recalled—that Mexico City was "overrun with North Americans" seems
to reflect less an empirical reality than the frustration that many participants
felt from missed connections and failed identifications.[18] Domitila recalled that
when she arrived at the NGO tribune, she expected to find "people like me . . .
people with similar problems, you know, poor people."[19] Instead, she found
women like Esperanza Brito and, of course, Betty Friedan. Participants experienced many such missed connections: Chicanas snubbed by Mexicans, a young
African American activist shut down by a veteran African American activist,
Allende supporters seeking an ally in the Chilean tribune director, Friedan hoping that if she could only sit next to a Chinese delegate "some woman-to-woman
things would get across."[20] Their frustration speaks to the fantasy that with the
right mix all participants would feel duly represented.[21]

The eagerness with which participants pursued these connections raises the
question of what they hoped to find in them. Partly they sought the grounds for
solidarity and allies in the struggles that inevitably lay ahead. They also sought to
establish the grounds of representation by establishing the salience of particular
social categories, whether "poor people" or "woman-to-woman." Identifications
did not necessarily follow color lines or nationalities, and they sometimes
emerged in unexpected ways—between two people who happened to sit next
to one another in a tribune session or to stand in line together waiting for boxed
lunches or to encounter one another in the loggia of the Centro Médico, where,
as development expert Irene Tinker recalled, "participants readily met, yelled,
or rested."[22]

Describing the event as a global consciousness-raising session invoked the
discourse of 1970s US feminism and gestured to the multiplying numbers of
grassroots activist groups that challenged the established NGOs that had collaborated with the UN since its earliest days and with the League of Nations before
that. Feminists from the United States, in particular, saw themselves as leading
this disruptive charge, specifying not only what counted as legitimate feminism
but also the path to feminist consciousness and policies: consciousness-raising
groups led to organizing led to demonstrations led to policy changes.[23] As the
Seattle-based feminist labor activist Maxine Reigel asserted in a widely reprinted
column, "Women in less developed countries will follow the leadership of more
advanced movements."[24] Many US feminists, including NOW president Karen
DeCrow, saw a pressing need to ensure that feminist perspectives received a
hearing in Mexico City, but for many Third World women, US feminists had
simply articulated their own version of modernization theory—one in which
women would follow a Western-determined path from tradition to modernity.

By 1975, a Third World critique of modernization narratives had taken hold
in the form of dependency theory; many participants in the IWY deliberations

expressed suspicions about the promise of feminist modernity and refused the label of "feminist" for themselves. Dependency theory framed underdevelopment not as an early stage on the path to modernization but rather as part of an extractive model in which underdeveloped countries remained poor precisely so that industrialized countries could remain wealthy. Andre Gunder Frank, the German economic historian who shaped economic reforms in Salvador Allende's socialist Chile, argued that as capitalist ideologies and market logics "effectively and entirely penetrated even the apparently most isolated sectors of the underdeveloped world," the metropolitan powers drained wealth from neo-colonial satellites.[25] The creation of new industrialized metropoles in places like São Paulo or Delhi would only further immiserate their provincial dependencies. This zero-sum logic of dependency theory shaped countless interactions at the UN conferences of the early 1970s on the environment, population control, and food shortage. In these venues, First World and Third World concerns competed directly. If modernization theory imagined a linear process of women's emancipation—starting with literacy programs and birth control and leading over time to the executive office suite—dependency theory imagined that population-control and environmental-protection programs existed principally to ensure that poor countries remained poor.

The *dependistas* ignored the fact that much feminist thought posed a more thoroughgoing challenge to prevailing capitalist models than dependency theory did. In these early days of what came to be known as neoliberalism, feminist economists such as Ester Boserup challenged the premise that conventional development schemes would cure all or even make life better for women.[26] Repeatedly during IWY planning, feminists such as the Australian Elizabeth Reid pointed out that UN economic data simply did not count vast amounts of women's uncommodified labor. While liberal development programs sought to incorporate women into the paid workforce, others wondered who would perform the subsistence labor that went uncounted but remained necessary every single day.

In this context, the IWY organizers' aspiration that the conference would attend to "women's issues" unadulterated by "politics" seems hopelessly—perhaps even willfully—naïve. The very session when the GA would vote on the IWY conference also included a historic visit by the Palestine Liberation Organization (PLO) leader Yasser Arafat, an episode that put the UN headquarters and its environs in virtual lockdown. This unlikely juxtaposition of consciousness-raising—that quintessential feminist practice of the moment—with Arafat, the figure who personified the minefield of international politics, distilled the central conundrum of the International Women's Year conference: what was the relationship between women's status and geopolitics? Participants and organizers from a dizzying array of backgrounds and convictions insisted upon focusing the agenda on what they deemed women's issues to be during the precious days of the IWY conference. Yet they varied widely on where "women's issues" left off and "politics" began. At least from the US State Department's perspective, "politicization" signaled a challenge to US interests beyond the "standard 'noise level' of politics which is found in all international gatherings."[27] Politics, many agreed, should be left at the conference hall door. Otherwise, the specter of Arafat would eclipse the insights of consciousness-raising.

This dispute about the relationship between politics and women's issues did not stem, as some organizers and participants asserted, from a desire to discredit or undermine the IWY efforts. But for many participants the idea that women's issues or anything else existed outside of politics would be like expecting to live outside of gravity: the pull of politics acted on everything. Even seemingly innocent issues led to political debates. Many background papers and news stories, for example, stressed the problem of women's literacy rates, which tended to lag behind men's and in many Third World countries remained quite low. Women's literacy seemed to many IWY supporters like a critical and progressive metric of development and the extent to which it benefited women in a given society. But it also disregarded non-literate forms of knowledge production and dissemination—the oral traditions commonly shared among women—and generally was measured only in the national language, in many countries the language of an imperial power. Literacy in Mexico was measured by ability to read and write in Spanish—not Tztozil or Zapotec or Purépecha—so large swaths of the population who read and wrote only indigenous languages were deemed illiterate.[28] So even this seemingly innocuous and widely shared metric of women's progress carried its own ideological baggage.

More conspicuously, the debate over politics and women's issues often assumed that some gains could be made only at the expense of others. In IWY terms, the themes of equality and development were imagined in opposition to one another. Demands for women's reproductive and sexual rights were cast as cultural imperialism and mutually exclusive with human rights and economic justice. The US and Mexican press alike expressed open disdain for women who would worry about career opportunities or lesbian rights when so many women struggled daily to supply their families with adequate food, water, and shelter. Feminist arguments about patriarchy—that women's exploitation resulted from men controlling every space from the bedroom to the UN Secretariat—were dismissed as distractions from class struggle and national liberation. The subject conjured later by decolonial feminists—the anti-racist, anti-imperialist, anti-capitalist, pro-sex feminist—remained impossible in this formulation: one could not simultaneously be anti-imperialist and pro-sex.[29]

The Mexico City gatherings arguably offer as close to an experiment as most historians can find for testing the impact of disorder. The two principal events—a government conference of instructed delegations and an open NGO tribune—allow a comparison of their historical importance. At least in the world of feminist thought and women's activism, the NGO tribune has had the more enduring and far-reaching impact. Indeed, there was a close correspondence between the looseness of the event and the longevity of the resulting ideas. Despite the futility of scorekeeping on such a contest, IWY seems to have chalked one up for disorder while also highlighting the critical role the UN has come to play in providing the venue and the infrastructure to stage that disorder. The NGO tribune exploded the idea that feminism or even womanhood had a fixed meaning, but it generated a far-reaching, decentered movement made possible, as UN veteran Margaret Snyder explains, "by co-opting the UN as their unlikely godmother."[30] In short, the free-wheeling, chaotic friction of NGO gatherings—what the *New York Times* described as "the scene of much shouting, scheming, plotting, and general hell-raising"—made the bigger splash, but they were only possible because of the structure, resources, and legitimacy that came with the UN conferences.[31]

The fact that the conference took place in Mexico—in Mexico City, in the very spaces haunted by both its colonial past and recent episodes of state repression and popular resistance—informed the tenor of the debates and offered material reminders of their stakes. The Mexican political elite, particularly its ambitious President Luis Echeverría facing his final year in office, fashioned the country as a regional and even global leader, poised to take the reins of the Non-Aligned Movement. Echeverría often consciously framed conflicts in terms of national and regional interests rather than countenancing Mexico's stubborn inequalities.[32] US feminists would describe it as the most macho country on earth, an unmeasurable characteristic that nonetheless demonstrates how the social and cultural milieu informed participants' expectations.[33]

Participants bring to conferences their own narratives and meaning-making experiences—understandings shaped by personal and collective histories, by performances and expressions of identities, and by diverse conceptions of the pacing and time horizons for social change.[34] Unlike the three subsequent UN women's conferences in Copenhagen (1980), Nairobi, and Beijing, IWY participants had no scripts to work from and were uncertain about the objectives. The gestures that constituted a performance of progressive or leftist politics varied as much as the performances of feminism and femininity. The accelerated, revolutionary time of national liberation movements collided with the methodical, reformist time of UN functionaries. The progressive time of development programs encountered the cyclical time of domestic labor. The UN had its own calendar of sessions and special sessions that shaped the imperatives of airing certain issues ahead of others. Many of the US-based organizers still had ringing in their ears Martin Luther King Jr.'s "fierce urgency of now" and his warnings against the "tranquilizing drug of gradualism"; many also would have been steeped in the stubborn futurity of modernization theory and capitalist invest-ment. Given the challenges of organizing the Mexico City conference, many par-ticipants suspected that this might be their only opportunity to have their views heard. Organizers hoped to hold subsequent conferences but had barely pulled off the Mexico City conference logistically and financially; participants could not presume they would attend another such forum in the future. For Domitila Barrios de Chungara it seemed to offer a once-in-a-lifetime opportunity to tell the world about atrocities committed in her corner of Bolivia. Interactions under these conditions of urgency and novelty took on an intensity rarely seen in UN conferences.

Reconstructing the story of the 1975 IWY gatherings brings in all their con-flict and messiness. The actions and interactions of participants such as Betty Friedan and Domitila Barrios de Chungara drew from experiences in their home communities as well as in the broader world and in the hallways and meeting rooms of the Centro Médico. Although both Domitila's influential *testimonio* and Friedan's suspense-driven account of IWY elide ambivalences and ambigui-ties, their stances take on more nuanced meanings within the context of the IWY events. This book explores how and why they fashioned dichotomies and carica-tures out of the complexity and chaos that appears in the documentary record. Why, for example, does Domitila insist upon setting up sexual rights in opposi-tion to human rights and see feminism as antagonistic to economic justice? Why does Friedan insinuate that anyone who opposed the "unity" program must have been manipulated by men? And why have scholars and activists so readily ac-cepted these representations?

Uncertainty is a persistent element in the story of IWY. Were the Ukrainian hunger strikers really Ukrainian or even really hunger striking? Were they paid by the Central Intelligence Agency (CIA)? Was Gloria Steinem, as the Redstockings charged in their notorious press release? Accusations that demonstrators or boosters were simply paid for their services—a practice not uncommon in Mexican politics—arose repeatedly. Accounts by several US feminists indicate that anyone who challenged them must have been paid off or duped or suffered false consciousness—what else, after all, could possibly explain the disagree-ment?[35] Beleaguered delegations from Chile and Israel claimed the charges against them were pure fabrications. In many ways the entire UN system rested upon fictions—and not simply because some components that claimed to be disinterested bureaucratic entities in reality fronted for discrete sets of interests. The General Assembly served a gatekeeping function but operated more as a forum for expressing competing ideals than as a deliberative, decision-making body. The tightly controlled Security Council ruled on peacekeeping interven-tions and all forms of sanctions, leaving the GA as more of a stage performance of global governance.

For cosmopolitan women and men from all over the world, the UN seemed to hold out the possibility of fulfilling their hopes for a world where geopolitical boundaries carried less meaning, even as everything about the institution rein-scribed nationalism. The US State Department operated in a fantasy world of its own in which extensive intelligence reports kept it in the know about allies and adversaries alike. The NGO tribune was meant to be autonomous from govern-ment intervention, but it was funded almost entirely by the State Department–allied Ford and Rockefeller foundations, and State Department personnel clearly expected the tribune organizer to coordinate with its message.[36] "This shadow war of secret funding and Potemkin NGOs," observes historian Mark Mazower of covert CIA and Soviet front organizations, "raised the question whether a genuinely autonomous NGO was even possible in the Cold War."[37] Many of those who participated in the NGO tribune were selected and funded by their home governments, often to represent state-affiliated women's organi-zations or labor unions; many panelists were also public functionaries. The diffi-culty of understanding what any given participant "stood for" when she stepped up to the microphone compounds the difficulty of interpreting these encounters in any formulaic manner.

This telling of IWY unfolds in three acts. The first act examines how the year came into being, how it came to include the Mexico City conference, and how the conference emerged as its signal moment. Every form of politics from in-dividual ambition to geopolitics shaped these developments. Because funding remained scarce, those with deep pockets—whether governments, foundations, or individuals—had outsized influence, but dedicated activists had a say as well. Women's organizations of all stripes had proliferated around the world. Some of them grew out of civil society; others, particularly in Eastern bloc and postcolo-nial nations, emerged from government agencies; most had a hybrid relationship to states, accepting public funds but keeping officials at arm's length. The coun-tries whose organizations played prominent roles in IWY—not only the United States but also Iran, Mexico, and Australia—exemplify the range of relationships between women's organizations and governments in the 1970s.

By the time IWY came about, several decades of national and social libera-tion movements had substantially diversified actors involved in decision mak-ing and knowledge production. More women had reached professional ranks in governments, foundations, and the UN itself, raising new questions and making new demands. Some of these women self-identified as feminists and cultivated a thoroughgoing critique of the power structures that they fought to join. The International Women's Year drew not only well-educated profes-sional women from around the world but also those for whom the UN symbol-ized a promise rather than a massive international bureaucracy. Particularly for women of the generation that had lived through World War II, many of them

Jewish émigrées who had narrowly survived the Holocaust, the UN stood for the institutional instantiation of the guarantee "never again." Divides of generation, ideology, and experience among the IWY supporters became evident well before they arrived in Mexico City, generating tensions throughout the planning process.

The second act recounts what happened after these players arrived in Mexico, particularly those events that exploded most dramatically or left the most enduring impact. The relationship between the intergovernmental conference and the NGO tribune reflected the complex relationship between states and civil societies in practice. Even those who considered themselves private sector actors could never fully extricate themselves from the diplomatic priorities and assumptions of their home governments. The interactions between the two forums also demonstrated that the NGO tribune benefited from the structured nature of the government conference, and the conference derived energy from the dynamism and entropy of the tribune.

The actors are important in this drama: women like Domitila Barrios de Chungara and Elizabeth Reid substantially altered the conversation in Mexico City and were, in turn, catapulted into international recognition. The media also became characters in this story, and not simply because "mass communications media" had become an important battleground for those looking to improve women's status. The Spanish- and English-language coverage of events often diverged sharply, creating two discrete publics and distinct understandings of what had taken place. Language itself underscored both literal and metaphorical problems of translation. Language practices, particularly sex-specific usage, became areas of contention, along with words such as sexism and Zionism.

The third act examines IWY's legacies, both immediate and long term. Several conferences followed IWY and created a repertoire from which transnational organizations drew later. Many ideas that burgeoned in Mexico City—such as women's microcredit and a new role for NGOs—have remained important but have taken several twists and turns over the decades. Most important, IWY fostered friendships and networks, many of them forged in struggle, that reshaped the landscape of feminisms around the world.

What follows, then, is a thoroughgoing reconsideration of the moment that many scholars and activists see as marking a new era in feminism and women's activism—a moment after which women would see their concerns as linked to a larger web of global issues and after which global policymakers could no longer ignore women. It is a story about how the subject of "women" was disintegrating even at one of its most conspicuous moments of reification—the first-ever world conference of women. It is a story about why "women's issues" have never fallen outside the scope of politics—formal and informal, local and global. It is a story about people looking at the world from what appeared to be the brink of revolution and trying to imagine their places in a world made anew. And it is a story of unintended consequences—about how an effort to devise a clear, coherent "World Plan of Action" incubated and finally unleashed an unpredictable, incoherent, yet further-reaching and more enduring movement without boundaries or borders.

ACT I

INTERNATIONAL WOMEN'S YEAR DESERVES NO LESS

Scene 1

WINGO Politics

International Women's Year was born of the Cold War, fostered by feminism, and adopted somewhat reluctantly by the United Nations. At the 1972 session of the UN's Commission on the Status of Women (CSW), the Eastern bloc-oriented Women's International Democratic Federation (WIDF) convinced a group of delegates to introduce a resolution calling on the General Assembly to proclaim 1975 as International Women's Year.[1] The Romanian delegation initiated the resolution, and the Finnish representative Helvi Sipilä quickly seconded it, pointing to the recent success of other thematic years on human rights, racism, and education. The resolution noted that in its twenty-five years of existence the commission had never taken stock of its achievements. By all accounts the CSW, while hardly immune from geopolitical rivalries, cooperated more than other UN bodies; if there was any rancor over the IWY proposal, it went unreported by the commission, which noted only unanimous support accompanied by various suggestions for a title.[2]

Although détente had softened Cold War enmities a bit by the 1970s, it could not reverse decades-long antagonisms held by those who had developed a chess player's apprehension of an opponent's every move. Perhaps no one was more leery of the WIDF's proposal than the patrician and cosmopolitan Mary Craig Schuller-McGeachy, who had only recently and narrowly defeated Sipilä to serve her third term as the president of the International Council of Women (ICW). Schuller-McGeachy had assumed the ICW presidency in 1963 as the "Western personification of the ICW in Cold War terms," according to her biographer, and her antipathy toward the WIDF ran deep.[3] Founded in 1888 by Susan B. Anthony and other US suffragists, the ICW claimed the title of the first international NGO dedicated exclusively to women's issues—what political scientists playfully dubbed a WINGO.[4] The WIDF was a relative newcomer to this field, founded in 1945. With the horror of Hiroshima and Nagasaki still fresh, the WIDF's socialist founders concentrated on disarmament and decolonization as vital to women's freedom from violence and discrimination.

In 1947, when the UN's Economic and Social Council (ECOSOC) created the consultative-status categories to give NGOs the capacity to participate in deliberations, the International Alliance of Women (IAW), the ICW, and the WIDF all shared Category B status, meaning that they focused on an area of special competence—as women's concerns were considered—rather than on broader UN objectives. Liberal and communist countries differed markedly, however, in their conception of NGOs and the relationship between states and civil society. From the Western perspective, communist-backed NGOs such as the WIDF and the World Federation of Trade Unions seemed too ideological and insufficiently autonomous.[5] In 1948, the US embassy delayed issuing a visa to the WIDF representative, causing her to miss the CSW's opening session, and limited her visa to "single entry and only for transit to United Nations headquarters site."[6] The following year, the WIDF's US affiliate, the Congress of American Women, came under attack by the House Un-American Activities Committee.[7] By 1950—as the Soviets boycotted ECOSOC over whether Taiwan or the People's Republic of China would occupy China's seat on the Security Council, and Cold War tensions mounted between the United States and the Soviet Union—the WIDF had become firmly associated with Eastern-bloc countries and the target of Western distrust

The ICW-WIDF rivalry reached a head in the early 1950s.[8] Perturbed by the "propaganda" the WIDF generated from its new headquarters in East Berlin and its campaign against the US presence in Korea, the ICW had begun to campaign against its presence in the UN.[9] In March 1953, the United States refused a visa to the WIDF representative to attend CSW meetings, arguing that she posed a "security threat"; the following year it issued a visa allowing the WIDF representative to travel only in the "immediate vicinity" of the UN headquarters and orchestrated the suspension of the WIDF's consultative status, which would not be not reinstated until 1968.[10] In an indication of shifting political winds in the intervening years, when ECOSOC reorganized consultative-status NGOs into categories I, II, and Roster to replace A, B, and C, the WIDF was admitted to the more prestigious Category I status while the ICW and IAW remained in Category II.[11] An appalled Schuller-McGeachy quickly launched a campaign to elevate the ICW's status as well, securing Category I status in December 1969. The victory could not have come at a better time for Schuller-McGeachy, whose rival for the ICW presidency, Helvi Sipilä, campaigned in favor of closer collaboration with the WIDF and against the shoddy budgeting that had left the ICW dependent on older, wealthy European women to cover deficits.[12] Schuller-McGeachy retained her office largely because of her success with ECOSOC. By the time Schuller-McGeachy learned of the IWY proposal and Sipilä's support of it, her "warily pragmatic" posture toward the WIDF had chilled into Cold War frostiness.[13]

Despite these tensions, CSW members had forged strong relationships over the years, particularly as they crafted the 1967 Declaration on the Elimination of Discrimination against Women (DEDAW). Most of them knew each other through transnational networks, since many countries sent WINGO leaders as CSW representatives. Sipilä herself had risen through the ranks of the ICW and Zonta International, an organization for professional women, while also representing the Finnish government on the CSW. Following UN protocols and learning from the four-year process of drafting DEDAW, commission members adopted a methodical strategy to construct a legalistic case at the General Assembly, deploying the stilted UN formulations of "noting," "considering," and "drawing attention to" various resolutions that had come before. Although WINGO leaders gained access to the professionalized, male-dominated world of power brokering and policymaking, they faced nested struggles for legitimacy—of women within the NGO leadership and at the UN, of NGOs vis-à-vis the UN and governments, and increasingly, of consultative-status NGOs against newer civil-society organizations that deemed them out-of-date and too establishmentarian.

The number and diversity of NGOs had mushroomed in the 1970s, and many feminist and women's liberation organizations saw the ECOSOC-affiliated WINGOs as too complicit with male-dominated power structures.[14] Organizations such as Zonta and the ICW formed part of CONGO (the Conference of NGOs in consultative status), which included only the most established NGOs invested in preserving UN protocols and protecting the privileges of consultative status.[15] They aimed to show that, unlike the rabble-rousing feminists, they could pursue women's interests through diplomatic and legalistic channels that would not unduly disrupt social norms. Many feminists saw the WINGOs' legalistic, common-ground strategy as too slow-moving and tradition-bound, resulting in women's concerns taking a back seat to issues of greater importance to men. The white-gloved volunteers who populated the WINGOs saw themselves principally as addressing other people's problems, such as poverty and illiteracy. The ICW framed reproductive rights as "responsible parenthood" and labor rights as "retraining women to enter the labour force," subordinating women's emancipation to concerns about population control and economic productivity.[16]

Despite all their frustrations with the UN and with their home governments, the women (and very occasionally men) who populated the CSW believed that the United Nations, through conventions, declarations, data gathering, and the activities of its affiliate agencies, could, in the fullness of time, improve the lives of all women. These instruments undergirded demands on both UN and national resources and informed how the CSW and consultative-status NGOs alike understood the process of achieving social change as gradual and often technical improvements that would alter the ethos surrounding women's rights. Language accumulated from one document to the next, with each proposal or background paper fastidiously citing approved resolutions by number. As new actors become involved in the IWY project—NGO veterans, national policymakers, and assorted activists who had not previously worked with the UN—they had to learn a new, more gradual pace for social change as well as a new language—UN-ese, as the IWY tribune organizer Mildred Persinger dubbed it.[17] Elaine Livingston would explain to her fellow New York City NOW members that just wading through UN documentation constituted a full-time job.[18]

CSW members also had to learn the complicated and sometimes shifting structure of the UN itself. Often referred to as the UN system or, more intimately, the UN family, it includes not only member states but also an array of specialized agencies that together make an alphabet soup of acronyms— International Labor Organization (ILO), World Health Organization (WHO), Food and Agriculture Organization (FAO), UN Educational, Scientific, and Cultural Organization (UNESCO), UN Conference on Trade and Development (UNCTAD), UN Development Programme (UNDP), UN Fund for Population Activities (UNFPA), to name only a few. Most of the world experiences the UN through the activities of these various agencies, which often supply financial support, training facilities, and expert advisors on issues relevant to their briefs. These entities related to the United Nations as a whole to different degrees and in distinct fashions, and all of them pertained to the CSW's concerns. The CSW itself is considered a "functional commission" that reports to ECOSOC, which makes recommendations to the General Assembly.

The WIDF's recommendation to "take stock" of the CSW's accomplishments seemed calculated to highlight that the commission, with its liberal emphasis on individual rights, had succeeded only in securing empty promises. As a first step, the proposers indicated, all UN member states should ratify the conventions related to women's status, underscoring the United States' refusal to sign the UN's humanitarian treaties, including the 1952 Convention on the Political Rights of Women and the 1957 Convention on the Nationality of Married Women.[19] The General Assembly's Third Committee, charged with considering social, cultural, and humanitarian issues, amended the CSW's proposal in two important ways. First, while the original resolution had sought to "promote equality between men and women" and to "increase women's contribution to national and international development," Greece and Guatemala proposed altering the language to securing the "full integration" in development and adding the aim of recognizing "women's increasing contribution to the development of friendly relations and co-operation among States and to the strengthening of world peace."[20] Second, representatives from India, Hungary, Iceland, and Mongolia called for all member states to ratify the ILO's convention calling for "equal remuneration

Figure 1.1 The IWY poster logo designed by Valerie Pettis appeared on posters, buttons, flyers, and even potholders throughout the year. Courtesy of PettisDesign.

for men and women workers for work of equal value."[21] Like the CSW's appeal for member states to ratify existing conventions, this latter amendment again challenged the United States. By November 1972, seventy-three member states—from Afghanistan to Zambia—had ratified the Equal Remuneration Convention, including almost all of Africa, the Middle East/Central Asia, and Latin America; the United States had not.

With these two amendments, the three IWY themes of equality, development, and peace took shape, symbolized, as several reporters observed, by a "plumpish peace dove with the mathematical equal sign where its tail feathers should sprout."[22] As anodyne as they must have seemed—"soporific platitudes" as one UN staffer described them—observers in the press, NGOs, and the foundation community glossed these themes as demarcating geopolitical interests, with the industrialized countries focusing on equality, G-77 countries emphasizing development, and the Soviet-bloc countries stressing peace. While this mapping reflected at least an impressionistic sense of rhetorical divisions and the UN's geopolitical balancing act, making these themes seem straightforward and mutually understood frustrated all efforts to describe even the basic contours of such abstract ideas. Did equality imply equal rights (which might ignore issues such as maternity) or equal opportunities (which might accommodate maternity demands)? Would protectionist nationalism or free-market liberalism best serve the objective of Third World development? Did peace mean an absence of nuclear weapons, an end to foreign occupation, or the curtailment of revolutionary violence?

Even within the UN orbit, a growing cadre of women interrogated conventional wisdoms. In a critical challenge to the modernization model, Danish economist Ester Boserup argued in her path-breaking *Women in Economic Development* (1970) both that the metrics used to gauge economic growth (i.e., GDP) systematically excluded most women's labor and that contemporary development schemes, with their emphasis on mechanization and commodities production, contributed to women's economic marginality and increased their labor burdens.[23] Working within the UN system, Boserup wrote largely for an audience of funding agencies and development experts, earning her a

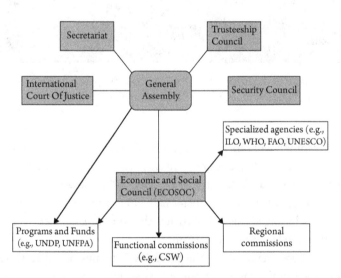

Figure 1.2 In 1975, the United Nations consisted of six principal organs (in gray) and dozens of specialized agencies, functional commissions, regional commissions, and programs, most of which report to ECOSOC.

reputation within economics circles for challenging Malthusian predictions about population and food supplies. By 1975, Boserup had galvanized the women-in-development movement; suddenly, women seemed indispensable to development projects.

If UN personnel—particularly those within the Secretariat—saw an opportunity to recruit women to support UN goals such as development, literacy, population control, public health, and food production, they also saw an opening to publicize the UN's own record of overwhelmingly relegating women to clerical positions and member states' practice of sending all-male delegations to UN deliberative bodies and conferences. The GA had proclaimed the 1970s as the Second UN Development Decade, encouraging the "full integration of women in the development effort," and two months later approved a program of "concerted international action for the advancement of women," accompanied by a chagrined resolution that the UN system should "set an example" by employing more women in senior and professional positions.[24] As CSW members and UN staffers alike frequently pointed out, Article 8 of the UN's charter specifies, "The United Nations shall place no restrictions on the eligibility of men and women to participate in any capacity and under conditions of equality in its principal and subsidiary organs." Taken together, these resolutions bore a striking resemblance to the initial IWY agenda. Had the UN lived up to its commitments, IWY might not have happened at all. The insistence on a thematic year and a central conference stemmed in part from vexation at repeatedly broken promises that women would become partners in international governance and development schemes. The IWY resolution proposed to the 1972 CSW meeting opened with the commission's frustration and disappointment that women suffered ongoing discrimination, despite this proliferation of UN instruments and conventions.

The IWY resolution also emerged out of frustration with the GA's constant hedging on the question of women's status. Even the 1970 program for "concerted international action," with its insistence on women's centrality to development projects and its promises of resources, concluded its preamble with the caveat, "notwithstanding the provisions of all the preceding paragraphs, that the family as the cornerstone of society, must be protected." The statement not only imagined family well-being in tension with improvements in women's status but also seemed to promise that, no matter what policies the UN advocated, conditions within the home would remain unchallenged. Indeed, intervention in family and cultural matters remained the third rail of UN politics; the personal would not be political there.

Emphasis on economic development dovetailed with growing alarm about the impending "population bomb"—signaled by Paul and Alice Ehrlich in 1968—and concerns that unchecked population growth, particularly in the Third World, would undermine development objectives and would lead to political instability and environmental degradation.[25] Population control had emerged as an Anglo-American priority: predominantly Catholic countries hovered somewhere between aloof and opposed; Eastern European and Central Asian countries were more concerned with declining fertility rates; Third World countries focused on industrialization and still had large swaths of their economies that depended upon labor-intensive production. Further, the class and racial politics of population control were complicated, as they targeted not the over-consuming populations of the North Atlantic but rather the impoverished and darker populations in poor and rich countries alike. While many well-intentioned enthusiasts of family planning saw it as a means to spare women from having more children than they wanted, the targets of these policies often experienced them as the imposition of elite and often racist concerns upon their very bodies. Throughout the IWY encounters, the meanings and policy implications of family planning—whether framed as population control or as reproductive freedom—remained among the most divisive issues. With attention to the twinned concerns of economic development and population control, the CSW saw an opening and stuck its collective foot in the door.

If CSW members envisioned IWY as bringing greater resources and new policies, the Secretariat focused instead on symbolic measures. Women, the Secretariat argued, had an image problem. It suggested inaugural ceremonies, commemorative stamps, film festivals and art exhibitions, radio and television spots, awards honoring women's achievements, distribution of copies of DEDAW, and the creation of an international symbol for the year. This focus on cultural efforts reflected both budgetary and political realities, since they cost less and required less political support than creating new bureaucratic structures to implement policy changes. Without enforcement mechanisms, cultural programs offered a more feasible means for pursuing IWY objectives.

In 1972, just as the IWY proposal wended its way through ECOSOC and then to the General Assembly's Third Committee, the Section on the Status of Women of the Human Rights Division of the Department of Social Affairs was upgraded to become the Branch for the Promotion of Equality for Men and Women under the new Centre for Social Development and Humanitarian Affairs.[26] This seemingly mundane bureaucratic shift had consequences: it moved the entity charged with providing "technical and substantive support" for the CSW and, later, for the UN women's conferences out of the political and juridical realm of human rights and into the technocratic economic development realm of humanitarian assistance.[27] Margaret Bruce—a Cambridge graduate and a consummate UN insider who had worked there since 1946—directed the Section on the Status of Women; when moved from the Human Rights Division to Humanitarian Affairs, UN staffers continued to refer to it simply as "Mrs. Bruce's division."[28] Responding to mounting criticism that the UN itself had failed to promote women within its ranks, Secretary-General Kurt Waldheim appointed Helvi Sipilä as Assistant Secretary-General for Social Development and Humanitarian Affairs, making her the UN's highest-ranked female official and the most powerful woman in the Secretariat. Although Sipilä reportedly faced "passive resistance" from fellow Secretariat members and resentments over the departmental restructuring, her appointment and the elevation of the women's branch seemed like progress.[29]

The Secretariat started from the three IWY themes of equality, development, and peace and followed the UN's standard four-step approach to theme years calling for "intensified action": specify targets, develop short- and long-term programs, establish machinery, and evaluate results. In other words, rather than pursuing structural changes, the UN sought to establish clear, measurable goals around issues such as juridical equality, legislative representation, literacy, educational and training opportunities, and equal pay; to develop strategies that would help UN agencies and member states achieve these goals; to develop bureaucratic structures and procedures that would sustain them; and to establish a mechanism to evaluate whether strategies had yielded results.

These developments reverberated on the other side of the planet from UN headquarters, as Australia felt the effects of the growing rift in civil society between WINGOs and feminists, the disputes within the UN between those who placed women's issues within the purview of human rights and those who saw them as falling under humanitarian concerns, and the shifting balance of power from those working within the rules of the game to those who wanted to change the game entirely. For her part, Julie Dahlitz knew exactly how best to mark the International Women's Year. Like many committed to the UN, she had been deeply affected by World War II and the Holocaust and had a cosmopolitan worldview, a privileged upbringing, and professional training. By the early 1970s, Dahlitz had become executive director of the United Nations Association of Australia (UNAA), one of the original members of the World Federation of United Nations Associations (UNAs) formed in 1946 as an NGO supporting the UN. Although not part of the UN system, the UNAs' letterhead and logos included the UN's iconic map nested in olive branches, and leaders often finessed the distinction between UNA and UN activities. Like other consultative-status NGOs, the UNAs provided a venue for semi-professionalized voluntarism and attracted their share of active and ambitious career women. At the earliest opportunity, Dahlitz formed a high-powered IWY Preparatory Committee chaired by the UNAA President, Major General Paul Cullen. Dahlitz set her sights higher, however; she spotted a chance to increase Australia's visibility on the world stage and make its reputation as a world leader in women's rights. As the political temperature rose in the General Assembly, the IWY offered Australia an opening to secure a role as an honest broker.

Dahlitz must have written to Elizabeth Reid the very day she read the announcement of Reid's appointment as the first-ever advisor to the Australian Prime Minister on women's issues.[30] She congratulated Reid and invited her to join the newly formed UNAA IWY committee. Almost in passing, she mentioned the possibility that Australia might host a major IWY event. "It is certainly timely and not out of keeping with the stated policy of the Government," Dahlitz explained, "that a United Nations sponsored world conference be held in this country. As well as enhancing our international image, this would undoubtedly give impetus to local improvements in many desirable ways."

Thirty years old when Prime Minister Gough Whitlam appointed her, Reid had already lived a remarkable life. She narrowly survived a tragic train accident at seventeen, and doctors had told her that if she continued her university studies she would end up "in a mental asylum."[31] After several months of sneaking back on campus, she finally convinced a sympathetic dean to readmit her and graduated with first-class honors in philosophy. She continued her studies at Oxford and was a senior tutor back at Australia National University (ANU) when the opportunity in Whitlam's government arose.

According to Reid's recollection, the idea for the position had come from one of Whitlam's closest advisors. "I've just spent time in the States," Peter Wilenski told Whitlam, "I've seen this burgeoning women's movement; it's going to be one of the greatest social justice movements in our century and I think you should bring onto your staff somebody that will speak with the voice of that movement."[32] Over 400 women applied for the job.[33] Reid later described the short list as "a diverse group of extremely impressive women" and speculated that "a pin was stuck in the list and it was announced that I would be appointed."[34] By then, Reid had already traveled widely, been married and separated, had a five-year-old daughter, become active in the women's liberation movement, done research on China, and gotten involved in activism around South African human rights and Australian Aboriginal land rights. Her efforts often combined her intellectual proclivities with her feminist convictions, performing research and offering adult education on women's role in society, paternity and maternity leave, and reproductive rights.

Reid immediately drew political fire. She had anticipated the attacks from the feminist left, which accused the government of tokenism and branded her as a sellout, and received a flood of letters from women—some congratulatory and others promising, as one put it, "the utmost in non-cooperation."[35] She found herself blindsided, though, by partisan assaults and misrepresentations in the press. Whitlam's press secretary recalled that Reid "found her views on life, love and sex spread across the headlines as industrious male investigative journalists trawled university student newspapers for her early opinions."[36] Decades later, Reid recalled her first press conference: "I was trained as a philosopher, I had extremely well elaborated views on all of [the issues] that had stood the test of lots of thinking and practice, so I told them exactly what I thought about abortion law and homosexuality and drugs and all this, and then I saw the headlines the next day, and that was the greatest shock of those years to see how questions that I had assumed were asked all in good faith were twisted and distorted and sensationalized . . . no subtlety or caveats or qualifications, or careful statements of this—just headlines in black and white terms."[37] A senator from the Catholic, anti-communist Democratic Labor Party took to the Senate floor to ask if Reid would advocate legalizing abortion, prostitution, homosexuality, and marijuana.[38] A representative from the conservative Country Party pressed Whitlam on Reid's "views and attitudes of womanhood," citing a piece that ran in the ANU student newspaper with the text of a lecture Reid had given about masturbation.[39] The talk itself—about as untitillating as a lecture on masturbation could be—typified Reid's philosophical approach, posing questions and unpacking them from conceptual and ethical angles and demonstrating a policy wonk's fascination with data.[40]

The generational gap between Dahlitz and Reid was wider than their twelve-year age difference implied, exemplifying the growing divide between established NGOs—the type that prized their consultative status and assiduously hewed to the etiquette of governance—and the new-model civil society of activists that sought to disrupt the staid and scripted performances of the CONGO crowd. Reid, often described as a revolutionary in a reformist's job, had embarked upon a cultural revolution. Dahlitz's UNAA meetings, meanwhile, exhibited thoroughgoing deference to protocol and to the status of the UN itself; its IWY committee had subcommittees, and its meetings followed the orderly formality of motions, committee reports, and resolutions. Attendance lists specified "Mesdames" and "Misses," while Reid faced endless questions about why she preferred "Ms." The UNAA committee's rules of conduct allowed four influential WINGOs—including both the ICW and the WIDF—veto power over any material published in the committee's name.[41] John Gavin, a Special Minister of State and convener of its IWY committee, reported from one UNAA meeting that he was struck by the "very heavy emphasis on formal procedure," that there was "very little of substance and there was no real bite to any of the deliberations," and that the committee had not "approached the year in anything like an enlightened, effective, or analytic way."[42] For her committee, Reid sought input from younger women, including those not involved in the women's movement, and described its preliminary meeting as "conducted on informal lines to allow maximum exchange of information and airing of questions. The result was a vigorous, day-long forum where participants were surprised and stimulated by the range and depth of discussion."[43] While Dahlitz and the UNAA wanted to show that women could operate in official settings as effectively as men, Reid wanted to shake up the whole system using feminist strategies of power-sharing and collaborative decision making.

Dahlitz clearly hoped to garner Reid's support for her idea of Australia's hosting a world IWY conference and secured a unanimous resolution at the first meeting of the UNAA's IWY preparatory committee, in May 1973, to ask the Australian government to proffer this invitation before the January 1974 CSW session.[44] A month later, she called the prime minister's office to report that at the recent ICW convention in Vienna, the Australian delegate had a "long discussion" with Helvi Sipilä about the possibility of something along the lines of the Bucharest population conference. Someone scrawled on the back of her phone message, "Cost of WPY1974 in Bucharest: upwards of $3m."[45] Dahlitz insisted that the tourist income would offset the expenses, but Labour and Immigration Minister Clyde Cameron explained that Australia was an unlikely venue given the travel expenses and the need to hold any major UN events in a developing country. Besides, he reiterated, "I would find it difficult to support holding a meeting in Australia if the cost were on the order of the World Population Conference which you cited as an example."

If Dahlitz and her committee seemed to think the Whitlam government failed to appreciate the value of a UN conference for elevating Australia's national stature, officials saw the UNAA as amateurs playing at diplomacy. One Department of Foreign Affairs staffer vented her frustration after a November 1973 UNAA meeting at which Dahlitz remained relentless on the matter. "The most obvious feature of the meeting," the staffer reported, "was a clear failure by the Committee to come to grips with basic issues. The Chairman (Cullen) had not thought of any program for IWY except the holding of a Conference in Australia. His Secretary, Mrs. Dahlitz, was clearly in favour of the idea as a means of attracting the Government's financial support. The Committee had deliberated a Conference idea at some length without once defining: (i) its purpose, (ii) the audience it was to reach, (iii) its subject matter, (iv) its source of funds." She observed that Reid deftly tried to "steer the Secretary's enthusiasm into a more practical channel" but cautioned Foreign Affairs against offering the group any material resources until it more clearly determined its plans and objectives.[46]

Like many of her counterparts in the United States and elsewhere, Dahlitz experienced a sense of relative deprivation as new actors occupied space within civil society and drew public officials' attention. She complained that "Ms. Reid had shown a total disinterest in the [UNAA IWY] Committee, and that it was clearly not the Government's intention to give financial or other support to it."[47] Dahlitz recognized the efforts to sideline her plans and traveled to Canberra to take up her grievances with the Department of Foreign Affairs.[48] Horace Perera, the president of the World Federation of UNAs, had secured her an appointment, but during the meeting Dahlitz demonstrated that she had "little idea of costing and had obviously made little attempt to obtain this information." When offered a "maximum grant" of $A5,000, she grumbled that she would "advise Mr. Perera" and unsuccessfully sought to press her case further.

As Dahlitz continued to badger ministerial offices, Reid prepared for a two-month tour of European and North American countries to survey IWY plans. She ended in New York at a UN-sponsored conference on women's role in population and development efforts.[49] She did not meet many fellow revolutionaries along the way. She noted that Canadians had paid too much for a publicity campaign that she dubbed "typical PR firm crap"—a characterization with which many Canadian women's groups appeared to agree—and that the cash-starved US center seemed to limit its aspirations to celebrating one notable woman a month starting with Amelia Earhart.[50] Reid set off a firestorm during the UN meeting. Appalled at the condescension with which the men treated the women present—including one who said he had come to learn about the "mysterious problem called the status of women and also what were the latest fashions"—she pointed out that women had left important jobs only to come to the UN and have men treat them like children. "We have had very little real opportunity to get together and discuss seriously the problems we were brought here at tremendous expense to discuss," she told reporters.[51] UN staffer Susan Jane Kedgley wrote her afterward, "Needless to say, your comments in the *New York Times* caused an unprecedented commotion amongst UN men—beginning in the secretary-general's cabinet meeting. You really shook the men up—they were furious and indignant and, incidentally, interested. IWY suddenly became an object of interest."[52]

While Reid was abroad, the minister of foreign affairs advised Whitlam to step up his IWY commitment. Citing UN requests that member states "intensify their efforts to promote equal rights for women and to increase women's contribution to national and international development," as well as the "growing domestic interest in women's matters and the Government's own declared policies," he proposed a National Advisory Committee (NAC) that would liaise between government departments and NGOs and recommended Reid as the "most suitable person" to chair the proposed committee. Following her performance in New York, Whitlam agreed.[53] For all the Whitlam government's progressive impulses, Reid still found herself swimming hard upstream. In June she wrote to Whitlam about the challenge of finding a ministerial home for the newly created NAC. "Basically, the Department of Foreign Affairs does not want it, the Department of Prime Minister and Cabinet does not want it, and the Department of the Treasury's mind has never been crossed with the thought that women might be worth spending money on."[54] Meanwhile, Reid received more correspondence than any minister, save Whitlam himself, and worked tirelessly to create openings for women in every policy consideration, while constantly battling illness and exhaustion.[55]

Reid must have been heartened, at least, by Whitlam's staunch support. When the treasurer proposed deferring NAC nominations until the next budget, Whitlam immediately acceded to Reid's cautions against further delays. "My dear Treasurer," Whitlam responded, explaining that he remained "convinced that we must stand by our commitment to the objectives of International Women's Year." Mapping out a plan to appropriate $A2 million, he elaborated, "Australia in the past has led the world in removing many areas of social injustice, and I believe that International Women's Year will be a welcome occasion to do so once again."[56] Although Whitlam portrayed the NAC as evidence of his government's support for civil society, UNAA affiliates and established NGOs dubbed it a "federal takeover" of their activities. Using nearly identical language, letters arrived pointing to the "vast store of knowledge and experience that has been built up by the women's organisations which have been working steadily to improve the Status of Women; many of these organisations have Consultative Status with the United Nations, being recognized as experts in the various aspects of this work. Their knowledge and experience should not be wasted or over-looked."[57]

The conflict between Dahlitz and Reid only intensified as their circumstances diverged sharply with the creation of the NAC. Dahlitz, a consummate establishmentarian, found herself on the outside, while Reid, a self-proclaimed women's liberationist and revolutionary, was on the inside. As Whitlam prepared to put Reid in charge of the NAC fund, Dahlitz informed her committee that the UNAA would no longer finance its activities and asked members to contribute donations to defray expenses "pending a financial allocation from the government."[58] Having burned her bridges with the Whitlam government, she began a public relations counteroffensive, giving interviews to sympathetic reporters and capitalizing on the public confusion about the relationship between the UNA and the United Nations to claim the UN imprimatur. The *West Australian* ran a headline, "PM's Adviser on Women Rebuked—By a Woman," and quoted Dahlitz as saying that Reid's public statements advocating greater inclusion in IWY planning were "misleading and contemptuous of the many thousands of Australian women who are involved in the planning of International Women's Year."[59]

Dahlitz's press statements spotlighted the growing tensions between her and Reid as well as their very different concepts of advocacy and activism. One activist who worked with both likened the widening split to the schism between NOW and the "outright revolutionary Women's Lib groups" in the United States.[60] Regarding plans for IWY, she raised concerns about the "division of women in Australia in two camps, those who belong to the old fashioned N.G.O.'s representing groups of women organised on state-national-international levels who have consultative status with U.N. and those newly come to the women's movement. The former are tightly structured, the latter opposed to hierarchical forms believing that they set up power systems wherever they exist."

The lack of adequate support from either the government or the UNAA itself began to pinch, and Dahlitz wrote to the members of her committee that the July 1974 meeting was postponed "for lack of funds." She implored subcommittees to meet in the interim "to ensure that the momentum of preparations for International Women's Year is not lost," but the wind was gone from her sails. In September, after returning from the World Population Conference in Bucharest, she extended an olive branch to Reid. Explaining that she no longer presided over the UNAA, she wished Reid success with IWY.[61] She may have realized during her interactions in Bucharest that Reid's star had risen in UN circles as Helvi Sipilä cited Australia as "leading the way toward equality for women."[62]

The UNAA's indignation did not subside with Dahlitz's departure, however. John Gavin reported that the September 30 meeting had a "mood . . . of suppressed outrage" due to the fact that the committee "appeared to have been overlooked and certainly until now, starved of funds" and that "members of the committee were for the most part the most senior office bearers of the women's organisations they represented" but had not been included in the NAC.[63] Concerned about "alienating such an influential group of women," Gavin struck a conciliatory tone. He emphasized the need for communication and collaboration and reprised the official line that the NAC sought a "blend and balance of expertise and experience" rather than to represent organizations or states. He heard later that the fact that Australia had developed its own IWY symbol—a stylized rose in lieu of the UN's "plumpish dove"—had "added to the general feeling of outrage."

When Sipilä visited Australia a week later, Gavin was "keen to give her some feeling" for the situation with the UNAA, but their discussion quickly turned to plans for collaboration with the Australian government.[64] Sipilä supported NGO activities but pointed out that the UN's imprimatur for an event required government involvement and praised the Australian government's exceptional commitment to IWY, particularly compared to the United States.[65] Like Julie Dahlitz and Elizabeth Reid alike, Sipilä held out hope that Australia might help steer IWY clear of the thicket of Cold War politics.

Scene 2

Choosing Battles in the Cold War

In February 1973, before Elizabeth Reid's position had even been created, two groups of consultative-status NGOs began almost simultaneously to plan IWY activities. One was a Geneva-based group that formed as a subcommittee of the NGO Committee on Human Rights and met in the Palais des Nations, the other a New York–based group that emerged out of CONGO's Sub-Committee on Women in Development and met in the Church Center for the United Nations, a twelve-story building owned by the United Methodist Church that housed mostly faith-based NGOs.[1] In many ways, these two groups reflected not only the WIDF-ICW rivalry that had simmered over the previous two decades but also the shifting center of gravity for women's issues at the UN as the section on women's status changed its affiliation from human rights to humanitarian and social affairs. The Geneva group convened within the UN's own space and linked women's status with broader human rights concerns, while the New York group met in a space populated by NGOs and concentrated on how to create new economic opportunities for women.

The Geneva group was led by one of IWY's original proposers, Shahnaz Alami, an Iranian exile and scholar of classical Persian poetry who had lived in East Berlin since 1953 and served as the WIDF's representative to the CSW and chair of the CSW's subcommittee on human rights.[2] In a January 1973 interview in the WIDF's monthly magazine, *Women of the Whole World*, Alami stressed the fact that seven other NGOs, including its rival International Council of Women, had supported its IWY proposal, in hopes of creating the impression that IWY was above geopolitical rivalries. The WIDF would celebrate IWY "with a happy heart," Alami explained, because it would coincide with the federation's planned World Congress of Women and the thirtieth anniversary of the WIDF's founding.[3] The Geneva committee started its campaign in May with a letter to the director-general of the ILO stressing the "particular importance" it attached to workers' rights and pressing him to include in the 1975 agenda an item on the "equal opportunities and treatment of workingwomen."[4] In late July, the Geneva committee submitted to the secretary-general a five-point IWY program that reflected the WIDF's priorities: a campaign to press member states to ratify and implement all existing UN instruments related to women, a special CSW session to evaluate the success of the UN's Second Development Decade regarding women's concerns, seminars on vocational training for rural women and on employment issues for women with family responsibilities, an aggressive literacy campaign, and a call for member states and the mass media to "mobilize public opinion in favour of *de jure* and *de facto* equality of men and women."[5]

The Geneva committee had an international profile from the outset, including participation by prominent figures such as Jeanne-Martin Cissé, a Guinean who had been the first woman to preside over the UN Security Council. The New York group, meanwhile, consisted overwhelmingly of New York–based women, most of whom also participated in planning the NGO forum for the August 1974 UN Population Conference in Bucharest.[6] The New York committee's second meeting ended with a call to invite "additional men and persons from other countries" to future meetings but seemingly without much effect.[7] The committee chair Esther Hymer, a longtime activist who had marched for women's suffrage while a student at the University of Wisconsin, by 1975 represented the International Federation of Business and Professional Women at the UN. CONGO president Rosalind Harris participated in the first meeting, Mary Craig Schuller-McGeachy took a leadership role as president of the ICW, and her former rival Helvi Sipilä attended as an honored guest representing the UN. While Hymer, Harris, and Schuller-McGeachy all had cosmopolitan orientations, they also situated themselves squarely on the Western side of the Cold War divide.

Correspondence between the New York and Geneva NGO committees remained sparse but cordial during 1973. In August, Alami wrote to Harris to thank her "very sincerely for the attention you have given to our work" and for documents forwarded from the New York group, imploring her to send information about any future undertakings. "We attach particular importance," she explained, "to close collaboration between the New York and Geneva groups, both of which are concerned with the advancement of women and their full participation in economic, social and cultural life at all levels."[8] The accompanying documents charted several issues where the two committees concurred, such as combating illiteracy, encouraging vocational training among girls and women, and assessing progress toward the UN's goals for its Second Development Decade. Other recommendations—public child-care facilities, wage parity, government influence over media representations, and, most important, securing ratification for all UN instruments relating to women's status—hinted at disagreements in their priorities. Still, Harris responded warmly to Alami's letter, saying what "great pleasure" she always derived from seeing her in Geneva and indicating that "the same ideas and programs are being considered both in New York and Geneva so that we ought to be able to demonstrate real strength."[9]

Although the two committees shared convictions about the orderly, well-governed manner in which change ought to occur, they diverged in obvious and subtle ways. Given Alami's own experience as a political prisoner, the committee unsurprisingly pressed for a program that stressed human rights concerns and social inequalities—issues that in IWY terms fell under the theme of peace—rather than the educational and political rights that preoccupied the New York committee. Women like Hymer and Schuller-McGeachy, however, saw these matters as politically loaded questions that distracted from the core women's issues; they focused instead on questions such as development aid and training programs.[10] When Margaret Bruce attended the second New York committee meeting to explain what role NGOs might play in IWY, she described IWY as centered on equality, development, and women's contributions to society. The emphases on peace, anti-colonialism, and anti-racism that loomed large on the Geneva agenda were not even part of the conversation in New York.[11]

Meanwhile, another rivalry had begun to dominate the UN General Assembly that would pervade every aspect of IWY. The GA's Third Committee included representation from every member state, so it expanded alongside the UN.[12] Similarly, ECOSOC, which had started with only eighteen members in 1946, had grown to twenty-seven in 1965 and jumped to fifty-four by 1973. By the end of 1974, General Assembly President Abdelaziz Bouteflika reportedly proclaimed, "The only thing left now to decolonize is the Secretariat."[13] When the GA convened in the fall of 1972 for its 27th session—the session that proclaimed 1975 as International Women's Year—the non-aligned countries forged solidarity around issues ranging from broadcast satellites to nuclear proliferation. They particularly homed in on racial and economic justice. The former was focused on efforts to marginalize the expanding state of Israel and the apartheid government of South Africa. The latter centered on a proposal from the Mexican delegation for a Charter on the Economic Rights and Duties of States promoting economic sovereignty under a New International Economic Order (NIEO), the bête noire of the industrialized countries.

These geopolitical tensions eclipsed IWY efforts until the US State Department came to see IWY as an opportunity, albeit one it embraced only half-heartedly, to burnish the United States' reputation at home and abroad. Pulled along by the demands of long-standing NGO women, feminist activists vigilant about the government's failures to uphold its commitments, and diplomats who questioned its policies, the State Department began to view women's rights as an arena where it might not only best the Soviet Union but also curry favor in the Third World. Secretary of State William Rogers made no mention of IWY in his detailed assessment of the GA's 27th session. He lamented that "most of our effort had to be expended on preventing bad situations from getting worse" and offered a litany of the ways the United States had become *patria non grata* at the UN, its representatives finding themselves "steamrollered on a number of issues that saw the have-nots pitted against the haves."[14] US Ambassador George H. W. Bush increasingly found himself isolated on political questions, although he thought that the United States triumphed over its Soviet rival on what he dubbed "motherhood" issues—world disarmament and strengthening international security—and achieved "damage limitation" on other matters. He noted the coming challenge posed by the "majority of poorer, weaker, smaller nations in UN who are aware that rich, large, powerful nations are in the minority and can be out-voted." Although he decried that "have-not nations" sought short-term rhetorical and psychological advantage, while "have nations" generally stood firm on the UN founding fathers' principles of the "sanctity of property, inviolability of contracts and agreements, constitutionalism and rule of law," he saw this dynamic as fostering a "certain mutuality of interest among 'haves' of varying ideology that did not previously exist."[15]

Increasingly frustrated with the behavior of non-aligned nations and the complicity of the UN Secretariat, President Richard Nixon recalled how General Assembly delegates had "jumped around" and "danced" upon the 1971 expulsion of Nationalist China. "It was revolting," concurred National Security Advisor Henry Kissinger. "Oh, yeah," Nixon mused. "A bunch of apes."[16] Nixon told Bush's successor, John Scali, that he recognized he "was not a popular figure in the UN" but that Scali should explain to the other ambassadors that the UN "should be even handed toward the US and smaller states should not 'gang up' against the big powers." Nixon and Scali agreed that Secretary-General Waldheim seemed better disposed toward the United States than his predecessor but could not understand the hostility from countries such as Mexico. "We do not ask other countries for their affection," Nixon complained, "but only to be treated fairly."[17] Scali reported to Kissinger that he was "getting through" to Waldheim, hoping he would "continue to 'run scared' in sure knowledge that we will not hesitate to lean on him, publicly if necessary, when his respect for our concerns is inadequate."[18]

In August 1973, Rogers anticipated that at the upcoming GA meetings "militant Arabs may press political offensive against Israel and US" and that the G-77 would "promote contentious trade and aid issues." Enumerating the questions around which the United States increasingly found itself at odds with the GA—including disarmament, the use of napalm, and the escalating Middle East crisis—Rogers could only offer, "We shall strive against mounting odds in 28th UNGA to minimize acrimonious debate, to arrest drift toward polemical tyranny of numerical majority, and to promote view that since north-south nations must live together and need each other, they should in mutual interest seek cooperation not confrontation."[19]

Anxieties at the State Department intensified in the fall of 1973, following the Algiers conference of non-aligned nations and the Yom Kippur War. "What is new and potentially alarming," observed deputy USUN representative William Tapley Bennett Jr., following the Algiers conference, "is the degree of mutual, unqualified, and generally effective support each group is giving the other on these respective issues [Israel and apartheid], and the success with which they have concerted their positions on more peripheral questions."[20] Through the mid-1970s, the non-aligned countries would link these two issues, branding Zionism as a form of racism and shifting the movement's center of gravity from India and Indonesia to an alliance between Arab and sub-Saharan African countries that traded allegiances, giving the bloc "votes to dominate most aspects of UN activities, and to paralyze the rest, if they so choose." Indicating the "spectacular exhibition of nonaligned solidarity" of twenty-two African states breaking relations with Israel, Bennett pointed to the non-aligned countries' practice of overriding the UN budget committee, which could potentially remove the "last barrier to eventual confrontation between [the] UN majority and its major contributors." Distressingly, non-aligned solidarity benefited the Soviets, who were "in [a] position to support Africans on African issues and Arabs on Middle Eastern ones and often go at it with stomach-churning obsequiousness." Bennett advised exploiting "centrifugal forces" and "fissures" in the non-aligned group by giving more US attention to the group's core issues of development, decolonization, and the Middle East, "if the US is not to be further isolated within the UN and if the UN is not eventually to be destroyed as an institution for constructive international cooperation."

Convincing the US government even to notice IWY amid UN politicking and widespread Vietnam War protests as well as the exploding Watergate scandal would require more than an appeal for women's equal rights—an issue that clearly held little interest for Nixon or Kissinger, despite the growing popularity of the Equal Rights Amendment. By the waning months of 1973, however, US diplomats were on the lookout for ways to break non-aligned solidarity and to divide the non-aligned group from the Soviets.[21] IWY planning had raised enough awareness in policymaking circles to induce the Senate Foreign Relations Committee chair, Senator J. William Fulbright, to ask Kissinger to appoint more women to the US delegation to the General Assembly, hoping to avoid the embarrassing appearance of tokenism.[22] On the House Foreign Affairs Committee, Minnesota Democrat Donald Fraser held a hearing in late October to discuss the international women's movement and its impact on US foreign policy. Most enduringly, Senator Charles Percy attached an amendment to the 1973 Foreign Assistance Act specifying that all bilateral US development aid would be predicated on the receiving country's progress in improving women's rights and incorporating women into the national economy.[23]

Although the official charged with developing UN policy urged ratification of the conventions related to women's rights, the State Department remained tepid about IWY as late as November 1973.[24] Efforts focused on an IWY working group and a commemorative postage stamp; officials congratulated themselves on having come up with a piddling $36,000 to fund a US Center for the International Women's Year through the following August under the leadership of the veteran China hand Ruth Bacon.[25] "As a matter of principle and of good operating procedure," the State Department explained, "it would be desirable to obtain additional funds from the private sector." IWY organizers were encouraged to seek support from "private sources and foundations for voluntarism." Meanwhile, the White House offered its "approval" of an IWY working group but "no money to support the project."[26]

As the January 1974 CSW session approached, one member of the US mission to the UN cautioned the State Department that its refusal to consider a UN convention on women's rights was "completely untenable" and would appear both at home and abroad "simply to be that of outright opposition."[27] Patricia Hutar, a Republican Party activist and ardent anti-communist, reminded State Department personnel that IWY coincided with the thirtieth anniversary of the WIDF's founding as well as its World Congress of Women, which the Soviet-aligned NGO organized every five years. "These two events," the WIDF proclaimed, "will climax International Women's Year, which undoubtedly will be of historic significance all over the world."[28] By late 1973, the possibility that the centerpiece IWY event might take place behind the Iron Curtain galvanized the State Department to take it more seriously.[29]

The twenty-fifth Commission on the Status of Women session—the meeting where Julie Dahlitz had hoped to propose an IWY conference in Australia—opened in New York on January 14, 1974, with "somewhat of a 'homecoming day' atmosphere." Most of the delegates knew one another, and the commission's relatively small size and shared struggle for resources within the UN fostered a camaraderie and cooperation that, particularly by the mid-'70s, had become increasingly rare in UN bodies.[30] Alice Paquier of the World YWCA described the atmosphere as "generally warm, in spite of differing views, and the contact between government delegates and NGO representatives was easy and friendly."[31] Mostly professional women served as CSW delegates, with men from members' New York–based UN missions occasionally stepping in as alternates, particularly on diplomatically sensitive issues.

Despite having been named to the CSW less than two weeks earlier, US representative Hutar quickly jumped into the fray, introducing during the session's first full day a resolution for the UN to sponsor a world conference during IWY.[32] The proposal might have seemed innocuous, given that the commission had pressed for a women's conference since its 1946 founding, but Hutar understood the strategic importance of seizing the initiative both to drive a wedge between the Soviets and their non-aligned allies and to prevent the

WIDF congress from becoming the principal IWY event. The UN conferences on food and population that would take place later in the year had drawn attention and resources to the issues; a major international event seemed key to moving IWY beyond being a series of art exhibits and seminars and commemorative stamps.

The proposal to host an IWY conference did not meet with the same unanimous support as the proposal two years earlier to sponsor a year. Many representatives, particularly those aligned with the Soviet bloc, argued that a theme conference was simply an expensive gimmick, a distraction from the need to ratify and implement the UN instruments that already existed to improve women's status. While Hutar contended that the Soviets simply feared that a UN-sponsored IWY conference would detract from the WIDF's East Berlin meeting, more seasoned participants recognized that thematic conferences had become an increasingly contentious issue at the UN. The General Assembly had resolved repeatedly since 1969 to slow the pace of theme conferences.[33] Member states had to pay to send delegations, at greater expense when held outside New York or Geneva, and the conferences themselves put a financial burden on both the UN system and the host country. Documentation and translation expenses alone were considerable. No one disputed whether the conferences took up compelling issues—recent gatherings had examined issues such as human rights, disarmament, racism, environment, and food supply as well as more specialized questions such as the law of the sea—but rather whether these conferences accomplished more than less costly and more localized efforts.

The idea to hold a world IWY conference had taken hold first among NGO leaders, particularly among those who, like Dahlitz, witnessed the impact of the planning for the UN's Population Year conference. Commenting in December 1973 on the secretary-general's proposed IWY program for the year, the New York NGO committee pointed out, "It has become the accepted custom for the designated Years to have their activities fashioned around a world conference—International Women's Year deserves no less." Although the committee recognized that the GA resolution designating IWY called for a program "within the limits of the existing resources," its members expressed deep disappointment that it did not "envisage a full-fledged World Conference as the centerpiece of the Year." They recommended holding one in a developing country both for its potential to yield more concrete, far-reaching results and its "great symbolic significance," urging the Secretariat to support the proposal and that "all efforts be made to obtain a financial commitment for a full-fledged world assembly worthy of the importance and meaning of the Year."[34] The suggestion was inspired, offering a means to recapture the IWY program as linking the interests of the First and Third worlds and casting support for the conference as a gauge of support for women's concerns more generally. This language would appear nearly verbatim in an NGO statement supporting the IWY conference proposal and anticipated Hutar's proposal at the CSW session.[35]

The Soviets, seeking to refocus discussions on issues that the United States considered political distractions, offered an amendment to the proposal suggesting that, in lieu of a separate IWY conference, the General Assembly include an agenda item to consider "the situation and role of women in society, with special emphasis on the need to ensure the equality of women and of the contribution of women to the achievement of the goals of the Second Development Decade, the struggle against racism and racial discrimination, the strengthening of international peace and the development of friendly relations and co-operation among States."[36] The Soviets argued that forcing the General Assembly to wrestle with women's issues would have a far greater impact than a conference, which ran the risk of allowing the GA to sideline women's issues and let unsupportive members off the hook. The Eastern bloc states advocated instead for focusing energies on securing the ratification and implementation of existing instruments such as DEDAW and maintained that resources could have greater impact if they targeted raising awareness and improving facilities in the places most in need rather than organizing a conference for well-heeled diplomats already supportive of IWY priorities.[37] Bacon found their position "surprising in view of the usual Soviet effort to be on the side of the developing countries on an issue of this sort" but speculated that the Soviets "wished to forestall any other women's conference which would reduce the propaganda impact of Moscow's effort."[38]

The CSW working group that considered the secretary-general's draft IWY program sidestepped both the US and Soviet proposals, deferring them for discussion by the full commission during the session's final days.[39] Jockeying over the fate of the proposed conference took place offstage over the two-week CSW session, sandwiched between discussions about issues such as how to transform DEDAW into a more binding convention, the UN's own failure to promote women in its professional ranks, the ILO's efforts to promote equal-pay laws, the merits of protective labor legislation, and the mass media's role in shaping attitudes toward women.

The challenge for the conference proposal arose, as ever, from the lack of funds. Third World countries demonstrated enthusiasm but could offer no financial support, and European countries were reluctant to commit to funding the accelerating parade of theme years and conferences, understanding correctly that the UN would seek still further commitments of resources on specific issues. The United States, having proposed the conference, did not even adequately fund its own Center for IWY, much less commit to another major appropriation for the UN.[40] "Three men talked all evening, arguing that the conference idea was not feasible because no country would offer a place," Esther Hymer recalled. "It was because the Soviets were planning a huge Congress of

Women in 1975, and didn't want to distract people's attention. So we sent for a Colombian representative, who returned after a while and said that the government would provide Bogota as a conference site. Then Russians said, O.K., but there's no money for the conference. . . . That's why the conference was held out of regular budget, a tiny sum of money, while millions of dollars would be allocated to other international conferences."[41]

When the IWY conference proposal returned to the CSW for deliberation, the United States had added a call for special attention to women in rural areas—to increase its appeal to Third World countries as allies—and secured the co-sponsorship of Chile, Colombia, Costa Rica, Dominican Republic, Kenya, Liberia, Nigeria, Philippines, and Thailand.[42] Recognizing the "deep differences in priorities and methods" between industrialized and developing countries, the proposal was "concerned especially with the basic needs of rural women, such as a water supply that does not have to be carried in daily from the village well, local health services within walking distance, elementary educational and training opportunities, etc."[43]

CSW members had lost patience with the endless short-changing of their objectives, and the IWY working group replaced the call for a conference "providing funding can be found" with a call to the secretary-general to provide support "by reordering priorities within available resources" and creating an IWY conference voluntary fund that could accept contributions from individuals, IGOs, NGOs, foundations, and member states—the UN's mechanism to support activities not included in its regular budget.[44] "It was generally agreed," the session report recounted, "that one of the key factors in the success of the Year and of long-term programmes was to ensure adequate funding." Women's organizations could not be expected to provide sufficient funding, and "several representatives remarked with regret that the Year was inadequately funded under the regular budget of the United Nations, that no extrabudgetary funds were available, and that there was a great discrepancy between funds allocated to International Women's Year and other Years, notably World Population Year."[45] The revised resolution simultaneously pressed the Secretariat by calling for a reordering of priorities and left room for the possibility of setting up a voluntary fund.

The resolution carried in the final vote, but the Eastern bloc countries maintained their opposition and several European countries expressed concerns about the potential cost. In the end, three countries—the USSR, Byelorussia, and Hungary—voted no, and six, including France and Belgium, abstained. Another twenty-one delegations—including one from the People's Republic of China, attending for the first time—supported the conference. US Ambassador John Scali crowed that the United States had won a rare UN victory by claiming a "new human rights leadership role on [the] issue of equal rights for women" and that the session "revealed clear Soviet bias against equality for women" resulting in a "realignment of old Commission voting patterns with support from LDCs [less developed countries] and PRC [People's Republic of China] for the US against socialists."[46] Scali, former Associated Press and ABC reporter who had gained notoriety by serving as an intermediary between the White House and the Kremlin during the 1962 Cuban missile crisis, had joined the Nixon administration as a foreign affairs advisor before being appointed UN ambassador. Having forged his political career during the most nail-biting moment of the Cold War, Scali viewed his diplomatic duties through the lens of the US-Soviet rivalry. The Soviets' "futile filibuster effort," Scali reported gleefully in his telegram to the State Department, was defeated by US diplomatic cunning, bolstered by Nixon's timely proclamation of support for IWY during the session's closing days, which "effectively stalled Soviet drive designed to focus worldwide attention on single Communist women's year conference."

For all Scali's triumphalism, the IWY conference still required approval in two bodies where it would be met with suspicion: ECOSOC and the General Assembly. Given the disagreements in the CSW and the GA's concern about the proliferation of off-site theme conferences, conference advocates feared they were unlikely to secure final approval before late 1974, leaving little time to organize, since Colombia had offered to host early in 1975. Reporting back to the Geneva committee about the CSW session, the WYWCA's Alice Paquier noted, "There seemed to be unease about whether ECOSOC would take a decision [about a conference] or make a recommendation to the General Assembly."[47] As Ruth Bacon noted emphatically in her report from the CSW, "The vote of ECOSOC this April is crucial."[48] The Secretariat's revised IWY task force report, issued just after the CSW session concluded, made no mention of a conference, offering instead a calendar of radio and television programs, seminars and discussion groups, and a touring photo exhibit highlighting "great women scientists, educators, political leaders, philosophers, humanitarians, artists and others." Cognizant of persistent budget constraints, the task force specified as part of its planning agenda, "Prominent women invited to become members of the IWY patrons' committee with the hope of using this device to raise funds."[49]

Hoping to upstage the East Berlin conference, the New York NGO committee shifted into high gear to press the Secretariat to sponsor a high-profile event that would include NGOs. At this point, its members envisioned a two- or three-day NGO conference prior to the hoped-for UN intergovernmental conference in Bogota, along with several "useful" regional NGO conferences in Paris, Addis Ababa, New York, and Sydney that would focus on implementing the IWY program. Committee members who had attended the CSW's IWY working group sessions found them "constructive" and "valuable" but noted with dismay that compromises had fostered a "greater emphasis on racial discrimination, apart-heid and self-determination" as well as a separate heading for peace alongside equality and development—all concessions to Eastern bloc and G-77 countries that they viewed as "politics" that adulterated the agenda of "women's issues." Asking themselves what their committee might do with the working group's re-port now that the CSW had accepted it, they decided to print an abridged ver-sion, "pick out what could be done on the national and local levels. Leave out political angles, translate equality into legal plans of action."[50]

The Soviet bloc opposition to the conference raised red flags for Mary Craig Schuller-McGeachy and intensified her suspicions of the Geneva group. "My dear Rossy," she confided to Rosalind Harris, "The reason for this note is that, rightly or wrongly, I have gained the impression that the [CONGO] Bureau may not attach much significance to [the IWY] subcommittee. This, in my view, would be a mistake." She explained to Harris about the WIDF's role in the Geneva group and its plans to "convene and finance" an NGO conference for IWY. She noted with alarm that "proceedings and reports of this group in Geneva are reported on W.I.D.F. letter-head, even when these are addressed to the Secretary-General of the United Nations." Schuller-McGeachy stressed that any IWY celebrations must be "truly representative" and that "the only hope of achieving this essential balance is to give the New York subcommittee its proper place and authority." She urged Harris to give "Mrs. Hymer's Sub-Committee" the same support enjoyed by NGOs working on the UN's World Population Year.[51] In May, Schuller-McGeachy reported with dismay that the WIDF had met the previous month at the UNESCO offices in Paris, where its leaders had resolved to hold the NGO congress in East Berlin in October 1975.[52]

Although "Mrs. Hymer's committee" imagined itself as above the fray of ide-ological conflicts and certainly above "politics," its composition and the tenor of its discussions belied its supposed universalism. In discussing how to ensure the success of the IWY conference and voluntary fund, it noted the opposition from the "Eastern group" and cautioned that its "influence may be felt again." Still, the New York group had reason for optimism: its membership had grown to forty-seven organizations from seventeen in early 1973—although it still had not attracted any international members—and it had launched a publicity cam-paign around the idea of women as an "untapped resource."

As animosities between the New York and Geneva NGO committees bub-bled up, the head of the Geneva NGO Committee on Human Rights wrote to Kurt Waldheim, copying Rosalind Harris, to stress the importance of involving Shahnaz Alami in any activities related to the "1975 Conference on Discrimination against Women." Harris responded with a curt note assuring him that Esther Hymer's committee met twice a month, consulted with the UN Secretariat, and included representatives from all but three of the WINGOs on the CSW—notably, the WIDF was among those three. She pointedly insisted that the IWY's themes were equality, development, and peace—"not discrimination, per se."[53]

Like calls for peace, demands to end discrimination had become a strategy for knocking Western powers—the United States in particular—off the moral high ground.[54] On November 20, 1963, twenty-two Third World and Eastern bloc states had introduced a GA resolution for the United Nations Declaration on the Elimination of all Forms of Racial Discrimination; two weeks later, the GA would call on the CSW to draft an analogous Declaration on the Elimination of Discrimination against Women.[55] As with the declaration against racism, DEDAW stressed the keyword "discrimination" and the contradictions of Western liberalism, highlighting the ways that an emphasis on individual rights remained insufficient in the face of widespread de facto exclusions. As economist and IWY participant Devaki Jain explains, "The declaration made the first attempt to define discrimination against women by referring to laws, customs, regulations, practices, and prejudice as being responsible for denying and limiting women's equality of rights with men. It viewed discrimination as incompatible with human dignity and the welfare of society."[56]

Demanding rights and fighting discrimination need not be mutually exclusive objectives, as the African American civil rights movement had demonstrated, but in the competing ideologies that defined the Cold War battlefields, a fundamental divide lay between the belief that social justice could be attained by protecting equal rights and opportunities and the conviction that it required a more thoroughgoing restructuring of economies and societies. The tensions between the New York and Geneva committees reflected this debate. While the Geneva group generally stressed broader structural problems and systemic factors— widespread female illiteracy, the undervaluing of uncommodified forms of labor, the particular burden that poverty placed on women, the social consequences of colonialism and of violent conflict—the New York group tended to concentrate on individual solutions that treated symptoms—encouraging family planning, facilitating self-help programs, and providing women with training programs or access to credit. While the New York committee focused on the status of women compared to men in the same circumstances, the Geneva committee gave more attention to the ways that inequalities among social groups and nations particularly affected women. The New York committee saw Geneva's emphasis on questions such as racism and structural inequalities as political distractions from matters that might properly be considered women's issues; from Geneva's perspective, the New York committee's solutions failed to address the underlying problems.

When the New York committee reconvened in April, anxieties ran high about the impending ECOSOC meeting.[57] Hymer urged committee members to contact any ECOSOC representatives they knew personally and meet with them before the upcoming debate on the IWY conference and voluntary fund. Rumors that Colombia's commitment to host appeared "far from definite" only compounded their worries [58] To give the committee an international perspective, Hymer invited the Filipina CSW member Helena Z. Benítez to report on recent meetings in London and Kenya. Calling for "all hands on deck" to promote IWY, Benítez advocated a position that enjoyed considerable support on the New York committee: promote equality to place more women in prominent professional and political positions, and development and peace would follow. Helvi Sipilä arrived for the latter part of the meeting to offer more tactical advice: try the "human rights approach" and the "development approach," stressing the "interrelatedness between development and population." The key to securing UN support for women's issues, Sipilä recognized, was to place them under the rubric of issues that already enjoyed support from powerful actors.

These discussions remained inseparable from the context of a GA special session in late April to vote on the New International Economic Order—an issue that sharply highlighted the conflicts between the United States and the non-aligned countries.[59] The State Department distinguished between the more radical non-aligned group (sardonically dubbed NAG), which achieved "consensus based on logrolling between Africans (on colonial themes) and Arabs (on Israel)," and the more pragmatic G-77, which emerged out of trade and development concerns and "concentrated on [a] tough, pragmatic approach to LDC economic aims."[60] Following the GA special session, however, State Department personnel fumed that the G-77 and NAG had joined forces to "steamroller" debate, preventing votes on US-sponsored resolutions.[61] Finding a wedge issue seemed more urgent than ever.

Finally, in mid-May, ECOSOC overwhelmingly approved the IWY, although divisive issues arose as soon as planning commenced.[62] The Brazilian and Argentine representatives struck references to family planning from the "development" section of the agenda, eliminating the call for social services including health, family planning, child care, social and community services that IWY advocates had hoped would draw support from the well-funded UNFPA. The Human Rights Commission objected to having discrimination against women fall within its purview. ECOSOC rejected the CSW's proposal to create a women's advisory committee to rectify the imbalance between men and women in UN professional positions, even as a group of UN employees issued a resolution demanding steady progress toward equal numbers of men and women in professional categories by 1980.[63]

Hymer's committee was jubilant at the news that the Bogota conference would take place, but Margaret Bruce immediately dampened its collective glee with her budget report. Existing funding amounted only to $266,000; by comparison, the UN had come up with $3 million for the Bucharest population conference and $900,000 for the Rome food conference. Bruce urged the NGO leaders to contribute to the newly created voluntary fund.[64] Committee members suggested selling IWY bracelets produced by Franklin Mint and asking as many women as possible to make small donations to the fund. Bruce and ECOSOC envisioned a modest technical conference for IWY, using $5,000 of the budget to pay consultants to help devise the agenda and indicated that the conference "findings" would be reported to the UN General Assembly. She outlined a series of regional preparatory seminars to be held before the conference and explained the need for an "action plan" that would recommend training programs and specific projects that governments could fund.

The members of the New York NGO committee knew that distracting attention from the East Berlin conference required something more ambitious. Hymer initially proposed a three-day pre-conference of consultative-status NGOs that would focus on findings from regional meetings, discuss the draft World Plan of Action, and make recommendations to the intergovernmental conference that would follow. Although only consultative-status NGOs would be allowed to vote on resolutions or reports, Hymer suggested they might include select national organizations to attend as observers. The committee resolved "without objection" to organize the NGO meeting in Bogota and sent the proposal to Geneva "for advice and comment."[65]

Anxious to push forward, Hymer sent Harris more detailed plans for the NGO conference, explaining that "Craig [Schuller-McGeachy] and others" had been "eager that this meeting take place" to eclipse the later one in East Berlin.[66] Hymer shared the concern about the Geneva group's interested politics and collectivist ethos and stressed to Harris that her organizing committee was "not a counterpart of the Geneva group but rather a working group of good individuals representing international and national organizations, the purpose being to promote the observance of IWY."[67] Although she perceived "pressures to prevent an NGO meeting in Bogota," Hymer's convictions had only grown after she witnessed the maneuvering in the CSW and bureaucratic delays in the ECOSOC Social Committee.

While Hymer understood the New York committee to be the legitimate body to oversee NGO activities for IWY, the Geneva committee saw it as a local organization that acted prematurely without proper consultation. Shahnaz Alami had called an "expanded consultative meeting" of the Geneva committee for all the major WINGOs to meet in early July at the ILO office; the New York committee would need to seek approval there.[68] Hymer contacted all WINGO presidents to drum up support, and the New York committee continued its work on a tentative program for the NGO forum.[69]

Hymer and Schuller-McGeachy cannot have been pleased with what they heard back from Geneva. The Berlin planning clearly had far outpaced the Bogota planning in terms of both logistics and fundraising. The organizing committee for the World Congress of Women met with Helvi Sipilä in Geneva to discuss the East Berlin congress. Sipilä "showed great interest in the Congress," which offered both a convenient location and the facilities for an event anticipated to draw 2,000 people "from all social strata and coming from all continents."[70] If the New York group seemed to have the ear of Margaret Bruce, the Geneva group clearly had the attention of the higher-ranked Sipilä. Three days after her appearance in Geneva, Secretary-General Waldheim announced Sipilä's appointment as the secretary-general for IWY, empowered to "act on Mr. Waldheim's behalf regarding the Year and the Conference."[71]

To make matters worse, the Geneva meeting had highlighted precisely those issues that the New York committee hoped to cordon off in the realm of politics to prevent them from adulterating the IWY proceedings. Dwain Epps, the president of CONGO's Geneva office, opened with his reflections on the "new era of NGO cooperation on matters of substantial importance—not just to the UN— but to peoples of the world."[72] Epps, the well-regarded executive secretary of the Commission of Churches on International Affairs, had developed a career focused on social justice while serving as a Presbyterian minister near Neshoba, Mississippi, in 1964 when three civil rights workers were murdered by white supremacists.[73] "Up to now, in UN-related circles," he told the gathered WINGO leaders, "we have tended to react to individual crisis situations, concentrating our attention on them for more or less specified periods of time. . . . But the facts are that, with very few exceptions, we have made pitifully little progress in any of the areas which the UN has singled out for special attention. . . . [W]e must begin to see the interrelatedness of each of these problems, and how they form parts of a single, generalized crisis. If we are unable to do so, we may be—quite literally—doomed." Epps saw the array of crises—inflationary spirals, food shortages, the looming nuclear threat, and the "so-called 'crisis of morality' in industrialized Western societies"—as all of a piece, and the NGOs' IWY program would need to address matters holistically. Overcoming these challenges without women's full participation, he argued, would be "like a person trying to swim up-stream with one arm and one leg tied together." Rather than mobilizing women and NGOs in support of the UN's and member states' priorities—"so often introduced in UN resolutions by the phrase, 'the role of women in . . .'"—Epps recommended a vast campaign of "'conscientization' work among women—and men—i.e. creating in them a critical awareness of their present situation and of their true human potential."

With Epps's opening address setting the tone, the assembled WINGO presidents agreed to an ambitious two-pronged strategy that centered on implementing existing UN instruments and ensuring that the IWY message reached "all women regardless of nationality, religion, social background and so on" through "day-to-day contact with women of all walks of life." Regarding the New York committee's plans for an NGO conference in Bogota, the WINGOs decided that they had neither enough information about the proposal nor enough time to consider it and "referred the matter to the [Geneva] Sub-committee and asked it to adopt suitable decisions." The abiding sense was that such events should not come at the expense of more quotidian efforts. As if the rebuff in Geneva were not worrisome enough, rumors started to reach the New York NGO committee that the results of Colombia's April presidential election had unsettled the plans for the Bogota conference.

The Bucharest population conference in August was a game-changer for IWY planning. It not only put women squarely in the middle of geopolitical considerations but also demonstrated the impact that NGOs could have on intergovernmental negotiations. Population control was thus widely seen as a pet issue of the United States, the strongest proponent of World Population Year. "Through foundations, private organizations, and later through USAID," writes historian Mark Mazower, "American population control enthusiasts went around the UN, eventually managing to set up what can only be described as a front organization within it—the UN Fund for Population Activities—which operated entirely outside the control of member nations."[74] Preparations for the November 1974 UN Food Conference in Rome drew notice to per-capita consumption rates in industrialized countries, even as the organizers for the population conference trained their attention on population levels with little regard for per-capita impact. Concerns mounted about a "grain drain" from the Third World to the First and steadily increasing levels of malnutrition and poverty in the former, putting pressure on the United States in particular to respond. State Department staffers foresaw conflicts in Bucharest, particularly arising from the pervasive perception that US population policies arose from "racism, economic imperialism and desire to maintain dominance." Third World complaints of the "alleged profligate use of the world's resources by the U.S. and other developed countries" meant that the US delegation "may be faced with demands for a reduction in their use and a more equitable distribution."[75]

Although IWY and even population matters did not figure among the State Department's headliner concerns, the United States actively sought issues on which it could demonstrate leadership and make common cause with Third World countries.[76] Diplomats tried out this new approach in Bucharest, deciding a few days into the conference that their policy of "maintaining a low profile was unproductive, and that a more active role should be taken."[77] The Bucharest conference convinced US policymakers that IWY offered the perfect opportunity to strengthen ties with Third World governments as well as a side door through which they could bring in population-control programs.[78]

Seeking strategies to defuse hostilities with the G-77, Kissinger arranged a lunch with leading development economists and international legal scholars, who drew strong connections among the population boom, the food crisis, and the Third World's growing militancy and audacity—a constellation of concerns that drew Kissinger's attention to the issue of women's rights. The US State Department's interest in IWY—as measured by financial commitment—grew as its officers perceived clear foreign-policy opportunities. Kissinger's executive secretary, George Springsteen, informed Nixon's counselor for women's programs, Anne Armstrong, that a State Department interdepartmental committee had called for establishing a national commission for IWY with a $500,000 budget.[79] While still paltry compared to the funding allocated other programs, this budget dwarfed the $36,000 that had been granted to fund Ruth Bacon's center. Springsteen was explicit about the funding's diplomatic purpose: to sway the ECOSOC vote in favor of the US proposal for IWY over Soviets opposition. Although Springsteen confessed that the "major obstacle seems to be finding funding for this program," he indicated that Bacon's center worked closely with an advisory group of thirty-five NGOs—presumably the New York CONGO group—that focused on fundraising and publicity.

For WINGOs, Bucharest had offered even more valuable lessons. When the New York NGO committee reconvened in September, its members were giddy from their Bucharest triumph. Sipilä described Bucharest as a "turning point in history, where governments in reality will be giving consideration to the issues: the status of women, equality of men and women, women in policy making positions and the integration of women in development." Noting that the first committee of the Population Conference added three paragraphs about improving women's status to the World Population Plan of Action, Sipilä proclaimed, "Now we can say that all governments strongly supported what IWY proposes."[80] She hoped, she told the New York committee, that Bucharest had set a precedent for a similar NGO meeting in Bogota. The New York committee members must have been relieved by her report that she met with the Colombians in Bucharest and would visit the Bogota facilities soon.

Despite the committee's collective enthusiasm, Esther Hymer struck a cautionary note. ICW members in Bogota reported that facilities would be quite limited and most likely would not accommodate an NGO forum similar to the one in Bucharest. Her appeal to NGO presidents had yielded minimal financial support; the UN liaison, Ann Heller, suggested selling IWY buttons to raise funds. Most distressingly, Hymer said that the WINGO meeting in Geneva had declined to endorse an NGO forum in Bogota. "It was suggested that Bogota was 'so far,'" Hymer explained, "and that the WIDF meeting in East Berlin would be easier to attend." Mary Craig Schuller-McGeachy tried to conjure a bit more optimism, arguing that, once Bogota plans became concrete, organizations would respond more positively. Any day now, she assured the committee, they should know more.

Relations between New York and Geneva NGO committees grew more mistrustful amid this uncertainty about Bogota. Geneva's WYWCA representative Alice Paquier wrote to her New York counterpart Mildred Jones that she had attended several NGO meetings in Geneva at which the topic of an NGO conference in Bogota had arisen. "There were some reactions," she explained, "mostly of disappointment and regrets that the New York small committee on International Women's Year has gone rather far in their organization of the NGO Bogota meeting without more cooperation with the Geneva Sub-Committee on Women, and especially with the NGO Bureau."[81] Paquier's reference to New York's "small committee" underscored differences about who legitimately represented the WINGO community. The Geneva group included a larger, more diverse array of members. By comparison, the New York committee seemed parochial, although its local membership allowed the committee to meet more frequently and plan more quickly.

Despite some conscientious efforts at diversification, the New York committee was primarily composed of New Yorkers and was overwhelmingly Judeo-Christian, with about a third of the NGOs represented claiming explicit religious affiliations.[82] The non-religious NGOs present included professional organizations, such as the International Federation of Business and Professional Women and Zonta International, as well as secular service organizations such as Altrusa International and the Pan-Pacific Southeast Asian Women's Association. Most of the organizations had been established and remained headquartered in the United States, and the rest were headquartered in London and various European cities. The New York committee included only one communist bloc NGO, the World Peace Council, and no representatives from the Third World. Over the coming months, the percentage of religiously affiliated organizations would grow, as would participation by population-oriented organizations such as the Population Crisis Committee and the Population Institute, which joined the International Planned Parenthood Federation (IPPF).

Upon hearing of Paquier's letter, Rosalind Harris moved quickly to defuse the brewing hostilities between the two NGO committees. She immediately sent copies of the New York committee's minutes to Shahnaz Alami, noting that it had been "quite active and generated several ideas" and stressing the importance of the two groups working together. She sent the same minutes to Elizabeth Palmer, the secretary-general of the WYWCA, explaining, "I understand there is considerable comment in Geneva about the activities of the [New York committee]. This Committee was approved by the Board of the Conference of NGOs (NY Section) following the request of several organizations for its establishment." She also sent the minutes to the UN liaison to the Geneva committee, noting again that they had been regularly conveyed and remarking curtly, "I suppose it is possible that there was some slip despite the fact that various people in Geneva referred to the contents of them occasionally." When she wrote to Alami again ten days later, she stressed the importance of NGOs' contributions to IWY and praised the Geneva committee's work but continued, "I note that your committee has not recorded any specific suggestions about the role of the NGOs, in connection with an IWY Conference. If you have any specific ideas perhaps you could let me know, because we must work with the UN on the possibilities."[83] Even the conference, as Harris well knew by this point, seemed quite uncertain. As she wrote to Anne Sieve of IPPF, "I understand that there are some real problems at this moment in connection with the whole Bogota idea as a result of the change of government. When we know more I shall let you know."[84]

Scene 3

Getting to Mexico City

Helvi Sipilä tried repeatedly to schedule a visit to Bogota to review the facilities and logistics, only to be put off by Colombian officials.[1] By early October 1974, it seemed evident that the Colombian government was no longer willing to foot the bill for the local expenses of a major international conference. Australia, Mexico, and Iran all volunteered to host the IWY conference should the Bogota option fall through. These regional leaders aspired to exercise more influence in diplomatic maneuverings, particularly in mediating negotiations between the powerful nations that held the permanent seats on the UN Security Council and the agitating G-77 countries. Leading diplomats from these mid-level powers spotted a chance to elevate their standing by showcasing their accomplishments in women's rights.

The question of a possible venue change remained confidential not only because of diplomatic concerns but also because the politics surrounding which countries would host UN conferences had become increasingly fraught.[2] The Secretariat could not simply assume the power to change a decision made by ECOSOC and the General Assembly. Sipilä preferred Mexico, which could offer better facilities and seemed like a more enthusiastic host, and was eager for a resolution, since she had been tiptoeing around the matter with NGOs and other interested parties. A week later, the Colombian ambassador cited new austerity policies when he notified Waldheim that Colombia would have to forgo the honor of hosting the IWY conference, a decision facilitated "by the generous offer made by a friendly country that would like to act as host to such an important event." Sipilä must have been relieved by this news, noting to Waldheim that it meant the "matter is therefore no more confidential except that we have to find a formula in which this change of host will be introduced to Member States." The General Assembly would affirm the venue change during the same session in which it voted on the Charter on the Economic Rights and Duties of States (CERDS), Mexico's proposal to codify the New International Economic Order.[3]

Perhaps no one was more pleased with this development than Mexican president Luis Echeverría, who had set his sights on international governance and openly jockeyed to succeed Waldheim as secretary-general. This combination of personal and national ambitions and the opportunity to demonstrate Mexican leadership on the world stage led the Echeverría administration to highlight the ways that Mexico's foreign and domestic policy dovetailed with the UN's own priorities and, by extension, the imagined "international community." Echeverría's Cold War allegiances were murky—both the CIA and the KGB courted him— but his ambitions to emerge as a Third Worldist political leader were clear.[4]

Echeverría had bolstered his credentials among the G-77 countries by introducing the foundational principles of the CERDS at the April 1972 UNCTAD meeting in Santiago, Chile. "Mexico's President Echeverria became closely identified with the Charter and accepted its approval as a personal victory in his campaign to extend his influence as an LDC leader," the CIA reported.[5] The Charter, which Echeverría and his supporters insisted on calling the Carta Echeverría, offered the NIEO a more legislative set of rules and regulations to promote sovereign control over natural resources and foreign investment as well as more equitable terms of international trade. Algerian president Houari Boumedienne had called for the NIEO at the 1973 Non-Aligned Conference in Algiers and again in his opening speech to the 1974 Sixth Special Session of the GA. Mexico and Algeria—both petroleum-producing nations with at least a nominal revolutionary tradition—benefited from both OPEC (Organization of Petroleum Exporting Countries)-induced petroleum price spikes and the GA's transformation into a G-77 stronghold. The two nations displaced India and Yugoslavia as leaders of the G-77, over which Mexico presided in 1973–74.

If the NIEO had been a call to arms, the CERDS seemed to offer a peace treaty, but one that threatened the holdings of US and European investors in the Third World as it sought to establish "generally accepted norms to govern international economic relations systematically and . . . to establish a just order and a stable world."[6] Calling for "the establishment of the new international economic order, based on equity, sovereign equality, interdependence, common interest and co-operation among all States, irrespective of their economic and social systems," the Charter was adopted in December 1974 with overwhelming support in the General Assembly.[7] "As to the differences in approach of countries to the NIEO on the one hand and the CERDS on the other," an Australian Foreign Affairs officer explained to Elizabeth Reid, "I am pretty sure the answer is the very simple one that the former is a collection of pious hopes and vague principles to which assent is easy because substantially meaningless, while the CERDS is much more specific and detailed and might therefore seem to impose obligations on states supporting it."[8] Its supporters recognized, moreover, that overcoming vocal opposition from the United States and Europe would require that its principles be reiterated at every opportunity. Hosting IWY, it turned out, would provide just such an opportunity.

It doubtless occurred to Echeverría that holding a women's conference on the themes of equality, development, and peace would not only whitewash his involvement in violent state repression but also secure his place on the international stage. The IWY conference would be the first major international event in Mexico City since the tumultuous 1968 Olympics, where sprinters Tommie Smith and John Carlos memorably raised their black-gloved fists in expressions of black power. The Olympics had taken place only ten days after the Mexican military had opened fire on a peaceful student demonstration in Tlatelolco Plaza.[9] Most Mexicans still consider Echeverría—then serving as minister of the interior—as the intellectual author of the Tlatelolco massacre.

The Echeverría administration and the long-governing Partido Revolucionario Institucional (PRI, Institutional Revolutionary Party) responded to UN concerns about population control with alacrity and a characteristically presidentialist approach. In March 1974, Echeverría created the National Population Council under the leadership of Luisa María Leal, who had had divided loyalties during the '68 movement as both a federal employee (and a PRIísta) and a professor of law and political science at the Universidad Nacional Autónoma de México (UNAM), where she supported student protests.[10] Women with backgrounds and convictions similar to Leal's would populate the Mexican feminist movement over the coming years, underscoring its ambivalent and ambiguous relationship to state power.

Amid rumors that Colombia might not host the IWY conference, Echeverría had introduced to Congress a constitutional amendment to grant women equal rights.[11] Adopted in December 1974, the amended fourth article of the Mexican constitution begins, "Man and woman are equal before the law. This will protect the organization and development of the family."[12] It goes on to guarantee the "right to decide in a free, responsible, and informed manner the number and spacing of children." It establishes the right to health care and underscores the government's responsibility for providing health services, the guarantee of a "dignified and decorous living," and parents' responsibility to "preserve the rights of minors regarding the satisfaction of their needs and their physical and mental health."

The day Colombia withdrew its invitation, the interior minister informed Mexican state governors that Echeverría had appointed Attorney General Pedro Ojeda Paullada to coordinate Mexico's IWY program.[13] He asked all governors to perform a complete review of women's juridical and social status and reminded them that a month earlier Echeverría had submitted constitutional and legal reforms to Congress to "eliminate the obstacles and inequalities [that] prevented women's incorporation into the collective life." He exhorted governors to pass legislation in their own states to support the IWY program and to urge municipal governments to do the same. Any queries regarding this initiative or IWY could be addressed to the newly installed Mexico IWY program offices in Mexico City.

Mexico's IWY program office inspired envy among IWY advocates. Rosalind Harris described the Mexican organizing committee as a bit too rigid but impressive in its "organizational capacity."[14] Lili Hahn reported to fellow members of the New York NGO committee the bustle and energy around all the planned activities. The phone rang constantly, and a photographer busily snapped pictures of the twelve-member staff. "*12*—hear that U.S. Center?" Hahn asked, referring to Ruth Bacon's still woefully under-supported US Center for IWY.[15] The photo shoot was doubtless for the office's glossy, full-color, tabloid-sized monthly magazine, the first cover of which featured a quarter-profile torso shot looking up at a smiling Echeverría, accompanied by the full text of his declaration of IWY.[16] IWY ambassadors toured the country to explain "Programa México" and ensure that local political leaders "achieved the best results in the celebration of IWY."[17] PRI-affiliated labor unions and rural organizations sponsored events to extol the government's efforts on behalf of women's rights and to praise first lady María Esther Zuno de Echeverría's activities promoting the welfare of rural women and children. Women who attended these events and the first lady's speeches about motherhood as the transcendental human mission received a free set of plastic cups and pitchers.

All of these endeavors—the concerted population-control efforts, the constitutional amendment, and the lavish IWY offices—seemed geared not only to show that Mexico hewed to UN priorities but also to challenge the idea that industrialized countries should tutor developing countries either in rights-based concepts of juridical equality or appropriate state responses to UN programs. Indeed, the amendment passed in the final days of 1974, just as the Equal Rights Amendment lost momentum in the United States. If the US government envisioned an IWY in which private funding and initiatives constituted nearly the entire program, and the Australian government offered its imprimatur with public funding for women's initiatives as well as the creation of a high-level office, the Mexican government advanced an IWY program intended to eclipse private organizations with state-orchestrated efforts. But the success of Mexico's postrevolutionary government depended upon its capacity to incorporate oppositional programs into its own. The constitutional amendment took up core demands of the feminist movement—reproductive freedom and equality before the law— but put them in the framework of protecting the sanctity of Mexican families. The point of all these official efforts was to credit Echeverría and the PRI, but the office created opportunities for activists to raise awareness about issues and make claims on public resources.

When leading Mexican feminists learned in November 1974 that the IWY conference would take place in Mexico City the following summer, they were outraged. Much as the civil rights movement had fostered a dominant strain of US feminism, Mexican feminism grew out of the struggles and frustrations of Mexico's 1968 student movement.[18] To feminist leaders, the idea that Echeverría would burnish his international image by holding himself up as an advocate of women's rights seemed a blatant attempt to coopt their movement. That he would do so by hosting a UN conference at the Ministry of Foreign Relations on Tlatelolco Plaza, the site where their comrades had been massacred, was as if Richard Nixon had convened a peace conference at Kent State.

Mexico's small but energetic feminist movement, dubbed the "new wave"— *la nueva ola*—of Mexican feminism, took on its inchoate institutional formation in 1970 with the founding of Mujeres en Acción Solidaria (MAS) under the leadership of Marta Acevedo, a leader during the 1968 movement who had witnessed the Tlatelolco massacre. Several leading feminists recall meeting the charismatic Acevedo after a lecture that US intellectual Susan Sontag delivered at the UNAM political science department, the headquarters of the '68 student mobilizations.[19] From its early days, this new wave had a strong cosmopolitan streak. Many feminist leaders had moved to Mexico City to escape authoritarian regimes or political unrest in places like Chile, Guatemala, and Argentina.[20] In addition to having contact in Mexico City with feminist intellectuals like Sontag, many women who led the new-wave organizations had lived or studied abroad, where they came into contact with feminist ideas such as the wages-for-housework campaign, feminist practices such as consciousness-raising groups, and feminist subjectivities such as lesbianism. Of the women who formed MAS, several came from the Mexican Communist Party or the Unión Nacional de Mujeres Mexicanas (UNMM, National Union of Mexican Women), Mexico's WIDF affiliate. In recollections published in Mexico's feminist press, women frequently linked their formation of feminist consciousness to a transformational encounter with ideas from outside Mexico.[21] Replicating many of the sectarian splits that fractured the Mexican left in 1970s, a minority group within MAS accused the majority of being "insufficiently Marxist." The majority broke off and formed the Movimiento de Liberación de la Mujer (MLM, Women's Liberation Movement) a name chosen, as MLM leader Marta Lamas recalls, because it "identified us with that international current."[22] This cosmopolitan aspect of the movement—combined with the internationalist influence of the communist and Trotskyist groups that loomed large within these circles—engendered a deep suspicion of Mexican nationalism, of the PRI, and of Echeverría in particular.

Feminists' suspicions of government cooptation also emerged from experience. The PRI-dominated Mexican state—already fueled by petrodollars and undergirded by a vast network of officially sanctioned popular organizations— could readily take control of the feminists' agenda just as it had so many others in the decades following Mexico's 1910 revolution and particularly since the 1929 formation of the ruling party. Echeverría's shepherding of the constitutional amendment echoed President Adolfo Ruiz Cortines's proclamation of women's suffrage two decades earlier, ignoring entirely the long-pending constitutional amendment for which activists had struggled to the point of a hunger strike.[23] While feminist organizations used Mother's Day as an occasion to demand reproductive rights and to protest the reduction of womanhood to motherhood, official events—and even the constitutional amendment—fashioned IWY as a celebration of the conventional family, albeit one reduced from its customary size.

For all its cosmopolitanism and efforts to create affinities with a global feminism, Mexican feminism was also refracted by its national context. The government's willingness to use repressive force had produced the intended effects of generating divisions within dissident movements and intimidating activists from demonstrating. Echeverría had campaigned for the Mexican presidency in 1970 under the slogan of "democratic opening," but even in this more tolerant climate women attended meetings but then shied away from participation in public demonstrations.[24] Lamas recalls that two-thirds of the MAS membership begged off the first time its leadership called for a public march.[25] Their reservations were well founded; declassified documents reveal that the Mexico's secret police kept close tabs on feminist organizations and reported names of those participating in meetings and demonstrations. Further, many US and European feminists' core demands did not resonate among their Mexican counterparts. While US feminists struggled for the passage of the Equal Rights Amendment, Echeverría effectively had decreed one in Mexico by fiat. While US and European feminists debated the merits of demanding wages for housework, Mexican feminists generally paid someone else to perform this labor.

Despite feminists' misgivings, hosting the IWY conference had induced the federal government both to plan a dizzying calendar of related events and to dedicate substantial funds toward creating resource centers, producing publications, sponsoring exhibits and other cultural events, and supporting services such as child-care centers and health clinics. Feminist activists struggled to keep pace with official programming.[26] Seeing the UN and Mexican state projects as a "lukewarm and opportunistic appropriation of feminist proposals," in March of 1975 a committed group of feminists drawn primarily from the left formed the Women's Front against International Women's Year.[27] The group traveled all over the country convening conferences, presenting street theater, organizing movie clubs, planning solidarity actions with female textile and transportation workers, meeting with feminists from various countries, and passing out flyers everywhere they could. Citing the official IWY themes of equality, development, and peace, the flyers proclaimed, "We do not want equality of conditions to be exploited in the same way as men; we do not want development that perpetuates economic, racial, and sexual inequalities; we do not want peace that only signifies the stability of the current system."[28]

Esperanza Brito de Martí, the leader of the Movimiento Nacional de Mujeres (National Women's Movement)—which distinguished itself from the MLM—later recalled that the level of state support also raised the stakes of opting out of the official program. After meeting with Attorney General Ojeda Paullada in late 1974 for an enthusiastic discussion of her organization's planned activities, Brito received a "gentle reminder" from his office that her proposals would only receive support if they became part of the official IWY program. Once the group signed on, the funding came pouring in. The group's collaboration came at a price, however. "We were rejected and discriminated against by members of other feminist groups," she would recall two decades later, "They accused us of being members of the PRI, which we never were, of being petty bourgeois because we didn't wear jeans, and of being reformist because we wanted to change the laws."[29] Brito and her *compañeras* explained that they did not share the PRIístas political convictions but did believe that PRI women merited the same support and respect as any others, a position that drew sharp criticism from the feminist left.

The criticism of the PRI's investments in IWY came from the right as well. María Elena Alvarez Bernal, the daughter of a Catholic militant who had taken up arms against Mexico's postrevolutionary government and the wife of a politician soon elected president of the conservative Partido Acción Nacional (PAN, National Action Party), explained to an audience of PAN loyalists that women found themselves trapped between a *machista* society that treated them as objects and the forces of consumer culture that saw them merely as vehicles for promoting sales. Women's liberation, she maintained, would come not from feminist activism, government intervention, or international programs but rather from the natural development of humanity. Her fellow panelist, the first female PANista federal deputy Florencia Villalobos Chaparro, stressed that the constitutional reforms were unnecessary. If God created men and women as equals in intelligence and capacity but with physical differences, it would be superfluous to underscore these facts in the constitution. While Villalobos applauded the benefits that IWY promised, she ironically reiterated Soviet objections when she expressed reservations about the waste of energy and public expenditure on meetings and hospitality that excluded those at the bottom of the social pyramid.[30]

All these factors—personal and national ambitions for global leadership, challenges from the right and the left, Mexico's complicated history of revolutionary politics and social justice movements—would shape dynamics at the IWY conference. Mexico City served as a microcosm of the global problems under discussion at the UN. The city's overcrowding and pollution problems illustrated the concerns of environmentalists and population-control advocates; between birth rates and rural-urban migration, the metropolitan area had nearly quadrupled its population in the quarter century leading up to 1975, when it joined Tokyo and the New York metropolitan area as the three UN-designated "mega-cities."[31] Squatter communities mushroomed virtually overnight; the municipality of Ciudad Nezahualcóyotl had grown from a population of roughly 40,000 in 1954 to nearly 2 million by 1975. The growing inequality that G-77 countries pointed to on a global scale had become increasingly visible in Mexico City. By 1974, the service-sector economy had outpaced the industrial economy, and roughly 70 percent of the economically active population earned minimum wage or less—barely a subsistence income.[32]

If the Echeverría administration hoped that the IWY conference would allow Mexico to showcase its efforts to address these intractable problems of inequality and population growth, it was less enthusiastic about the prospect of hosting scores of NGOs. "In those days," recalls Iranian UN mission member Zohreh (ZuZu) Tabatabai, "member states were worried about NGOs being radical revolutionaries; the idea that they might be cooperative was not seen as an option, they were viewed more like rabble-rousers."[33] The New York NGO committee needed to convince the Mexican government of the wisdom of inviting thousands of activists to Mexico just at the moment when the Echeverría administration hoped to draw international attention. As Lili Hahn reported back to fellow committee members, "After describing what kind of 'animal' an NGO is I caught one cautious if anxious question, something like 'any politicos'? This indicates to me that neither this busy planning committee in Mex nor the powers that be at the UN relish the thought of demonstrations."[34] Indeed, as ECOSOC discussed the Secretariat's IWY plans, the paragraphs regarding possible NGO meetings drew particular questions and concerns about which NGOs might participate and in what capacity. The Soviet delegate insisted that the UN not issue invitations to NGOs until after approval of the final list during the spring ECOSOC session, which would conclude only a few weeks before the IWY conference itself.[35] The NGO tribune, which operated autonomously from the UN, could of course issue invitations whenever it wanted but would need permission from the Mexican government, and some participants would require visas. The tribune organizers had their work cut out for them, but at least the IWY conference had taken one important step toward becoming a reality.

Rosalind Harris enlisted two high-powered allies to allay the Mexican government's concerns about an NGO event. The elder statesman Antonio Carrillo Flores, who had served as secretary-general for World Population Year and the conference, wrote directly to Attorney General Pedro Ojeda Paullada to sing Harris's praises and heap commendation upon the NGO tribune at the Bucharest conference. "The event was very lucid and very lively since participants there

acted in a personal capacity," he explained. "I believe I remarked upon it the evening that I had the pleasure of having you to my house, which is your house, just
last month."[36] Harris also secured the support of Marcial Plehn-Mejía, a Mexican
diplomat who had worked at UNDP and UNCTAD in Geneva and had served
as secretary of the World Population Plan working group in Bucharest. Just after
the new year, Plehn-Mejía reported to Harris that the Mexican government
"welcomed the tribune" and, while it could not offer funding or accommodations, it would provide a convention space at the National Medical Center; local
support personnel; simultaneous translation; and the translation, reproduction,
and distribution of documents.[37]

The conference's relocation to Mexico changed the dynamics around IWY
in ways that seemed to mark a US victory over the Soviets. Although the GA's
IWY resolution ultimately split the difference between the US and Soviet proposals, calling for both a conference and a special session, the Mexico City conference became the year's centerpiece rather than the East Berlin conference or
campaigns to ratify existing UN instruments.[38] It also bolstered the New York
committee's leadership for an NGO event, since its more nimble structure and
proximity to UN headquarters made a critical difference as time grew short.
Issues that animated the Geneva committee—those generally included under
the IWY theme of "peace," such as disarmament, anti-racism, anti-colonialism,
and human rights—were pushed to the margins and often overlooked entirely
in conversations in both the Secretariat and the New York committee. Margaret
Bruce reported to the GA's Third Committee that the Secretariat had developed
an IWY conference agenda of "three main substantive items": the "achievement
of equal rights, opportunities and responsibilities," the "integration of women
into the development process as equal partners with men," and the finalization
of a World Plan of Action.[39] Despite reassurances to the Soviets, peace had van-
ished in this formulation.[40]

As word spread about the conference's relocation, the buzz grew in the NGO
world. "I am hopeful that more substantial UN action will take place now that
Mexico City has finally been designated as the Conference site," Susan Doerr of
the American Freedom from Hunger Foundation wrote to the YWCA's Mildred
Persinger. "However, a lot remains to be done, and I think that the YWCA could
utilize this opportunity to great advantage."[41] In an apparent effort to bury the
hatchet, the New York and Geneva NGO committees decided to blame the
postal service for their poor relations. "Obviously, for reasons nobody could really understand," explained WYWCA's Alice Paquier, "reports and letters sent to
and from Europe and New York seemed to have never reached their destination."
As a conference in Mexico City now seemed certain and the intergovernmental
conference would be planned from UN headquarters in New York, "everyone
agreed" that the New York group should plan the NGO tribune.[42]

Planning still continued apace for the East Berlin conference. Given all the budgetary and logistical challenges that even the official UN conference faced, not to mention the NGO gathering, if ideology and geopolitical rivalries could have been set aside it would surely have been more sensible simply to hold the IWY conference in East Berlin and organize it from Geneva. The decision, then, to persist in organizing separate events reflects the New York committee's strong conviction that the communist bloc not claim women's equality as a byproduct of communism. "If the IWY is not a success," Paquier wrote to her New York counterparts, "it certainly will not be for lack of meetings."[43]

For women like Esther Hymer, these meetings were hardly interchangeable. The main purpose in wresting IWY control away from the Geneva group was to offer an education in individuals' role in securing authentic social change. The ethos informed even her thank-you notes. "You have made a tremendous contribution to the work of NGOs this past year and I for one express deep appreciation for your understanding and skill to bring about creative and constructive action," she wrote in a New Year's Eve note to Rosalind Harris. "You have carried too heavy a load but progress comes from effective action of individuals not of groups." She appended an essay for discussion at the next NGO committee meeting: "How to Reach the Grass Roots," by Eleanor Roberts of the Associated Country Women of the World. "When the term was first used," the essay began, "it summoned a vision of a vast countryside, peopled by sturdy pioneers whose integrity and resourcefulness could be called upon to wage whatever campaign was being fought."[44] The essay went on to call for an emphasis on outreach and education, an approach that coincided with the New York committee's priorities rather than the structural emphasis of its Geneva counterpart. Whatever activities the New York–based NGOs planned for IWY, they would bear the deep imprint of these two ideas: that NGO leaders advocated not for themselves but for other, presumably less fortunate women, and that this advocacy would principally take the form of training and organizational programs that would encourage these "sturdy pioneers" to help themselves.

By December, the New York committee could model the NGO tribune's format on two recent UN gatherings: the August Bucharest Population Conference, where NGOs convened in a separate forum and lobbied government delegations, and November's Rome Food Conference, where NGOs participated directly in the government conference committees and working groups. The Bucharest NGO forum had required more significant financial and logistical resources, but whatever they decided would have to sit well with prospective funders. Competition for funding resources compounded the considerable challenge of raising the estimated $200,000 necessary to run the NGO tribune. Not only was the UN itself passing the hat for contributions to the IWY voluntary fund, but two other activities slated to precede the conference—a seminar on women and development organized by the American Association for the Advancement of Science, and a journalists' "encounter" organized by the UN's Center for Economic and Social Information—required support as well.[45]

In order to pull off an NGO tribune in Mexico City, the New York committee needed to form a smaller, more focused organizing subcommittee and—more urgently—to find funding. The first stop was a few blocks away at the Ford Foundation, which was in the thick of its own feminist uprising, with program officers objecting to the foundation's lack of commitment to women and women's issues.[46] The tribune organizers offered funders an instrumental justification, describing NGOs as the critical link between the UN's idealist proposals and their implementation. "There is now consensus among the governments of the world," the committee wrote to the Ford Foundation, "that solutions to the problems of food and population are to a large extent in the hands of women. Unless these hands are strengthened, massive threats to human survival may not be confronted in time."[47] The foundation had underwritten the Bucharest NGO tribune, which it considered "an exceedingly cost-effective grant."[48] Program officer Adrienne Germain and others at Ford seemed to welcome the opportunity of an encore performance in Mexico City and met with a small group from the NGO committee. "This group is calling itself an advisory committee," Germain noted for the files, "to establish a Tribune (plan an agenda, undertake registration, raise funds, etc.). An official chair has yet to be nominated (I bet on Ros Harris) and it will probably not have the relatively well-structured administrative backup that the Population Tribune had; nor is it likely to have international representation because time is so short."

Germain most likely was not the only one surprised when Esther Hymer announced at the January NGO committee meeting that Mildred Persinger would chair the tribune organizing committee.[49] Persinger was not among the die-hard committee members who had attended since its early days as a subcommittee on women and development; indeed she had first attended a meeting in mid-April 1974 and sporadically over the summer, pinch-hitting for her fellow YWCA leader Mildred Jones.[50] A member of the National Board of the WYWCA who had marched on Washington in 1963 and been active in peace and human rights organizations, she had served as a public member of John F. Kennedy's commission on the status of women and had been chosen by USUN ambassador Charles Yost for a Nixon commission on UN relations.

Persinger first drew attention at the New York NGO committee when she delivered an animated account of the NGOs' victory at the Bucharest conference, gaining her entry to the inner circle of IWY planning.[51] When the New York NGO committee gathered in mid-September for a pre-meeting luncheon featuring a lecture by Margaret Mead, Persinger jotted down the world-famous anthropologist's maxim, "Every time you liberate a woman, you

liberate a man," and calls for greater "budgetary recognition" of IWY, containing population growth, and involving men in subsistence labors.[52] Following
Sipilä's report on Bucharest, Persinger recounted that women badgered delegates for five straight days to include a section on women's status in the conference documents. "The Plan of Action didn't seem to know who had the
babies," she explained, noting repeated instances in which population experts
had treated women as simply part of a problem. In the end, she told the committee, "Most of what we hoped for, we accomplished."[53] Hymer responded
with a warm note of thanks and an invitation to follow-up meetings with Sipilä
and other UN personnel.

Persinger received "various informal overtures" about planning the NGO
forum but had demurred, citing WYWCA commitments.[54] She agreed in the
end, with assurances that Harris would continue "more-or-less in charge," and
she turned out to have been an inspired and consequential choice. While committee members such as Hymer and Schuller-McGeachy retained a Cold War
mindset complete with antipathies toward the WIDF and the Geneva committee, Persinger's work with the WYWCA, as well as her pacifist and anti-racist
activism, earned her respect and trust across ideological divides. Her personal
correspondence, like that of Elizabeth Reid, demonstrates a warmth, gracious-
ness, and humor that endeared her to people around the world.

Most important, while the CONGO faithful strove to protect the prestige
and exclusiveness of consultative-status NGOs, Persinger seemed determined
to open things up. She began the first official meeting of the tribune organizing
committee with several critical announcements. First, logistical support from
the Mexican government made it "feasible to undertake a crash program to hold
an NGO Tribune concurrent with the World Conference of IWY." Gone were
the plans for a two- or three-day pre-conference and recommendations to inte-
grate NGOs into UN meetings. Gone too were suggestions to limit participation
to consultative-status NGOs. Persinger envisioned an "open forum for private
citizens" that would yield unexpected results and consistently stressed the critical importance of having a diverse array of participants. Mexico City would
have a full-length NGO meeting "open to all interested persons," preferably with
a two-day orientation for those unfamiliar with UN proceedings, and would require pre-registration.

Second, Persinger told the group, "Informal consultations with Geneva
NGO representatives resulted in agreement that organization of NGO activities in Mexico City for IWY should be done from New York, given the proximity of the site and shortness of time." Persinger's leadership and WYWCA ties
surely helped to secure this truce. As a result of the definitive sidelining of the
Geneva group, the tribune took on the pragmatic ethos of the New York committee, which agreed, "The Tribune program should probably take a functional

approach, with emphasis on strategies for reaching objectives." Ongoing correspondence with members of the Geneva committee, however, clearly indicated
that the Geneva organizers imagined a far more active role for themselves than
the New Yorkers did. Even as Persinger's committee mapped out the program
for a concurrent two-week tribune, the Geneva committee deliberated over the
structure and purpose of a three-day pre-conference, sending its decisions to
Persinger for consideration.[55] When the New York committee discussed the out-
lines of the tribune program, nobody even mentioned the Geneva committee's
carefully deliberated suggestions.[56] The immense pressures of time and limited
resources would further limit consultation between the two groups as the conference drew nearer.

Finally, Persinger stressed the importance of fundraising and emphasized,
"The major budget item will be travel and expenses for participants from less
developed countries who could not otherwise attend."[57] She seemed to ask everyone who corresponded with her about strategies for bringing more Third
World women, and Harris exhorted members of the NGO committee to use
their organizations' resources to sponsor the attendance of Third World participants.[58] Several funding entities would specify that their support should be earmarked for this purpose.[59] The emphasis on bringing in Third World participants
served a didactic purpose, although a quite different one than some envisioned.
"The explicit purpose of the Tribune is to show how diverse women's problems
are; that women in different parts of the world have different needs and aspirations," reported Ford Foundation program officer Elinor Barber in her memo
supporting the committee's approach. "Since there is some apprehension about
the domination of the NGO Conference by women from the U.S. and perhaps
from other developed countries (who are assumed to lean towards Western-
style 'Women's Lib'), an implicit purpose is to educate these Western women
about the problems of other women, especially those in the Third World."[60]

Not everyone agreed that increasing the number of Third World participants
would contribute to the tribune's success, however. When she received the draft
tribune program, organizing committee member Fanny Simon, a New Yorker
representing the International Council of Social Democratic Women, wrote
to Persinger, "My own first reaction was: 'Heavens! Are we reproducing in
the Tribune the conditions in the General Assembly?' A substantial number
should be from developing countries, especially as the emphasis of the World
Conference will be on development. And yet, is not a distribution of about 70 to
30 per cent rather excessive? Those from the developed countries can learn from
the developing but so can those from the developing from the developed." She
commented that Persinger "certainly must have gone out of [her] way to minimize the participants from North America" and objected, in particular, to the
program including no panelists from Israel.[61]

Limitations of time and money meant that the NGO tribune organizers relied heavily on their existing networks and working relationships. They particularly mined two veins. First, because of the strong ties from the recent triumph in Bucharest, most of the committee's ideas about the tribune agenda, funding sources, and additional personnel came directly from that experience. In mid-March, when the committee finally secured resources for a staff director, it quickly hired on Marcia-Ximena Bravo, a Chilean living in New York City who was on loan from the Population Council and had worked at the World Population Conference. When the organizers set their sights on organizing an IWY newspaper, they first asked those who had edited *Planet*, the newspaper in Bucharest. Many of the participants who appeared on the tribune program—particularly Third World participants—came through population-control organizations. Second, progressive Christian organizations offered the other set of networks that supplied Third World participants and strengthened working relationships. For Mildred Persinger, the WYWCA offered the obvious quarry.[62] In addition, Unitarian Universalists (UU), the Commission on Churches in International Affairs, Church Women United, and the Quaker Friends all played important organizational roles.

Once Bravo joined the team, the tenor of the tribune began to emerge, cultivating a festive atmosphere that combined education with celebration. The program would include not only panels of "resource persons"—people with either research- or practice-based expertise on specific issues—but also films, music, art and dance exhibitions, craft displays, and slide shows. Noting the absence of restaurants near the Centro Médico, Persinger and Bravo stressed the importance of arranging a food service at the facility so that tribune participants could have chance encounters and informal exchanges. Persinger reported to the Ford Foundation, "Under [Bravo's] creative hand the program is taking a lively form, and individuals with very impressive credentials are daily declaring their intention of participating."[63] She urged the organizing committee not to get bogged down in concerns about whether too many people would overwhelm the tribune facilities and to focus instead on the "function of the tribune—to spread information and concern." Unless she saw evidence that excessive participation posed a problem, she noted, "everyone is welcome and so are financial contributions."[64] Persinger wrote to the Ford Foundation's Elinor Barber, "We do not expect [the tribune] to be an extravaganza, but by no means a run-of-the-mill event."[65] Ten days later, Ford made a "core support grant" of $25,000 for the NGO tribune.

The decision to resist scheduling the tribune's last few days reflected Persinger's imaginary of an event that could "achieve the successful integration of such free-wheeling activity and produce an energizing experience for participants."[66] As soon as word got out about the open tribune, Persinger and Bravo found themselves steadfastly fending off scholars and activists seeking to claim some portion of the program: a Kuwaiti graduate student living in Fort Collins, Colorado; a woman from Ohio living in Mexico City who described herself as "acutely aware of women's problems here"; an Ecuadorean International Relations student married to an Irish historian of Europe and living in Minneapolis, Minnesota; university faculty members and municipal officials, some of whom were big fish in their respective ponds. The experience of the Bucharest Tribune, Persinger explained to Barber, "suggests that some participants will arrive with their own agendas, for which they will seek support. Different goals then surface, and the cross-cultural negotiation of a consensus appears to be one of the valuable contributions a forum of this kind can make to motivating participants to work on a broader agenda at home. Others will be seeking to ally themselves with the like-minded and will conduct their own workshops and formulate their own action plans." The final unscheduled days would allow these diverse networks of alliances to coalesce.

Scene 4

Follow the Money

The UN General Assembly voted on the IWY conference amid one of the most tumultuous sessions in UN history that included not only Arafat's historic visit but also votes on the Charter on the Economic Rights and Duties of States and the suspension of credentials of South Africa's apartheid government.[1] "The United Nations was in turmoil," reported leaders of the American Association of University Women (AAUW), which had organized a seminar to educate US feminists about the UN on the eve of the International Women's Year.[2] Seminar attendees relocated from the UN building to a nearby hotel to accommodate security measures and settled in for keynotes by Helvi Sipilä and Margaret Bruce. Bruce predicted that IWY would "result in a worldwide consciousness raising, a realization that equal rights for men and women are a matter of social justice and vital to the progress of any society," bringing the feminist practice of consciousness-raising sessions to the growing confrontations among intergovernmental policymakers. These intimate circles had fostered the adage "the personal is political," airing grievances about domestic and sexual violence, uneven labor burdens, and the sexism and misogyny lurking even in the most liberal-minded organizations. A global consciousness-raising session, Bruce conjectured, would reinsert the "personal" into international policymaking, collapsing the scale of politics to include intimate questions of reproductive freedom and household budgets alongside global issues of oil prices and decolonization.

Anne Tuckerman, veteran UN reporter for Agence France Presse, tried to explain to her audience what it was witnessing. "What kind of place is the UN which is transformed today into a fortress, and where the main speaker of the day arrives by helicopter like James Bond?" she asked in her keynote address. "It is a place of revolution, a place where the most militant wing of the Third World is waging its struggle against the old establishment, and winning, at least in words and on paper, and words and paper help, when they are loud and repeated and backed by Arab oil."[3] Demands for a new economic order, Tuckerman explained, emerged from "countries long held in sub-standard living conditions clamor[ing] for a part of the wealth monopolized by the affluent society." The fact that Arafat would be welcomed as a head of state during the very week that the General Assembly voted 125 to 1 to suspend South Africa offered powerful evidence that a new era had dawned at the UN. Tuckerman concluded with a caveat for the activists in the audience who hoped this transformed UN would prove to be a feminists' asset. "The UN can be a highly useful tool for governments that seek an international seal to diplomatic moves or for those that want a public forum to air their grievances," she explained. "For individuals, rebelling against established authorities, it is and most likely will remain unavailable."

Although the IWY conference resolution had been overshadowed by other business, it still drew fire. The Lebanese-born, New York-adopting, long-time Saudi delegate Jamil Baroody described American men as "slaves" to American women.[4] The *New York Times* reported, "'My Government will not contribute a cent to an International Women's Year conference,' said Mr. Baroody, shaking a finger at officials of the observance, who are women. 'Women all over the world enjoy unwritten privileges and men do not want to hold a conference to point out or negate those privileges,' he declared."[5] Although one UN aide told the *Times* reporter that Baroody expressed "fairly widespread apprehension about somebody trying to impose Western ideas of equality on the rest of the world," he seems to have been the most outspoken objector.

This political upheaval and accusations of cultural imperialism bedeviled General Assembly deliberations about representation at IWY—who would be invited to the conference, who would be appointed to various decision-making bodies, who would populate the delegations. As new nations emerged out of dismantled colonies, the guest list was not entirely obvious. The GA agreed easily that all member states should be invited, but consensus was more difficult on the question of national liberation movements. If the UN included them as observers, as had become common practice at UN conferences, then it opened the question of which movements to include, since several often vied for legitimacy. The GA resolved, in the end, that the Organization for African Unity and the League of Arab States would tap the movements from their respective regions.[6]

Conference organizers grew exasperated watching the GA deliberate during the autumn of 1974 as planning time for IWY dwindled. Short of both staff and funds—IWY had been allocated a UN staff of eight, while the Population Conference had a staff of 125—the Secretariat's office charged with producing a provisional conference agenda ("Mrs. Bruce's division") had made little headway. The Iranian delegation proposed the creation of a sixteen-member consultative committee in hopes that a small but representative and well-versed committee could produce a clear IWY plan with maximum efficiency.[7] Given how little time remained to prepare for the IWY conference, the proposal resulted in a consultative committee that would exercise substantial influence over its agenda.

Far more than the GA's official rosters, every budgetary decision determined who would have a say in defining the IWY agenda. An official UN gathering—even of a small consultative committee—would require translation and reproduction of documents as well as simultaneous interpretation for participants, all of which would come out of the still-minuscule IWY Voluntary Fund.[8] Moreover, few UN delegation members could speak with any credibility about issues likely to arise at the consultative committee. If the committee were to include representatives with knowledge about women's issues—anyone who might fit the description of "highly qualified representatives with special expertise in this field"—it would need to import talent. Governments would have to cover the travel and accommodations of any representatives not already in New York. Although the consultative committee would abide by UN rules governing diverse geographic representation, participation would be limited to those governments willing or able to pay expenses. The Iranian delegation transformed the discussion by volunteering to cover two-thirds of the consultative committee's expenses, including "travel and subsistence" of committee members.[9] Iranian mission member ZuZu Tabatabai offered an additional reason to create the consultative committee: to mollify Princess Ashraf Pahlavi, the Shah's twin sister, who was "furious" that Iran had not been chosen to host the IWY conference. The consultative committee was created "so that Iran could play a role."[10]

The UN's structure reifies regional blocs that correspond loosely to continents—the Latin American group, the African group, an Asia-Pacific group that stretches from Jordan to the Pacific Islands, an Eastern European group comprised mostly of the Soviet Union and its satellites, and the awkwardly defined Western Europe and Others (WEO) group that includes not only Western Europe but also the United States, Australia, New Zealand, Canada, and Israel. Seat allocations for the consultative committee generated arguments and horse-trading. WEO countries perceived an anti-Western bias. The Australian mission cabled Canberra that if Foreign Affairs was serious about securing a spot on the consultative committee, this would be a good moment to announce its planned contribution to the IWY Voluntary Fund; the next day, Canberra pledged A$50,000 (USD$40,000), securing a spot for Elizabeth Reid.[11] Secretariat staffer Susan Jane Kedgley was elated by the news. "Fantastic about Australia getting on consultative committee," she wrote to Reid, "could transform it from a Princess Ashraf gimmick into something really worthwhile."[12]

Although popular with many feminists as the founder of the Women's Organization of Iran (WOI) and the first Iranian woman in modern history to appear in public without a veil, Princess Ashraf generated controversy even within close, like-minded friendships. Betty Friedan had visited Teheran at Princess Ashraf's invitation in 1973.[13] In June 1975—just before the IWY conference opened—Friedan published an upbeat account of her visit, indicating that the state-sponsored WOI was leading Iranian women into the modern world.[14] Only a year earlier, Friedan's publicist, Jacqueline Ceballos—who attended the consultative committee meetings as a NOW liaison to the IWY organizing committee—had campaigned against the detention of Iranian sociologist Vida Hadjebi Tabrizi. Pointedly dismissing the WOI, she explained, "Iran is a hotbed of male supremacy of the worst kind and women there badly need our help. There are feminists, but they dare not surface. Finding help for Ms. Hadjebi is not easy, as she is divorced and does not generate sympathy that a wife/mother figure does in our patriarchal world. Of course there is no help from our government, for the Shah is a valuable friend. It is up to us, the feminists, to respond to her cry for help."[15]

One can imagine the anger and betrayal Shahnaz Alami—the Iranian dissident who first suggested and promoted IWY—must have felt when Princess Ashraf stood up at an official ceremony honoring Human Rights Day on December 10, 1974, and presented Waldheim with a declaration of support for the International Women's Year signed by fifty-eight heads of state.[16] Then, after Pahlavi pledged a million dollars in support of IWY activities, she became chair of the agenda-setting consultative committee.[17] To someone like Shahnaz Alami, the script probably looked all too familiar: money and power had trumped activist dedication.

As voluntary-fund contributions remained quite modest, a million dollars bought quite a bit of influence.[18] The UN-published *Development Forum* described Pahlavi as a "well-known figure around the UN" who had "helped to lead the drive for the consultative committee," which would develop "a world master-plan for the attainment of equality between the sexes."[19] *Delegates World Bulletin*, a privately published newspaper that served up commentary and gossip about goings-on at the UN, reported, "The expectation is that Princess Ashraf . . . will be named chairwoman of the consultative committee's meeting. Iran, whose newly flexed financial and political muscle is being exercised increasingly in UN affairs, is a committee member. It is also expected that, following her election as committee chairwoman, the princess will announce an additional Iranian financial contribution to IWY activities."[20] Although Pahlavi's million-dollar pledge certainly appeared to purchase agenda-setting authority, she left nothing to chance. As the time to convene the committee drew near, the Australian mission informed the prime minister that the Iranian mission sent a note requesting support for Pahlavi's candidacy. "We assume," the ambassador wrote, "that you will want to respond warmly and affirmatively to the note. There seems no doubt that she will be the only candidate."[21] Australian feminist Germaine Greer would quip later to a television reporter that Pahlavi had "purchased us lock, stock, and barrel."[22]

As the Secretariat drafted its Plan of Action in preparation for the consultative committee meetings, UN officials traveled to Mexico City to work out a tangle of logistics—everything from diplomatic protocols to shuttle-bus service.[23] Member states submitted aggrandizing reports about how much their governments had accomplished in improving women's status, often appending speeches by heads of states or their spouses or ministers. Industrialized countries boasted about women's participation in the paid labor force, attendance at universities and vocational programs, and growing presence in conventionally male-dominated professions. Less industrialized countries stressed literacy rates, maternal health data, and, often, progress made toward Western ideals of monogamous marriages and smaller family sizes. Back at UN headquarters, staffer Susan Jane Kedgley reported to Elizabeth Reid, "Things are a trifle frantic here, but IWY lumbers on and receives amazing press and attention despite government indifference. The UN made the mistake of discussing something that has grassroots interest and support—IWY could go down in herstory as the only UN-proclaimed year anyone can remember."[24] She urged Reid to meet with Persinger—"a very good woman"—when she was in New York for the consultative committee and expressed optimism that the NGO tribune might allow the conference to "turn into a happening."

The UN's own fundraising for the IWY still had a bake-sale feel about it, despite Princess Ashraf's support. Helvi Sipilä told the NGOs in Geneva that if every Finnish woman contributed one mark, it would cover the implementation of the entire Regional Plan of Action for Africa. WYWCA leader Katherine Strong complained that Sipilä seemed not to see much of a role for NGOs in shaping the World Plan of Action but did expect them to contribute to the IWY voluntary fund, noting that until then only ten governments and no NGOs had contributed.[25] *Delegates World Bulletin* reported that member states had been slow to pledge support and even slower to come up with the actual cash, but the IWY voluntary fund had received a steady stream of "small, personal contributions—some for as little as $2."[26] A group of UN staffers tried to pull together a women's pop concert to raise money for the IWY voluntary fund but soon realized that securing headliner acts on such short notice would be impossible.[27] Despite the UN's insistence that IWY was about women and men, NGO and UN organizers alike seemed to understand that women would foot the bill. Indeed, even the voluntary fund's single largest contribution came not from the Shah of Iran but from his sister.

IWY planning drew attention to the UN's own poor record on discrimination against women. "In an apparent frenzy of self-revelation," novelist Shirley Hazzard wrote in the *London Times*, "the United Nations is sponsoring 'International Women's Year.' International women will be particularly grateful since, without this exercise, the acutely discriminatory practices of the United

Nations itself might have been obscured for yet another decade."[28] Twenty-seven hundred UN staffers signed a petition from the Ad Hoc Group on Equal Rights for Women to the secretary-general demanding increased professional opportunities and an independent grievance procedure. Throughout the consultative-committee meetings, the group protested outside the Secretariat building with placards reading, "Never Too Late for Article 8!," referring to the UN Charter's call for "men and women to participate in any capacity and under conditions of equality in its principal and subsidiary organs."[29]

Susan Jane Kedgley wrote to Elizabeth Reid that she would arrive to a festive atmosphere in New York, including a "March for IWY" on International Women's Day.[30] Before the consultative committee, Reid participated on a panel dubbed an "international encounter" on the theme "Women and Men: the Next 25 Years"—an event that included public officials such as Ghanaian Supreme Court Justice Annie Jiagge and public intellectuals such as Germaine Greer and Alvin Toffler, the author of *Future Shock*.[31] "Women of the Third World are not being divided from women of the developed world over equal pay for equal work," Jiagge explained to the audience. "But we are being separated by value judgments.

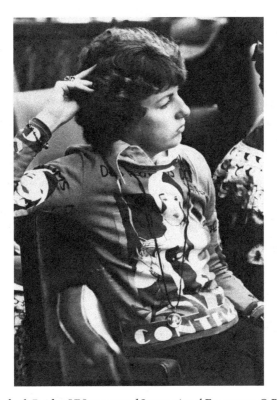

Figure 4.1 Elizabeth Reid at UN-sponsored International Encounter. © Bettye Lane. Courtesy of Schlesinger Library.

Today, one-third of the world makes use of two-thirds of the world's wealth, and then tell them to manage on that. As a result, we are faced with starvation and a struggle for the basic necessities. You are so concerned with equality, but you do not see the injustices of this set up, and that's where our basic differences lie."[32]

The question of whether the plan of action should emphasize the equality or development theme manifested itself in tensions between Margaret Bruce and Helvi Sipilä, who spent considerable time trying to raise awareness and funds for IWY. "Ms. Sipila is really hanging in there with the concept of 'development', while [Sol] Nahon and Bruce orient towards the concept of equality," one staffer confided to Betty Friedan. "In other words, (and please keep this confidential) that is where the split has taken place. We women in the house [i.e., at the UN] do not feel affinity towards Sipila because she has not been helpful in concrete terms (or otherwise) to women in the house."[33] UNESCO staffer Shawna Tropp similarly reported that the "diversity of Mrs. Sipilä's activities as well as her heavily promotional conception of her job, has apparently precluded intensive planning for the year, including regular communication with [Bruce]. . . . This has left the Section's Director, Mrs. Bruce, in an embarrassing position."[34] Decades later, Bruce confirmed that she had "personal difficulties" with Sipilä leading up to the conference but declined to elaborate.[35]

The Secretariat's draft World Plan of Action reflected Bruce's stronger influence "in the house." It privileged equality over development, imagining the

Figure 4.2 Helvi Sipilä, Margaret Bruce, and Rasil Basu at IWY Consultative Committee meeting. UN Photo by T. Chen in possession of the author.

former as requisite for the latter, and all but dropped discussions of peace as well as considerations of colonialism, racial discrimination, and apartheid. The Australian mission reported to Canberra that it had "not been particularly well received," with some delegations troubled about the "absence or inclusion of particular political matters (Eastern Europeans, United States, Africans, Mexico)" and others concerned that it reflected the "particular professional expertise of those taking part (Sweden, France, British)."[36] Its recommendations centered on practical mechanisms by which the UN and its member states could set targets and assess progress toward them, resulting in a technocratic document that reflected an Anglo-American modernization ideology that societies would evolve from traditional to modern practices and that the World Plan of Action should map out a plan to facilitate and expedite that transition.[37]

Following the model of W.W. Rostow's "stages of economic growth," the plan envisioned a progressive achievement of women's equality from access to health and nutrition, to literacy, to education and vocational training, to professional and political participation.[38] Although it gestured toward the UN Charter and concerns about "sex discrimination as fundamentally unjust, an offence against human dignity and an infringement of human rights," it adopted an overwhelmingly functionalist approach that saw women as a critical part of the modernization machinery. Noting widespread concerns about poverty and corollary problems of malnutrition, underemployment, housing shortages, and infrastructural deficiencies, the draft plan pointed to evidence that "improvements in the situation of women may be a vital factor in the alleviation of the problems." It went on to specify that improving women's health, education, and training would allow them to become "productive" contributors to economic development by joining the wage labor force or adopting more efficient modes of food production that would allow them to sell more at markets.

The plan recognized the widespread feminist critique that women did, in fact, make important contributions to their economies—often in the form of child-rearing and eldercare, subsistence food cultivation, and the daily provision of meals, water, and firewood—but that those efforts were systematically excluded from economic data. It recommended that data be gathered about these activities as well as women's participation in informal economies but offered no explanation for how this labor might be valued or what practices or policies might ensue from recognizing its value. Instead, the modernization model advocated well-trained and educated women joining the ranks of paid laborers and salaried professionals. Apart from gestures toward technological and infrastructural improvements and the advisability of child-care centers, the plan made no mention of who might perform this everyday labor once women entered the commodified labor force.

The draft plan nodded to the problems of inequality in industrialized countries as well as the UN itself, but it principally targeted "traditional," Third World societies. "It is recognized that some of the objectives of the Plan have already been achieved in some countries, while in others they will only be progressively accomplished," the draft plan stated. "As societies evolve from a traditional economy to various levels of modernization and industrialization, women may, initially, be adversely affected by the process," the plan explained, acknowledging Boserup's influential findings. "For example, their roles may become less defined, their spheres of economic activity as producers of food and handicrafts may be reduced; their recognized rights to the use of land may be abolished; and their living standards may be lowered by migration to overcrowded urban areas." Governments, NGOs, and UN agencies would take responsibility for mitigating these ill effects and meanwhile would train women in entrepreneurial skills, including marketing and how to gain access to credit.

The draft plan also touched on culturally rooted and deeply familial concerns such as education, food practices, and fertility. It favored co-education and mixed-sex training programs, and curricula for boys and girls that would be "identical" even in sex-segregated schools. Women would be taught to "contribute more efficiently to production of proper types of food through vegetable gardens in rural and urban areas through the provision of better tools, seeds and fertilizer," and media campaigns would introduce "previously unacceptable nutritious foods into the daily diets of people." Pointing to the World Population Plan of Action, the draft IWY plan called for a "change in certain crucial demographic variables, such as age at marriage, age at birth of first child, total number of children and the interval between births, and age at termination of child-bearing." To implement all of these profoundly personal changes, the Secretariat recommended that governments form commissions of experts, the UNDP send in advisors, and "trained women" circulate among countries in a given region "on a voluntary basis" to share expertise. "Countries with different political, economic and social systems and cultures and at differing stages of development," the draft plan explained, "have benefited from the common knowledge of problems, difficulties and achievements and from solutions worked out jointly." The draft plan struck many who read it as both too long and too vague, especially with its passive-voice formulations. In an effort to avoid the thorny question of how to pay for improvements in services and infrastructure, it offered nebulous suggestions of voluntary efforts and reprioritizing expenditures.

The most pointed criticism of the draft plan focused on its underlying principles. If the 1960s had witnessed widespread faith in the power of industrialization and modernization schemes to improve quality of life, by the 1970s the limitations and uneven results of these schemes had become obvious, particularly with regard to their effects on women. ZuZu Tabatabai, the Iranian mission member whom Rockefeller advisor Joan Dunlop described as "young (30ish), very energetic, smart and indignant about the lack of sophisticated attention being paid to IWY—both in and out of the U.N.," formulated a twelve-page summary of this critique that she convinced Princess Ashraf to use as a working paper to structure discussion during the consultative committee meetings.[39] Drawing heavily on the Secretariat's draft, Tabatabai upended the plan's paradigm from modernization theory to dependency theory. Poor women were disadvantaged not simply because they had not followed the prescribed stages of development but rather because they were systematically denied the benefits of progress.[40] In place of exhorting women to cultivate "proper types of food" and to serve their families "previously unacceptable nutritious foods," the working paper focused on women's need for labor-saving devices and access to credit. It conceded that "women involved in the production of food need both agricultural training and nutritional education" but went on to emphasize that "women in high-consumption societies need not only education about nutrition but also education regarding the consequences of unnecessarily high consumption, especially of proteins, on the world's total food supply." In this formulation, Third World women were not seen as a problem to be solved but rather as the victims of large-scale theft.

While the Secretariat's draft concentrated on training women to enter labor markets, the Iranian working paper problematized the very category of productive labor. "Thus, we see, for instance, from the statistics of one African country that only 7% of the women in that country were 'economically active.' In actual fact most of the agricultural work of that country was carried out by women." Further, employers consistently categorized women's wage labor as less skilled and therefore lower paid. The working paper laid out recommended policies, many of which overlapped with the Secretariat's—such as increased technical training and access to credit—but altered the emphasis. In the section on education the Iranian proposal stressed, "Boys as well as girls should receive training in homemaking and child care so that men might carry their share of duties and responsibilities and help relieve women of the 'double burden' that inhibits their full participation in economic life." In stark contrast to the Secretariat's draft, which highlighted the health risks of "too many pregnancies or pregnancies at too close intervals or at too early or too late an age," the Iranian proposal included no mention of family planning but focused instead on pre- and post-natal care, the provision of mobile and stationary clinics, and the introduction of labor-saving devices such as wells and milling machines.

Most strikingly, whereas the Secretariat's draft plan had concluded with a set of technocratic recommendations about how to feed the plan into the machinery of UN bureaucracies, the Iranian working paper ended by underscoring issues that the Secretariat had tried to bracket as too political. "With the very survival of the human race being threatened by weapons of mass destruction, deterioration of the biosphere, the exhaustion of non-renewable resources and the potential for more widespread starvation than ever known in human history, the capacity to respond to problems must be augmented by every possible human resource." Repeating a common IWY refrain that men got the world into this mess and pointing to women's activism in efforts for world peace, environmental justice, and human rights, the Iranian paper urged "a future of true human equality where no person will suffer discrimination because of sex, race, religious belief or political conviction."

The Secretariat's draft and the Iranian working paper aligned most closely on women's legal and political rights. They agreed that member states needed to ratify and uphold the major UN conventions on women's status and that cultural and practical factors opened a "tremendous gap" between de jure and de facto recognition of women's rights.[41] Both documents pointed to the importance of developing a comprehensive international convention guaranteeing women's rights, converting DEDAW into a more binding convention. The Iranian paper did point out, however, that the gap between women's de facto and de jure status pervaded societies of all types. In her opening statement to the consultative committee, Pahlavi drew on Tabatabai's dependency analysis sprinkled with a distinctly feminist perspective and elements of liberalism. "The true emancipation of women," she averred, "begins only with their economic independence. To give them the intellectual and technical equipment to earn their living directly, without depending on men, is to lay the foundations for their liberation."[42] Reaffirming calls for geopolitical self-determination, she insisted on this independence as a "fundamental human right."

Although Pahlavi presided over the consultative committee, the Mexican and Iranian delegations formed a working group "largely aimed at putting the detailed work in hands other than those of Princess Ashraf," chaired by Elizabeth Reid, who remembers it as "the most difficult meetings I was ever to chair."[43] The Mexican representatives insisted on incorporating language from the CERDS into the draft IWY plan of action. "The atmosphere tensed immediately," Reid recalled, "and the forces lined up on either side of the working table, one side insisting that the demand had absolutely no relevance to women and no place in that particular arena and the other side insisting that it had every relevance."[44] Nearly four decades later, Reid still remembered the intensity of the conflict. "To describe the atmosphere as tense or hostile barely captures the feel of the meeting—which to this day still returns when I think back," she explained. "The Mexican Attorney General was there, relentlessly and threateningly insisting on the references being included. The US was equally intransigent and hostile (and I felt this was particularly directed at me for not falling in behind the US line). As chair, my constant ruling was that any links between a political position and women had to be made before wording could be included and the wording included had to include the links to women."[45] The US representative Patricia Hutar's objections provoked what Ambassador Scali described as a "shrill extemporaneous diatribe from Venezuelan rep who attacked US position as unsympathetic and insupportable." Scali expressed frustration that deliberations had "in general avoided polemics up to that point" but sometime allies such as the Jamaican MP Lucille Mair and the Philippine ambassador Leticia Shahani had openly sided with Mexico over the United States on this issue.[46]

In an effort to skirt these conflicts, Reid finally convened an informal working group that met without simultaneous interpretation to hammer out a "compromise position." The US representative argued that the conference should concentrate exclusively on reducing the de facto gap between men's and women's status within each country and that all other issues constituted political distractions. Third World countries joined Jamaica and Mexico in arguing that women's advancement would only come with a new economic world order, including an end to colonialism, foreign occupation, and racial and ethnic discrimination. The Soviet representative insisted that the conference should include a discussion of détente and the GA's recommendation of a 10-percent reduction in military expenditures to make funds available for assistance to women and children. The compromise position, proposed by Sweden and Australia and supported by Iran, Philippines, and Sierra Leone, called for changes in traditional roles of both men and women, which would "necessarily evolve from some change in the international order, including a reexamination of the classical conception of development and development assistance."[47]

The informal working group reviewed the draft proposal's "Recommendations for Action" section-by-section, questioning many of its assumptions and prescriptions as inappropriate for particular contexts.[48] Although everyone supported women's increased political participation, for example, the recommendation of quotas came in for strong opposition. The working group stressed that "population was not *as such* a scourge" but rather was a problem of resource allocation and that structuring policies around nuclear families and heads of household was "outdated" and "did not reflect the realities of society." Although the working group agreed with the importance of research and data collection about women, it rejected efforts to define the research agenda, insisting instead that it should respond to local and regional concerns. While some of the working group's additions were predictable—more child-care services to allow women to work and attend school and training programs, less sexism in school textbooks and career counseling, the enforcement of equal-pay and minimum-wage laws, a section on prostitution—others marked significant challenges. The additions called, for example, for an end to employment discrimination on the basis of sex, age, sexual preference, or marital status, making it one of the earliest recommendations that the UN prevent discrimination based on sexual preference. In short, the working group, drawing heavily on Tabatabai's working paper, significantly contested many of the premises of the Secretariat's plan, including its evolutionary notion of women's emancipation and its narrow conception of family and social life.

This challenge energized the consultative committee meetings, substantially altering the dynamic from the staid CSW sessions to one that resembled a feminist political meeting. Describing the working group's deliberations as "fascinating," the UNESCO representative Shawna Tropp confessed, "I think I may be on the verge of taking feminism seriously—at least, as it is formulated by some delegates."[49] Tropp was referring in particular to Elizabeth Reid, who had drawn attention both because of the Australian government's commitment to IWY and because of her combination of candor and diplomatic dexterity. In her address to the consultative committee, she adopted the language of the non-aligned movement, describing women as the "oldest colonial and under-developed group in the world" and insisting, "Development cannot and must no longer be measured in terms of Gross National Product and economic growth rates alone. Development has a human face, not a harsh, pragmatic, economic one."[50] Reid described many of the equality-oriented proposals—equal educational and occupational opportunities, maternity leaves, and child-care centers—as falling short of the "radical revolutionary demands" necessary to restructure society. She called instead for a thoroughgoing cultural revolution that would grant men and women alike limitless possibilities for organizing their social, political, and economic lives. "Notions such as that of the breadwinner and the homemaker, the values of ambition, prestige, status, and incessant promotion, the dichotomy between the public and the private, work and the home, between the personal and the political, must be challenged," she exhorted the committee. "Both men and women must be made aware of our habitual patterns of prejudice which we often do not see as prejudice but whose existence manifests itself in our behavior and in our language." Her address lit up the room. "You have consciousness-raised this whole committee," her friend Susan Jane Kedgley scribbled to her, "and have changed it from traditional rhetoric to something fundamental and important."[51] Indeed, Tropp's report to UNESCO headquarters in Paris cited extensively Reid's critique of the "conventional conception of development" as "of particular interest to Unesco."[52]

The consultative committee ran out of time before it could fully revise the draft World Plan of Action or respond to delegates' concerns. "Because of the many pressures on U.N. Secretariat," Reid reported after the committee meetings, "it is difficult for them to produce anything but the lowest common denominator plan of action."[53] Development, she explained, "didn't get much of a run at the Consultative Committee and then only in standard economic (GNP) terms"; she predicted that "the political issues of peace, disarmament, racial discrimination and new world economic order are likely to get a large amount of the time of the Mexican conference." Ambassador Scali, concerned that the IWY conference would be "deflected from its purpose to satisfy political ambitions of President Echeverría," saw the writing on the wall. "If [the] US and Western view is to achieve maximum support at [the conference]," he explained in a telegram to the State department, "US [delegate] believes our best tactic, as revealed in microcosm by events in this committee, is to emphasize those interests which women share in common and avoid those issues which divide them. Otherwise, the majority of [delegates] will be driven into ideological camp of President Echeverría and conference will become politicized to detriment of women everywhere."[54]

The US Center for IWY boasted that the United States Information Agency (USIA) agent Mildred Marcy, who had taken the reins of the newly created US Commission for IWY, was "doing her best to keep the agenda on specific women's issues, not such things as disarmament, food production, ecology, politics ad infinitum. These items all have their specific forums and we should have ours."[55] If Scali was exasperated by the supposed intrusion of political matters into the IWY plan, Marcy must have been a bit more ambivalent. She was, as State Department veteran R. G. Livingston observed, "scrambling like everyone else at State to get attention at the top," and the explosion of polemics over economic sovereignty would likely "draw more high level attention" in a way that women's political rights and educational opportunities simply would not. Livingston noted with admiration that Marcy "understands the barriers and also how to get through the hierarchy," an acumen that certainly would have made her cognizant of using the geopolitical conflicts to hold the State Department's attention.[56]

Criticism of the draft World Plan came not only from government representatives or from the Third World. The World YWCA argued that the language of integration implied that women would "adjust to the established patterns," but IWY was necessary precisely because the "structures of society are made by and for men . . . all around the world," requiring a thoroughgoing reconsideration of all the challenges "practical, psychological, cultural, sociological, economic, etc." that women face.[57] An open letter from the Washington-based, liberation-theology inspired Jesuit Center of Concern succinctly articulated reservations that resembled others' objections: that it considered women principally in terms of child-bearing and rearing rather than their "full personhood"; that it concentrated on women's impact on issues such as food and population rather than "because she is important in her own right"; that it framed development solely as economic growth and industrialization, implying "that worth as a human person is to be considered solely in economic terms"; and that it completely ignored calls for disarmament and the extent to which "industrial and national establishments are selling arms on a scale unprecedented in history."[58]

In late April of 1975, the Secretariat released the revised World Plan of Action, which would structure deliberations in Mexico City. The new document incorporated some of the working group's suggestions, including those on prostitution and the role of the mass media, but the technocratic tenor remained, along with much of the modernizationist, evolutionary language.[59] The Mexican government, seeing that the revised document still marginalized non-aligned concerns, took advantage of a regional seminar on women in development in Caracas to issue a declaration that echoed the Iranian working paper—reasserting language about economic sovereignty, decolonization, disarmament, and the elimination of racial discrimination.[60] The emphasis on the international economic order, "rather than distracting the attention of the world community from the urgent issues examined in this seminar, reveals them in their true dimensions." The solution, in Mexico's view, could be found in the Charter on the Economic Rights and Duties of States, which promised the "elevation of the standard of living of millions of people in Latin America, half of whom are women, to a level consistent with human dignity, and the elimination of all forms of colonialism, neo-colonialism, foreign domination, foreign occupation, and racial discrimination."

At the end of the seminar, the Mexican delegate Carlos Rico informed Patricia Hutar, recently named co-head of the US delegation for the IWY conference, that Mexico would present the Caracas Declaration at the IWY conference "to show Latin American solidarity on economic issues."[61] Hutar had made US reservations clear, refusing to support the consensus because of the language of "general and complete disarmament," the use of the term " 'neo-colonialism' as a term which lacks definition and which has been used loosely and irresponsibly by some countries to attack others," and, unsurprisingly, any mention of CERDS. She informed Rico that if Mexico insisted on pushing the Caracas Declaration in Mexico City, it would precipitate a confrontation and risk causing the entire conference to end in failure.

Mexican diplomats were eager to avoid a blowup at the IWY conference but far from willing to abandon their geopolitical objective of seeing CERDS become as much a part of accepted UN policy as the Declaration of Human Rights. They made plans to reconvene thirteen members of the consultative committee to consider both the Caracas Declaration and the World Plan of Action.[62] The diplomatic chatter around the invitation centered on whether accepting would signal endorsement of Mexico's position or offer a glimpse of Mexico's strategy. Describing the Caracas Declaration as "weak and pointed in the wrong direction," the State Department underscored its opposition to "the degree of linkage between economic development and women's rights issues" and expressed concern that "the Mexico conference might become yet another forum for developing countries to emphasize economic grievances."[63] Hutar told a mid-May US congressional symposium that the US strategy regarding the new economic order "would be to stifle it wherever possible and to restrict conference business to what [US delegates] regard as the status of women."[64]

ACT II

THE CONFERENCE

Scene 5

Opening Acts

Mexico City was uncharacteristically dry for mid-June as the Chinese, Cuban, and Korean delegations arrived nearly a week before the conference. Seasonal thunderstorms held off for a few days as delegates streamed in from Iran, Australia, and countries throughout Latin America and Africa, arriving in time for pre-conference negotiations about rules of procedure and who would hold the conference offices of president, vice-presidents, committee chairs, and minute-taking rapporteurs. Official participants arriving for the government conference were greeted at the Benito Juárez Airport according to elaborate diplomatic protocols that entailed an honor guard for heads of state but perhaps only the wife of a cabinet member for lesser ministers. Mexican secret police carefully noted the point of origin and destination of every arrival.[1]

As the US delegates packed their suitcases, Mildred Marcy sent First Lady Betty Ford one last note and an extensive briefing book in hopes that she might, in the end, accede to Marcy's imploring invitations.[2] Ambassador John Jova offered assurances that Mrs. Ford could stay in the diplomatic residence's guest suite and "could arrive at a time of her choosing, retire to her quarters to rest if she wished and surface when she chose." Despite Marcy's exhortations that her presence would offer "evidence of high level US interest in the proceedings," Mrs. Ford sat out the Mexico City conference. The Mexican press noted her absence.[3]

Journalists and activists arrived in a somewhat less decorous fashion and with considerably less scrutiny than official participants. US feminists Linda Fowler and Carol Lease had driven all the way from North Carolina, where they had visited Fowler's parents and covered the Joan Little case that had become a cause célèbre on the feminist left. Sending an optimistic letter to her compatriot Robin Morgan as they continued their journey to Mexico, Fowler signed off, "kisses and revolution."[4] Another feminist group caravanned from Philadelphia.[5] Celia Herrera Rodríguez, a returning student at California State University-Sacramento, learned about IWY at a Communist Party meeting and called her friend Frances Romero, an activist in the Teatro Campesino movement in Fresno. Together, they hitchhiked to the border and took a bus from

Tijuana to Mexico City. By the time they arrived, they had only four dollars between them and "shacked up" at Herrera Rodríguez's mother-in-law's house, commuting from her working-class neighborhood to the NGO tribune, where Herrera Rodríguez sold her artwork to cover expenses. "I really felt that I knew nothing about Mexico and yet it was home," Herrera Rodríguez later told an interviewer, explaining why she would undertake a journey at such hassle and expense. "There was something that was almost like a spiritual feeling to it that I wanted to go."[6]

Arriving participants would readily have perceived the political unrest and social tensions. If they picked up a newspaper in the airport or a kiosk or at one of the tony hotels along the Paseo de la Reforma, where most conference and tribune participants stayed, they would have learned that the attorney general declared that the two youths shot to death at the university had been members of the guerrilla 23 of September Communist League, political unrest roiled Argentina and India, and Chilean dictator Augusto Pinochet had proclaimed that elections would not take place during his lifetime.[7] Many participants were struck by conspicuous manifestations of poverty, particularly women who begged for alms or sold goods on the street with children sleeping in their laps. Australian delegation member Sara Dowse recalled walking along the red carpet into the posh Hotel María Isabel, passing indigenous women selling handicrafts and produce as she puzzled over warnings not to buy anything from them.[8]

These encounters with daily news reports of state violence and pervasive evidence of abject poverty reminded conference-goers that they had arrived in a city engaged in an uneven and ambivalent process of modernization, a process that shaped the very landscape of the IWY gatherings. The official, intergovernmental conference would take place at Tlatelolco Plaza—called the Plaza de Tres Culturas (Plaza of Three Cultures) because it includes ruins of the Aztec city as well as a sixteenth-century Spanish cathedral and the Mexican Ministry of Foreign Relations—which lent its name to the Treaty of Tlatelolco, the 1967 agreement proscribing nuclear weapons in Latin America and the Caribbean, and the notorious 1968 student massacre.

Three miles to the south of Tlatelolco Plaza stood the cylindrical, mid-century modernist Centro Médico, the icon of Mexico's modern welfare state that would host the ancillary events—the NGO tribune, a seminar on Women in Development, and the UN-sponsored journalists' encounter. Those arriving for the pre-conference gatherings crossed the broad esplanade, where an enormous, carnation-pink cube bearing the IWY logo had been erected, and climbed the stairs to a vast, airy exhibition hall leading to wood paneled auditoriums and marble staircases that echoed with locals hustling to complete arrangements for the NGO tribune, installing translation booths and sound systems, and hanging a welcome banner across the building's façade.

Figure 5.1 Delegation leaders giving a press conference in Tlatelolco Plaza with the structures representing three cultures as a backdrop. © Bettye Lane. Courtesy of David M. Rubenstein Rare Book & Manuscript Library, Duke University.

Four days before the conference commenced in earnest, First Lady María Esther Zuno de Echeverría inaugurated the Women in Development seminar organized under the auspices of the American Academy for the Advancement of Science and the leadership of the development expert Irene Tinker, an acolyte of economist Ester Boserup and anthropologist Margaret Mead.[9] The development seminar, a quiet, wonkish opening act to the more boisterous and contentious IWY gatherings, would generate some of the event's most enduring and transformative ideas, some of which—such as the Women's World Banking— would be realized in the months and years ahead.

The next morning, nearly 200 coffee-fueled journalists filed into one of the smaller conference rooms for the journalists' encounter—open to any accredited journalist—that dedicated one day to each of the IWY themes of equality, development, and peace. The UN Centre for Social and Economic Information (CESI) sponsored fifty media fellows from Third World countries as part of its broader mission within the UN's development agenda.[10] The brainchild of CESI deputy director Snowden Herrick, a Yale graduate who had served as an information officer for the US Army and then the International Labor Organization, the encounter formed part of a broader media strategy organized in conjunction with UNESCO to promote understanding of and support for UN programs. Amid the chaos of the last-minute preparations for the NGO tribune, Herrick

Figure 5.2 Xilonen editor Marjorie Paxson on the Centro Médico esplanade. Paxson, Marjorie, B., Papers, 1844-2008 (C4078), State Historical Society of Missouri Manuscript Collection.

sat on the presidium for the inauguration, along with Helvi Sipilä, Mexican Attorney General Pedro Ojeda Paullada, and the Colombian senator turned UNESCO envoy Esmeralda Arboleda de Cuevas Cancino.[11]

More than just locale linked these two gatherings. The seminar on women in development and the journalists' encounter simultaneously reaffirmed and sought to transcend the divide between the First and Third Worlds. Both wrestled with the implications of a major cultural and intellectual transformation that had spread around the world: the rapidly proliferating sites of knowledge production and dissemination combined with a growing suspicion, among feminists and postcolonials alike, of the authority of expertise.[12] Together, these two gatherings showcased the fundamental structural and cultural issues around women's status, highlighting some of the major challenges that the ensuing conference would try to tackle.

Although the development seminar included many professionals who would participate later in the NGO tribune, they did not share the tribune participants' ambivalence about expertise. The seminar broke into five closed-session working groups that would produce proposals to consider, as one group put it bluntly,

"Does development help or hinder women?"[13] As Tinker explained to reporters, "The Western development model exports a middle-class image of what work might be considered appropriate for women that does not always correspond to her needs. . . . The vast majority of women are performing more restricted economic functions now than within the pre-development economy."[14]

The seminar delved into a central concern that troubled feminists and development specialists alike: how to recognize the vast amounts of subsistence and caring labors that overwhelmingly fell to women and that appear nowhere in the economic data. These responsibilities included not only feeding and caring for children, elders, and adult males but also performing agricultural labor, hauling heavy loads of water and firewood, and bartering or marketing to meet household needs. These activities only appeared in economic statistics when, for example, a woman sold household agricultural or artisanal products in a recognized market or performed caring labors for wages in someone else's home. Far more often, these labors fulfilled subsistence needs or quietly slipped into the informal economy. Within economic systems in which commodification offered the only metric of productivity, the failure to account for all this labor created the appearance that entire regions—and women in particular—remained "unproductive."

In her opening remarks to the development workshop, *la señora* Echeverría invoked what had become common sense among IWY planners: that women remained a "wasted resource" in development that must be tapped to achieve the UN's and the world's development objectives.[15] Helvi Sipilä put the matter more starkly, indicating that policymakers must "motivate women to participate in development and change society" rather than "enslave" themselves to domestic life.[16] She drew from the Finnish model to advocate public services, particularly child care centers, to replace much of women's uncompensated labor. Many development experts and quite a few feminists shared the view of the labor market as emancipatory for women—that it would improve their status (through access to income), their national and local economies (by boosting measures of productivity), and their self-esteem (by allowing them to build skills and independent lives outside their homes).[17] The NGO UN We Believe had launched an IWY ad campaign showing a man in profile and a woman shadowed behind him with the tagline, "Half the brainpower of the world is out of service." The ad's text explained, "Half the minds on *earth* belong to women. Who knows the penalties of holding back their development? Who knows what product of human thought will never see the light of day?"[18] NOW sponsored a similar campaign with the tagline, "Womanpower: It's much too good to waste."[19]

Discussions of "working women" generally included only those women who commodified their labor in exchange for wages, salaries, or payment at markets. Sociologist Alexander Szalai presented findings from an extensive time-budget study showing that—despite improvements in labor-saving technologies and

Half the brainpower of the world is out of service.

It is perhaps the oldest human disorder.

Yet even today...even at this late point in the twentieth century, the condition hasn't really cleared up.

Who can deny it? In obvious ways or in subtle ways the advancement of women continues to be blocked just about everywhere.

The barricades can be visible. Or invisible. They can be thrown up in a woman's early years. Or in her later years. But there are always barricades.

Never mind how immoral that is. Think how wasteful it is.

Half the minds on *earth* belong to women. Who knows the penalities of holding back their development? Who knows what product of human thought will never see the light of day?

It could be anything. A precedent-shattering technique for creating more food. A brilliant new symphony. A breakthrough in the fight against disease.

Human brainpower is the most precious resource of them all.

Waste it and it isn't only women that are being robbed.

It is humanity that is being robbed.

 The UN has officially proclaimed 1975 as International Women's Year.

Help break down the barricades. Mail $1 to UN WE BELIEVE, 33 East 43rd Street, New York, New York 10017. In return, we'll send you information on International Women's Year and a pin like the one shown here.

UN WE BELIEVE

Figure 5.3 UN We Believe ran a series of advertisements describing the failure to use women's talents as "immoral" and "wasteful." Courtesy of UNA-USA and Tamiment Library.

prepared foods—many women spent more time on household labor than their mothers had, particularly if they also engaged in paid labor. Women in the paid labor force worked on average more than an hour longer than men in their households on work days and two and a half hours more on days off.[20] The seminar's working group on food production and small technology listed as its first recommendation "that governments rethink and redefine the concept of economic activities to include the vast production carried out within the domestic sphere."[21] The urban living group similarly recommended "that all persons performing domestic service (including housewives) and other unpaid work in the informal sector should be brought within the national labor and social security laws, and the monetary value of their contribution added to the statistics of national accounting systems."[22] After all, the entire World Plan of Action would be a dead letter without a feasible strategy for either recognizing or alleviating women's subsistence labor burdens. Literacy programs and technical training and efforts to involve women in the political process would be meaningless so long as women remained buried under these obligations and threatened with everything from shame and stigmatization to outright violence if they failed to perform them.

Seminar participants disagreed about which economic system might best resolve this problem. While Tinker herself questioned whether a New International Economic Order would be any more sensitive to women's needs than the current systems, the seminar's working group on health, nutrition, and family planning opened its report with an affirmation of the Charter on the Economic Rights and Duties of States and a call to "redirect resources that are presently applied for defense and war to peaceful development of all nations."[23] Women from socialist and communist countries—at both the development seminar and, more vocally, the journalists' encounter—insisted that socialism offered the answer, with states providing public child-care facilities, communal kitchens, and health clinics.[24] Patricia Hutar told reporters gathered in front of the Hotel María Isabel that it was "absurd" to believe that socialism provided a better system for integrating women into development, since capitalism offered women a "greater number of opportunities to improve themselves and achieve their development."[25] Despite the brief popularity of the wages-for-housework campaign, nobody at the development seminar proposed commodification of this labor as a serious solution.[26]

The question of subsistence labor challenged not only extant economic models but also prevailing family structures. "In many places the relation between men and women is equivalent to that between master and slave," grumbled Mexican journalist Esperanza Moreno de Brito Foucher. "And none of that master-slave dialectic, according to which a moment arrives when the master's dependency on the slave's services is such that it is unknown who is the slave of whom; surely, with all its consequences, the slave would prefer to be master."[27] Participants deliberated extensively about the extent to which incorporating women into formal economic and political life required a wholesale reconsideration of nuclear families. Like many population-control advocates, Cecile de Sweemer, the Belgian director of the Ford Foundation's family planning efforts in Lagos, argued that current family sizes led to a vicious cycle of malnutrition, infant and child mortality, and women's increased unpaid labor obligations. Renowned sociologist Rodolfo Stavenhagen editorialized in one of Mexico City's principal daily newspapers, "The problematic does not consist so much in greater equality for women (either in the abstract or on the purely individual level) but rather in a redefinition of the structure and role of the family in modern society." Pointing to the Chinese commune and the Israeli kibbutz, he called for a radical rethinking of the relationship between subsistence labor and family structure. "It is unlikely that the International Women's Conference will dedicate itself to such a creative activity," he lamented, "but it would be a great opportunity."[28]

The seminar's working groups emphasized widely expressed critiques of modernization approaches: that development practices should emerge from local knowledge and understandings and demonstrate greater sensitivity to local social, cultural, and economic needs. Development programs raised suspicions that they merely served as vehicles to create new markets for devices produced in industrialized countries. "We think three times when [Westerners] try to sell us something, women as well as men," Shanti Solomon of New Delhi told a reporter. "We are tired of exploitation."[29] As the working group on organizations stressed, development projects should "bear in mind the need to provide continuity and understanding between new and traditional ways of doing things."[30] The working group on education described development programs as "elitist" and argued that mass communications media crowded out local creative expression and technical expertise, amounting to a "major form of cultural domination and confusion."[31]

Attention to media coverage tapped into a long-standing concern shared by feminists and Third World nationalists that a small handful of powerful interests cultivated an inaccurate portrayal of women and postcolonials alike as irrational and politically immature.[32] Concerns about the media had been linked to IWY from the beginning. The same CSW session that resolved to designate 1975 as the International Women's Year also noted that "deep-rooted attitudes in men and women" posed one of the greatest obstacles to improving women's status and that "these attitudes are due to cultural patterns which to a certain extent determine their way of thinking and feeling and which are disseminated on a vast scale today as a result of the technical advances in mass communication media."[33] Recognizing the difficulties of discerning media influence apart from "other socializing factors," the commission nonetheless urged the UN and its agencies and member states to perform a thoroughgoing review of the ways that media represented women in relation to family, polity, and workplace.

By 1975, UNESCO, under the leadership of former Senegalese education minister and vocal media-reform advocate Amadou-Mahtar M'Bow, had become a hotbed of G-77 activity and concentrated on amplifying the voices of Third World intellectuals.[34] If people like Margaret Bruce imagined the journalists' encounter as a gathering where reporters learned about IWY objectives to become partners in a struggle against "traditional attitudes," people like M'Bow had a different goal—to educate Westerners about women's struggles in the Third World and to showcase the talents of Third World journalists.[35] Third World intellectuals and policymakers decried "electronic colonialism" based on metropolitan control over communication hardware and software, media outlets, and the definition of normative social and cultural practices that depicted the Third World as unruly, violent, and incapable of self-governance.[36] Of the five existing wire services, four—AP, UPI, Reuters, and Agence France Presse—were based in NATO countries, and the fifth was the Soviet Union's wire service TASS. The advent of satellite broadcasting threatened to exacerbate this information divide. "The communications media distort the objectives of equity, equality, and balance of the underdeveloped countries due to their high levels of commercialization," explained Mexican Communications and Transportation Secretary Eugenio Méndez.[37] Deliberations at the journalists' encounter achieved greater reach than M'Bow or Herrick could have imagined when the documentarian Martha Stuart secured funding to make two half-hour shows—one featuring a handful of encounter media fellows and the other "key women" at the conference—that would air in the United States as part of her popular *Are You Listening?* series and circulate worldwide.[38]

The UN itself tried to shape press coverage of IWY, particularly through its Office of Public Information and CESI. Its agencies, such as the World Health Organization, the Food and Agriculture Organization, and the UN Development Programme, produced glossy, abundantly illustrated magazines to highlight their efforts. Beginning in July 1974, the Secretariat produced the *IWY Bulletin*, which showcased what various UN agencies and member states had planned for IWY. These UN publications clearly demonstrated working assumptions about how IWY might accomplish the structural and cultural changes that its organizers sought. The *IWY Bulletin*'s first issue featured a cover photo of a long row of women under beating sun with picks raised high over their heads, with the caption, "Man's World, Woman's Work: Road Building in Lesotho." The next issue featured a cover photo of a young woman in a Western-style coat and a headscarf surrounded by women wearing garments fully covering their heads, faces, and bodies. The caption identified the place as Kabul, Afghanistan, and explained, "Young women are discarding 'chadari' while older women still wear it in public."[39] The IWY issue of *Development Forum* included various photos of women engaged in development projects and featured a cover photo of an African (or perhaps African-descended) woman driving a tractor. None of the women are identified even by country, allowing them to stand in for all poor, non-white women. The cover photo is captioned, "Through equality, women can contribute to their countries' development."[40] To counter pervasive images of women as white, middle-class homemakers and consumers, in other words, the UN offered images of non-white women confidently and productively occupying a "man's world."

Governments also generated their own media messages about IWY. Although the US government produced nothing so ambitious as Mexico's glossy monthly, it did create an elaborate press kit touting US accomplishments on women's issues. Between the former news reporter John Scali as UN ambassador and the USIA officer Mildred Marcy at the State Department, they kept a watchful eye on how US actions would appear to domestic and international audiences. Marcy acknowledged that the United States faced "public-relations challenges" related to the NIEO and disarmament that "may get out of hand," but she also saw the IWY as an opportunity to "give our nation and the world something to think about as to whether this super-power, the United States, will be perceived both here and abroad as muscle-bound with hoary traditions of status-quo-ism; or, whether, on the eve of our nation's Bicentennial it demonstrates once again a profound responsiveness to a new current which is on the side of constructive change."[41]

As broadcast media grew more prevalent and satellite technologies concentrated influence in the hands of the few media outlets that could afford them, groups who felt misrepresented by the mainstream media turned their attention to creating alternative representations. Feminist groups, particularly in the United States, launched campaigns to shape media messages. NOW had a standing committee on the "Image of Women in the Media," and the Boston Area Socialist Feminist Organization launched a "major media project" that would inform press coverage, train socialist-feminists to interpret and manage the media, and launch a newspaper to "promot[e] our politics."[42] Countless women's groups produced newspapers and newsletters not only to communicate with each other but also to critique mainstream media coverage and popularize a new discourse including terms such as "sexism" and "marital rape." Elizabeth Reid saw the media as a key battleground and had arranged for the Australian government to host a UN seminar on women and the media in late 1975. In Mexico, as the Movimiento Nacional de Mujeres prepared for the IWY events, activists produced background papers on the national media's role in reproducing sexism.[43]

Figures 5.4 Cover photo of *IWY Bulletin*, No. 1 (July 1974) shows women in Lesotho constructing a road. Courtesy of UN Photo.

In addition to countless mimeographed newsletters, the IWY inspired two ambitious efforts to create alternative media: Women's International Network (WIN) News and Hotline IWY. Fran Hosken launched WIN News out of her Lexington, Massachusetts, home in January 1975 to mark the beginning of IWY. She envisioned a feminist alternative to commercial wire services like AP and Reuters that would feature "world-wide communication for, by and about women; to share their problems and their proposals for change. Though social, economic and cultural conditions greatly differ between nations and regions, the human needs of women are compelling everywhere. Our common human goals will overcome all divisions and will persuade men everywhere to join our

Figure 5.5 Cover photo *IWY Bulletin*, No. 2 (October 1974) captioned "Kabul, Afghanistan. Young women are discarding 'chadari' while older women still wear it in public." Courtesy of UN Photo.

just cause."[44] The tireless, obstinate, over-achieving, and often irascible Hosken liked to rub elbows with those in power. As she prepared to put the first issue of WIN News to bed, she wrote to Kurt Waldheim as a fellow Austrian, dropping names of friends in common and giving him ten days to produce something for the first issue, in which she was "holding a space" for him next to a promised column by Helvi Sipilä. Waldheim's aide wished her luck but did not submit a column.[45] Hosken secured support from USAID and proudly reported to Persinger's organizing committee that she had sent materials "to Washington for approval" and that she enclosed "the information that USAID agreed I could send out about IWY."[46]

WIN News aligned with the New York NGO committee, which largely hewed to the liberal belief that social problems stemmed from misinformation. In other words, if all parties involved simply had access to the same information, they would inevitably reach similar conclusions about how to proceed. WIN News's aesthetic matched this common-sense feminism. Printed with a simple, sans serif masthead and headlines and minimal graphics, WIN News conveyed a simplicity that seemed to assume that if women around the world could share enough information, then politics and ideology would fall away. The bulletin's editorial content, however, exhibited Hosken's establishmentarian and Western orientation: it effaced the WIDF's role in establishing IWY and omitted the East Berlin conference, instead linking IWY to the efforts of Helvi Sipilä and Ashraf Pahlavi. The lengthy regular column of "Reports from Around the World" focused overwhelmingly on Western European and North American women's accomplishments. The first issue also included short sections on women in the Philippines, India, Kenya, Japan, and the Republic of China (Taiwan) but omitted any news from the People's Republic of China and Eastern European socialist bloc countries. Perhaps as a projection of her own experience, Hosken focused principally on individual activist women and the organizations they directed.[47] Like Julie Dahlitz, she advocated a feminism that respected diplomatic protocols and demonstrated women's ability to work within established conventions.

Unsurprisingly, WIN News drew fire from the women's liberationist left, which deemed Hosken's feminism fraudulent and complicit with repression. "One of WIN's major political objectives is to interpret and even speak for the 'inequality' of working class and Third World women," chided an open letter from the Anti-Imperialist Women Against Population Control. "Princess Ashraf Pahlavi of Iran, we are told, can perform this function." Enumerating a litany of WIN offenses—from claiming representative authority to accepting USAID support to endorsing the UN and World Bank strategies for population control—the letter concluded, "We may find ourselves laughing at [WIN's hypocrisy], if it was not clear that another bitter pill of co-optation had been manufactured and we were designated targets for swallowing it. . . . Because of their visible ascendancy as champions of women's equality during 'International Women's Year,' our working class and Third World sisters in different regions of the world, including North America, are being politically manipulated and the ground for their further oppression is being laid by the new attractive breed of 'American women's liberationists.' "[48] The criticism was overblown and not entirely accurate, but the battle over what constituted legitimate feminism continued.

The other IWY-inspired approach to media was the prescient Hotline IWY— a computer network that would link the conference in Mexico City to participating computer nodes around the world. Glen and Mildred Leet ran Hotline IWY out of their New York City apartment.[49] The Leets—along with their staunch supporter Margaret Mead—envisioned vast computer networks connecting people all over the world to international conferences, allowing them to participate and to bring the conference ideas and objectives back to their home organizations and communities. Hoping to involve a broader array of individuals and organizations in discussions about international issues, the Leets sought to make international conferences "serve as launch pads rather than as splash downs to keep the interest and action at a high level."[50] As Mildred Leet told Esther Hymer's NGO committee, "You can take part in the IWY Conference in Mexico without going there." Groups would simply need access to a computer terminal for a few hours a week, and Hotline IWY would help them establish a "linkage center" in their area. "If NGOs at the Conference need facts," Leet explained, "a call in to the HOTLINE can be made, and answer given."[51] Much like Hosken's WIN News, Hotline IWY broadcast a liberal feminist common sense that would grow organically out of the field seeded with shared information and ideas.

By the time of the IWY conference, the Leets had organized several such hotlines and expressed confidence in the system's promise to radically expand participation in international deliberations and policymaking. For Mexico City, they set up focal points in ten US cities and Vancouver. They had plans in other locales ranging from Ames and Denver to Tehran and Manila, but the abbreviated planning period left them short of time and funds. In addition to finding a networked computer, groups had to pay fifty cents per minute to participate, an amount prohibitive in many parts of the world and certainly burdensome in most, particularly as technological and logistical glitches caused complications. Phone calls from Mexico City—intended as part of the networking experiment—were often delayed. Several communications reported problems due to phone lines and weather. The Vancouver group reported getting repeated error messages and being unable to access the Hotline index. The group assembled at Sears Tower in Chicago messaged, "Coming on line . . . hopefully." The Mexico City–based Hotline committee reported, "Having difficulty transmitting. Due to garbage on telephone line. Will attempt to file short report on journalist encounter."

If endeavors such as WIN News and Hotline IWY ended up, if only inadvertently, as platforms for US-based women, the CESI journalists' encounter was intended as a counterweight to Western-dominated media. For an audience of prominent media and diplomatic figures as well as other journalists, the Third World media fellows all produced background papers describing women's status in their home countries.[52] Some produced detailed accounts of legal rights, others of marriage practices, and still others of economic and labor rights. The authors portrayed the vast array of cultural and structural challenges that women faced around the world as well as the ambivalence that many women expressed about the dramatic changes that women's movements fostered. Although the media fellows titled their papers by national conditions—women's status from

Argentina to Zambia—the papers themselves offered very particular perspectives based on experiences of class, religion, party affiliation, and the like. Many of them, particularly those written by journalists from recently decolonized nations, highlighted women's participation in struggles for national liberation and the extent to which women's status had changed under new governments.

The encounter offered a preview of issues that would arise during the conference and NGO tribune. A reporter from Zaire called for "liberation according to each country's own reality," rejecting a perceived "equality pure and simple" principle that had taken hold in Europe and the United States.[53] A Tanzanian reporter opened with an explicit explanation of sequencing and priorities: "Like in most African developing countries, the conscious struggle for the emancipation of women came with the arrival of political independence in Tanzania."[54] "To conserve the true spiritual values and to harmonize itself with a modern and global civilization," wrote the Moroccan fellow, "that is the challenge every young country faces."[55] Guyana's information minister, Shirley Field-Ridley, stressed the need for women to fashion their own development programs, even if that meant rejecting "assistance from developed countries that came with strings attached."[56]

As at the development seminar taking place down the hall, one journalist after another underscored the problem of not valuing subsistence labors.[57] The media fellow from Cameroon described how women in her country "yearned for liberation from household drudgery" but rejected the "slavish imitation of the morals and customs of advanced countries."[58] A Ghanaian journalist pointed out the indispensable labor of illiterate women food vendors to the functioning of modern labor markets.[59] The Kenyan fellow stressed that the "high rates of profit made by all employers would not be possible except for the unpaid labour of the wives of their African workers, who feed, clothe, and care for themselves and their children at no cost whatsoever to the companies."[60]

Like the CSW, the New York committee hoped to use the media to bridge this divide between First and Third World experiences and began reaching out to media personalities and morning talk shows and brainstorming "techniques for changing the attitude of mass media."[61] Persinger and the other NGO tribune organizers particularly hoped to mitigate geopolitical and class tensions with the production of a newspaper that would cover events in the NGO tribune and government conference and promote mutual understanding among all participants by fostering a common, "reasonable" discourse.[62] From its earliest proposals to the Ford Foundation, the tribune committee designated a fifth of its budget to run a conference newspaper that would not only improve communication between the government conference and the NGO tribune but would also shape the news coverage by newspapers and wire services.[63] The Ford Foundation's Adrienne Germain helped drum up additional support both within the foundation and elsewhere.[64] Pointing to the "emphasis placed on international political questions (armaments, international economic order)" at the consultative committee meetings, Germain argued that the IWY newspaper could play a balanced, educational role in Mexico City and serve as "virtually the only avenue" for giving civil society a hand in shaping policy decisions. "Press reports on the Tribune," she argued to potential donors, "should help broaden public awareness and understanding of the breadth and depth of the issues beyond narrow feminist concerns."

Planet, the successful conference newspaper at the Bucharest conference, served as Germain's model when approaching other funders. "There is consensus," Germain explained, "that *Planet* was one of the most useful aspects of the Tribune and provided the only source of information on all relevant happenings." Funders expressed concern, however, about whether the model for the IWY conference paper would be *Planet* from the Bucharest conference or *PAN* from the Rome conference, which had highlighted global wealth disparities, including "grotesque cartoons" and comparisons of the caloric intake of conference participants and the world's poorest populations.[65] Their apprehensions intensified when it became clear that *Planet* editor Fran Dennis—the guarantor of cool-headed deliberation—had no intention of undertaking another daily newspaper. Dennis doubted that the IWY conference would draw the "subject interest" that the population conference had, particularly given the "paltry" financial support it received compared to the population and food conferences, and she noted the "indications of aggressive activity by women lib groups in North America, many of which have their own well-established media outlets."[66] The most that she and the International Planned Parenthood Federation could offer was to coordinate with Herrick and the encounter journalists to produce some coverage to include if a newspaper materialized.

Less than two months before the conference was scheduled to open, Persinger and Bravo were still scrambling for an editor, a printer, reporters, and funding. Bravo's Spanish fluency facilitated negotiations with the Mexico City daily *Novedades*, which also published Mexico City's only English-language daily, *The News*, to provide typesetting, printing, and distribution services. She also tapped her networks to secure an editor, Marjorie Paxson, the assistant metro editor for the Philadelphia *Bulletin*. If organizers and funders worried about "women's libbers" but still wanted someone who stood up for women's rights, Paxson fit the bill. With a graduate degree from the University of Missouri's highly regarded journalism program, she was an experienced journalist who had professionalized the major women's journalism organization and moved "women's page" coverage from society items and domestic advice to an emphasis on workplace issues; and she did not prominently identify with any strain of the US feminist movement.[67] "Marj Paxson was bubbling with delight at the prospect of getting her teeth into the paper—and I am sure you have made a wise choice," a mutual friend wrote to Mildred Persinger. "She is one of the most professional newspaper women I know."[68] In mid-May—just a month before the conference inauguration—Bravo wrote to several staffers from *Planet* to line up reporters, photographers, and a cartoonist. The lineup did not entirely quell funders' anxieties, but other funders seemed interested; Persinger, Harris, and Bravo forged ahead in faith that somehow, in the end, all the bills would get paid.

When the newspaper staff gathered for its first meeting in Mexico City just before the opening of the journalists' encounter and the development workshop and four days before the conference inauguration, the newspaper still had no name and insufficient funding. Most funders had earmarked their donations for specific expenses, particularly for travel expenses of Third World participants. Several foundations and a handful of women newspaper publishers had declined to offer financial support.[69] Paxson and Bravo wanted a Spanish name but had ruled out any that seemed too political or were used by Mexican newspapers. The name of the Rome food conference newspaper gave them the idea of using a deity's name and, after consulting with Mexico's National Museum of Anthropology and History, they landed on the name *Xilonen*, the Nahuatl name for the Aztec goddess of tender corn.[70] On June 19, Elinor Barber cabled her Ford Foundation colleague Adrienne Germain at the Hotel Montejo in Mexico City: "Tribune grant approved. Please inform Marcia Bravo. See you Sunday."[71]

Scene 6

Inauguration Day

By 10:30 on the morning of Thursday, June 19, men and women poured into the Juan de la Barrera Gymnasium for the inaugural ceremonies. As some 8,000 bodies filled the vast, enclosed arena, audience members sought ways to keep stuffiness at arm's length; by the time the ceremony started, thousands of fans, from silk to paper, stirred the air. At least one woman squinted through opera glasses hoping to catch a better glimpse of the historic moment.[1] As she scanned the arena, her field of vision filled with many more women than usually appeared at UN conferences; she saw much more color and fabric and hair piled high on heads adorned with baubles ranging from demure hoops and pearls to dangling earrings and ornate beadwork necklaces. The scene's novelty drew reporters' attention as well. Princess Ashraf, reporters noted, wore a "modern, fashionable suit and modern hairstyle" while several Japanese delegates demonstrated the "ancient Japanese concept of feminine beauty: tiny feet, a timid modesty in walking with hands over their chests, and their fabulous and monumental hairstyles."[2]

President Echeverría, Secretary-General Waldheim, and IWY Secretary-General Sipilä took their places on the dais against a backdrop of UN and IWY symbols and a crowded array of the flags of UN member states, highlighting that this was, above all, a gathering of nations. Echeverría must have basked in reports that several countries had endorsed him to become the next secretary-general, although Waldheim himself declined to comment on the possibility.[3] The dignitaries' spouses followed, taking their seats in the first row of the audience, followed by a parade of functionaries and honored guests.[4] The din of chatter and scraping chairs rose as those fortunate enough to secure an entry ticket through luck or connections joined the official delegations and observers. Despite organizers' concerns that first ladies' participation might give the conference a ceremonial feel, many led delegations, since their official roles often included overseeing "women's affairs" in their home governments.[5]

The prickly question of who would be included in the official delegations to the IWY conference touched on every aspect of the surrounding political issues.

Figure 6.1 IWY conference inauguration in the Juan de la Barrera gymnasium. Courtesy of UN Photo.

Recognizing the likelihood that governments might not take the conference seriously, Waldheim directly contacted heads of state urging them to send delegations to Mexico City consisting of equal numbers of men and women and "government officials and national leaders at the highest political and technical levels."[6] As the *New York Times* headline explained, "U.N. Wants It to Be More Than a 'Ladies Meeting.' "[7] Mexican authorities urged participating governments to limit their delegations to four people with leaders of "very senior, preferably Ministerial" rank.[8] The delegations' composition reflected geopolitics as well as the politics of patronage and nepotism. As governments acceded to political expectations, their delegations threatened to grow beyond what the Tlatelolco facilities might accommodate and certainly beyond the three seats allocated to each government for the inauguration. Those who saw themselves offering technical expertise—about literacy programs or development economics, for example—were dismayed by the prominent roles assumed by the wives and sisters of world leaders, many of whom had spent far less time than Ashraf Pahlavi considering issues related to women's rights and status. US feminists referred to the first ladies at the conference as the "wifey-poos."[9] In addition to the incongruity of Princess Ashraf or Filipina First Lady Imelda Marcos representing Third World women's concerns, more policy-oriented women like Reid worried that IWY would become a mere charade of attention to women's issues—with all of the media and public attention focused on the participation of well-recognized figures and little to no attention and resources dedicated to structural and policy changes that would affect women's lives.

Even amid the optimism of the opening ceremonies, observers anticipated conflicts. Journalists highlighted the possibilities for both personal and geopolitical battles, perhaps because the prospect of global conflict offered a gripping story line or perhaps because many of them had witnessed tensions at previous gatherings. "While the mood was festive at the opening session," reported the *Washington Post*'s Marlise Simons, "conference officers expect the coming days to produce some bitter debates before a proposed 10-year plan of action is approved."[10] The problem, as ever, was that no one agreed on which matters should be corralled into the pen of politics.

Even the space itself highlighted the complex interplay of politics and history. Mexican authorities had moved the inauguration from the Ministry of Foreign Relations to the Juan de la Barrera Gymnasium to accommodate more people and avoid diplomatic slights as Echeverría chased votes in the General Assembly. The gymnasium was part of the athletic complex used for the 1968 Olympics, a moment meant to showcase Mexico's arrival as a modern nation but remembered instead for Black Power protest and state violence. One of six facilities named after the *niños heroes*, six young soldiers who, legend has it, died while defending Mexico City against US invasion in 1847, the Juan de la Barrera Gymnasium would have conjured—for Mexicans at least—more than a century of lopsided encounters and fraught modernization efforts.

As Waldheim's speech writer, the conservative British politician Robert Rhodes James, confided in a note accompanying the draft of Waldheim's inaugural address, "One of the major difficulties in preparing this speech has been the remarkable impression—and disagreement—among the organizers of the Conference about what its priorities are and what they hope it will achieve. Furthermore, they have become so obsessed by this issue that they cannot effectively relate it to other concerns of nations and the international community." Rhodes James warned Waldheim that the IWY organizers—presumably Margaret Bruce, Helvi Sipilä, and their ilk—did not "sufficiently appreciate the suspicion and hostility of many developing countries towards the essentially 'advanced Western' point of view which dominates their attitudes." He urged the Secretary-General to "steer a careful course between the Scylla of vague generalities and the Charybdis of precise, and highly controversial, recommendations."[11]

As Waldheim praised Echeverría for his global leadership on the NIEO and for hosting such an important conference on the UN's thirtieth anniversary, he was interrupted by the chants of protesters outside the building. The Mexican Youth Movement and Chile Solidarity distributed flyers printed in English, and the Spanish Women's Liberation Movement agitated to free women political prisoners jailed under the authoritarian Franco regime.[12] The demonstrators also

Figure 6.2 Women holding signs for the Movimiento Femenil Margarita Maza de Juárez demonstrated outside the inauguration. © Bettye Lane. Courtesy of Schlesinger Library.

included a caravan of roughly 200 women wearing threadbare, rural clothes who marched barefoot under the banner of the Margarita Maza de Juárez Women's Movement, carrying signs with slogans such as "Plan your family," "Mexico welcomes you," and "Discrimination against Third World women must end."[13]

When the group tried to force its way into the gymnasium, purportedly to show its support for Echeverría, security forces dispersed the demonstrators.[14] The entire episode underscored the surreal quality of the Mexico City gatherings, introducing early on the prickly question of what constituted "authentic" political expression. At least one reporter as well as the photographer Bettye Lane took the demonstration at face value and described it as a sincere expression of popular patriotism and Third World feminism.[15] IWY participants and even security forces described the group as a shell organization of women who had been bused in for the event (and paid for their troubles) and that existed only to create the illusion of popular support for the Echeverría government and the conference.[16] In a subsequent, participant-organized session at the NGO tribune, several Mexican participants accused the group's president of manipulating indigenous Otomí to participate in the inaugural demonstration.[17]

Yet the group's performance perhaps became a bit more improvisational than anticipated. "The demonstrators, who were obliged to leave their market stalls in the Vallejo neighborhood to shout cheers of welcome to the visiting delegates," reported *Excélsior*, "protested because they had been left in the street with

Figure 6.3 Some demonstrators, like this one holding a sign bearing the Mexican government's slogan to promote family planning, seem to have been hired. © Bettye Lane. Courtesy of David M. Rubenstein Rare Book & Manuscript Library, Duke University.

banners and signs, under the inclement sun."[18] The women gathered outside the massive glass doors until their numbers were great enough that they could force their way in, sending police officers scurrying to secure the sliding doors that allowed entry to the central arena. As Waldheim spoke from the podium, they reached the periphery of the audience and shouted, "We, too, are women!" Journalists ran from door to door, ignoring Waldheim's speech as they tried to ascertain what was happening, security agents shoved the demonstrators out of the arena, and the women "unleashed an intense clamor of insults" as audience members rose to peer toward the doors to discern the cause of the ruckus.

The first act of this performance—the lively but orderly carrying of banners emblazoned with regime-approved slogans—seemed to follow the well-rehearsed choreography of PRI-sponsored political rallies staged to create the illusion of popular support by securing participation at the price of tacos and beer.[19] It seemed calculated to counter the skepticism that the IWY conference had anything to offer impoverished, indigenous women. Even the PRI-supporting newspaper *El Universal* expressed doubt, running an editorial cartoon showing two indigenous women in long skirts and elaborately embroidered blouses with their children strapped to them and an array of fruits and cactus leaves stacked in pyramids before them, apparently for sale. One market-woman explains to the other in broken Spanish, "So this thing about the women's year, I think it's something like a leap year."[20]

When the women breached the barriers to the inner sanctum of the inauguration, they seem to have gone off-script. Uniformed guards, plainclothes officers, and *edecanes* (female hostesses) covered the inauguration as well as both the conference and tribune venues, hoping "to ensure . . . a cordial and tranquil atmosphere" to counter Mexico's international image as the site of chaotic protest and unrest.[21] However, Mexican security forces had also been well trained to suppress dissent. When the spectacle of humbly dressed women supporting the regime's policies gave way to the spectacle of humbly dressed women clamoring for recognition and being forcibly removed from the inauguration, the curtain parted a bit to reveal the Mexico that lay behind Echeverría's lofty inaugural rhetoric of "democratic opening."[22]

Waldheim finally gave a sharp bang of his gavel to bring attention back to the inaugural proceedings and return reporters and rubbernecking audience members to their seats. Dismissing arguments that women's issues constituted a "luxury" concern that pertained only to wealthy countries, he wove together the instrumentalist and human-rights arguments, describing discrimination against women as "unjust, offensive to human dignity, and an infringement on human rights" as well as having "severe consequences for the economic and social development of nations."[23] After rehearsing the "practical considerations" of exploiting the "talents, experience, and wisdom" of half the world's citizens, he highlighted that, while racial discrimination was generally considered "contemptible," discrimination based on sex remained widely accepted. He pointed to the struggle against racial discrimination as among the UN's "most notable achievements"—although hardly complete—and called on the world community to embark on a similar campaign against sex discrimination. "We know that we are confronted by a very formidable and complex task," he cautioned the audience. But he urged his listeners to help make their shared goal more than a "pious aspiration" by using the two weeks in Mexico City to devise strategies for translating lofty objectives into meaningful action and to close the gaping divide between the many UN resolutions on women's status and the lived experiences of women around the world.

While Waldheim stressed the central role the UN could play in improving women's status, using its fight against racial discrimination as a model, Echeverría followed by striking a note consonant with his claims as a Third Worldist leader—stressing structural problems, expressing doubts about technical and technocratic solutions, and highlighting disparities between poor and rich countries rather than class differences within them.[24] Although he pointed to women as a "great revolutionary reserve" and "natural allies in the struggles against all forms of oppression," he quickly moved on to underscore the risks of focusing on the concerns of women in "rich countries" rather than the "rest of the planet, who cannot count on medical attention for their children, nor hygienic homes in which to shelter them, nor sufficient preparation to orient them in life." Only a global economic restructuring could rectify the economic marginality of Third World women. He called upon women in wealthy countries to bring their "powerful moral force" to become the "internal rebels of a system that determines the precarious and marginal existence of the majority of nations." He intermingled invocations of motherhood with challenges to traditional gender roles, which offer a deceptively "comfortable refuge." His speech—interrupted repeatedly by standing ovations and bursts of applause, most of them initiated by his wife—extended his structural assessment to the household level, warning against the "fallacy that only incorporation into the labor market" would liberate women and the "technocratic mirage" that technological advances would solve the problem of reproductive labors.[25] It would not do merely to "hand out prescriptions that mitigate the severity of the symptoms without treating their causes. To remedy women's situation," he concluded, "would demand profound changes." The US delegation, reported the *New York Times*, "was conspicuous in not applauding."[26]

Following Echeverría's speech, the delegates formally elected Ojeda Paullada as conference president, per UN protocols that the leader of the host delegation preside over plenary sessions. As his first official act, Ojeda Paullada introduced Sipilä, who countered Waldheim's and Echeverría's emphases in her brief remarks, exhorting them to clean up their own houses first. Describing women as "the most underdeveloped of all human resources," she insisted, "I do not see a conflict between the prevailing conditions in developing and industrialized countries as regards the real aspirations of women for social justice and a better life." Instead, she stressed men's role in sustaining women's subordination. "Men cannot claim an exclusive right to shape the future of our world," she argued. "It is high time for them to accept the challenge and share with women in the decision-making process. . . . It is high time to acknowledge that the denial of women's rights and opportunities is at the very root of our development problems and socio-economic ills—including illiteracy, malnutrition, mass poverty, and unchecked rates of population growth."[27] Stressing that the conference had only "two weeks to break with centuries of tradition," she steered away from issues outside its stated objectives and counseled against repeatedly redefining the problem. "Let us now focus on their practical solution," she concluded.[28]

Countless laudatory feature articles about the sixty-year-old Sipilä stressed that she was married with four grown children—"lawyer, diplomat, wife, and mother"—and had specialized in family law; neither her biography nor her public statements posed a threat to conventional family formations.[29] (If reporters noted the apparent contradiction between her own family size and her ardent support for population control, they did not comment upon it.) "She is quick to point out," the *New York Times* reported, "that she is not a rabid feminist and that she sees herself as 'defending the rights of both men and women—there should be equality of men and women, equal opportunities.' "[30] She favored liberal divorce laws but thought abortion should only be used in extreme circumstances. In her comments to the IWY newspaper she offered pointed counsel to participants, explaining, "I have always said that the ideal would be that women participate in decision-making positions. . . . If, counting in these efforts on the participation of so many brave women, we don't reach a satisfactory result not just for the future of our *compañeras de sexo* but for the future of the world, we will have failed."[31]

After all the speeches and ceremony had concluded, government delegations reconvened at the Ministry of Foreign Relations to attend to procedural matters, including the election of conference officers. While UN veterans dubbed some of these positions—such as vice-president and committee vice-chair—as "sleeping positions," meaning they proffered honorary status but carried little power, positions such as committee chair or rapporteur framed the language of documents that became the foundations for UN policy and practice going forward. The experience of the consultative committee had demonstrated to participants such as Elizabeth Reid and Zuzu Tabatabai the critical importance of the seemingly scribe-like position of rapporteur. The conference would hold plenary sessions but also would convene as two committees: the first charged with developing the World Plan of Action and the second charged with considering the integration of women into development and the impediments to women's equality. No committee was charged with considering the item on women's role in strengthening peace and eliminating racism, but it would receive considerable attention in the plenary sessions.[32] Jeanne-Martin Cissé, the Guinean schoolteacher-turned-diplomat and mother of six who had presided over the UN Security Council in 1972, would chair the first committee, while the Australian

John Campbell served as rapporteur. Ashraf Pahlavi notably ceded her position as chair of the second committee to an Iranian Baha'i member, Shapour Rassekh, and the Jamaican Phyllis Claire MacPherson-Russell would serve as rapporteur.

As the official delegations assembled at Tlatelolco shifted from the pomp of the inauguration to the scripted, rule-bound discussions of procedure, the NGO tribune inauguration at the Centro Médico featured a mariachi band and a marimba player to accompany the opening of folk art and photography exhibitions. Tribune organizer Mildred Persinger endeared herself to the audience by opening her remarks in halting Spanish before offering a welcome in English, laying out the ground rules for the tribune. She explained how to schedule rooms and suggest topics for the final, unscheduled sessions and stressed that the NGO tribune would not issue a final statement and that no one was authorized to speak for it. With that, she rang open what she dubbed "two weeks which could ultimately change the world."[33] Sipilä stressed the critical role the NGOs would play in converting the World Plan of Action into policy and practice at home. The First Lady repeated her husband's call for a global structural transformation, pointing out that in many places women face a "depressing choice" between renouncing their creativity to become "reproductive being[s]" or to sacrifice motherhood and family.[34] Exhorting the media to abandon the "anachronistic sentimentalism that presents women as a paradigm of abnegation, as the sum of all her anxiety and suffering," she insisted, "Women should not continue being wasted potential, outside of civilization and the creation of history."

Many women envisioned the tribune as a space where their views would get a fair hearing. Trinidad and Tobago's Leonora McShine, who had advocated women's rights since the mid-1950s, told the Washington Post, "I would not be interested in listening to a lot of government people talk. I would rather talk to the feminists, and I have prepared a paper on the bad conditions of women in Trinidad just in case."[35] McShine exemplified the type of postcolonial cosmopolitan Persinger sought. The founder and first president of Trinidad's Women Voters, she had traveled in 1953 to Britain to study women's organizations and received a UN grant to pursue research in New York City. During her stay, she had joined 500 other women for the lively three-day biennial conference of the National Council of Negro Women in Washington, DC. Perhaps this juxtaposition between her experiences in New York and Washington had convinced McShine that the most relevant work for her priorities would occur among the NGOs at the tribune rather than among the official delegations at the government conference.[36]

By populating the tribune with women like Leonora McShine, the organizers hoped to foster an atmosphere of productive exchange among people of diverse experiences. "We have two ground rules," Marcia-Ximena Bravo explained to a *Xilonen* reporter. "Everyone has an obligation to listen and learn, and everyone has an obligation to explain themselves fully. It's a two-way process. Every woman who comes here is an expert in the issues here by the way she's lived her life as a woman—and every man is an expert by the way he's lived his life surrounded by women. This is not a paper-producing conference. It will be as open as possible and have an atmosphere of personal testimony."[37]

Many women anticipated the types of rap sessions and consciousness-raising experiences that Bravo described, but others naively expected to have a voice in UN proceedings, despite Persinger and Sipilä's efforts to disabuse them of this notion. While corresponding with prospective attendees, Persinger had explained that the latter consisted of instructed delegations selected as representatives of their countries, while at the former "participants are self-selected or will be sent by their organizations—but not as delegates since the Tribune will take no action in its own name."[38] She urged members of the NGO committee to instruct their members on this distinction, and all tribune materials—brochures, registration forms, programs, funding proposals—specified that no one would be authorized to speak for the tribune. The tribune would submit a final report to funders but would not take minutes nor issue a final declaration. This policy was critical for ensuring open and candid discussions. Freed from having to represent any official positions, participants could check their politics at the door and concentrate on women's issues.

If the organizers had hoped to keep the IWY proceedings sealed off from ambient political conflicts, the impossibility of such isolation became evident at the inauguration. As the president and First Lady departed Tlatelolco, members of the Communist Party–organized Mexican Youth Confederation heckled them about recent shootings at University City; several attempted to climb into the presidential car before being removed by security detail.[39] After the tribune inauguration, the *El Universal* reporter peppered Marcia-Ximena Bravo with questions about her thoughts on the Pinochet government. Having left Chile eleven years earlier, at age fifteen, Bravo tried to dodge his questions. "She pursed her lips, reddened, and averted her gaze," he recounted. She insisted that her role required her to remain impartial; she pleaded ignorance. A crowd gathered as the reporter badgered her to take a position on capitalism, finally eliciting the terse comment, "In capitalism, the woman can liberate herself."[40] Finally satisfied that he had extracted a confession of sorts, the reporter left her in peace.

The elaborate rituals of both inaugurations—the slow, ceremonial entrances of the principal players, the dramatic display of member states' flags behind the dais and the UN logo affixed to the lectern, and the carefully crafted speeches of world leaders—fueled participants' expectations that serious work might be accomplished at these gatherings. By the time delegates and activists scattered through Mexico City to dive into the work ahead or to collapse, exhausted, in their hotel rooms, or perhaps to raise a glass of tequila with new-found friends, hopes ran high that by the closing ceremonies the exchanges would effect a substantial improvement in women's status around the world.

"Betty Friedan versus the Third World"

By Friday morning, Attorney General Ojeda Paullada's election as conference president had emerged as a sort of litmus test of views on the centuries-old conflict over sex equality and difference. These arguments reignited long-standing debates about whether women needed separate spaces—schools, labor unions, activist organizations—as well as separate legislation—protective labor laws, maternity benefits, political party quota systems. Such questions had bedeviled the United Nations from the outset. Fearing the marginalization of women's concerns, US representatives to the UN—including luminaries such as Dorothy Kenyon and Virginia Gildersleeve—had opposed specifying women's rights in the UN Charter in 1945 as well as the creation of a Commission on the Status of Women the following year.[1] At the inauguration itself, nobody raised an eyebrow over Ojeda Paullada's appointment, but US feminists could not fathom a justification for having a man preside over a conference about women.

Even before the conference opened, on the second day of the journalists' encounter, Betty Friedan led the way in forming the Feminist Caucus to "reintroduce and reaffirm the principal [IWY] themes from a feminist perspective."[2] Denouncing the organizers' decision to encourage men's participation, the Feminist Caucus sought to create women-only spaces to "open up channels of communication among women from all over the world."[3] On the evening of Ojeda Paullada's election, the Feminist Caucus passed a resolution to protest the election and sent Friedan a note urging her to speak out against it.[4] Friedan called a press conference to denounce the decision as ludicrous and outrageous. "What's happening here illustrates just what this conference is all about," she fumed. "If we have [IWY] in the land of machismo, then let the wife of the president run the conference. Mrs. Echeverria herself is an activist and a feminist."[5] The *Washington Post* noted that "snide comments are heard" about two men speaking first at the inauguration and "almost everyone agrees that insult was added to injury when a man . . . suddenly emerged as president of the conference."[6]

The problem was that not everyone agreed, although it had become the common sense among many US feminists. *El Universal* conducted a "survey" (of unspecified size and method) that found that 99 percent of Latin American women supported Ojeda's election. Rubíe García and Elena Villarreal de Porras of Colombia agreed that his willingness to take on the role reflected men's commitment to improving women's status. Their compatriot Isabel Carrasco de Gómez joined the Venezuelan Martha Regalado in arguing that women's advancement required participation by prominent men. In an adjacent article, the Mexican congressional deputy Aurora Navia Millán challenged Friedan, insisting that women's liberation needed the effort of an entire society and that Ojeda had "performed his role well and sensibly."[7]

Ojeda responded directly to Friedan's objections in a brief press conference, insisting that the conference was for both sexes and rejecting her assertion that his election evidenced "machismo."[8] Monday's edition of the PRI's newspaper, *El Nacional*, reiterated Ojeda's statement, editorializing, "She can opine freely, and her opinion is heard with absolute respect. But it is not true that some principle has been transgressed by the fact that men and women participate in this event. In no moment was it thought that the Conference was exclusively a women's meeting."[9]

Tribune organizers and funders had expressed concerns that US feminists and "women's lib" types—media-savvy, relatively well resourced, and already mobilized by the abortion-rights and ERA campaigns—would overwhelm other participants and, to the consternation of US feminists, openly sought to limit their participation.[10] When tribune organizers notified travel agencies that they could not use the IWY logo for commercial purposes nor claim to be an official IWY travel agency, they received indignant responses from women citing their activist credentials and objecting to the letter's officious tone.[11] To the organizers' dismay, the Los Angeles-based Womantours promised travelers a visit not only to the NGO tribune but also a threatened Mexican feminist counter-conference.[12] UN staffer Sonia Nusenbaum confided to Friedan her "indignation" that Persinger and UN Secretariat staffer Ann Heller "both seem to be rather concerned that American feminists will take over the conference and be imposing on the representatives of the 'developing nations.' "[13] As in the consultative committee meetings and the UN more generally, US participants in the NGO tribune experienced a sense of relative deprivation as the postcolonial moment required that US and European participants cede space and speaking time to their Third World counterparts.

Other US feminists shared Persinger's qualms. The AAUW's Carol Leimas, who had participated actively on Esther Hymer's committee since its earliest days and directed the UNA-USA efforts on IWY, urged AAUW members to make a concerted effort to understand and empathize with women's concerns in other parts of the world. "The objective of such an exercise," she explained, "is, first, to understand why their problems are often quite different from ours and, second, to help them in ways they want to be helped (the international version of 'Lady Bountiful' is just as obsolete as her well-meaning domestic counterpart)."[14] Activists Charlotte Bunch and Frances Doughty argued that although "some radical and lesbian/feminist presence is vital" at the IWY conference and, in particular, the NGO tribune, they cautioned their fellow feminists to remain cognizant of the dynamics at such an event. "The presence of large numbers of women from the U.S. presents serious problems," they explained. "No matter whether the individual is conservative or radical, she will be a part of an overwhelming U.S. presence and domination of the conference which will be resented by many. This is the reality of American cultural and economic imperialism."[15]

Persinger and Germain need not have worried too much over radical feminists, most of whom dismissed the IWY events as too patriarchal. US socialist feminists largely ignored IWY, scheduling their own national conference in Dayton, Ohio, during the Mexico City conference.[16] As one Philadelphia feminist newsletter reported, "Many radical feminists had pronounced the concept of the IWY bourgeois and planned to ignore it."[17] The women's liberationist publication *off our backs* ran an article titled, "International women's year is anti-feminist," and argued that it advocated individualist solutions rather than drawing on the "collective power of women-identified women."[18]

NOW, however, had taken a notable interest in both the UN and IWY. "NOW has gone international!" proclaimed Patricia Burnett, the former Miss America runner-up and GOP activist who chaired NOW's International Committee, to the NOW national board. With encouragement from Margaret Bruce and UN staffers frustrated by their dim prospects for advancement, Burnett convinced the board to seek Category II consultative status with ECOSOC to gain access to "key women all over the world" and a "constant flow" of expert reports on women's status, which NOW could convert into a political project of "the women's movement."[19] Burnett envisioned NOW representatives bringing to the UN a sorely needed "strong feminist organization to help them put through some of the reforms they have failed in so far."[20] Jacqueline Ceballos explained to the New York chapter, "NOW is planning a miniconference to decide strategy while [in Mexico], as there are problems with both Third-World men and with UN women who are frightened by NOW. Betty Friedan will attend."[21] NOW president Karen DeCrow sought a $5,000 budget allocation "as NOW's contribution to this worldwide feminist effort" to police the boundaries of authentic feminism. Reporting to the executive committee of NOW's national board just after the consultative committee adjourned, DeCrow explained, "There will be, in

Mexico City at the same time [as the governmental conference], a conference of NGO organizations. During this period of time many women will be in Mexico City from all over the world. Also, many men. Not too many feminists. It is essential that the feminists of the world get together to discuss (not foreign affairs) but ways in which we can cooperate to assure legal rights for women, the right to choose abortion, child care, equal opportunities in education and training, getting feminists into politics and government, and so forth."[22] DeCrow petitioned President Ford to sponsor an international feminist caucus at the conference but, according to the *Washington Post*, "Mr. Ford pocketed the request and nothing came of it."[23]

NOW members were not the only feminists worried that women's concerns would take a back seat to geopolitics. Even Charlotte Bunch, who opted not to attend the Mexico City IWY conference for fear that there would be too many US women there, in 1972 expressed her deep frustration with efforts to combine feminism and anti-imperialism. "Men have carried on endless struggles over race and nation, using women and keeping us in servitude," she lamented, citing an example of a Bangladeshi woman who was raped during the liberation struggles and then shunned by the victorious liberation movement. "This will not change until women demand it—with our lives. This begins quietly today with every feminist's decision how to spend her time, what struggles will be her priority. Our oppression doesn't give us the luxury to keep choosing to put a little energy here and a little there, dabbling in all the worthy causes and also carrying out an offensive against sexism. We must choose to win this time."[24]

Still, in a letter to the author Robin Morgan, feminist health activist Carol Downer dismissed what she saw as NOW's campaign to hijack the women's movement. "I think we are going to see the fruition of their efforts to pre-empt, co-opt, obfuscate, and distort the feminist vision at that Mexico City U.N. Conference in July," she wrote. "I expect to see Friedan, the World YWCA, the Population Crisis Committee (a similar organization to [Gloria] Steinem's) running the show. Planned Parenthood has footed most of the bill, of course. We will find ourselves in the interesting position of being on the outside of the outside (the Tribune is the parallel non-governmental conference). Of the several thousand American women who are attending, I doubt that most of them will perceive the contradictions. . . . I expect to see my sisters doing the tourist bit. We will be staying with a small, beleaguered band of feminists in Mexico City who are disgusted with the whole thing."[25]

Friedan had raised particular concerns among IWY planners on both the government and the NGO side. In the weeks leading up to the conference, Aída González at Mexico's Ministry of Foreign Relations had heard that as many as 6,000 people might come for the tribune, "including such 'radical' elements as Betty Friedan and NOW."[26] She implored the US government to "prevent such elements from coming to Mexico," although she assured the State Department that Mexico's borders remained open to tourists and admitted that its government "really could do nothing to exclude those who were determined to attend." US Ambassador John Jova doubted that the Mexican government "could afford politically to act to discourage attendance" at the IWY conference and parallel activities. "It is interesting to us, however," he cabled the State Department, "that there is such concern over possible disruption—or perhaps simply distraction—by radical women's groups." He was curious whether the State Department found any credibility to the rumors of boycotts and counter-conferences and the estimates of several thousand "bouncing back and forth between us and Mexicans without much substantiation."

NOW member and WIN News founder Fran Hosken had rebuked Friedan after the "International Encounter" that took place before the consultative committee meetings, "I heard your statements yesterday at the UN Encounter, where you spoke *though you were not invited*." Chastising her as an "ugly American" who had not bothered to read the UN documents before speaking out, she continued, "It is utterly *irresponsible* that you muscle in and begin to shout at an audience that, had they wanted you to speak, would have asked you. This kind of behavior is intolerable internationally and you must consider that you do not speak for yourself: there are a majority of American women who do not want you to speak for them; and you are not doing yourself or feminists or the feminist movement any favor at all: you will be publicly repudiated and your divisiveness is utterly damaging to those of us who are trying to keep a low profile which is essential in international affairs. Especially with the USA position what it is. And especially at the UN. You should also finally realize that the position of American middle class women or their views of 'liberation' including yours are entirely irrelevant to the majority of women around the world and simply have nothing to offer to their way of life, culture or well being. You should LISTEN and not shout at them." Hosken sent a carbon copy of the letter to Mildred Persinger with an explanatory note pleading, "Someone must get to her before Mexico."[27]

Friedan certainly had gone to Mexico City expecting to lead a feminist charge. "The women's movement for equality, which began in the U.S. a dozen years ago with my book, is now spreading worldwide," she had boasted in a letter to *New York Times Magazine* editor Gerald Walker asking to cover the IWY events.[28] Imagining herself battling the "male establishment of the Communist and Third World (Arab, Africa, Latin America) and, of course, the Vatican," she explained, that "from tales around the U.N., the last months, one sometimes gets the idea that the main "enemy" from which they want to protect their women is the likes of me: the feminists." Women within the UN and involved in IWY planning had come to her "with SOS'es," she informed Walker. Describing herself as an "ambassador-without-portfolio for women," she told him, "I am obviously going to be in the thick of it—out front in the non-governmental Tribune, and privy to the behind-the-scene maneuvering of the official conference, where the new women-politics cuts across the usual lines. At the very least, a kind of journal of my own encounters and reactions (which is probably the best way to write it) will dramatize the common, or different, interests of women in the four worlds, as they meet in large numbers for the first time—and the new political dynamics of womanpower as such confronting, meshing with or crossing the usual power interests." She closed with a prescient query: "The modern women's movement did begin in America—but when I'm asked to help women organizing in their own countries—or in Mexico—am I an agent of American imperialism?" Still, Friedan brushed off concerns that US women would overwhelm the NGO tribune, explaining to a *New York Times* reporter, "We are our sister's keeper."[29]

Jeanne-Martin Cissé was not so sure she wanted to be kept by the likes of Friedan, who seemed to disparage the work of homemakers and to pit women and men against each other. In an interview during her tenure as president of the Security Council, she explained, "According to the natural role of women, we are citizens. But we don't want to be doctors, engineers, astronauts and prime ministers. We want to remain the woman, the mother, the spouse. As mothers, we give more importance to security and peace. I am an ambassador, but I am also a mother."[30] More pointedly, in another interview describing the July 1972 African Women's Conference in Dar es Salaam, she explained, "We have some firm positions on Afrikan problems. There are no feminists around. We are not looking, like the whites, for competition with the men. We're certain the conference does not want any competition with the men."[31]

Organizers' concerns about distractions by US feminists were realized even before the conference and tribune opened. During the journalists' encounter, the US radical feminist group the Redstockings renewed accusations that panelist Gloria Steinem had collaborated with the CIA, only to be shut down with warnings that US feminists' parochial disputes were of little interest at a global conference.[32] For her part, Steinem told the audience that the United States had not exported feminism, but if it had, "it would have been the best thing the country had sent abroad."[33] Steinem left Mexico City after the journalists' encounter, before the conference even started.[34]

When the Feminist Caucus issued its manifesto during the journalists' encounter, it entered into this fracas, sparking debate in the pages of *Xilonen*. Australian Germaine Greer dubbed the statement "phoney" and lambasted the presumption of issuing a manifesto before most participants had even arrived in Mexico City.[35] Her critique focused on the manifesto's call for a "sexist ghetto in the service of female chauvinism" and the inappropriateness of making declarations before the consciousness raising session had begun; it conspicuously omitted the well-worn reproach that the Feminist Caucus represented a narrow, Western point of view. The Nigerian-born, London-based actor and magazine editor Taiwo Ajai nonetheless responded as if she had. "It is presumptuous of any one to assume that women of the Third World are unable to articulate their own outrage on any issue which concerns them," she wrote. "As a member of the Third World I repudiate this patronising attitude and particularly the underlining intellectual imperialism. Women in the Third World do not need any more champions. We are bored and tired of all Great White Hopes."[36]

Ajai's accusations spoke to the widespread and not unfounded view that US feminists sought to impose their particular conception of women's emancipation as just another form of cultural imperialism. In the same issue as Greer's critique of the "Feminist Manifesto," *Xilonen* reported in Spanish (but not in English) that more than 100 NOW members had pledged to keep watch over the intergovernmental conference to ensure that "forces outside of feminism" not have any influence at the official meeting. NOW's Karen DeCrow could only have reinforced the expectations of many readers when she declared, "I don't want to seem jingoistic, but it is evident that the women of the world are trying to follow the behavioral patterns of the North Americans." As proof, she pointed out that four out of Greece's eight female senators sought to include equal rights in the country's new constitution.[37] She seemed unaware that Mexico had already enshrined equal rights in its constitution, and women representing US Chicana organizations told reporters that US legislators might actually learn from their Mexican colleagues about promoting women's juridical equality.[38]

Many observers at IWY saw feminists like Friedan as trying to have things both ways: they wanted to insist upon equality but also perceived a difference between having a man or a woman presiding over the conference. Dismissing Friedan as "a Yankee who is crazier than a pack of billy goats," an *El Universal* columnist conceded that her accusations of machismo "may be true, upon reflection, since one would have to be very manly to get mixed up in the arguments of so many women and still want to control them." The "true absurdity" was that "in a country where appalling injustices are committed daily, [he] was commissioned for this meeting as if there were nothing else to do."[39] The next day, *El Universal* editorialized that US feminists had shown their true colors in objecting to Ojeda Paullada and needed to remember that "the woman needs the man to be a woman, and the man needs a woman to be a man."[40]

The government conference responded quickly to Friedan's objections. Nine government delegations made an official statement supporting Ojeda Paullada.[41] Princess Ashraf told the *New York Times* that his election served "as a striking example of cooperation between men and women" in promoting female equality.[42] Sirimavo Bandaranaike, the Sri Lankan prime minister and only female head of state to participate in the IWY conference, told reporters that she did not consider

Liberación Bajo Control

POR MARINO

Figure 7.1 "Liberation under Control" depicts Attorney General Pedro Ojeda Paullada holding handcuffs. *Excélsior*, 20 June 1975, 6-A.

it an insult that a man would preside over the conference but rather indicated real cooperation between the sexes while ending men's monopoly over dialogue and decision making.[43] "Complementarity of men and women perhaps offers a better alternative to the overly rigid concept of equality," she asserted in her speech opening general debate. "The participation in paid employment does not constitute the only means of women's personal realization and expression."[44] Patricia Hutar pointedly opened her speech with congratulations to Ojeda Paullada—a line added since the draft she had sent to her delegation—and offered a widely quoted assertion that "women cannot wait, with arms folded, for men to achieve a new order before women can achieve equality."[45] Meanwhile, Egyptian First

Lady Jehan Sadat told the plenary that the "excesses of Western feminism" did not sit well in her country, and the leader of the Peruvian delegation, Carmen Oviedo de Sarmiento, elaborated, "Women's equality with men cannot be conquered only through feminist movements that make demands centered exclusively on divisive aspects of women's human condition."[46]

Even Elizabeth Reid—arguably the delegate most sympathetic to US feminists' concerns—opened her remarks with congratulations to Ojeda Paullada and continued with a critique of the equality framework. Pursuing Australia's diplomatic aspirations as a mediator between the non-aligned and the industrialized West, she praised the politics of NIEO and CERDS while stressing the importance of moving from rhetoric to action and insisting that "women as well as men must benefit from this revolution."[47] What she saw in the reports from regional IWY seminars in Africa, Asia, and Latin America was not an embrace of sexism, Reid explained, but a rejection of what would later be dubbed neoliberalism. "Those women who reject the western pattern of development—the increasingly larger institutions, distant workplaces, inflexible hours, a dehumanised environment which suppresses the social, spiritual and cultural lives of its workers—must work towards patterns of development which do not demand productivity and efficiency at any cost." She pointed to the deep inequalities created in developed countries that effectively rationalized masculine and feminine domains.

Like colonialism and racism, she insisted, sexism was enforced through pervasive violence, including "rape, immolation, forced sterilisation, indecent assault, infibulation, unwanted pregnancy, clitorectomy, unnecessary surgery and wife beating and shackling as well as mental violence." Most often, she noted, these acts were perpetrated not by some "sick stranger" but by members of their own households. In this climate, she argued, "equality is a limited and possibly harmful goal," one that might legitimate sexist oppression rather than eradicate it. "Even if we, each of us here, were dedicated, sensitive and understanding," Reid concluded, "we could only hope to touch the outermost limits of the experience of most women. This realisation commits us to enabling women to determine the shape of their own lives, not because it is our favourite political theory but because it is the only way the decisions made will be the right ones."

As delegation leaders orated in the plenary and other official delegates planned their work in committees up in Tlatelolco, the esplanade in front of the Centro Médico had already taken on a carnival atmosphere, with impromptu music and dance performances circling around the enormous pink sculpture of the IWY emblem and mariachis for hire offering to have their pictures taken in *charro* costume of bandoliers and oversized sombreros.[48] The Mexican Youth Movement distributed flyers protesting the presence of "representatives of the fascist [Chilean] Military Junta," while the Bolivian Democratic Committee of Mexico passed out mimeographed sheets decrying the state of affairs in its home country.[49] A small group with the outsized name World Congress for Free Ukrainians would occupy one of the meeting rooms in protest but dispersed when no one took notice. Security officers frantically collected samples of all the protest literature, most of which they could not read. The tribune organizing committee expressed dismay at "acts of hooliganism which are taking place at the Tribune," including the destruction and defacement of national exhibitions. "Such acts of irresponsible and provocative behaviour," they proclaimed, "contradicts the spirit and objectives of the International Women's Year and undermines constructive discussion in the framework of the Tribune. We request (insist) that such actions be stopped."[50]

Roughly 4,000 women poured into the Medical Center for the opening sessions of the NGO tribune—starting with the illustrious lineup of Ghanaian Supreme Court Justice Annie Jiagge, Bulgarian Justice Minister Svetla Daskalova, Dutch Development Minister (and NIEO advocate) Jan Pronk, and the director of Mexico's new National Population Council, Luisa María Leal. The afternoon brought a similarly high-profile panel of participants discussing "Women across Cultures." Elia Borges de Tapia, a former representative to the Venezuelan Congress, called on women not to wait for changes in economic structures. "If the working class had thought like that," she insisted, "it would be in some countries a

Figure 7.2 The esplanade in front of the Centro Médico was the site of both planned and chance encounters at the IWY tribune. © Betty Lane. Courtesy of David M. Rubenstein Rare Book and Manuscript Library, Duke University.

wage slave and not the powerful class it is today."[51] Yugoslav Health Minister Zora Tomic said that women had achieved equality in political and cultural life but that the state had not done enough to alleviate women's labor burdens. The Japanese feminist leader Shikeyo Inoue explained that women had gained equal rights in Japan but that workplace discrimination remained a problem. Betty Friedan spoke last and perhaps surprised her audience by sounding more like Luis Echeverría than Patricia Hutar. "The struggle for women's emancipation is not a revolution against men," she argued. "It is against economic and political reactionaries who have impeded their development." Crediting women of color as the "true initiators" of the feminist movement in favor of equality, she laid the blame squarely on "large economic interests and North American policies that try to maintain inequality between men and women for the benefit of their own interests."[52]

Tribune organizers had hoped that the "Women across Cultures" would demonstrate the diversity of challenges women faced while still establishing some common ground on which to build a truly global effort. Unlike the instructed delegations in the government conference, the NGO *tribunistas* could speak candidly about policies and practices in their home countries. Even Tomic, presumably careful not to run afoul of Josip Broz Tito's government, conceded that "little has been done to liberate women from manual labors."[53] Borges de Tapia, despite her own public officeholding, expressed disappointment in government action. "We are poised to begin the structural changes, and as long as this moment does not arrive, we [women] should act as the advance sector," she argued. "We cannot wait for our governments to exhort international organizations to attend more to the woman problem."[54] As the panelists concluded their prepared remarks, they seem to have reached a consensus about a shared frustration with government inefficacy that might unite women across their otherwise disparate experiences.

When the session opened up for comments from the audience, an unidentified Latin American woman pierced this illusion. "In Latin America," she objected, "for the excluded, greater or lesser discrimination doesn't affect the educated. The problem is not that men are in power but rather that the great imperialist powers cling to their privileges. For you, the most important problem is to liberate yourselves while maintaining your standard of living; for the underdeveloped, it is to liberate ourselves to be able to eat. . . . You ask for solidarity among all women: tell me, can a servant and her mistress unite?"[55] Offering its own illustration of dependency analysis, *El Universal* juxtaposed its coverage of the episode with an article explaining that 30 percent of *campesinos* were malnourished, accompanied by two unrelated photos of well-heeled women eating, one captioned as showing a tribune-goer "devouring a *gelatina*."[56]

Apparently hoping to blunt expectations that she would stoke a war between the sexes, Friedan held a press conference just after the panel to highlight the importance of collaboration, stressing that women's exploitation hurt men as well.[57] She need not have bothered. Most newspapers led off with her objection to having a man preside over the conference, immediately setting off rumors that she would lead a protest march of thousands of women down the Paseo de la Reforma and ending in Tlatelolco Plaza, reenacting her famous march down Fifth Avenue five years earlier.[58] Pacifica Radio highlighted the anticipated geopolitical divide, titling its broadcast of the press conference, "Betty Friedan vs. the Third World." As she would many times during her two weeks in Mexico City, Friedan emerged as a caricature, a flattened symbol of equality-based liberal feminism that insisted unwaveringly that women be treated exactly as men. She stood in for the most literal partisans of the equality theme and fueled the anxieties of those participants who perceived not only an assault on conventional family structures but also a denigration of the labors that consumed most women's time and energy.

The Mexican press depicted Friedan flouting gender conventions. *El Universal* noted her "pink outfit" as if it were a form of drag that failed to disguise her "deep voice, hard and decided facial features" and how her "short, ashen hair frames her broad face. Her long, bulging nose gives her eyes a sad expression, but this image is erased as soon as she opens her mouth and speaks with her powerful voice."[59] Another reporter noted her "masculine wristwatch, a dress like an oversized shirt, gray hair, and agile words," while pointing out that she retained her husband's surname even after their divorce.[60] This fascination with Friedan's purported manliness often took on a low-grade anti-Semitism. The Mexican print media—which exhibited no difficulty spelling names such as Sirimavo Bandaranaike—identified Friedan by a dizzying array of Semitic names, including a few nicknames evoking the Mexican tradition of *lucha libre* fighters: Friedag, Betty "La Terrible" Freaman, Betty "La Amenaza" [The Threat] Friedman.[61]

As Friedan wrapped up her press conference, tribune participants scattered for the evening, many of them making plans for the weekend when the tribune would not hold sessions. Up in Tlatelolco, as the conference meetings stretched from Friday night into the wee hours of Saturday morning, delegates peeled off. By a quarter past midnight, only 150 remained of the 800 who had attended the first plenaries. Licelot Marte de Barrios, heading the Dominican Republic's delegation, reminded the few weary remaining delegates of other feminisms that predated NOW and Friedan and to reimagine families in ways that would alter women's status.[62]

As the last delegates spoke in the sparsely populated auditorium, Dorothy Height and the US National Council of Negro Women (NCNW) convened a three-hour closed-door meeting in a suite at the Hotel Alameda.[63] While the Ford administration disregarded US feminists' requests for support, USAID offered the NCNW a grant—the only group to receive one besides the AAAS grant for the Women and Development workshop—that allowed the group to reserve a "large hotel suite" where eventually groups of fifty to sixty people regularly gathered for two hours or more to compare notes and strategize. "We were funded to bring a group of women from African countries and Latin America and the Caribbean together at the tribune for the opportunity to have them meet together and to look at the concerns that were on the agenda, really from the viewpoint and perspective of black and other third world women," Height told an interviewer a few months later. Interpreters allowed participation in Spanish, French, and English.[64] But the "perspective of black and other third world women" was as contested as the perspective of women more generally. Even on the flight to Mexico City, Height had encountered a group of activists encouraging her to join their protest against the US delegation.[65] As the following morning's events would demonstrate, the question of who might represent the "perspective" of any group remained a bone of contention.

Scene 8

"This Is an Illegitimate Delegation"

The day of the conference inauguration, the US delegation had circulated a bulletin inviting tribune participants to take part in an "encounter" at the US embassy on Saturday morning.[1] Several hundred people streamed past the Marine guard outside the imposing, fortress-like embassy on Paseo de la Reforma—only a few blocks from many conference-goers' hotels—to the embassy's inner patio, where the US delegation members sat prepared for an "informal dialogue" with NGO activists.[2] The fact that the gathering happened at all underscored the popular expectation of democratic engagement and the increasingly important role of rapidly proliferating NGOs, which were alternately viewed as the "private sector" or the new frontier of participatory democracy. Patricia Hutar introduced herself and her fellow delegation leader, USAID director Daniel Parker. When she announced that Parker would speak first, since he needed to leave early to catch a flight, the audience cheered.

The fact that the US delegation was co-led by a man had been widely considered a misstep by the State Department. Parker had been selected to provide a "strong male presence" in Mexico City and because USAID took principal responsibility for implementing the Percy Amendment's commitments to incorporating women into development projects.[3] Ambassador Jova wrote to Kissinger to suggest that a woman lead the delegation alone. Having a male delegation head would put the United States in the questionable company of only a handful of countries, including Swaziland and Botswana—new nations that purportedly could not send women leaders. If Parker spoke at the conference plenary as planned, he would most likely be the first male speaker during the general debate, following the likes of Sri Lankan Prime Minister Sirimavo Bandaranaike and Jamaican First Lady Beverly Manley. Jova did not need to spell out for Kissinger how that would look on a world stage and underscored his recommendation that the "titular head" of the US delegation be a woman.[4] Jane Sidney Oliver echoed the sentiments of many letters to Kissinger when she cabled, "Nomination Parker insults betrays women. Deplore your gross insensitivity. Send Barbara Jordan." Across one such letter, an assistant had penned, "Daniel Parker flap/no action required."[5]

Oliver was not the only one imagining the African American congresswoman Barbara Jordan leading the US delegation. The media-savvy Mildred Marcy reported on the "current atmospherics surrounding question of who speaks for the United States at the International Women's Year Conference," stressing, *"This is the crux of the present problem. . . .* The main question is why a woman of acknowledged national reputation and rank is not speaking for the United States."[6] The State Department had repeatedly expressed interest in having Betty Ford appear at the conference, especially given her support of the Equal Rights Amendment. Even better would be a surprise appearance by Kissinger himself. "It would be a coup of the greatest magnitude as far as American women are concerned," Marcy explained, "and, because unexpected, would have far-reaching international implications for many U.S. foreign policy goals." She also suggested asking Barbara Jordan. "She must know intimately the problems of minorities who are doubly disadvantaged by sex and color, and sensitive to discrimination based on national origin. . . . Her very presence, even briefly, would say volumes about the United States system in practice and its ideals to the Group of 77, the Third World, the non-aligned, the Communist and socialist countries, to all the so-called 'oppressed peoples'—but, most importantly, to the western industrialized democracies and Japan—about this country and its willing responsiveness to changing attitudes and aspirations." Understanding that images had come to dominate media coverage, Marcy recommended that the United States could burnish its reputation by having Representative Jordan share the dais with Betty Ford. "The two of them by their presence—the First Lady and the 'lady from Texas'—[show] evidence of healing in this country in spite of the violence and anguish rooted in the civil rights struggles of our recent past." While Marcy conceded that temporal and political restraints rendered this unrealizable, her fantasy highlighted the extent to which the image of demographic representation informed State Department decisions about its delegates' roster.

Until nearly a week before the conference inauguration, the White House dangled the possibility that the First Lady might deliver the delegation's address to the IWY conference.[7] Two days later, however, the White House announced the elevation of Patricia Hutar as delegation co-chair and spokesperson, attributing the feminist protests to an "assumption" by the press (one shared by Jova and the State Department) that Parker would offer the keynote as the delegation's senior member. Hutar herself brushed off the presumption of Parker's leadership as a "procedural error" in the State Department.[8] Since at least early May the State Department had known that Parker and Hutar would co-lead the delegation for the first three days, at which point Hutar would lead it alone; apparently only the distant hope of Betty Ford's attendance prevented it from definitively specifying its spokesperson.[9] Despite Hutar's partisan allegiances this alteration seemingly assuaged many women's concerns across the political spectrum.[10]

Gloria Steinem voiced the view held by many feminists that the official delegation reflected the conference's broadly establishmentarian orientation. "We would have preferred to have an international feminist conference instead of a conference of government representatives, who may or may not represent the point of view of women," she told reporters during the journalists' encounter. "But this is what we have. And we will try to make the best of it." She expressed disappointment that the US government had not consulted women's groups in formulating its agenda and delegation. Hutar insisted that the US position resulted from "dialogues" between government representatives and "private organizations."[11] Of course, Steinem and Hutar were talking about completely different sectors of what had long been imagined as civil society—Steinem had in mind the recently formed feminist organizations including women's liberation organizations, NOW, and women's civil rights groups, while Hutar meant that she had consulted groups such as the International Business and Professional Women's Federation, Church Women United, and NOW's more conservative splinter group, the Women's Equity Action League.

No one in the State Department appeared concerned that appointing two delegation leaders violated the UN's rules for such conferences, which allowed each member state to send one delegation leader and a maximum of two other representatives.[12] Nominations for delegation members poured into the State Department within days of the UN's announcement of the Mexico City conference. By April, the Office of International Conferences had established the principal criteria for selecting delegates: "active participation in women's affairs, a thorough knowledge of U.S. policies on issues which will be discussed at the Conference, an ability to present U.S. positions, and an ability to negotiate effectively in an international forum."[13] In the end, the State Department sent the two delegation heads, two other accredited representatives, twelve alternate representatives, four congressional advisors, and seventeen further advisors for a total of thirty-seven members, making it among the largest at the conference.[14]

Parker had made population control a particular priority for USAID, but internal strategy papers also stressed the importance of improving women's status and recognizing their domestic roles.[15] Parker, a Republican activist who had directed his family's Parker Pen Company before being appointed director of USAID, had received a practical education through discussions with Secretary Kissinger and Ambassador Scali about the politics of development aid. When the United States failed to match Iran's support for the UN's special fund for food aid, Kissinger testily queried Scali, "Well, what do we have in mind when we talk of helping the less developed?"—to which Scali replied, "Nothing." Parker mentioned the bilateral, government-to-government aid programs, but Scali and Kissinger focused on making US contributions more visible abroad without raising hackles at home.[16] As MIT political scientist Eugene Skolnikoff reminded one such gathering, "A few years down the road the situation could be worse. We could face a painful choice of either slowing down US meat consumption or halting our food aid program." When Parker had suggested linking food aid to population control, National Academy of Sciences president Philip Handler had chided him, "How do you do that internationally without appearing racist? You have to convince the LDCs [less developed countries] that population control is in their interest not ours."[17] Indeed, the first half of the 1970s had generated countless stories—particularly in the feminist press—about forced sterilization campaigns targeting African American, Native American, Chicana, and Puerto Rican women as well as the ways that population control had become a central tenet of US development policy.[18]

So Parker might have anticipated some hostility when he stepped to the microphone in his coat and tie before murmuring audience members and scribbling reporters.[19] Before he even began to speak, Wynta Boynes of the Congress of Racial Equality (CORE) stood up to accuse the delegation—and Parker in particular—of illegitimately representing US women and of advancing US imperialism. Boynes spoke for three full minutes, lambasting USAID's Office of Public Safety and accusing Parker of collusion with the CIA.[20] As she spoke,

Figure 8.1 Wynta Boynes (right) and Esther Urista led the protest at the US embassy.
© Bettye Lane. Courtesy of Schlesinger Library.

some people cheered her on, while others shouted her down; Parker waited uncomfortably by the microphone. When finally allowed to speak, he opened with a wonkish description of the Percy Amendment and other policies intended to improve women's status and control population growth, explaining in monotone the role of impact statements and development appropriations.[21]

Parker had spoken for just over four minutes and was in the midst of designating girls and women as "the most pervasively deprived" when Boynes stood up and interrupted him again, insisting, "You're not addressing yourself to the issues that we raised. You're a cover up, a cop out." Parker asked—amid supportive applause—that she allow him time to speak, but Boynes shouted over him, "Cover up, cop out! You talk about the oppression of women outside the United States. You oppress women—dark, Spanish-speaking, Chinese, Asian, Native American women right in the United States." Parker and Boynes continued to interrupt one another as the encounter erupted into chaos. Someone in the audience insisted, "Everyone! When you undermine that man, you undermine America!" Someone else barked, "Shut up!" Carole de Saram from New York City NOW stood up and proclaimed amid boisterous cheers and applause, "I'm a woman of the United States, and I don't need a man here speaking for women. . . . With all these women in America, with the accomplishments they've done—our congresswomen, our doctors, our lawyers—we have to have a *man* come from America?"[22] Someone in the audience piped up, "This conference is for men and women, women and men." As arguing and murmuring continued, Boynes took control of the floor again. "You!" she yelled at Parker, "First of all, you're not even a woman; second of all, you're not oppressed as a woman." Parker finally took advantage of his obvious technological advantage and said into the microphone, "As far as I'm concerned, I'm honored to be here. I'm honored to be a person in this group." As audience members applauded, he continued, "I wish you well because this conference is far too serious, and the objectives are far too meaningful to let it . . . ." Shouting erupted yet again, at which point Parker simply stated, "I do wish you well, and I—good luck. Thank you," and left the room among cheers and boos.

As Parker escaped to the airport, Patricia Hutar stepped to the microphone and attempted to restore order. Explaining that the delegates had "other meetings" to attend, she turned to the planned program. Although the boisterous audience continued to interject comments as she spoke, Hutar offered a brief history of the CSW and the Bucharest conference, expressing hope that they could replicate what came about there through collaboration between NGOs and government delegations. Notwithstanding Boynes's critique of US policy, Hutar addressed her audience as if they all shared a national agenda that they sought to advance together. With her characteristic equanimity and a hint of condescension, she explained, "I think that if we can keep our cool and exchange ideas

Figure 8.2 US delegation members (left to right) Jewel Lafontant, Patricia Hutar, Joan Goodin, and Arvonne Fraser. © Bettye Lane. Courtesy of Schlesinger Library.

and get formulations put together and work closely together communications-wise and talking with delegations such as you'll be talking with us—many of you are members of international organizations, you have friends in other delega-tions. And those are the people you've got to address your concerns to also. If we don't work together, we're not going to come out with the kind of World Plan of Action that we need." As ever, the "we" in this statement remained ambiguous.

When Hutar ceded the microphone to Rita Hauser, a delegation member with a background as an international lawyer and co-chair of the New Yorkers for Nixon 1968 campaign, Boynes stood again. "Wait, wait, wait," she insisted, turning to someone to warn, "Don't touch me!" As Hutar attempted to deter Boynes, assuring her an opportunity to speak later, Boynes shouted, "No! The United States delegation is an inadmissible, racist, and discriminatory collection of men and women." The audience erupted again, drowning out both Boynes and Hutar. A group of women stood up around Boynes and began to speak along with her both to amplify her message and to demonstrate that she was not a lone objector. As some audience members applauded enthusiastically, Hutar seemed on the verge of losing her patience. She asked whether any of the protesting women had ever actually met any of the delegation members and scolded, "If you'd be quiet, you could have a chance to talk with them, and we want to be able to talk with you throughout this, but don't show prejudice against others until you know what they're like and where they're coming from."

Hauser finally calmed the crowd by promising them time at the microphone within a few minutes. "Let's just try to get a little semblance of order because no one is hearing anyone on anything at this point." The protests subsided as Hauser began to introduce the delegation, which she described as representing "a very broad cross-section of American womanhood." When a protestor interjected a comment, Hauser turned and snapped, as if to a child, "Cool it—let's try to do this in an orderly way." She explained the relationship between the intergovernmental conference and the NGO tribune, reiterating—belaboring, even—how keen the official delegates were to meet and exchange views with "members of the private sector." Hauser underscored that everyone gathered in that courtyard should consider themselves privileged because they enjoyed the right to challenge their own government. Boynes and her supporters proceeded to exercise that right. Hauser attempted to subdue Boynes, indicating that there were many women in the room with many different priorities for the conference and that they all wanted the opportunity to be heard. Explaining the challenges of developing a World Plan of Action for women "coming from very different economic, developmental, and social backgrounds," she stressed, "That is the unity that has to come out of this international conference." Having served for three years as the US representative for the UN Commission on Human Rights, Hauser could attest to the ways in which IWY had forced the UN and its member states to at least feign respect for women as political and economic players.

Before allowing audience members to come to the microphone, Hauser insisted on introducing one other delegation member, Jewel LaFontant. A Nixon appointee as the deputy solicitor general at the Department of Justice, LaFontant had been a late addition to the delegation leadership, replacing former Michigan congressional representative Martha Griffiths, and was given a speaking role at the conference.[23] Although she had no particular involvement with women's issues, LaFontant had served as a representative to the UN General Assembly in 1972 and had a formidable background in both Republican Party circles and Chicago legal circles as the first African American woman to graduate from the University of Chicago Law School. To the extent that the official delegation put on a political performance for a domestic audience, LaFontant may have offered an even more inspired casting choice than Barbara Jordan, effectively reclaiming the civil rights issue from the Democratic Party.[24]

As LaFontant stepped to the microphone, one of the protesters called out, "Let the black lady speak next, huh?" To which LaFontant promptly responded, "Yes, I'm black; and, young lady, I'm proud I'm black. And, let me tell you this: I'm glad that I look black so that no one can say that I'm anything else but black. . . . Likewise, I'm female, and thank God that's obvious." She then turned to the protesters to tell them that she had been a founding member of CORE in Chicago. "That's letting you know how long I've been active in the movement," she chided them. "Long before you were born. Now, I don't often brag about being black and being female, and I don't often brag about my age, but I wanted you to know that I've been working in the vineyards for a long time." Citing racism as the "biggest problem in America," she insisted upon the principle of fighting the system from the inside. Offering to meet with anyone who had ideas to offer, she cautioned, "Let's not be thrown off from our task here. The world is looking at us, and we don't want to act like what they call 'emotional, dumb women.'"

The moment LaFontant stopped speaking, the room erupted again, and Hauser began calling with some desperation, "Where's Gilda? Where's Gilda?" Gilda Bojórquez Gjurich, the sole Mexican American member of the delegation, had not yet arrived. Gjurich was not the only (or even the most fluent) Spanish speaker on the delegation. The labor union leader Joan Goodin spoke briefly in Spanish, having lived for five years in Peru. Carmen Maymi, a Puerto Rican who had grown up in Chicago where she worked as a community organizer, represented the Department of Labor as the director of women's affairs, but her arrival in Mexico City had been delayed because of ILO meetings in Geneva, where the equal-pay resolution was under discussion.[25] Gjurich, a successful Los Angeles–born businesswoman affiliated with the Chicano nationalist Raza Unida Party as well as the well-established League of United Latin American Citizens (LULAC), was nowhere to be found. She was scheduled to return to Los Angeles on Monday morning; arguably her principal obligation in Mexico City was to bolster the delegation's legitimacy at this event. Virginia Allan, a former president of the NGO National Business and Professional Women who oversaw relationships between the State Department and women's NGOs during the Nixon administration, reassured the protesters that Gjurich was on her way but had been held up by a press conference.

While she waited for Gjurich to arrive, Hauser called the other delegation members to the front "so they can get a look at you." Delegates strained to establish "minority" credentials to legitimate their status: Muriel Berman, the vice-chair of the Women for Pennsylvania Bicentennial, claimed minority status as a Jew; Nira Long, the USAID lawyer overseeing implementation of the Percy Amendment and the only other African American, seconded LaFontant's argument that people "on the inside" still work alongside those "on the outside" and stressed that she had marched in Selma, Washington, and Los Angeles; Hauser described Carmen Maymi's background; Arvonne Fraser, founder of the Women's Equity Action League and wife of Senator Donald Fraser, claimed minority status as the lone remaining Democrat.

Gjurich finally showed up about forty-five minutes into the meeting and rushed to the microphone, greeting her *hermanas* in Spanish and answering shouts of "Qué viva la raza!" She apologized for her tardiness, explaining that she just could not get out of bed as early as she once did; responding to an audience member, she explained, "No makeup, dear? I need it at my age. You make your choice; I'll make my choice." After apologizing for her limited Spanish and stopping briefly to introduce herself, she went on, "I don't know what's going on, and I came in late, but this delegation has been the greatest thing for me. Only in the United States could a woman like me rise and be counted and be able to speak for the Spanish-speaking, the blacks, and the Orientals." Someone from the audience shouted out that she spoke for whites, too. She then quickly tried to yield the microphone to the next speaker but was stopped by questions from the audience: "How do you represent us? How to you represent Chicanas?" As she rattled off her activist credentials—in addition to Raza Unida and LULAC, she worked with the Hispanic veterans and civil rights organization GI Forum as well as the Comisión Femenil de Los Angeles—someone from the audience interrupted in Spanish to offer her endorsement of Gjurich as "muy buena gente" [good people], strong, and confidence-inspiring.[26]

The interventions by LaFontant and Gjurich seemed to quell the protests a bit. As Jova cabled Kissinger, "As each member took mike and revealed long and productive careers in women's movement, often from underprivileged beginnings, tide of opinion turned in favor of delegation."[27] Carl Hemmer—one of the two other men on the delegation—initially drew groans when he introduced himself as working for USAID. "Yeah, I know how you feel," he acknowledged. Explaining that many "Third World women" have much larger families than they want, he described USAID's efforts to make voluntary abortion and sterilization available to all women as a "humanitarian act on the part of our country." Someone queried from the audience, "Have you had a vasectomy?"—to which he promptly responded that he had and elaborated on the important role that men had to play in family planning. The audience howled and applauded his candor, but several objected when he went on to insist that they "give credit" to the US government for humanitarian motivations.

Given the fraught discussions about the delegation's composition, its leaders had likely foreseen the melee that would ensue; or perhaps they hoped the exchange would forestall open hostilities among US participants that would belie claims of national unity and healing following decades of violence and betrayals. These wounds remained raw, however, and activists arrived at the embassy with bitter knowledge of the consequences of being denied political representation. When the delegation leaders finally allowed one audience member from each group to come to the microphone, Wynta Boynes unsurprisingly claimed the first spot.[28] With Hutar looking over her shoulder, occasionally fingering a long string of pearls, Boynes began to read an eleven-point statement from the Coalition of Unrepresented Women. "The United States delegation is an illegitimate delegation," she explained. "It is impossible for the men and women of this delegation to understand what oppressed women in the United States are about." Although USAID funded Dorothy Height and the NCNW, Boynes asserted that the State Department had failed to consult any recognized organizations representing minority interests and had ignored all petitions for greater diversity. "This delegation is nothing more than an offshoot of AID," she declared. Several speakers underscored her concerns, some speaking in Spanish and others in English.

Amid a parade of speakers lambasting not only the delegation for failing to represent them but also the US government more generally for acts of imperialism and oppression, a counter-narrative emerged from a different group. Mary Beth, a spokesperson for the Ukrainian National Congress who grew up in Michigan, explained that her illiterate parents had come from Ukraine "when Ukraine was free" and found opportunities in the United States. She called for unity among IWY participants and with the reproof "shouting doesn't help," she turned to Boynes and her compañeras and rebuked them, telling them that if they thought women in the United States were oppressed, they "ought to get a taste of the oppression in other countries." Maria, a Yugoslavian immigrant, echoed Mary Beth in her accented English, "You talk about freedom? Believe me there is no freedom like there is freedom in the United States." But Mary Jo McConaughy, reporting for *Ms.* magazine and Pacifica Radio, returned the discussion to issues Boynes had raised at the outset, asking about AID's work with police forces in authoritarian countries like Brazil and Chile and its collaboration with the CIA, particularly with regard to population programs.

By Jova's estimation, the encounter lasted a full three hours. He judged that the delegation had clearly won the bout, emerging with "heightened prestige for the way in which they conducted themselves and for having improved rapport and understanding with non-governmental sector." He offered fulsome praise for the entire delegation, particularly Parker, who "absorbed minority's heaviest fire" but remained "supremely composed and patient." Hutar had handled the commotion with "poise and confidence," and the "special contributions of delegates LaFontant and Gjurich effectively destroyed argument that delegation failed to include representation of U.S. minorities and their interests." But Jova argued that the challenges from people like Boynes played a critical role in making the encounter a "free and uninhibited exchange" that made a "valuable contribution to mutual understanding and confidence-building." He and Hutar agreed that the session would be worth repeating, not least because it offered "an impressive and persuasive example of U.S. participatory democracy at work."[29] Hutar repeated this line nearly verbatim in her comments to *Xilonen*. She described the episode as "remarkable, an example of freedom of expression, of democracy in action" but revealed her irritation with the activists' protests. "We need their input," she explained, "and there is no time for a leisurely debate."[30]

Not everyone shared Jova's assessment of Hutar's performance. For the feminist lawyer Nancy Reeves, who attended the conference as a journalist, Hutar lacked an understanding of both diplomacy and feminist thought. "Mrs. Hutar was all dolled up and the rest of it but she couldn't really deal with the conference because she didn't have the diplomatic background," Reeves told an interviewer upon her return to Los Angeles. "Hutar was a cupcake who had been a committee woman. She may have had the gray matter for the job, but she didn't have the background." Describing Hutar as a "lightweight" compared to Elizabeth Reid, who "is a philosopher by profession, an extremely intellectual woman. Reid has studied feminism in depth, whereas Hutar's views of feminism is a suburban view of the issues—whether women get jobs, things like that."[31]

As in the embassy confrontation, challenges about legitimate representation did not follow only racial or ethnic lines—although those conflicts attracted the most notice, particularly in the US press—but also divides of class, of generation and experience, of insiders and outsiders, and of people who wanted to reform decision-making systems versus those who found the current systems too dysfunctional and damaged to be salvaged. Ethel Payne, the veteran civil rights reporter for the *Chicago Defender*, must have noticed these divides but tried to suture them to whatever extent possible. Whereas Jova's report spotlighted the moment when LaFontant called out the CORE protesters, Payne depicted the disruptions as feminist-led and downplayed the generational disagreements among CORE leaders, describing the "disruptions over . . . representation" as "dissident feminists seized the lectern and shouted that the [official delegation], including [LaFontant] did not represent their best interests."[32] In a more retrospective article, she mentioned LaFontant's "spirited defense" of the US delegation when challenged by a "young, positive and black" woman but omitted any challenge to the CORE leadership, instead stressing Friedan's role as a "gadfly" with "a genius for both making news and managing to alienate whole segments of people."[33]

The frustrations and challenges to legitimacy expressed by activists and delegates alike were hardly confined to the US participants or even to interactions with official delegations. Elizabeth Reid received angry letters from aboriginal women saying that Ruby Hammond, an activist in the Council of Aboriginal Women and Aboriginal Legal Rights Movement, was not a suitable representative to Australia's IWY National Advisory Committee.[34] The official Chilean delegation—representing Augusto Pinochet's military government, which many UN member states, including Mexico, did not recognize—drew challenges throughout the conference and tribune, where the widow of overthrown president Salvador Allende consistently drew cheers from supporters. Mexican feminists staged a series of protests against the composition of the Mexican delegation. Tribune participants remonstrated against their lack of participation at the intergovernmental conference; many of them also objected to caucuses emerging within the tribune that claimed representative status.

The problem of representation seemed bottomless, particularly in these settings where policymaking itself was largely performative. Much in the way that Imelda Marcos and Ashraf Pahlavi seemed inappropriate representatives of the Third World, Wynta Boynes and the activists who rallied around her did not find suitable representation in Jewel LaFontant and Gilda Gjurich, despite their activist credentials. Many participants came to the tribune hoping to, as one Chicana participant recalled, "share a common sisterhood."[35] It remained unclear, however, what could serve as the foundation for such kinship.

Scene 9

"Other Kinds of Problems"

Domitila Barrios de Chungara finally made it to Mexico City on Monday morning on her own search for representation. She knew from the Bolivian newspapers that the IWY events were divided between an intergovernmental conference and an NGO tribune. She figured that the "upper class ladies" would attend the conference, "making fancy statements, saying that in Bolivia more than any other place, women had achieved equality with men." She planned to attend the tribune, where "people like me would be, people with similar problems, you know, poor people."[1] Her journey from her tin-mining community had taken, it seemed, a lifetime. Her years of struggle as a leader in the union's Housewives' Committee drew attention after her appearance in a 1971 documentary, *El coraje del pueblo*, about labor conflicts in the state-owned Siglo XX mine. The filmmaker "liked what I said," Domitila explained in her widely read *testimonio*, "and she said it was important that everything I knew should be said to the rest of the world."[2] Mildred Persinger's tireless search for more Third World women and fewer "elite people" to participate in the tribune turned up Domitila, who agreed to attend the IWY conference if the filmmaker could find money to pay for her to travel.[3] She then forgot about the invitation, assuming it was another of many well-intentioned promises by outsiders sympathetic with their struggle.

When a telegram arrived inviting her to the tribune, the "surprised and disconcerted" Domitila called a meeting with her compañeras, who agreed that she should go. With financial support from the miners' union, she and some compañeras traveled to La Paz to begin the frustrating process of securing a travel permit from the Ministry of the Interior. When union leaders arrived on the day of the IWY conference inauguration and found Domitila still in La Paz, mired in bureaucracy, they brandished her "invitation from the United Nations" and demanded, "What's happened here? Is it or isn't it International Women's Year? Do our wives have the right to participate in this conference, or can only your wives go there?"[4] They threatened to stage a work stoppage in protest and to file a complaint with the United Nations. The ministry begrudgingly granted her visa, but, as she boarded the plane in La Paz, a ministry employee reminded her ominously, "Your return to the country depends a lot on what you say there. So it's not a question of talking about any old thing . . . you've got to think it out well. Above all, you've got to think of your children who you're leaving behind. I'm giving you good advice. Have a good time."[5]

Leaving Bolivia for the first time in her life, Domitila zigzagged her way from La Paz to Mexico City, changing planes in Lima and again in Bogotá. On her last leg, she met an Uruguayan woman also en route to the conference, and her excitement grew as she anticipated the opportunity that lay before her. "It was like a dream for me! Goodness, I said to myself, I'll be meeting peasant women and working women from all over the world. All of them are going to be just like us, oppressed and persecuted."[6] Persinger recalled Domitila's long-awaited arrival as "the most memorable thing that happened in Mexico."[7] Having been warned that the Bolivian government might not allow Domitila to attend because she was "something of a revolutionary," Persinger had fretted that Domitila might not make it after all. As Persinger stood in the main corridor of the Centro Médico with tribune participants buzzing all around her, speaking in several languages and jostling to read the messages on the increasingly crowded bulletin board, Domitila entered and was introduced to her. As Persinger recalled, they both cried from exhaustion and anxiety and relief that Domitila had finally arrived.

Persinger's and Domitila's memories of this episode diverge in telling but not necessarily contradictory ways. Domitila recalls receiving an invitation through a radical Brazilian documentary filmmaker who had seen her in *El coraje del pueblo*; Persinger remembers the suggestion to invite her coming from a Catholic Charities social worker from the mining camp. Persinger describes the social worker bringing Domitila to the tribune "to see that she got there," and Domitila recounts her arrival with an Ecuadorian, quite possibly the activist Marisa de los Andes. Perhaps misled by her own assumptions about what a Housewives' Committee might do, Persinger seemed to have misunderstood the nature of Domitila's activism. "She was the wife of a tin miner," she later told an interviewer, "and she had started a project among the women to bake a special kind of biscuit that is very popular, in Latin America and sell them. And they were making money and for the first time, she had organized them to do this, and for the first time they were able to send their children to school because you have to buy school uniforms and other supplies for school."

If Persinger imagined that Domitila—whose militancy included arguments over the Sino-Soviet split, hunger strikes, and violent confrontations with army personnel that had landed her twice in jail, where she endured savage beatings— had spent her time organizing a bake sale to pay for children's school uniforms, she was quickly disabused.[8] "The minute she came to us in Mexico, within five minutes, she was on the floor in the big meeting and she was ranting and raving about the injustices that were done to the peasants in Bolivia," Persinger remembered. "Everybody was only allowed to speak five minutes, then you were supposed to have a discussion from the whole audience. Well, okay, she spoke the five minutes, and . . . the chairman started to pound her down, and then there was such a roar from the audience. . . . I wasn't getting exactly what she was saying, but I could tell by the tone of voice and also the rest of the folks who were listening to her insisted she had to go on. The person in the chair had enough sense to let her go on or we would have a riot. She was fiery."[9]

But Domitila recalls having been alienated into silence on her first day at the tribune.[10] She and her Ecuadorian *compañera* crowded into the back of a meeting room, perching on some stairs when they were unable to find seats. "It was my first experience and I imagined that I would hear things that would make me get ahead in life, in the struggle, in my work," she explained. To her horror, however, "a *gringa* went over to the microphone with her blond hair and some things around her neck and her hands in her pockets" and told a cheering audience that she and other prostitutes deserved "a thousand and one medals" for having "the courage to go to bed with so many men." Domitila and her compañera fled the conference hall and went to another room only to find themselves face-to-face with lesbian activists. Having come to Mexico City to share stories and strategies with other women from exploited countries and other liberation movements, Domitila recalled she was stunned to "run into those other kinds of problems. . . . I felt a bit lost."

Although Domitila seems to have jumbled together several episodes that would play out over the chaotic and cacophonous days of the tribune, her retrospective conflation highlights the extent to which the debate over the relationship between politics and women's issues emerged as a false dilemma over whether to prioritize First World concerns, which Domitila boiled down to sexual liberation and fighting against men, or Third World concerns, which centered on human rights and economic justice. "This conference is political—and thank goodness it is!"proclaimed Ojeda Paullada. "Peace obviously is in itself a political preoccupation, development is a political preoccupation, and equality is also a political preoccupation," he explained.[11] Vicente Lascurain, who had taken refuge in Mexico after fleeing the Franco regime in the 1930s, put the division even more starkly in his column in the ruling party's *El Nacional*. "Those themes that have been dubbed political are the preoccupation of those nations that include themselves in the so-called Third World, and those more particular to women's conditions are raised by the rich nations," he explained. "If women disagree over what is most important, it is because in their personal lives and as members of a national community, they live out of sync because of different levels of development. Something similar would occur if there were a world conference on consumer culture or waste: the women from the Horn of Africa, India, and Latin America would immediately politicize the theme, and it would be impossible to discuss the advisability of having two cars among those who form a fourth world of hunger and desperation. Like it or not, the female condition is not an instrument of planetary unity and the Conference is destined to have the same results as nearly all the other international conferences that are held."[12]

Although Domitila would emerge in coming years as the embodiment of discord at the IWY events, her participation reflected one area of widespread agreement: concern about what Lenin had famously dubbed "the barbarously unproductive, petty, nerve-wracking, stultifying and crushing drudgery" of domestic labor.[13] The filmmaker who arranged Domitila's invitation to the IWY tribune was Helena Solberg-Ladd, the Brazilian-born, New York–based filmmaker who interviewed Domitila for her documentary *La doble jornada* (The Double Shift), a film about the "second shift" of women's reproductive labor.[14] Countless newspaper accounts, foundation reports, and background papers attested to the amount of time and energy that women spent collecting water and firewood, cultivating crops and tending livestock, and caring for family members young and old. *Xilonen* featured an article entitled "The Harsh Life of Rural Africa," accompanied by a cartoon of a woman frantically peddling a Rube Goldberg contraption that allowed her to grind corn, wash clothes, bathe a child, and study all at once.[15] Nearly every one of the Third World media fellows who participated in the journalists' encounter described the alleviation of this labor as one of the most pressing concerns among women in their home countries. Mexican feminists made similar charges, arguing, "Unpaid domestic labor is noxious from every perspective. It gives rise to an extreme exploitation of servants and postpones the socialization of housework, a necessity to end the servitude of all women."[16]

In more industrialized areas, many women experienced the isolation and alienation that Betty Friedan had famously identified in *The Feminine Mystique*, although journalists often dismissed these concerns as whining, implying that only privileged women in wealthy countries worried about domestic hardships. "The poor cannot afford the dubious luxury of a feminine mystique," Jennifer Seymour Whitaker quipped in *Foreign Affairs*.[17] James Sterba of the *New York Times* disdained issues such as equal pay and child-care centers as "luxury" concerns and lamented US women's unfamiliarity with Third World hardships.[18] But these glib comparisons—Third World women walk five kilometers to find water and then have to carry it back to their homes, while First World women turn a tap; Third World women spend hours grinding grains, while First World women buy bread at a supermarket—obscured what the vast majority of IWY participants agreed was a critical structural similarity: the overwhelming amount of labor that fell on women's shoulders and that appeared nowhere in national economic data. Despite dismissals by Sterba and others, Third World women repeatedly raised issues such as equal pay and the availability of child-care services.

The subject of "Women and Work"—as the tribune program dubbed it—brought to the surface one of the thorniest issues in both feminist and development circles. Development programs concentrated on getting women into the "productive" labor sector, and discussions at both the tribune session and the conference centered not on whether but how women would enter the labor market. Kalmen Kaplansky, the Polish-born Canadian representing the International Labor Organization (ILO), urged member states to ratify the ILO's equal-pay convention and to enable vigilant enforcement.[19] The tribune session led off with a short documentary about the exclusion of women's labor from the calculation of gross domestic product (GDP) and then continued with a discussion about the pace at which women might be incorporated into the paid labor force so as to minimize disruption to both family life and the economy.

This approach left unanswered the question of who would perform the vast amounts of labor left behind by women entering the paid workforce, creating a disjuncture not only between the experiences of First and Third World women but also between urban and rural women. Leaders of five Latin American delegations described rural women as the "Cinderellas among Cinderellas" because they continue to serve as men's domestic servants.[20] Even the chair of East Germany's IWY committee, while touting communism's many gains in women's status, conceded, "It is not always easy for women having children to meet all demands resulting from work and family life. That requires more than just the wish to combine everything in a harmonious way."[21] As Dorothy Height of the National Council of Negro Women recalled, "We [from the United States] were talking about work in one sense and those [Third World] women were pointing out that they never show up in any labor statistics. But women who have to carry water two miles up and two miles back for whatever they and their children drink, whether they are sick, pregnant, or whatever, are involved in work."[22]

This issue sparked debates over possible solutions—structural and cultural, individual and state-managed. Articles such as "The Politics of Housework" made the rounds in the US feminist press.[23] The more radical among these regularly referred to "domestic enslavement" or created equivalences between marriage and prostitution, citing court cases that saw wives as contractually obliged to fulfill domestic duties. The wages-for-housework campaign had gained popularity in some feminist circles, although many feminists expressed concern that, as the anthropologist Carole Lopate argued, it would "only serve further to embed women (and men) in the clutches of capitalism."[24] The Mexican poet and ruling-party politician Griselda Alvarez deplored the distribution of household labor—along with the violence that too often enforced it—but insisted, "This is not about demanding a salary from the husband for the work the woman performs, no. We repeat, it is not about this but rather about a transformation in customs."[25] To Domitila, the discussion of wages for housework seemed absurd if divorced from a broader discussion of capitalism. Speaking after a screening of *La doble jornada*, she explained that she received a "family subsidy" from the mining company of fourteen Bolivian pesos per month—enough to buy two bottles of milk or a half box of tea. In a low-wage economy, wages for housework were still poverty wages.[26]

As Domitila underscored, many participants in the IWY tribune could attend because they paid someone else to perform domestic labors—a luxury that women like herself could hardly afford. Annie Jiagge, described by the *New York Times* as well educated, of regal bearing, and from the aristocracy, told the reporter, "In Africa, you have house help. You pay through the nose for it, but you have it."[27] The South Korean diplomat Sookja Hong later boasted to reporters that she never learned to cook because "we had housekeepers."[28] Meanwhile, a Mexican domestic worker named Raquel Núñez reminded the 1,600 people attending the "Women and Work" tribune session that paid domestic workers remained the most marginalized and long-suffering members of the labor force.[29] Tribune participant Josephine Hulett, of the US-based National Committee on Household Employment, had explained to a reporter for the *Chicago Tribune*, "Since the housewife has not been paid for her work, she doesn't think someone doing her work is worth that much. Most housewives do not have money of their own; they're given a certain amount of money to run the house, and they oppress women beneath them."[30]

Women like Domitila faced challenges in their own households. "One day I got the idea of making a chart," she explained in her memoir. "We put for example the price of washing clothes per dozen pieces and we figured out how many dozen items we washed per month. Then the cook's wage, the babysitter's, the servant's. We figured out everything that we miners' wives do every day. Adding it all up, the wage needed to pay us for what we do in the home . . . was much higher than what the men earned in the mine for a month."[31] In a subsequent account, she related a far more combative episode during which she went on strike, suspending all domestic labors when her husband objected to her union activities. The following month, she resumed her domestic labors but presented her husband at the end of the month with a bill for 240 pesos—three times his monthly wage.[32] Barrios de Chungara clearly recounted these stories in part to highlight the impossibility, in her world, of commodifying her caring labors but also to stress the principle of that labor's value to household, community, and nation. A Mexican feminist pamphlet issued in advance of the conference situated the issue within G-77 priorities, underscoring the importance of "a just valuation of women's work, as much in the home as in the factory or the office" and calling for twenty-four-hour child-care services and "the preparation of a document that captures the rights and obligations of the couple before society and that could be included in the Charter of the Economic Rights and

Figure 9.1 Josephine Hulett (left), National Committee of Household Employees,
sharing a translation headset at the Tribune. © Bettye Lane. Courtesy of David
M. Rubenstein Rare Book and Manuscript Library, Duke University.

Duties of States, defender of the Third Worldist countries and the oppressed
classes."[33]

For the most part, however, even the most impassioned advocates of ame-
liorating women's labor burdens remained vague on the details, resorting to the
passive voice or abstractions. Many agreed that men should do more. Some favored the Swedish model, which set up incentives for men to stay home with
children and for companies to hire men and women into jobs dominated by the
opposite sex.[34] Margaret Mead argued that men would need to take up more of
the domestic burden, which she hoped would be alleviated by efforts to reduce

fertility.[35] The trade unionist Beatrice von Roemer explained to conference delegates, "The participation of both sexes in domestic tasks would help the woman participate more actively in the labor market. The duties performed predominantly by women are often undervalued. This work should not be assigned solely on the basis of sex."[36] Acknowledging that the age-old division of household labor would not change overnight, Mexican politician Griselda Alvarez proclaimed, "In sum, we must propose and obtain a change in family customs, pulling the old molds out by the root with the help of progressive men who are man enough not to fear this change."[37] Others, particularly those from socialist countries, stressed the provision of public services and technological solutions.

The only country that had addressed the issue head-on as a policy concern was Cuba, which had, after lengthy deliberations, passed the Family Code, which took effect on International Women's Day, March 8, 1975 but surprisingly drew no attention at the IWY gatherings. Vilma Espín, herself a revolutionary and the leader of the Cuban Women's Federation, was identified in *Xilonen* and the *New York Times*, both of which misspelled her name, only as Raúl Castro's wife.[38] The *Times* listed her among the women whom US feminists had dubbed "wifey poos," while *Xilonen* offered an article focused entirely on her dress and behavior during a performance by Cuban prima ballerina Alicia Alonso. Given the near-universal concern about the problem of women's subsistence labors, it is surprising that no one thought to interview the woman who had just orchestrated a five-day congress for ten to thirteen hours a day discussing precisely this issue.[39] Her plenary address—which included praise for the Soviet Union, a shout out for the upcoming East Berlin conference, and hearty congratulations to the Vietnamese delegations—enumerated the steps the Cuban government had taken to achieve the educational, labor, and family rights sought in the World Plan of Action. "But we still are not satisfied," she insisted, "and so that this equality can be fully exercised, we have worked in a systematic way to elevate women's educational levels and erase the last traces of backwards misunderstanding about her role in society."[40] The Family Code discussions in Cuba had signaled an even deeper change afoot in Cuba and elsewhere, an issue that erupted at the IWY tribune: shifting cultural and social ideas about sexuality and gender roles.[41]

The panel that Domitila and her comrade stumbled into, the session she found so disorienting and alienating, focused on socialization and cultural attitudes toward women. The panel chair, the Bangladeshi scholar Rounaq Jahan—who at age thirty-one had chaired Dhaka University's political science department and was on her way to a year-long fellowship at the University of Chicago—told the audience that women remained "too submissive in bed" and urged men to learn to listen better. While the session next door on law and women's status remained orderly and restrained, the session on cultural attitudes grew increasingly rowdy.[42] Jahan and the other panelists often had to shout over audience members who interrupted presentations. Guatemalan poet and essayist Luz Méndez de la Vega called for women to "take up arms" in the "war of the sexes." Chilean author Isabel Allende and her Mexican comrade Berta Arenal sparked enthusiastic applause with their call for solidarity with Chile and for the rejection of the official Chilean delegation representing the Pinochet government.[43] This would not be the last time that Chilean dissidents would indicate that tribune-goers should attend to issues of human rights rather than issues of sexuality.

Jahan recalled "something like four hundred people lining up behind the two microphones on the floor to speak," forcing her to interrupt speakers who veered off topic. "When I cut short the seventh speaker on Chile as she started to read out a lengthy critique of U.S. foreign policy," she reported, audience members expressed the views with "clappings and counter clappings for half a minute."[44] Jahan was not the only session chair struggling to keep the Chilean situation from becoming a focal point; from the first day of the journalists' encounter, Chileans had spoken out about the horrific events of the previous two years, hoping to galvanize international intervention by citing Pinochet's mockery of the UN Declaration on Human Rights.[45]

In the first half of the 1970s, Chile had become an international cause célè-bre. In the first years of the decade, activists and political leaders cheered the first democratically elected socialist government of Salvador Allende. After the 1973 military coup, as reports came out of human rights abuses committed under the Pinochet dictatorship, the outcry against the regime grew louder. At the 1974 General Assembly session, twenty-one countries of varying geopolitical orientations—from Australia and Britain to Yemen and Yugoslavia—had signed a resolution protesting human rights violations in Chile and calling for a UN investigation.[46] The Soviet delegation leader Valentina Tereshkova had reiterated Soviet opposition to the Pinochet coup soon after her arrival in Mexico.[47]

The Mexican press anticipated a face-off between the Chilean representatives and the sizable Chilean exile community in Mexico City.[48] Organizations such as Mexico's UNMM added Chile, along with Vietnam and Palestine, to the list of countries needing solidarity. As the IWY conference drew near, Mexico's Popular Socialist Party petitioned the Mexican government to reject the credentials of the official Chilean delegation and instead accredit Salvador Allende's widow, Hortensia Bussi de Allende, to lead the Chilean delegation.[49] While this petition had no chance of success, the Mexican government did deny a visa to a Chilean journalist who formed part of the official delegation and directed the junta-controlled daily, La Patria.[50] As Isabel Allende and Bertha Arenal received cheers in the tribune for demanding the expulsion of Chilean officials, Swedish Prime Minister Olof Palme stepped to the podium at the government conference and decried the "atrocities being committed against the men and women of Chile."[51] Just the day before, Sergio Méndez Arceo, the liberation theology-inspired bishop of Cuernavaca, had delivered a homily describing Chile as a "limit case of the present moment" and led a prayer for the Chilean women who suffered terror and exile.[52]

As reports of US involvement in the Pinochet coup leaked out from the Senate's Church Committee hearings, concern mounted within the United States. Ford Foundation field officers reported unsettling encounters with members of the Chilean police and military who arrived unannounced at their offices and residences, and the foundation wrestled with whether to suspend operations in Chile over objections from Henry Ford himself.[53] Sympathetic US feminists—mostly socialist feminists—set up Action for Women in Chile to raise international awareness about female political prisoners and conditions under the junta.[54] Several feminist newsletters reported on the fate of women in Pinochet's Chile, and NOW passed a resolution protesting the "sexual torture of Chilean women political prisoners."[55]

In short, protests against the Pinochet regime and US support for it were as much a part of the conference that Domitila Barrios de Chungara encountered as were the prostitutes and lesbians she describes so vividly in her *testimonio*. In fact, at the moment Domitila recalled encountering the prostitutes at the tribune, the leaders of the staunchly feminist, San Francisco-based prostitutes' rights group COYOTE (Call Off Your Old Tired Ethics) were en route to Mexico City. The "prostitution workshop" that so horrified Domitila and her friend would not take place for several days.[56] At any rate, COYOTE's political commitments certainly trouble the opposition that someone like Domitila or Isabel Allende saw between social justice and sexual rights: the previous summer, COYOTE members had refused services to a Chilean ship docking in the San Francisco harbor, claiming it had been used as a "floating prison" by Pinochet's junta.[57]

Ever media savvy, COYOTE leaders Margo St. James and Flo Kennedy gave an interview to *El Universal* describing COYOTE's origins and highlighting the hypocrisy of anti-prostitution laws passed and enforced by men who patronize and profit from prostitution.[58] With St. James cursing like a sailor and Kennedy sporting orange dungarees and a cherry-red shirt over a yellow T-shirt, the pair hardly conformed to the reporters' conceptions of demure femininity, never mind Kennedy batting her "enormous false eyelashes." Explaining that they wanted the right to organize legally for benefits such as social security—"to avoid having the government as our pimp"—the two stressed their solidarity with a broader feminist movement. Kennedy, an active NOW member and close comrade of Gloria Steinem, distributed photocopies of critically annotated *New York Times* articles about IWY, underscoring what she saw as liberal misrepresentations and assumptions.[59]

Figure 9.2 Flo Kennedy hailing a taxi in Mexico City. © Bettye Lane. Courtesy of David M. Rubenstein Rare Book and Manuscript Library, Duke University.

If COYOTE organizers troubled the presumed trade-off between sexual liberation and human-rights activism, Chilean officials were anxious to demonstrate that not everyone from G-77 countries welcomed discussions of politics at the conference. "Our delegation is concerned because the world conference on women has shifted from its objectives and has fallen into the terrain of the political," Chilean delegation leader Alicia Romo Román told reporters who stopped her in the stairwell of the Tlatelolco chancery. "But we will struggle to make the projected conclusions for this meeting into a reality so that women truly reach places of authority and decision-making."[60] As Chile's CSW representative, Romo had ardently supported the US proposal to hold an IWY conference, but she doubtless regretted that position once the conference had moved to a country openly hostile to Chile in a city that famously hosted exiles from military dictatorships around the world.[61]

In short, Romo found herself in enemy territory. She proclaimed that what looked to the outside world like a war on Chile's own people was, in fact, peace. "Peace has a deep significance for us," First Lady Lucía Hiriart de Pinochet had proclaimed in her speech inaugurating IWY in Chile. "We are horrified to see that it does not exist in other countries; we knew we had lost it but today have recovered it; we want it fervently for all the world."[62] Romo told reporters that the Pinochet regime had saved Chile from economic chaos. To questions about persecution of political opponents, she simply responded, "Many things are said in the world." Women, she assured reporters, worked enthusiastically for Chile's new regime.[63] Dismissing the reports about Chile as Soviet propaganda, Romo declared, "Chileans cannot be told about democracy because we know what it is: a very painful experience. But we are going to rebuild the order that was destroyed through the treason committed by Salvador Allende. . . . The current government is the only one that can save Chile from the situation it faces, and we support it with faith and with effort because it is the only government we can have in this stage of convalescence."[64]

Romo was not alone in defending military authoritarian regimes. By 1975, most of South America was governed by militaries; the delegation leaders of Peru, Guatemala, Brazil, and Panama joined Romo in a public statement about the value of military regimes in promoting development, controlling inflation and instability, and preventing political nepotism and corruption. Military governments, they argued, offered the best guarantees for equality, development, and peace. Ana María Vargas, leading the Guatemalan delegation, described civilian governments as having too many commitments to foreign interests. "They are run by unscrupulous politicians who are in no way patriots," she explained. Brazil's Marilia Mota added, "In Brazil there is no *gorilato* [i.e., excessive use of force], and if the people support militarism, it is because the government has controlled inflation and grants as many liberties as the people demand."[65]

While defenders of military regimes clearly found themselves on the defensive in Mexico—where a different variety of authoritarianism held sway—they raised questions about where the boundary lay between authoritarian repression and the preservation of social peace. Reporters and demonstrators badgered Mexican officials with questions about violence against student demonstrators, but many Mexicans had had their fill of student uprisings, not to mention guerilla movements. Within the past two years, guerillas had kidnapped—among many others—the First Lady's elderly father and the US consul-general in Guadalajara. An Indian delegate, who would speak to reporters only while hiding her name badge and away from the intergovernmental conference, described the attacks against Indira Gandhi as the work of a "reactionary minority" acting at the behest of a discontented minister.[66] The Argentine activist Analía Pairo told reporters that 8,000 university professors had been fired for "political activities or mere ideological affinities," more than twenty periodicals had been shut down, 1,386 political prisoners tortured and another 500 killed, mostly at the hands of the Argentine Anticommunist Association. The previous March, she claimed, there had been one assassination every two hours and 24 minutes. She warned that Argentina was "becoming a dictatorship like Pinochet's."[67]

Most conference-goers would not have countenanced a military government in their own countries. "We had a disastrous experience," explained Ana Sixta González, leading the Colombian delegation. "In some countries militarism will be good, but for Colombia, ¡no!"[68] Still, the explanations offered by military regimes' supporters made some sense even to detractors—the problems of inflation, rising unemployment, social instability, and political corruption extended well beyond the Southern Cone. Alicia Romo Román's response to accusations by Salvador Allende's sister and widow might have come as easily from Patricia Hutar or even the French delegation leader Françoise Giroud. She described the criticisms of her government as the "machinations" of political groups that wanted to prevent women's incorporation into development and had put up smoke screens to distract their attention. "We have one week left to put the conference back on the correct course," she cautioned.[69]

Scene 10

The Politics of Peace

At the end of a twelve-hour shift observing the Hotel Camino Real on June 24, Dirección Federal de Seguridad (Federal Security Directorate, DFS) Agent 259 Fernando Solórzano Martínez reported calm. Having observed some 200 hotel guests shuttle off to the IWY events and Swedish Prime Minister Olof Palme leave to bid farewell to President Echeverría before returning to Stockholm, he reported, "Until now, no incidents have been provoked; there have been no visits from functionaries, student groups, political parties, nor journalists. Treatment by the [police] agents as well as hotel personnel had been courteous and amiable."[1] Solórzano's colleagues at the Medical Center, however, could offer no such reassurances, submitting reports of one protest after another.[2] The newspaper *El Universal* described it as a veritable Tower of Babel as the meetings quickly disintegrated into impromptu, specialized gatherings, precisely as Persinger and Bravo had hoped.[3]

As demonstrators continued to crowd the esplanade and the Centro Médico, the flyer emerged as the political weapon of choice. The Ukrainian women distributed flyers demanding justice and liberty for political prisoners in the Soviet Union. Flo Kennedy and Margo St. James, having been told to leave the Medical Center's hallways because they "distorted International Women's Year," distributed COYOTE's flyers calling for legalization of prostitution.[4] When the guards again asked them to leave, they "went peacefully" and, playing off the media's tendency to collapse the two groups, promised to return the next day to demonstrate with the lesbians. The International Communist Group, the Socialist League, and the Women's Leninist Group passed out flyers lambasting the IWY gatherings as official theater that excluded those who might address "true women's problems." The groups invited tribune-goers to attend a gathering four miles away in the Casa del Lago cultural center of Chapultepec Park to speak out on issues they insisted Echeverría would find "scandalous": legal, state-funded abortion; twenty-four-hour, public child-care; equal opportunities in work and education; equal pay for equal work; liberty for political prisoners; opposition to sterilization and forced birth control; and protest against the "antidemocratic formation" of the Mexican delegation.[5]

By Tuesday morning, one of the tribune's most conspicuous logistical problems had come to a head. Tribune organizers and security officials had worked out an elaborate system of pre-registration and color-coded badges—blue for employees of the Ministry of Foreign Relations, white for delegates to the government conference (who would also have access to the NGO tribune), "Mexican pink" for tribune registrants, orange for "tourists" who only planned to attend for one day, and gray for "observers."[6] Security personnel had been instructed to bar entry to anyone not wearing the appropriate badge. The day before the tribune inauguration, everything seemed manageable; about 600 people had pre-registered, and buses would carry people among the tribune, the conference, and the hotels. Mexico's Department of Federal Security warded off disruptions and demonstrations by deploying personnel posing as participants as well as 308 name-tagged hostesses to assist visitors.

The number of attendees mushroomed to roughly ten times the number of pre-registrants.[7] The registration and badge pick-up took place inside the Medical Center; so participants who had not pre-registered or arrived on the first day of the tribune had no way to obtain the requisite badges, and many who had badges lost them in the first few days.[8] Contributing to the confusion, Mexican women were required to register off-site, purportedly to limit the number who attended, lest they overwhelm the tribune. On Tuesday morning, roughly forty women led by two Chicana activists, Maura Palma de Apodaca of César Chávez's movement and Elvira Hernández from Cal State Northridge, picketed in front of the Medical Center with signs demanding "equal treatment for our Mexican sisters" and insisting "all of us will enter or none." Margarita Troncoso Valles and Encarnación López Solís led a separate group of *campesinas* from the far north of Mexico's Federal District demanding title to lands they occupied. The *campesinas* joined the Chicanas, adding their pickets and voices to the demonstration.

Given the logistical difficulties, tribune organizers had decided to forgo the badge requirement, opening the NGO events to anyone who showed up. To security officers, this policy change created precisely the headache they hoped to avoid. They already had their hands full fending off indigents and vendors; checking ashtrays, washrooms, and flower arrangements for possible explosives; and ensuring that visitors' experiences remained unmarred by accidents, robberies, or "scandalous arguments by people in a state of inebriation."[9] At 1:30 in the afternoon, María Urquidi, a Mexican feminist and employee of the US-Mexico Chamber of Commerce, decided to test whether security personnel hewed to the new policy, concealing her own badge as she attempted to enter the Medical Center. When guards prevented her from entering, she argued loudly in English that there should be no distinctions made in a free tribune. The security guards then removed her by force, according to Urquidi's account, "pulling her down the front steps, across the plaza, twisting her arms while trying to prevent photographers and newspaper people from getting to her. She was being dragged away when a group of women from the conference voiced their objections and physically pulled [her] away from the police, who at this point released her."[10]

Amid this tumult on the esplanade, inside the Medical Center the policy-oriented NGO tribune sessions calmly focused on issues of health and nutrition in one room and agriculture and rural development in another—central concerns of IWY that seemed not to galvanize audience members the way the previous day's sessions on cultural issues had. Roughly 1,700 filed in for the agriculture and development session featuring illustrious participants from the Women and Development workshop: Danish economist Ester Boserup, Tanzanian feminist development expert Martha Bulengo, Mexican economist Gloria Brasdefer, and British development specialist Elizabeth O'Kelly, who had gained her expertise working in Africa and South Asia. Panelists agreed that without transforming the distribution of training, technology, and land tenure in rural areas, women would remain on the losing end of most development schemes.[11]

The tribune sessions reflected the immense care that organizers had taken to achieve geographic diversity among the panelists, although they remained predominantly professional-class cosmopolitans. "We have an elite class that has had the benefits of education and also income improvement," development economist Devaki Jain explained to an interviewer, "and very often we take the decisions for the rest, and we also influence world opinion on what is necessary in our countries. I feel now that this must be changed because our concerns are very different from those who are, say, the fifty percent of India's population who are in rural areas living very traditional lives, where labor is not male/female but family labor."[12] The small group that showed up for the afternoon session on health and nutrition would have found a panel of Katharine Focke, the West German minister of women, youth, and health; the Mexican nutrition specialist Miriam Múñoz de Chávez; the Peruvian gynecologist Luz Jefferson Cortez; and Victoria Mojekwu, the chief nursing officer for the Nigerian ministry of health. Having trained as a midwife and a pediatric nurse in the United Kingdom and the United States before returning to Nigeria in 1972, she railed against those who would restrict women's access to abortion and contraception, dismissing them as blinded by religious prejudice.[13] "Religion is a disease of the world," she fumed, "Religion was made by men, interpreted and misinterpreted by men and worshiped by women."[14]

Despite the impressive lineup of panelists, the tribune organizers became victims of their own success as informal gatherings drew participants away from the carefully curated tribune program. By the afternoon, only about 100 people—of an estimated 5,000 or 6,000 tribune-goers—occupied seats scattered around the auditorium for the health and nutrition session.[15] Other participants presumably had dispersed to the dozens of other gatherings—of the American Friends Service Committee or the International Association for the Right to Abortion or the Coalition of Unrepresented Women, the group Wynta Boynes and Esther Urista spoke for at the US embassy confrontation. The biggest draw was the Coalition of Latin American Women, which set out to establish priorities distinct from those of Betty Friedan and the Feminist Caucus and discussed a wide range of issues, such as abortion, US imperialism, premarital training, women's libraries, and military-inspired toys. After four hours of discussion and debate, the group resolved to return the next day at noon in anticipation of wrapping up deliberations and defining a program before one o'clock.[16]

While the NGO tribune fostered disorder and even occasional pandemonium, in Tlatelolco some 600 delegates attended the plenary sessions, where the carefully scripted choreography of instructed delegations held sway.[17] "The speeches are frequently interminable," Judy Klemesrud reported in the *New York Times*, "the rhetoric rolls on, and the delegates often snooze with their earphones still plugged in."[18] Even the security personnel thought all the speeches started to sound alike. After dutifully detailing the main points of a half-dozen speakers, one report noted that from 3:30 to 6:30 in the afternoon, representatives from Sri Lanka, Mali, Botswana, Hungary, Central African Republic, Oman, the Holy See, UNESCO, and the WHO "agreed in their interventions with the previous speakers." The report summarized that evening's speeches by Senegal, Canada, Gabon, Bulgaria, the WIDF, the Democratic Republic of Vietnam, and Bahamas as calling for the "recognition of women around the world on an equal plane with men."[19]

At least one speaker, however, kept her audience riveted. The Soviet cosmonaut Valentina Tereshkova had arrived in Mexico City on the twelfth anniversary of her historic space flight to enthusiastic paparazzi that gushed over her beauty, her intelligence, her readiness to answer any question. Even as Tereshkova insisted that in the Soviet Union women had achieved complete equality with men—"no nation has put women in a higher place," she said, referencing her space flight—reporters offered detailed descriptions of her dress (green silk print), her jewelry (a garnet ring, a wedding band), her hair (styled and discreetly dyed red) and nails (long, painted).[20] The society pages noted what she ate at an official dinner (smoked turkey from Chihuahua) and how she responded to the folkloric Mexican dancers (enraptured).[21]

Tereshkova used this platform to highlight the theme of peace, the issue that the Soviet Union had insisted—with limited success—retain a central place during IWY.[22] As one Mexican newspaper editorialized, "development is the new name for peace."[23] Tereshkova pressed the Soviet demand for general, unconditional nuclear disarmament. "All of us who live on planet Earth," she told

Figure 10.1 Valentina Tereshkova greeting an admirer at the UN conference. © Bettye Lane. Courtesy of Schlesinger Library.

reporters upon her arrival, "have an obligation and the weight of the grave responsibility to keep it free of the human egotisms and antagonisms, as well as to avoid by any means the unleashing of a fratricidal war that would terminate Humanity."[24] Tereshkova repeatedly pointed to her extraterrestrial perspective to legitimate her advocacy for nuclear disarmament.[25] She elaborated in a press conference, "I went up and I saw that the Earth is a beautiful place, and I am calling on the men and women of the world to unite their efforts with the aim of saving our planet and not permitting it to be covered in the black ash of atomic bombs."[26]

Discussions of peace at the IWY conference could not be severed from the geopolitical context in which Soviet-bloc countries calling for peace and disarmament, sponsored peace organizations and congresses, and, according to the US State Department, used peace issues as a "front" to influence and infiltrate non-communist organizations.[27] The Vietnam War had given anti-war demands a central place in left-leaning activism more broadly. Mexico's WIDF affiliate consistently organized demonstrations and conferences to oppose the US intervention in Vietnam and to express solidarity with Chilean socialists. Japanese participants similarly recounted that their activism started in pacifist movements and opposition to the US military presence.[28]

If official delegations and tribune-goers still deliberated over the definitions and implications of the IWY themes of equality and development, they agreed even less on what they meant by calls for peace. They were not mere rhetor-ical abstractions —Pakistani First Lady Nusrat Bhutto exhorted the plenary to support disarmament only a year after India staged its first successful nuclear tests—but the theme encompassed everything from nuclear disarmament and a reduction in armed conflict to the elimination of racism and colonialism and the protection of human rights.[29] In short, it became the catch-all theme for issues that Western countries—and the United States in particular—wanted to bracket for the purposes of IWY deliberations, dismissing them as political distractions from core women's issues. Thus, struggles against racial discrimination and im-perial domination fell under the rubric of "peace" rather than "equality," where they might have found a better fit.

Instrumentalist arguments asserted that just as development schemes' suc-cess depended on the appropriate incorporation of women, the promotion of peace and international cooperation would require women's involvement. From the Secretariat's earliest proposals for IWY through every iteration of the World Plan of Action and ancillary proposals, all started from the assumption that women would make the world a more peaceful place. A research group submit-ted a proposal to UNESCO ambitiously titled, "Women, peace movements, and the reconceptualizing of the social order," which involved women researchers examining women in peace movements and in the political process.[30] "If the women of the world—from socialist, capitalist, neutralist countries or from wherever—would vehemently and in unison insist that swords be beaten into plowshares, they just might be," editorialized the English-language Mexico City News. "If man remains impotent in this question of future survival, may women exercise a role more far-reaching, more significant than any perhaps meritorious, if unilateral, self-centered 'Lib' movements many are seeking."[31]

While the "substantive items" of the UN's IWY agenda focused on the themes of equality and development, the matter of peace had largely been left in the hands of NGOs, several of which devoted themselves to peace advocacy.[32] When the secretary-general first requested commentary on a draft IWY pro-gram, seven of the twenty-three responding NGOs had peace as one of their principal objectives, and five others were Catholic or otherwise Christian or-ganizations that placed a high priority on pacifism.[33] These numbers would only increase as organizations such as WILPF (Women's International League for Peace and Freedom), the World Peace Council, and the World Council of Churches submitted suggestions. "Women have a particular interest in peace and disarmament," WILPF advised the consultative committee. "Militarism and chauvinism are almost exclusively a male ethic. Women and children are pre-dominant among the civilian population which is increasingly being made the target of modern war planning and recent conflicts in all parts of the world."[34]

While discussions about equality and development explored ways to minimize differences between men and women, discussions about peace often presumed a profound and biologically rooted sex difference rooted in maternity. The controversial Bulgarian cultural minister Lyudmila Zhivkova asserted at a press conference that "only woman can safeguard peace in the world, because she is mother and creator of life, and her destiny is in large part oriented toward preserving the human species."[35] A member of the Mexican delegation, Octavio Salías, claimed that women's political participation would "contribute to world peace because her sensitivity as the founder of the home had permitted her throughout time to understand and demand peace for human society."[36] The Argentine congressional deputy Silvana María Roca reassured the NGO tribune that reports of violence in Buenos Aires had been exaggerated but that any incidents could be attributed to "the masculine influence" of the military.[37]

Certainly some observers expressed skepticism about the equation of femininity with an absence of violence. As the US magazine *The Nation* editorialized after the conference, the repressive tactics employed by Indian Prime Minister Indira Gandhi and Argentine President Isabel Martínez de Perón—both prevented from attending the conference due to unrest in their countries—"dramatically demonstrated that women are not immune to the attraction of power despotically exercised, which is hardly news."[38]

The anti-essentialist arguments came most powerfully from women who had participated in armed struggle as part of national liberation movements taking place all over the world. The language of national liberation and decolonization was ubiquitous both metaphorically—in aspirations to "decolonize women's minds" or liberate the "fourth world" within industrialized nations—and literally. The North Vietnamese had secured a victory earlier in the summer, Angola was on the eve of independence, and Mozambique gained independence during the conference's first week, prompting a hasty invitation to join the proceedings.[39] Puerto Rican and Panamanian *tribunistas* demanded an end to US sovereignty over their territories. Armed resistance and even terror campaigns had formed part of every independence movement, and liberation movements saw no advantage in conceding to their oppressors' exclusive claims to the legitimate use of force. Indeed, pointing out women's roles in these campaigns seemed to strengthen not only the movements' claims to legitimacy but also women's claims to citizenship within post-insurgency governments. Vietnamese delegate Ha Van Lan boasted that women had contributed actively to military campaigns to secure independence, and an Indonesian participant in the tribune similarly described women's participation in national liberation movements.[40] "Being citizens, we want to play a role, as men do, in the struggle in Afrika," Jeanne-Martin Cissé had explained in an interview while presiding over the Security Council.

"Because in Afrikan liberation struggles, men didn't liberate Afrika by themselves. They did need the woman's part in the struggle."[41]

At any rate, for most women involved in pacifist activism, their commitment stemmed less from an essentialized conception of their own femininity than from sustained concerns about human rights and about the allocation of public resources that militarization required. Many tribune participants disparaged the guns-versus-butter trade-offs between military spending and public health. Exiled Chileans protested that the Pinochet government had gutted the education budget to fund the military, and an Uruguayan activist informed the NGO tribune that 400 to 500 children died every year from diarrhea while half the public budget went toward the police and army.[42] In the tribune's opening session on the "constitution of the human community," the audience gave a thirty-second standing ovation when Annie Jiagge decried the "great powers' extreme expenditures on armaments" while many countries were unable to feed their populations. Pointing out that the average life expectancy of a Ghanaian was thirty and that many "by the grace of God" die before the age of five, she argued that allocating a mere 20 percent of the world's arms budget to development in sub-Saharan Africa would allow it to produce its own food.[43] Esther Aviles—a PhD in chemistry, vice-president of Ecuador's Association for Family Planning, and the deputy director of Guayaquil's leading daily, *Expreso de Guayaquil*—insisted that with enough energy and decisiveness, women would halt the arms race among industrialized countries, freeing funds to combat hunger. "From this day forward," Aviles insisted, "women's universal, primordial function is to increase efforts to end arms proliferation and obtain the greatest amount of food for the world population."[44] At a press conference intended to tout the Percy Amendment and US commitment to development aid, US delegates were pressed to answer questions about the percentage of GDP stemming from military and arms production.[45]

Despite WINGOs' long-standing commitment to pacifism, only one scheduled tribune session addressed issues of peace and disarmament, and of the 192 participant-initiated sessions that requested meeting space during the tribune, only five explicitly addressed the question of peace.[46] Mildred Persinger delegated the tribune session's organization to the WIDF secretary-general Fanny Edelman, who, perhaps pondering the growing unrest at home in Argentina, pointed to the horror of militaries using arms against their own populations in countries plagued by "uncontrolled fascism." She argued that all schools and educational centers should promote "absolute and total antiwar instruction." Misika Tonaka, a member of the Japanese Communist Party, described the inhumanity of the US attacks on Hiroshima and Nagasaki and indicated that the Japanese government had ignored both the increase in neonatal deformities since World War II and the "excesses" committed by US troops.[47]

The peace-related issue that loomed largest in Mexico City, however, was the conflict between Israel and its neighbors. Fatima Issam Abdul Hadi, the first woman to serve on the PLO's Central Legislative Council, insisted, "The occupation by international Zionism and the torture, imprisonment, and other human rights violations should be vigorously denounced by the international community. The women of the world should unite themselves to achieve peace. As long as there is no peace in Palestine, there will be no peace in the world."[48] No one paying attention in Mexico City would have been surprised to see the issue of Zionism arise, but the PLO intervention set the stage.[49] According to US intelligence reports, the General Assembly had spent much of the spring of 1975 attempting to "isolate and reject Israel from the international community, the UN, and other international organizations." Although the Egyptians seemed "to have soft-pedaled their campaign" in the weeks just prior to the IWY conference, there was "little doubt that the Arabs [were] keeping the expulsion/suspension option open."[50] Amid the coverage of IWY debates, intrigue, and social events, Mexican dailies ran banner headlines that Israel had claimed the Golan Heights and the Gaza Strip as within its permanent borders.[51] The Greek delegation to the intergovernmental conference warned that the conflict could "become World War III."[52]

Observers kept a close watch on First Ladies Leah Rabin of Israel and Jehan Sadat of Egypt; speculation about whether they might meet and shake hands turned into "one of the big guessing games of the conference."[53] Mexico sent its own diplomatic signals, sending only the wife of the minister of foreign relations to meet Rabin but sending her, along with the wives of the minister of government, attorney general, and chief of staff, to meet Sadat while their husbands greeted the only participating female head of state, Sri Lanka's Sirimavo Bandaranaike, with an honor guard.[54] Reporters awaited each of the First Ladies as they arrived at Benito Juárez International Airport, hoping to catch a glimpse of the fireworks. They pounced when Rabin told a press conference that Israel wanted only peace and posited that if more women held positions of power, the world would have less violence and fewer wars. "Can you imagine two brigades of women fighting each other?" she asked. "Of course not! War is only for men." Responding to a reporter's question about how she explained Golda Meir's role in the 1973 Yom Kippur War, she explained that Meir was "not a tyrant" and had to abide by her cabinet's consensus.[55] Sadat highlighted the reporter's question, explaining, "In reality, the woman in power is not much different from the man."[56] Asked why Arab countries did not celebrate women's bravery in the way that Israel did, Sadat responded, "We do not pride ourselves on carrying rifles and machine guns. These are arms that a man ought to carry, and we have plenty of men to carry them. In reality we women work in silence; we don't make propaganda."

If Sadat's remarks stung, it was in part because she and Rabin agreed on one front: the gendered order of things should remain intact. As Sadat responded when a reporter asked whether she believed in liberation movements, "I think that an intelligent woman can obtain her rights within the home."[57] At a subsequent press conference, she warned that women's liberation "should not consist of hysterical cries demanding a revolution" and said that the "battle of the sexes as it is conceived in the Western world does more harm than good, since we need to find an equilibrium within the family and in no way stage a revolution against men but rather work together."[58] In her own remarks to the press, Rabin sounded the same note: "Women must be granted the means to work and intervene in politics, but I am not an extremist of women's liberation, nor do I think that men should be washing the diapers."[59]

The press itself took sides. The day after its mannish and obliquely anti-Semitic depiction of Friedan, El Universal ran a glowing piece about the two women who formed the Mauritanian delegation.[60] Aissata Toure, the delegation head, was described as "tall and thin as a gazelle" with a "silk scarf that allowed glimpses of her curling hair" and hands "like reeds swaying in the wind." Turkia Ould Daddah was described as "intelligent and beautiful as her compañera." No mention had been made of Friedan's three children (only her divorce), but the feature on Toure and Daddah highlighted that they had five and two children, respectively. These divergent descriptions obscured the remarkably similar content of the interviews. "I can't see the difference between men and women; both are human," explained Toure, president of Mauritania's leading feminist organization. "In Mauritania, the government favors promoting women through laws, but men discriminate in practice, by custom or old habits or from feeling superior to us." Drawing parallels between sexism and racism, she insisted, "When I am successful, men respect me and realize that I am not simply a body but a mind as well. Each woman is obliged, to support her liberation, to set a good example and show that she is a true human being." Daddah seemed to disagree somewhat, adding, "This makes me furious. In all countries, men's typical reaction to intelligent women, to women who work, is not to take them seriously. I have been conscious since childhood, but women's struggle today consists in gaining consciousness that we have a right to an equal place in the world alongside men."

The media coverage of Sadat and Rabin continued in this vein but the English- and Spanish-language coverage markedly differed, even within the pages of the IWY newspaper Xilonen.[61] El Universal ran long, front-page interviews with both Rabin and Sadat on the same day.[62] Both women proclaimed their commitments to peace and then offered their divergent opinions about the fate of the Occupied Territories, recounting familiar narratives of who threw the first punch in the Middle East conflict. Although the interviews had parallel formats, the interviewer fawned over Sadat, appreciating her stylish suit, delicate pearl earrings, and hair elegantly pulled back into a tortoiseshell comb; she concluded by telling Sadat how much Mexicans admired her beauty.[63] *La Prensa* similarly carried a headline, "The beautiful Sadat rejects the occupation of her country."[64] By contrast, the *New York Times* featured a photo of a smiling Rabin with the caption, "Leah Rabin, who said she was willing to talk to Jihan el-Sadat," alongside one of a scowling Sadat captioned, "Mrs. Sadat, who said she still wasn't willing to talk to Mrs. Rabin."[65] The *Washington Post* quoted an anonymous European diplomat saying, "Mrs. Sadat has called for peace in the Middle East, but she will not even greet her Israeli counterpart right here in the hall with her."[66]

If the editorial boards of US newspapers had hoped to minimize the slight as personal pettiness, developments in Mexico City would make that increasingly untenable. On Friday morning, Sadat spoke to a welcoming audience in Tlatelolco as reporters and delegates waited to see what she would say about Egyptian relations with Israel. She did not disappoint. Making an analogy that sent a clear signal to anyone who had followed recent UN developments, she stated, "We cannot speak of development and equality while there is no peace, and there will be no peace as long as Arab territories continue to be occupied, the Palestinians have no home, and the vestiges of neocolonialism and racism, such as apartheid, persist in South Africa and other parts of the world."[67] Rabin stayed for the whole speech, arriving half an hour late to her own press conference to avoid leaving before Sadat's plenary address had concluded, although reporters seemed to notice not that she had stayed but how quickly she had departed.[68] Sadat, after all, had assured reporters that she would not leave the session while Rabin spoke.[69]

On Tuesday evening, as Leah Rabin stepped up to the podium to deliver her plenary speech, hundreds of delegates from African, Asian, Latin American, and Eastern bloc countries left the auditorium, waiting in the foyer until she had completed her address. "We shall wait until the exodus is over," Rabin said, as she paused for the conference hall to empty out. "I know there are conflicts and misunderstandings between countries, but not even wanting to listen to each other is truly missing the objectives and goals of this convention."[70] In the pandemonium of the NGO tribune, such demonstrations had already become commonplace; in the deliberative, protocol-bound governmental conference, the episode underscored that the IWY conference would not escape the tensions that defined the General Assembly meetings in New York City. Jehan Sadat was not among those waiting in the foyer during Rabin's speech; she had left Mexico City that morning to return to Cairo.[71] Exhausted, Rabin herself would depart the following afternoon, waving off questions from reporters about her reaction to the previous day's walkout.[72]

Rabin's address and the response to it—not only the walkout but also accusations by the Syrian, Sudanese, and Ugandan delegations that Israel falsely represented its desires for peace—renewed calls that politics had eclipsed women's issues.[73] The Australian and New Zealander delegations repeatedly insisted that all resolutions and amendments, regardless of their political implications, have some clear connection with women's status, and the veteran US diplomat Catherine East passed Elizabeth Reid a note lamenting, "The Conference and the Tribune both seem in a very unsatisfactory state." Describing the upheaval in the tribune and the "bogged down" working committees at the official conference, East implored Reid, "Some of us more aggressive types in the U.S. delegation hope you will do something about it. You seem to be the only woman in the government delegations with enough leadership capacity and courage to turn things around."[74] The issues that had "bogged down" the committees were precisely those that the US delegation had hoped to contain. Committee One considered a resolution signed by fifteen African nations protesting the situation of women in South Africa, Namibia, and Rhodesia and referring to the apartheid policies as "genocide" and "crimes against humanity" and calling for immediate sanctions.[75] Such liberationist language ran headlong into the lawyerly attention to linguistic precision as the Canadian and US representatives questioned whether the situation met the technical criteria for genocide and crimes against humanity, not to mention whether the IWY conference could impose international sanctions.[76] But the committee was still only in the quagmire's shallows; that afternoon it would begin to consider the controversial document that would become the Declaration of Mexico.

Scene 11

The First Rule of Fight Club

The NGO tribune had a very clear policy from the outset: nobody was authorized to speak on behalf of the tribune. Persinger had explicitly avoided including rapporteurs or even substantial plenary sessions and insisted that the tribune would not issue a report. The policy appeared in letters of invitation, in the registration materials, in *Xilonen*, and in Persinger's opening remarks. Persinger and Bravo reiterated it every chance they could find. The reason for the policy was obvious: those assembled at the tribune could hardly be considered representative. Many had ended up there by chance because a filmmaker or a Ford Foundation field officer or a YWCA leader had passed along a name to Persinger. Some came simply because they had the resources and the will. Some tribune participants were internationally renowned and others were unknown. None of them had been elected. A few had been funded by their organizations or even their home governments (raising questions for at least one reporter about how non-governmental the tribune really was).[1] The participants had been encouraged to create a global consciousness-raising meeting, an enormous rap session, not to engage in the deliberative crafting of policies and programs.

Nonetheless, by Wednesday, the halfway point for the conference and the last day on which amendments to the World Plan of Action could be proposed to the First Committee, tribune-goers clamored to have a say in decisions taken at the conference. Given the widespread suspicion that many harbored toward their governments and, by extension, the instructed delegations, it seemed imperative that the discussions taking place at the Centro Médico somehow inform the policies being hammered out in Tlatelolco. The tribune had, after all, drawn seasoned activists intent on being heard and accustomed to defying orders that they sit back and wait for their turn to speak. It seemed like a squandered opportunity to leave something as ambitious as a World Plan of Action for women in the hands of the government conference, which many feminist activists dismissed as gathering of flunkies, political appointees, and "wifey-poos" controlled by puppeteers in their home governments.

Those who ended up at the Mexico City NGO tribune largely represented the 1970s zeitgeist, particularly pronounced among feminists, of the importance of working around rather than through governments. Amid the Watergate scandal, mounting evidence of nepotism and corruption in postcolonial governments, and growing authoritarianism in many corners of the world, governments seemed like more of a problem than a solution. To many at the tribune, collaboration between NGOs and the UN seemed to offer a promising, perhaps even radically democratic, alternative. Two days earlier, at an open forum with Senator Charles Percy about his eponymous foreign-assistance policy, a group of women from several Third World countries, including Tanzania, Trinidad-Tobago, Ghana, Ecuador, and Argentina, pressed for development aid to be disbursed through UN-coordinated NGOs.[2] Four hundred tribune participants signed a proposal calling on ECOSOC to establish a new Secretariat that would monitor implementation of the World Plan of Action, receive complaints about violations, and conduct follow-up analyses.[3] Such proposals demonstrated the growing faith that NGOs and intergovernmental organizations offered a more promising means of influence for those who had opted out of or been systematically excluded from decision-making circles.[4]

Many tribune-goers had some sense of the conference through *Xilonen* or forums such as the one held with Senator Percy or the morning briefings that UN staffers held at the Medical Center, but these were generally one-way encounters that amounted to reports rather than exchanges. Those more confident in their government delegations tried to work through them but generally with minimal success; delegates themselves raced between meetings, often to negotiate with other government delegates. "Many frustrations exist within the Tribune," one participant reported back to the Chicago Hotline IWY focal point at the beginning of the week. "The women feel that they want to be involved in amendments to the World Plan of Action but in many instances cannot reach their official delegations. A group has formed to study the World Plan of Action and make recommendations to be presented at the government conference later this week; more to follow on Wed."[5] The absence of a formal vehicle of exchange between the tribune and the conference meant that those who had connections could leverage them, often to the irritation of those who did not.

The difficulty of communication between the government conference and the NGO tribune exacerbated these tensions. The Mexican government had arranged shuttle buses to run between the two venues as well as private cars and drivers for distinguished diplomats, but the physical distance between the governmental and non-governmental gatherings would compound the events' metaphorical distance. Lucile Schuck, who attended both the conference and the tribune as a consultative-status NGO representative, found the effect aggravated by Mexico City's altitude and the smog. "There were many steps and no elevators at the Conference or at the Tribune," she reported. "One needed a midday siesta but the traffic was so congested, transportation arrangements so irregular, and the two meetings so far apart that one could seldom find five minutes to relax." The Mexico City metro system stretched directly from Tlatelolco to Hospital General, about a half mile north of Centro Médico, but travel by metro required a ten-minute walk at either end, often under soaking summer rains, and "was so jammed that one had to drop all dignity and wrestle the crowds for a place."[6]

The altitude, smog, and travel distances were not the only factors discomfiting participants. "The delegates spent one third of their waking hours imprisoned in their official cars, glumly wondering if their mental stupor was another effect of the altitude or how long they could hold out in the endless traffic jams before setting off on foot in search of a toilet," quipped Germaine Greer. "The virulent Mexican version of tourist tummy laid low some of every delegation all of the time. The fourteen hotels which housed the delegates roared like Niagaras as they strained the plumbing to the utmost."[7]

As the conference of official delegations bumped up against the expectations of participatory democracy emerging in the tribune, the question of representation became increasingly vexed. Although Persinger and Bravo had stressed that the tribune would issue no formal statements, their own exhilarating experience of the NGOs influencing the official document at the Bucharest Population Conference must have made even them ambivalent on the issue. On the tribune's first day, a staff assistant to Oregon State Representative Pat Whiting wrote to Persinger, "It has become increasingly evident during the course of the International Women's Year Tribune that the original stance of not issuing policy statements is inadequate. The feeling of the Tribune participants is one of the exigency of ACTION."[8] Not waiting to hear what the scheduled tribune panel on population issues might yield, she enumerated four demands that she assumed all tribune-goers would support: family planning services, public medical clinics, the repeal of abortion laws, and sex education. She may have missed the article in *El Universal* that day about involuntary sterilizations performed on Mexican American women at Los Angeles County Hospital, or the participant-organized tribune session in which the Federation of Puerto Rican Women complained of being used as "guinea pigs" for contraception experiments.[9]

The self-proclaimed Feminist Caucus, led by Betty Friedan, had flouted the rule about representation before the tribune even opened, issuing its first proclamation on the second day of the journalists' encounter. Having sprinted off the blocks well before the starting gun, the group quickly became the best-organized caucus at the tribune. In addition to holding gatherings throughout the public areas of the Medical Center, the group established its center of operations at the Hotel Marbella, a few short blocks from the Medical Center, and met there every evening at nine o'clock to discuss and vote on its position on issues as they arose at the conference and tribune. When too many disagreements arose at those gatherings, a caucus-within-the-caucus called meetings at the Hotel del Prado, where many NOW members including Friedan stayed, in the ritzier neighbor-hood near the Bosque de Chapultepec.[10]

On Monday, the group had organized a "global speakout" to allow more discussion than the long lines standing at microphones in the formal sessions. It cajoled the organizers into assigning the group a room by arguing that the speakout would draw hecklers of the sort who protested at the US embassy on Saturday and might otherwise disrupt Senator Percy's panel.[11] On Tuesday, the

Figure 11.1 Some members of the Feminist Caucus gathered at the Hotel del Prado to strategize. © Bettye Lane. Courtesy of Schlesinger Library.

group, numbering roughly 300, had broken into eight working groups on issues such as population, peace, education, and family. By Wednesday, the Feminist Caucus, which renamed itself the United Women of the Tribune, was ready to make a public statement.[12] Still stinging from Ojeda Paullada's selection to preside over the conference, and no doubt antagonized by his statement in the previous day's *Xilonen* that nothing new or noteworthy was happening in the tribune, the United Women held a mass meeting attended by over 2,000 people who approved "by acclamation" a set of proposed amendments to the World Plan of Action. The meeting lasted upward of two hours as women lined up at microphones and frantically passed Friedan messages encouraging her, criticizing her, or just hoping to get a moment's attention to offer an opinion.[13] Friedan, who co-chaired the meeting with three other prominent feminists—Nigerian health minister Victoria Mojekwu, renowned Japanese journalist Yayori Matsui, and South Korean diplomat Sookja Hong—described it not as the product of careful and tireless organizing but rather as a spontaneous assembly of those frustrated that their voice was not heard at the UN conference.[14]

The gathering captured many tribune-goers' sense that they needed to seize this opportunity before it slipped away. As one of the chairs put it, "We women must show men we can work within limits. If we can't do anything within the next hour, we won't be able to do anything for the next hundred years."[15] The meeting culminated, as ever, with a press conference to explain that the United Women of the Tribune planned to issue a set of proposed amendments it would deliver to Tlatelolco and a letter demanding Ojeda Paullada's removal as conference president and replacement by a woman, recommending someone from the delegations of Colombia, Ethiopia, or Greece.[16]

The guiding principle of the United Women, as the name implied, was that women across divides of experience, ideology, and culture shared fundamental commonalities around which they could and should join forces. Friedan later recalled attending the Mexican government's reception at the Museum of Anthropology and History in Chapultepec Park, where she mingled with fellow delegates and ancient sculptures.[17] She and US delegate Jill Ruckelshaus tried to converse with Chinese women whose unfreedom they perceived by the fact that they "wore blue uniforms and no make-up; the head of the delegation had square-cut black hair; a younger one had light-haired pigtails; and they were flanked by men in identical uniforms."[18] Undeterred by language barriers and apparent efforts by the Chinese ambassador, who "like blocking a tackle in a football game," put himself between Friedan and the women on the Chinese delegation, Friedan remained convinced that she could make common cause. "She was a woman. I didn't accept the impossibility of talking to her," Friedan recounted later. "Maybe if I could sit next to her, some woman-to-woman things would get across."

Figure 11.2 Leaders of the People's Republic of China delegation. © Bettye Lane. Courtesy of Schlesinger Library.

Although the United Women caucus prided itself on its international membership, conspicuously pushing Third World cosmopolitans like Mojekwu, the Indians Sudha Acharge and Zarina Bhatty, and the Mexican Antonieta Rascón to the front row during its press conferences, many other tribune participants objected to having the caucus speak for them.[19] No matter how many concerns women may have shared across geopolitical or even class lines, many resented the group's arrogating to itself the authority to speak for the tribune on issues ranging from the Ojeda Paullada's presidency to the utility of the US women's movement as a model. If the tribune itself could make no representational claims, the self-appointed United Women could assert even less authority to do so. At Wednesday night's regular evening meeting of consultative-status NGOs, Esther Hymer tried to dissuade the United Women from going forward with the plan to present proposals to the conference, but to no avail. Indeed, at least one participant speculated that Hymer's consistent efforts to shut down non-consultative NGOs and to "treat [them] like schoolchildren" only contributed to the United Women's commitment to bypassing official channels.[20]

Other groups formed to object to the United Women's representational claims. The Coalition of Latin American Women, with the polymath, bi-national writer Sol Arguedas Urbina as its spokesperson, met at the same time as the United Women in the next room and issued its own statement of IWY objectives.[21] In many ways, the Latin American Caucus, as it became known, emerged as a sort of loyal opposition to the United Women. The two groups agreed on principal concerns such as women's right to control their own fertility and to participate in political life, and they shared demands for an end to the commercial and sexual exploitation of women's bodies. The Latin Americans also raised several additional issues, such as immigrants' rights, the treatment of political prisoners, and pensions and unionization for rural workers.

They diverged on two critical issues: the role of nationalism and the problem of reproductive labor. Whereas the United Women imagined a deracinated, placeless movement based on cosmopolitan universalism, the Latin Americans insisted upon working through national movements to form a "Latin Americanist consciousness." Laura Allende, the sister of martyred Chilean president Salvador Allende, underscored the importance of sovereign control over national wealth.[22] And whereas the United Women sought to resolve the reproductive-labor dilemma by gaining rights for women as autonomous individuals—equal pay for equal work, educational and occupational opportunities, access to technologies—the Latin Americans committed themselves to "strengthening the family as the moral nucleus of society and the psychological determinant of the individual." Rejecting the family's "character as an economic cell based in the arbitrary division of labor," they called for the socialization of domestic tasks through the creation of public child-care centers, kitchens, and laundries as well as of cooperatives for the production and consumption of basic goods. In short, they concluded, "We propose to realize our struggle together with men as an expression of true integration and human equality within the context of our Latin American realities."

Another group emerged on Wednesday calling itself Women against Imperialism, a decidedly disloyal opposition to the United Women. This more assertively Marxist group, dubbed by the press the "Group of 200," included Domitila Barrios de Chungara; Jehan Helou, a member of the PLO delegation and of Fatah; Puerto Rican journalist and independence activist Norma Valle; several unidentified North American women; and a member of the Chilean resistance.[23] While some participated in the more moderate Coalition of Latin American Women, the group expressed open animosity to the liberals of the United Women. Over four hours on Wednesday evening, participants shared critiques of US imperialism, "pointing to aggressions suffered in places like Vietnam, Puerto Rico, Angola and Chile."[24]

As the United Women of the Tribune, the Coalition of Latin American Women, and the Women against Imperialism coalesced into factions, challenging one another and seeking to have their voices heard up in Tlatelolco Plaza, the US-based tribune organizers favored the United Women, displaying their own understanding of where the dividing line lay between politics and women's issues. They began to impose more control over proceedings, in hopes of containing "political" interventions, requesting that session chairs require people to submit signed, written questions from the floor.[25] Egyptian-born, Los Angeles-based sociologist Nadia Youssef managed to achieve "notable order" as she chaired the morning session on "Women and Work."[26] Much as the Mexican press amplified the voices of women from non-aligned countries, *Xilonen* seemed increasingly to become an organ of the United Women, refusing to publish statements by the Women against Imperialism or even cover its activities.[27] Its article about the United Women of the Tribune meeting gushed, "Betty Friedan once again demonstrated her leadership gifts to convince so many women that it was better to unite than to fight among themselves." Of the Coalition of Latin American Women meeting next door, the newspaper sniped, "Without respecting the agreement not to involve political issues, the Chilean Laura Allende took the floor to denounce imperialism (as she had been doing during the entire Conference)."[28]

For many at the tribune, this escalating hostility between the Allendes and the leaders of the Feminist Caucus felt familiar. The Chilean sociologist Michèle Mattelart had published a widely circulated article in a special IWY issue of a Cuban journal describing Allende's overthrow as a "feminine coup" that resulted from bourgeois women taking to the streets, the famous "march of the empty pots" organized by Poder Femenino.[29] The article likely received more attention than it might have otherwise because Mattelart's husband, Armand Mattelart, had co-authored with Ariel Dorfman the wildly popular "How to Read Donald Duck," a critique of US imperialism that first appeared in Spanish in 1971 and in English in 1975.[30] Mattelart and Dorfman highlighted the ways that the Donald Duck stories effaced women, family, and labor, replacing them with markets, commerce, and consumption. In this context, it was a small step to read the opponents of the Women against Imperialism as the Women Favoring Imperialism, or at least as the Women Supporting Pinochet.

Despite organizers' efforts to restrict its scope, the tribune became increasingly raucous and contentious as frustrations mounted in all camps. Groups jockeyed for access to meeting spaces at the Medical Center. A ruling party deputy from Mexico State, María de la Paz Becerril de Brun, complained that the US-dominated tribune organizing committee "treats the Mexicans from here as if we were Mexicans living there," underscoring the class differences between the two groups.[31] While a Panamanian *conjunto folclórico* played in the esplanade, COYOTE's Flo Kennedy spoke out against US imperialism after being denied entry to the tribune. Frustrated that their petitions had gotten no traction, the Women for the Freedom of Ukraine, one of the few groups that secured a meeting room, voted to transform their anti-Soviet protest into a hunger strike. Two hours later, seven Ukrainian women gathered on the Medical Center's esplanade with a sign proclaiming, "Hunger strike in support of the Ukrainian women prisoners in the USSR," although no one apart from security forces seemed to pay much attention.[32] Tribune attendance dwindled throughout the day, starting with an estimated 3,500 participants for the morning session and dropping to about 2,000 in the afternoon. Only 500 remained by 7 P.M., and sixty diehards were still deliberating when the security guards finally closed the building at 11, asking the remaining Ukrainian hunger strikers and Women against Imperialism to congregate elsewhere.[33] With no group authorized to represent the tribune, spectacle and media attention increasingly became the principal means by which participants could convey their messages beyond the walls of the Centro Médico.

Scene 12

Coming Out Party

The next morning, nearly 3,500 bleary-eyed tribune-goers filed past the Ukrainian hunger strikers to attend sessions at the Medical Center amid mounting tensions and chaos as every effort to define a unified message seemed only to spin off another dissident faction.[1] Three days earlier, participants and press had filled the largest auditorium for the morning session on "Attitude Formation and Socialization Process"—the session that Domitila Barrios de Chungara had wandered into that developed into an everything-but-the-kitchen-sink session ranging over discussions of textbooks, sexuality, and family formation punctuated by interjections about poverty, human rights, and economic imperialism.[2] Among the hundreds of people that Bangladeshi political scientist Rounaq Jahan struggled to manage as they lined up to speak, Laurie Bebbington, a twenty-one-year-old who held the newly created position of National Women's Officer of the Australian Union of Students, had managed to secure time at a microphone. In her work, Bebbington had set her sights on sexism in education to "raise student consciousness," as she told a reporter; she stressed that issues such as child care were not women's issues but rather "people's issues and therefore involve men."[3] Her tireless work traveling throughout the country had drawn Elizabeth Reid's attention, and Bebbington made it onto a list of only eight women whom Reid nominated for government funding to attend the NGO tribune.[4] Bebbington had stood up at the tribune armed with a typescript copy of an address she had titled "Lesbian Speech . . . To the Tribune" and introduced herself, "amid whistles and jeering," as a lesbian feminist.[5]

Sexuality per se had not been on any official agenda in Mexico City. The closest that organizers of either the conference or the tribune dared to go was in passing attention to the often-conflated issues of prostitution and trafficking and the nearly obsessive concern with fertility and population control. Questions about pleasure and desire and even sexual identification would only fuel concerns that the UN operated as a vehicle for cultural imperialism that sought to impose Western models of family formation and sex roles. Even worse, observers feared that IWY acted as a Trojan horse that smuggled in unacceptable sexual freedoms. The Mexico City daily *Excélsior* cautioned in its lead editorial about the IWY inauguration that women's liberation "should be understood as the full development of women and not in the distorted form of sexual libertinage."[6] The Salvadoran participant in the journalists' encounter similarly indicated that "women's liberation" was often taken as a synonym of libertinage that "severed women from their rightful obligations as mother, spouse, sister, or daughter."[7] Others implied, if more subtly, the same anxieties about what modernizing sex roles implied about sexuality. "Certain feminists understand, for example, that to reach equality, domestic occupations should be shared between spouses, while others fight so that abortion will be a right for all women," explained the Zaire media fellow. "The youngest, however, seek a liberty that expresses itself as the relaxation of parental authority through a sexual life without barriers. There is a difference that we should underscore, given our policy of return to authenticity and our effort to restore the value of our good mores and customs, all those values that we do not want to disappear."[8]

Bebbington had not been the first lesbian to speak at the tribune. Frances Doughty, a leader of the National Gay Task Force in the United States who coordinated the US lesbian presence at IWY, had spoken up during one of the very first tribune sessions, expressing her desire to meet and share ideas with other lesbians.[9] Over the weekend between Doughty's intervention and Bebbington's,

Figure 12.1 Laurie Bebbington (left) and Frances Doughty spoke out as lesbians at the IWY tribune. © Bettye Lane. Courtesy of David M. Rubenstein Rare Book & Manuscript Library, Duke University.

they had gotten organized. "By the end of that first weekend," Doughty recalled, "three days later, we had met with a group of lesbians and homosexuals who wanted to start a gay liberation movement; we had met with the more radical segment of the Mexican women's movement; we had discovered that in certain Indian villages in Mexico there are women-sorcerers who pass their information from mother to daughter and who are lesbians; and we had appeared on the front pages of the Mexican press. 'We' evolved into the International Lesbian-Feminist Caucus."[10]

On Monday, Doughty stood up with Bebbington as she questioned "the fundamental assumption that all women wish to find fulfillment through marriage and motherhood," highlighting the ways in which the tribune itself had reinscribed traditional norms of femininity and marginalized those who did not conform. "In this room there are single women, there are childless women, and there are women who choose to love other women," Bebbington reminded participants. "Acceptance of a compulsory marriage and motherhood for all women not only denies us the possibility of choice. It downgrades and insults the lifestyles of many of our sisters present here." She acknowledged the ways that Australia's comparative wealth meant that she could "economically afford to talk about the social and psychological aspects of oppression," but she asserted that the "insistence on arbitrary cultural uniformity is a form of cultural imperialism." She concluded her remarks with a declaration that would set off a firestorm in the coming days: "I am proud to say that I am a lesbian . . . that I have chosen to love other women. My Australian lesbian sisters and I reject the idea that we are abnormal, sick or destructive. We would suggest that the only destructive relationship, both personally and politically, is one based on oppression and exploitation." Upon finishing her speech, Bebbington was surrounded by women sporting "radicalesbians" T-shirts, who showered her with hugs and kisses.[11] Some audience members cheered; others booed; a few simply walked out.

Bebbington's speech drew notice at least in part because it was particularly eloquent and well prepared, and she spoke willingly with reporters. She proudly sent Elizabeth Reid clippings of all the coverage, no matter how insulting. For a group that had struggled for visibility, there seemed to be no such thing as bad publicity. She also had been surrounded by a sizable and identifiable group who cheered her on and congratulated her, highlighting the fact that she represented a burgeoning movement.

Although Bebbington had echoed media expectations that only First World women would focus on cultural issues while their Third World sisters would concentrate on economic issues, that division did not always hold. To be sure, Domitila's Ecuadoran compañera told reporters after the panel that the tribune was not addressing the issues that most directly affected women, and the Mexican communist Adelina Zendejas cautioned tribune participants to "put

aside issues that would make the assembly into 'un show.' "[12] But other participants seemed to welcome the discussion of sexuality, and the popularity of this
session and subsequent similar gatherings that ensued indicated an appetite for
these conversations.

While Bebbington's comments barely attracted notice in *Xilonen*, and security agents made no mention of her in their report, they quickly drew the attention of the Mexican press.[13] Participants and reporters alike frequently perceived
any gestures toward female separatism as a dangerous Western import that
threatened not only to distract from efforts to fight poverty and injustice but
also to upend the social order and denigrate the roles that many women held
dear.[14] "There ought to be a conference rule that it not allow in so many dykes
[*marimachos*] that look like men," editorialized Roberto Blanco Moheno in *El
Universal*; in an accompanying editorial, the priest Samuel Bernardo Lemus
extolled women's domestic simplicity and maternal virtues.[15] Bebbington's insistence on women's liberation from men and from obligatory maternity seemed
to alarm these observers even more than her open sexuality.[16]

The following day, tribune-goers piled into auditorium four, where the
National Gay Task Force held a forum "to discuss their marginalization and
the need for governments around the world to recognize their rights as human
beings."[17] The organizing committee had initially assigned the forum a tiny
meeting room on the Medical Center's second floor, but it was relocated. Over
150 people squeezed into one of the smaller auditoriums on the main floor—
crouching on stairs, crowding in the doorways, and spilling out into the halls.
One participant suggested that they create more space for the women outside
by barring journalists and photographers; the suggestion was met with shouts
of agreement from the audience, but Nancy Cárdenas—Mexico's most visible
lesbian activist—dissented. "Compañeras," she explained, "it is necessary for
the press to be present, since in a country as 'machista' as Mexico, these themes
need to be discussed in the open."[18] So the reporters stayed as several lesbians
recounted their experiences, and Cárdenas argued that lesbians accomplished
more because they did not waste all their time trying to get married. Brazilian
sociologist João Guilherme Corrêa de Souza raised his hand to insist that he
had never met a "feminine lesbian" but was denied the floor. As the time ran out
on the session, the argument reignited between Corrêa de Souza and several
participants, tumbling out into the corridors. Over participants' objections, a
reporter interviewed Corrêa de Souza, who explained that homosexuality was
determined by social systems and had a "historical character," while heterosexuality was a "biological phenomenon."[19]

While the fourth estate did not have the salutary effect Cárdenas had anticipated, her participation drew attention to the lesbians' efforts. Cárdenas—a
Yale drama school alumna who had lived in Poland, traveled around the world,

and marched with Marxist radicals—exemplified the type of cosmopolitan that dominated the IWY events. In 1971, the noted Mexican dramaturge and theater director had helped to establish Mexico's first openly gay organization, the Frente de Liberación Homosexual, and, in a 1974 interview on the nationally televised talk show 24 Horas, Cárdenas publicly proclaimed herself a lesbian. After the Monday panel where Bebbington first spoke out, some "visiting lesbians" urged Cárdenas to participate in the following day's forum on lesbianism. "They told me that the Communists, my own compañeras from earlier in the party, abandoned the conference hall when an Australian girl said 'I'm a lesbian feminist,'" she recalled later in an interview. "They said, 'Throw out the sickos, we're out of here.' . . . That seemed to me to give an incomplete image of Mexico, because I was also a leftist militant, was a lesbian, and I had another position and raised my finger."[20] Inspired by what she deemed the "guerrilla model of the US women's liberation movement," Cárdenas had acceded to the visitors' request for her support and invited "all the foreign lesbians" to her house to meet Mexican lesbian activists and to strategize about both immediate questions of how to address the tribune as well as broader strategic questions such as whether to align themselves more closely with feminists or with gay male activists.[21]

With Cárdenas taking the lead, the lesbian caucus called another forum, a 9 A.M. session that Xilonen's calendar of events for Thursday, June 26, listed simply as "Lesbianism." This time the organizing committee scheduled the meeting before the tribune sessions started and in one of the largest auditoriums in hopes of accommodating the expected crowd; the forum organizers barred men and members of the press. An estimated 250 women looked on as Cárdenas presented the Declaración de las lesbianas mexicanas, pointing to sexual recognition as a critical form of social liberation and lamenting that "unconstitutional police actions" and widespread persecution had made it impossible to organize effectively. "We trust, nonetheless, that the tactics of struggle used by our brothers and sisters in other parts of the world will help us to find our own path."[22]

Both the declaration and Doughty's press statement about the event stressed the mutual inspiration and collaboration across geopolitical fault lines, challenging the persistent representation of lesbianism as an import from industrialized, capitalist countries that embraced a feminism characterized by sexual liberty and moral dissolution. Doughty explained, "Most of the women attending did not speak English; many of them had never before heard an open discussion of Lesbianism." The audience's enthusiastic response, she insisted, "shows the concept that Lesbianism does not exist in non-Western and developing countries to be false."[23] Guatemalan Luz Méndez de la Vega seconded this view in her contribution to Xilonen, blaming both the "extreme oppressiveness" of the left and the "spectacular prudishness" of the right and citing the forum on lesbianism as one of the few that really addressed issues of interest to women.[24]

Outside the meeting room, a group of Mexican women claiming to represent the Mothers' Society of Cuauhtémoc Delegation elbowed out the Ukrainian hunger strikers to picket against Cárdenas with signs reading, "Out with that Antisocial and Disoriented Cárdenas," "*Lesbianas y Homosexuales* ¡Go Home!" and "Death to Nancy Cárdenas" and distributed pamphlets calling on the delegation to close Cárdenas's drama schools.[25] Cárdenas described it afterward as a "mediocre act" put on by delegation head Delfín Sánchez Juárez.[26] Recounting the press response as she left the event, Cárdenas recalled years later, "Suddenly, I had forty or fifty reporters around me, like Sophia Loren in Via Appia! I couldn't think. The assault was aggressive: are you a lesbian? Who else is? Why did you agree to come? What does this mean? It was one question after another. I couldn't even answer. The only thing I managed to tell them was: so long as the laws of my country do not offer guarantees for homosexuals, neither I nor anyone can answer your questions."[27]

Although Cárdenas had been most dismayed by such anti-lesbian vitriol coming from the Marxist left, criticism came also from religious conservatives, particularly those concerned that lesbian sexuality posed a challenge to traditional practices of motherhood. Catholic historian Carlos Alvear Acevedo editorialized in *Excélsior* that both the "materialist societies of supercapitalism" and the "dehumanized societies of Marxist totalitarianism" encouraged women to seek "false and ignoble solutions" including sexual freedom and the "consequent perversions and aberrations." True freedom, he counseled, would come through Marian devotion and the exaltation of motherhood.[28] Another Catholic editorialist, Alejandro Aviles, lamented after the conference concluded that "many groups of women abandoned their issues to be manipulated by political issues of the right or the left"; most regrettably, "certain North Americans have broken the record, such as the 'radicalesbians' and those who promote the oldest profession in the world"—referring, in part, to Flo Kennedy's equivalence between marriage and prostitution.[29] Methodist evangelical Gonzalo Báez-Camargo, writing under the pen name Pedro Gringoire, complained in *Excélsior*, "some extremists have assumed the exorbitant pretension of converting woman into a *marimacho* [dyke], totally repudiating maternity and home."[30]

The mounting interest of the Mexican press in the lesbians' activities grew in proportion to the size and intensity of tribune participants' interest. No other national press paid them nearly so much attention, and even *Xilonen* made only passing mention in its coverage and ran a short opinion piece by US-based activists Linda Fowler and Carol Lease in its "contributions" section.[31] Very few newspapers mentioned Doughty's solo intervention when it occurred, although the episode garnered more coverage as the "lesbian issue" picked up steam; no media mentioned that a lesbian spoke up during the confrontation at the US embassy.[32] The two lesbian forums far exceeded expected participation and interest,

Figure 12.2 "Lesbians, prostitutes, homosexuals, abortion—at least in language we are plenty liberated." *El Universal*, 28 June 1975, 5.

not only filling rooms beyond capacity but also drawing vocal protesters and supporters.

Some of the press interest seems also to have been prurient, as the Mexican press consistently conflated any issues related to women's sexuality. *El Universal* ran three front-page articles side by side about the questions of lesbianism, legalized prostitution, and abortion rights as well as editorial cartoons linking the issues.[33] After the first lesbian forum, *El Universal* ran a photo montage of unnamed speakers and audience members as if to show the curiosity of actual lesbians; only sociologist João Guillherme Corrêa de Souza was named.[34] Noting the general absence of perfume and makeup customarily found in women's meetings, the reporter incongruously wrote of the fresh-faced, predominantly young women who appeared in the photos, "Most of the women wore pants, and the features of their faces were hard, lacking that goodness that turns into coquetry." Coverage of lesbians was often accompanied by coverage of prostitutes, in particular the dynamic and charismatic COYOTE leaders, Margo St. James and Flo Kennedy. Reporters and editorialists alike seemed to collapse the groups into twin embodiments of the depravity wrought by women's liberation.

Bebbington clearly touched a nerve when she told the audience that initially she "had relations" only with men. "How is this?" the *Diario de México* reporter wondered in print. She explained, "Homosexuality is a choice, and I chose it. I'm not ashamed but rather proud to be a lesbian."[35] Participants in the lesbian forum called for sperm banks that would allow women to have children without having to deal with men.[36] Fowler and Lease reiterated this discourse of choice in their *Xilonen* contribution. Pointing to the ways that heterosexuality reinforced a patriarchal status quo, they contended, "For these reasons, lesbianism is more than a bedroom issue. It is a highly political position that many women choose to take."[37] These explanations—echoing the aphorism widely attributed to US women's liberationist Ti-Grace Atkinson that "feminism is the theory and lesbianism is the practice"—seemed to be, for many Mexican reporters and editorialists, their first exposure to feminist separatism.

Gonzalo Báez-Camargo ("Pedro Gringoire") expressed dismay that the tribune sought to repudiate men and replace women with "insemination plants, incubators, and nurseries, substituting the family with the raising of human livestock." Rather than demanding rights for lesbians and prostitutes, he maintained, women should recognize that the limitations they face derive from the general socioeconomic situation. "Before [these limitations], the struggle for emancipation is not exactly against men but rather alongside them." Instead, he saw the tribune giving "free rein to all the passions, including the most aberrant and depraved." He quipped that the lesbians must have wandered into the wrong room at the Medical Center "because right there are clinics that could have treated them." But far from repudiating the lesbians, Báez-Camargo railed, the tribune organizers granted them meeting space. The only thing missing from the tribune, he inveighed, was a pornography exhibition.[38]

Excélsior columnist Antonio Delhumeau insisted that unlike class conflict, "women's lib" (written in English) created a false dichotomy that set women against affective ties to their children, erotic commitments to men, and responsible social participation, resulting in the repression of love, tenderness, and desire.[39] Alongside the editorial reproaching US feminists for their challenge to Ojeda Paullada's presidency, *El Universal* ran an unsigned editorial titled "Extremist Feminism" about the Society for Cutting Up Men (SCUM) accompanied by a large cartoon titled "Modern Ideas" of a sinister-looking woman fantasizing herself as a happy cavewoman dragging a caveman whom she has apparently bludgeoned with a club.[40] Modernization, it would appear, involved a detour through the Stone Age.

In the editorial, SCUM appears not as the fictional entity of feminist satire but rather as a "strange feminist corporation formed in the United States"; it treated the "SCUM Manifesto" author Valerie Solanas—best known for her attempt to murder Andy Warhol—as the leader of a functioning and even influential

Idéas Modernas   *Por Carrillo*

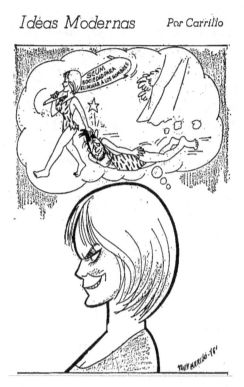

Figure 12.3 "Modern Ideas: SCUM, Society to Eliminate Men." *El Universal,* 24 June 1975, 5.

organization within US feminist circles. While lauding IWY's efforts to "dignify the feminine," the editorial lamented that "to convert the exaltation of the feminine into the emasculating denigration of the masculine, there is an abyss."

Perhaps someone tried to explain to *El Universal*'s editors that it was a joke, that SCUM never existed outside of Solanas's mind. The next day, the paper ran another editorial, describing it as "not a very extensive group" in the United States with Solanas as its leader.[41] (As Solanas explained later in an interview, "It's hypothetical. No, hypothetical is the wrong word. It's just a literary device. There's no organization called SCUM.")[42] Since Solanas was a "frustrated assassin," the manifesto "could not pass as a joke," the editorial insisted. "Is this feminism, or is this the future of feminism?" Distinguishing the imaginary SCUM members—the "strange women" for whom he could not come up with a "publishable term"—from "normal" feminists who sought equal juridical, economic, and social rights with men, he saw their victory as the only calamity not predicted even by Nostradamus.

The Mexican press was clearly fascinated and horrified by the joyous spectacle of it all, which provided a striking contrast with the sheer tedium of the

Figure 12.4 Flo Kennedy leading chants outside the NGO tribune. Courtesy of UN Photo.

government conference and the tribune's dire accounts of poverty, human rights abuses, and forced sterilizations. The morning featured lesbians chanting, "I'm gay and I'm beautiful," while the afternoon brought Flo Kennedy and Margo St. James leading choruses on the esplanade while passing out flyers on prostitutes' rights. Ironically, Kennedy and St. James became a particularly prominent spectacle because the security personnel repeatedly refused them entry to the Medical Center.

The lesbian forum vacated the meeting room in time for it to be used by a group calling itself Democratic Chilean Women. The audience listened in stunned and respectful silence as three women recounted their experiences of detention and torture following the Pinochet coup. "They took me in a closed van," explained the first woman. "They began with the blows and the groping until I arrived, blindfolded, to the 'softening room,' where they stripped me, gave me electric shocks, beat me with a wire, hung me from my feet and hands; they raped me." She talked about a *compañero* being forced to watch while guards raped his sisters. Another woman, twenty-three-year-old Viviana Uribe, described people finding the bodies of their parents and siblings floating in rivers and canals or strewn in the streets.[43] Afterward, a coalition of left-leaning Latin American and internationalist organizations held a press conference inviting one and all to a counter-conference the following Sunday at the Hidalgo Theater on Mexico City's historic Alameda Central. The spokeswomen explained the need for a counter-conference because "the panels all consist of UN officials, restricting free expression for non-governmental groups, with the purpose of making the Conference fail and distorting the Tribune with attention to the themes of lesbianism and prostitution, distracting from questions of importance and transcendence."[44]

Although some of those attending the "lesbianism" forum may well have stayed to attend the Democratic Women of Chile session, the juxtaposition of lesbians demanding rights while Chileans catalogued atrocities appeared consistently as a zero-sum choice that women either could support sexual rights or they could support other forms of social justice; the two were mutually exclusive. The *New York Times* dispensed with the geopolitical framing that typified the Mexican coverage but retained the basic message: "The woman alone in American society," the editorial board wrote the day after the lesbian forum, "struggling with the breakdown of social institutions and the need to raise a family on unequal pay and under covert discrimination, has very real problems—considerably more serious than those of the overprivileged few who worry about specialized forms of sexual liberation and exalted executive expectations."[45] Much like the persistent effort to parse politics and women's issues, sexual rights seemed always to be portrayed as coming at the expense of more pressing concerns, as though forgoing housing, family, and employment rights for lesbians would somehow make potable water available in Tanzania or prevent human rights violations in Chile.

Scene 13

Chaos in the Tribune

By Friday, a slow-burning fuse ignited an explosion in the NGO tribune. As word got out that Betty Friedan had led a group to Tlatelolco on Thursday to present Helvi Sipilä with a list of amendments to the World Plan of Action, tribune participants became incensed by her presumption to represent the whole despite the clear rules that individuals and groups could speak only for themselves and not for the tribune.[1] "I didn't head the group," Friedan protested to a reporter grilling her at the museum reception Thursday evening. "I joined a movement led by a black lady—the representative from Bermuda [Marjorie Bean]—and all I wanted was dialogue."[2] Many tribune-goers had never heard of the United Women of the Tribune, much less seen one of the few copies of the proposed amendments that circulated only in English. The Coalition of Latin American Women offered reporters no comment on the proposed amendments, never having seen them.

Friedan remained a lightning rod. "Betty Friedan arrived with an aura of fame from her book, *The Feminine Mystique*, which she has exploited," Argentine Edith Reynaldi told a reporter.[3] Some tribune participants described her as "dictatorial and closed to dialogue," and a group of Latin American women circulated a petition calling for rotating leadership roles and censuring the "authoritarian" and "manipulative" tactics used by a few women.[4] Confirming that the petition referred to Friedan, Mexican María Eugenia Echazarreta explained, "We consider Betty Friedan's value to be as a writer and as a vanguard feminist, but we don't feel she is representative of us."[5] Without naming Friedan, Phyllis K. White and "25 USA feminists" echoed the Latin American petition in a letter to *Xilonen* explaining, "Rotating leadership and working roles is a basic tenet of feminism, enabling all people to be heard and to use their skills. The authoritarian tactics of a few feminists at the Tribune have alienated feminists. . . . The purpose of our gathering [the United Women of the Tribune] was to unite feminists and not to force conformance and confrontation under self-appointed leaders."[6] A Bolivian tribune-goer, Ingrid Koster Urioste, told *Excélsior*, "Friedan is against real feminism; all she wants is for men and women to learn how to fry

Figure 13.1 Helvi Sipilä (center) in press conference with Betty Friedan (left) and Marjorie Bean (right). © Bettye Lane. Courtesy of Schlesinger Library.

eggs together."[7] Members of CORE and the Raza Unida Party demanded an apology from Friedan for her accusation during Thursday's "global speak-out" that dissenting Chicana and African American women had been paid to disrupt the tribune.[8]

African Americans and Chicanas extended their criticism from Friedan to the tribune organizers for having excluded African Americans, Native Americans, and labor organizers from the tribune program—an accusation that overlooked the participation of panelists such as Madonna Gilbert of the American Indian Movement, Dorothy Height of the National Council of Negro Women, and Puerto Rican political scientist and labor specialist Isabel Pico de Hernández but that highlighted the limits of representation across divides of politics and ideology that had been evident during the confrontation at the US embassy. Jacqueline Ceballos of NOW had written Friedan a frantic note during one of the speak-outs saying that women from *Ms.* had organized an alternative feminist caucus. Some NOW women "think we should meet with women leaders to discuss this government co-optation and control of feminist movements."[9] Friedan repeatedly told reporters that the CIA had orchestrated the division between women concerned about economic issues and those focused on women's issues, and she and her allies kept alive the Redstockings' accusations about Gloria Steinem's collaborating with the CIA, implying that only sufficient distance from the state allowed one authentically to speak for the US feminist movement.[10]

While *Xilonen* had been at pains, particularly in its Spanish coverage, to stress the international composition of the delegation that had gone to Tlatelolco, the Mexican press attributed the campaign entirely to Friedan, describing the group she "commands" as composed primarily of US women who had come to Mexico City on IWY tour packages and sought to subordinate the more political concerns that preoccupied Third World women to the "secondary issues" that interested US women. While *Xilonen* reported the group assertively but diplomatically pressing for negotiations, *El Universal* described it attempting to "invade" the government conference and shouting to be admitted.

During the Friday morning tribune session on family formations in the Medical Center's main auditorium, Dutch sociologist Ruut Veenhoven predicted that conventional family formations would become obsolete as homosexual unions, communes, and other formations arose to take their place. Describing Latin America as clinging to family structures prevalent in Holland and England "a thousand years ago," he foresaw that modernization and urbanization would transform social structures as "people realize that human happiness is more important and they tie themselves to the people they love."[11] Veenhoven's intervention doubtless would have received more attention but for the fact that just as the session was ending an argument broke out near one of the microphones over the document presented to Sipilä the previous morning.[12] The United Women of the Tribune were scheduled to meet in the auditorium during the lunch break, but before the session could start, Argentine Adriana Puiggrós dashed to the presidium and grabbed the microphone to make a "clarifying pronouncement about the document that has circulated in the name of the tribune."[13] Mexican feminist Antonieta Rascón, who had participated in the United Women caucus, wrestled Puiggrós for the microphone, inspiring some "colorful" insults from Puiggrós and an "unpublishable" exchange of words.[14] Members of the audience shouted for Rascón to allow Puiggrós to continue reading the statement signed by Latin American women, which she tried to do amid shouts and intermittent failures of the sound system. Reading in a voice "reminiscent of the great Latin American speeches to the masses," Puiggrós enumerated the more radical set of demands of the Women against Imperialism—peppered with denunciations of imperialism and exploitation. The group called for "a Latin Americanist conscience committed to revolution, not to the model of the Latin American woman who promotes imperialism." Rosa Luz Alegría, Echeverría's daughter-in-law, who had served as a panelist during the education session, grabbed the microphone and took to the presidium in a desperate effort to soothe tempers. "All the cameras and newspapers of the world are focused on us," she insisted, "to show we cannot organize ourselves—this is a very poor example, really."[15]

Indeed, the press could not resist the image of two women fighting over the microphone. An Associated Press photographer snapped the picture and, to the chagrin of AP reporter Peggy Simpson, sent it out over the wires. It would become the most widely circulated photograph from the IWY events.[16] The accompanying New York Times article described it as "a typical scene at the Tribune," but the photo carried a caption implying that the conflict had occurred among official delegates at the government conference.[17] Cropped in a way that highlighted the intensity of the conflict, the photo seemed to illustrate a narrative that already had emerged in the press (See Figure 1.1). New York Times reporter James Sterba lamented after the first days, "National grandstanding, regional bickering, arguments between socialists and capitalists, and a rift between women from rich and poor lands have drowned out the voices of unity and turned the first United Nations World Conference on Women into a political forum."[18] Drawing his observations largely from the pages of Xilonen, Sterba rehearsed Germaine Greer's objection that "political bickering has submerged major unifying feminist issues," oddly criticized official delegates for representing their governments' positions, and derided tribune participants for "squabbl[ing] for command of the microphone to push one esoteric cause after another." The grounds of the unity he sought—the "major unifying feminist issues"—remained elusive. Sterba implied that unity might have been achieved, paradoxically, by including a more diverse cross-section of societies, particularly more poor women.

This episode emerged as a sort of Rorschach test revealing the variety of ways in which observers understood the events. Accounts vary starkly depending on perspective and often include speculations and accusations of conspiracy on all sides. In one of the strangest instances where the Spanish and English coverage diverge in Xilonen, the English version identifies Rosa Luz Alegría as a tribune panelist and education expert who finally quelled the ruckus by chiding the audience. The Spanish version identifies Alegría only by name, apparently assuming readers' familiarity, and recounts that she "suddenly . . . named herself the feminist leader and stirred up women from more than eighty countries who had already worked together to edit a list of demands [and] returned to discussing two themes that had divided them: capitalism and economic domination. The support of the sound technicians was clear as the sound was cut from the women on the presidium and given only to señora Alegría. An attitude unworthy of the gentlemen who were contracted to serve women and not political games."[19]

A retrospective account written by Joan McKenna, a communications consultant who attended IWY as both a member of the press and a representative of a UNA chapter in the San Francisco Bay Area, offered an even more sinister account.[20] In a section she titled "Sabotage," McKenna described a shadowy plot in which Rascón—who seems to be conflated or perhaps confused with Puiggrós in this account—and Alegría were in cahoots in a game of good cop/bad cop, with the sound technicians and security guards as the supporting cast.[21] As the unfairly maligned Friedan sat quietly in the audience, Rascón "began ranting, accusing the Tribune of having been co-opted by Yankee imperialists, that the document did not represent the views or perspectives of Latin women, that the Tribune was a farce unless it spoke to the causes of oppression and condemn those countries, cultures, political and economic systems that imposed their wills on developing nations."[22] McKenna distinguished between "legitimate dissenters"—the Latin American Coalition that had been willing to work with the United Women—and the "disrupters," who purportedly had been instructed by their authoritarian governments to undermine the tribune and IWY as a whole. "It seems that calls were coming into the Mexican government from leftist and rightist dictatorships throughout the world with the message to disrupt and discredit the Tribune," McKenna explained. Unlike the more easily contained government conference, "the voices of women bringing a message of unity to the broadest spectrum of the people is indeed dangerous."[23] Both McKenna and Friedan, whose accounts align quite closely, perceived threats of violence by "men with guns" (the ever-present security guards) or a monkey wrench left at a government delegate's desk "and the threat of brutality it signified."[24]

The mêlée subsided when Sipilä arrived to respond to the United Women's petition to address the Tlatelolco conference and suggest amendments to the World Plan of Action. She explained to the assembled tribune-goers that they would not be allowed to address the government conference, for reasons of both protocol and logistics. Given the care and negotiations that had gone into deciding which groups apart from member states would have different types of representation and the particular order of speakers in the plenary, it was not plausible that the government conference would accredit a self-appointed delegation of spokespersons to address a plenary session.[25] Further, the speakers in Tlatelolco already ran far behind schedule, and the First Committee had been inundated with 894 amendments proposed by government delegations and faced an impossible task of trying to sort through them in a few debate-filled days. She reminded them that UN documents were only binding to the extent that they could hold their governments accountable. It was as though she had pulled back the curtain to reveal that the Wizard of Oz was just an ordinary old man whose powers derived from those who imagined him as powerful. "You must not think you are less important than the conference," she told the audience. "The UN is nothing when it comes to implementation. We cannot change your laws, your education, your economic plans. You are the ones who can elect people to the parliaments and the municipal councils where all the decisions are made—the UN cannot. You should be involved in national planning and you should be heard." The audience rose to a standing ovation as she concluded, "Let us create a network of women for the future. This is not the end—it is the beginning."[26]

As soon as Sipilä left, however, chaos broke out again, forcing the planned session on peace and disarmament including Nobel laureate Séan MacBride to move to a smaller room, where a scant 300 people would attend.[27] The two Latin American groups faced off, one accusing the other of being too timid and complicit with imperialist powers. The Mexican press—particularly the ruling party's *El Nacional*—could explain this division within the ranks only as a result of a nefarious conspiracy, although not of the sort that McKenna perceived. "We could cite a thousand excuses to justify what occurred among Latin American women," wrote journalist Sylvia Sayago, "but suffice it to say that the Latin women were not the initiators of the scandal but rather women who, based on their nationality, in the Spanish language, and their physical characteristics belong to our race, who sow the discord and disorder that they take as their directive. Those who want to distort the aims of this event for their own mean-spirited interests will not succeed. . . . Those who madly or foolishly intervened in the disturbance, exchanged views, realized their error and the manipulation to which they were subject, and decided to support each other more than ever."[28]

If women like Sayago did not see the protesters as authentically "Latin," the reverse charge was made as well. Members of the Women against Imperialism faction, such as Domitila Barrios de Chungara, increasingly saw themselves—not the Latin American Coalition—as speaking for Latin American women. When one of the Mexican participants approached her, urging her to make common cause, Domitila recalled replying, "All right, let's talk about the two of us. But if you'll let me, I'll begin. Señora, I've known you for about a week. Every morning you show up in a different outfit and on the other hand, I don't. Every day you show up all made up and combed like someone who had time to spend in an elegant beauty parlor and who can spend money on that, and yet I don't. I see that each afternoon you have a chauffeur in a car waiting at the door of this place to take you home, and yet I don't. And in order to show up here like you do, I'm sure you live in a really elegant home, in an elegant neighborhood, no? And yet we miners' wives only have a small house on loan to us, and when our husbands die or get sick or are fired from the company, we have ninety days to leave the house and then we're in the street. Now, señora, tell me: is your situation at all similar to mine? Is my situation at all similar to yours? So what equality are we going to speak of between the two of us?"[29]

The idea that class—or at least consuming power—brought influence was not limited to critics like Domitila but often carried the opposite implications. Sympathetic accounts of the United Women's campaign frequently stressed that the group consisted of many women who had paid their own way to Mexico City, seemingly entitling them to a greater say in proceedings.[30] "To the women of the Tribune, many of whom had endured personal hardship in the cause of women's rights and who had, by and large, financed their own ways across the world to be at this event," Joan McKenna explained afterward, "it was unreasonable that they would have no voice in the creation of the World Plan of Action—the Plan that they must implement in their own countries."[31]

Such expectations revealed a surprising ignorance about how the UN functioned, but the United Women's supporters stressed the procedural trappings of the group's meetings with the clear purpose of giving it representative credibility. McKenna drew on a parliamentary lexicon to describe the working groups, amendments proposed from the floor, and votes—presumably voice votes—by the "body-of-the-whole," meaning the subset of tribune-goers who attended the meeting. She generously estimated that the vote represented 4,000 of the 5,000 women who had registered.[32]

Despite all these efforts to establish the United Women's procedural legitimacy, the context made it impossible. The already overburdened Mexican facilities declined to translate, reproduce, and distribute copies of the United Women's proposed amendments, precipitating feminist objections that Ojeda Paullada simply wanted to silence Friedan and her allies. The US embassy volunteered to produce the copies. As a result, the copies distributed widely both at the tribune and the conference carried an annotation, "Printed courtesy of the American Embassy, Mexico City, Mexico"—a formality intended to foster goodwill that only fueled rumors that the United Women of the Tribune had all along been choreographed by the CIA.

The United Women's proposed amendments themselves were not necessarily the problem. Those protesting against them objected not to their contents, which most had not had the opportunity to read, but rather to the fact that the group had claimed representative status at all. As for the amendments, their sins, such as they were, had been largely those of omission: failing to mention the legacies of imperialism and the effects of global—rather than household—inequalities and offering no comments on the section about international and regional action. Most of the amendments sought to strengthen the plan's language, substituting "must" for "should" and calling for the "equalization" of employment conditions rather than merely a "marked improvement." They urged the creation of a new UN office of Under-Secretary General for Women's Concerns; this would oversee a team of consultants consisting of at least two-thirds women. To the plan's section on national action, the United Women added, "Women of each nation must act in a vigilante capacity to assure that their government" creates an agency to enforce the plan, budget sufficient funds, and submit annual reports.[33] In several places, the United Women proposed changes that emphasized women's exclusion, saying, for example, that public-service campaigns should "inform" rather than "enlighten" women about political issues.

Most of the United Women's proposals called for a shift in the World Plan's emphases rather than wholesale transformation. Some reflected an effort to expand the plan's focus from rural women in poor countries, recommending that "and urban poor" be added wherever "rural" appeared and suggested replacing "villagers" with "people." The group struck the language that training and technology would "reduce the drudgery of their daily lives." Other proposals challenged what some saw as too instrumental an approach to women's incorporation into development schemes. Rather than seeking ways that women might contribute more to society and the economy, they suggested, the plan should seek ways that societies and economies might better support women. They called for educational materials to treat women as "self-determining human beings with the inherent right to achieve their total human potential, rather than being viewed as an economic instrument for achieving nationalistic goals." They asked that art be added to school curricula along with the plan's current proposals of economics, agricultural technology, and "responsible parenthood."

While the United Women's proposed amendments generally hewed to the grammar of the World Plan of Action and the protocols of "UN-ese," at points their recommendations contrasted starkly with its technocratic language. Calling for educational programs that advanced the "emotional, social, and physical health of all individuals," the group elaborated, "Educators must be in touch with their own emotional, social, and physical selves to further this human development in others." To the plan's recommendation that women be informed of available health facilities, the United Women added, "Women must be given freedom of choice with regard to their reproductive processes and must be protected against the violation of their bodies by rape and cliterectomies and tribal, political and religious sanctions which physically harm women."

Some of the proposed amendments clearly touched a nerve already exposed by earlier events at the tribune. In the sections on political participation and employment, the United Women added "sexual preference" to the list of proscribed forms of discrimination. They repeatedly called for the replacement of the word "families" with "people" or even "individuals," recommended changing "mothers" to "women," and suggested including the "childless family" among those family formations where women's rights should be protected. They eliminated the paragraph describing the home as a primarily feminine space and instead offered that housing improvements would benefit "all human beings." Any family allowances, "motherhood awards and similar measures," the group insisted, "should not be used as incentives to keep women bound to traditional roles." The United Women also pointed to the "inadequate technological and medical attention to male contraception."

The Coalition of Latin American Women offered an addendum to the United Women's proposals. "Our struggle for liberation has a dual character," they explained. "As women we face the questions raised by the feminist, universal movement; as citizens, we face a Latin American reality based on economic exploitation and cultural penetration." The group's addendum reiterated the importance of a "Latin Americanist consciousness" to accompany a feminist consciousness, its "commitment to strengthen the family as a moral nucleus of society and as a determinant psychological factor of the individual," and its efforts to "fight against its economic character that arbitrarily divides housework." They called for the socialization of domestic tasks through the construction of infrastructure for child care, community kitchens, and production and consumption cooperatives. While the United Women called for educational programs that would allow women to achieve their "full human potential," the Latin American women invoked the famed Brazilian education theorist Paulo Freire in demanding that "educational systems be revised in order to promote a liberating consciousness that will foster the necessary structural changes in society."[34] The group renewed its calls for more humane treatment of immigrant workers and amnesty for all political prisoners—the types of issues that the United Women had decided not to touch. The Latin American Women's statement closed with a strong reassertion meant to distance the group from separatists, insisting they were "carrying out our struggle side by side with men as an expression of our genuine spirit for human integration and equality within the context of our own Latin American reality."

By the time the crowds at the Medical Center dissipated on Friday afternoon leaving participants were increasingly uncertain about who they could count as allies. Supporters of the United Women consistently depicted protesters as organized (possibly paid) dissidents who merely ventriloquized the positions of their authoritarian regimes, or possibly just those of Ojeda Paullada. These accounts repeatedly insist that what most threatened the powers behind these women was the prospect that women would unite behind a single political project.[35] They viewed the "orchestrated dissension" as calculated to undermine the most constructive effort in Mexico City, the group that made steady progress through the World Plan of Action while the government conference got bogged down in committee debates and the opposition offered nothing more than critique and polemics.

Opponents of the United Women depicted the plan as tone deaf at best and at worst the product of a nefarious scheme by the State Department or the CIA. To many it seemed like yet another effort to push aside alternative conceptualizations of women's rights—particularly those that did not see women in a battle against men or seeking individual opportunities but rather as a push for recognition of sexual difference. For many Latin American women, whose countries had so frequently been the targets of US intervention and manipulation, the US takeover of the NGO tribune seemed to follow a 150-year-old script. These dissenting views surely reflected in part the ways in which the informal structure of the United Women left significant numbers of women feeling unrepresented.[36] For many participants, the afternoon's episodes simply left them perplexed about what had happened and what would happen next.

Scene 14

Counter-congresses

By Saturday morning, exhaustion had set in for government delegates and tribune-goers alike. While many of the high-profile official delegates—such as Olof Palme and Daniel Parker—had already left to attend to other commitments, the weekend brought the departure of significant numbers of tribune participants who had taken a week away from work and families but needed to return home. Many who stayed decided to leave Mexico City for day trips, venturing to nearby Cuernavaca or Tepoztlán or to climb the famed pyramids at Teotihuacán. The First Committee, having decided not to revise the World Plan of Action beyond its introduction and first chapter, took a break for the weekend, although the Second Committee—tasked with considering more than sixty resolutions related to changes in women's status and obstacles to women's equality—soldiered on.

During the Saturday meeting of the Second Committee, Rita Johnston—a delegate to the OAS's Inter-American Commission on Women and a member of the US National Commission on the Observance of IWY—proposed that sexism be listed among the obstacles to women's equality, alongside "alien and colonial domination, foreign occupation, racial discrimination, apartheid, and neo-colonialism in all its forms."[1] An Iraqi delegate had proposed that Zionism be added to the list; he would later withdraw the proposal, but it raised the question of what might reasonably be included in that catalogue of offenses.[2]

This was not the first use of the term "sexism" during the IWY proceedings; Elizabeth Reid had conspicuously highlighted the concept—a term that had not yet been broached in UN deliberations—during her plenary address on the first full day of conference proceedings. She knew that the term could raise hackles and had spent months systematically introducing it into Australia's political vocabulary.[3] In her plenary speech, Reid made an often-cited analogy with racism, defining it as the "artificial ascription of roles, behaviour and even personalities to people on the basis of their sex alone. . . . The basis of racism, racial discrimination, colonialism and neo-colonialism, alien domination is similar to the basis of that violence against women which we call sexism. It is based on the need, which may well be a learnt need, for power over other human beings."[4] The prevalence of patriarchy, what Reid dubbed "a colonization by mute consent," within sexist societies "does not simply create differences but inequalities." Women had fought "time and time again" alongside men for dignity and national liberation only to find "their brothers in struggle carry within them the roots of treason, the myths and prejudices which keep women in their place."

The term certainly had gained some purchase outside of strictly feminist circles. The World Council of Churches had organized a conference in Berlin on "Sexism in the 1970s," and its representative explained to the New York IWY committee that he had come to understand the concept through the analogy with racism.[5] US civil rights leader Dorothy Height described to reporters the links between sexism and racism—although El Universal generally put "sexism" in scare quotes but omitted them from the term racism.[6] The word also had gained usage outside the Anglo-European world. Several of the papers submitted to the journalists' encounter, including those by participants from Mexico and Zaire, stressed the role of communications media in promoting sexism.[7] The Pan Africanist Congress of Azania, a South African black nationalist organization, had used the term in its presentation to the First Committee, explaining that racism and sexism reinforced one another.[8] Annie Jiagge told the New York Times that the elimination of sexism and racism were equally important. "The two things are one and the same," she explained. "It's a fight against injustice. If you want to root out the evil, it's injustice you want to root out."[9]

If delegates like Johnston and Reid saw the elimination of sexism as simply part of the progress toward modernization, many others read it as yet another absurd Western effort to efface sexual difference. In many parts of the world, language itself reinforced a sexual binary with every utterance; El Universal ran a front-page story mocking a resolution by the tribune's Committee on Language Revision calling for "unisex" language and recommending a "'non-sexist' vocabulary" that would avoid associating leadership with masculinity.[10] While the Second Committee deliberated over sexism, Ghanaian biologist Letitia Obeng of the UN Environmental Programme urged women in her plenary speech not to become "carbon copies" of men but rather to "try to resolve the world's problems using our sensibility that is so distinct from men's." Pointing to the widespread problems of air and water pollution as well as the desertification of parts of Africa, she invoked women's stronger ties to nature and commitment to future generations to motivate a struggle for "an environment more pure than today's."[11] The Uruguayan former senator and suffragist Sofía Alvarez Vignoli de Demicheli cautioned women to proceed prudently with their own liberation. "The woman who wants to compare herself to man in everything either speaks from rote or doesn't know what she says," she told an interviewer for El Nacional. "The result is so absurd that the man that she wants seems in all ways like a woman. Women in pants, men in skirts. Unisex. *Hijo de mi vida*, those are aberrations."[12]

Johnston's proposal was met with objections from the Bangladesh and Bulgarian delegates that the term was too vague and appeared nowhere else in UN documents; Johnston replied defining it as discrimination based on sex. New Zealand delegate Mary Sinclair added that the term racism was itself a recent addition to the UN lexicon and that anyone who did not understand what sexism meant had no business at the IWY conference. The Soviet delegate dressed down Sinclair for not taking deliberations seriously and invoked Valentina Tereshkova who, he was certain, did not want the word sexism in her vocabulary. The Somali delegate explained that the word implied animosity between men and women and that he saw it as a "nasty North American neologism which we could do without."[13] (Those losing interest in the discussion might have opened up that day's issue of *El Nacional*, which featured a full-page editorial—complete with charts—about "Machismo in Latin America: Myths and Realities of Supposed Male Supremacy," by Chilean physician and sociologist Hernán San Martín.)[14] The proposal to include sexism among the obstacles to women's emancipation failed—twenty votes in favor, twenty-six against, and ten abstentions—to the delight of most Eastern bloc and non-aligned delegates and the consternation of Anglophone and Western Europeans. "Hopefully," Patricia Hutar told a press briefing regretfully on Monday, "a result of this effort will be a consciousness-raising of the United Nations itself to the substitution of this term [sexism] for the more traditional wording currently in vogue."[15]

Meanwhile, Alicia Romo Román, having been relegated to a Saturday speaking slot, stepped to the podium to offer her formal address at the plenary session in Tlatelolco. Once again, the auditorium emptied out in protest. US ambassador John Jova remained, along with a smattering of representatives from other Latin American dictatorships, including Uruguay, Paraguay, and Nicaragua. "Chile has committed a grave crime against Soviet Marxism and will never be forgiven," Romo sighed.[16] She dismissed Pinochet's critics as the "servants, puppets, and useful idiots" of the Soviet empire who spun a vast web of lies about Chile. She described Bussi de Allende as a false widow, having only "played the role of a wife" during the Popular Unity government, and lambasted the audacity of Antonio Fernández, representing the Soviet-aligned World Federation of Democratic Youth, claiming he had deceived the plenary with a litany of abuses by the Pinochet government.[17] Romo branded as "inconceivable" the accusations of torture and executions of women "supposedly detained and victims of Chilean barbarism." While Romo spoke to the plenary, the Mexican, Algerian, Yugoslavian, and Dutch delegations submitted a joint resolution to the Second Committee expressing concern about the "news about the degrading and humiliating conditions to which [Chilean] female political prisoners are subject as well as the tendency toward extensive repression of the families of the perse-cuted to oblige them to submit."[18]

"Insolent! Degenerate fascist!" Laura Allende shouted to a crowd on Sunday, describing Alicia Romo. "If she's not afraid, let her come to the tribune, where we can answer her."[19] Allende spoke to an anti-Pinochet protest that took place at the Teatro Hidalgo next to Mexico's Alameda Central, featuring an all-star cast of communist leaders, including Valentina Tereshkova, Vilma Espín, and Fanny Edelman. The estimated crowd of 950 included demonstrators from North Vietnam, Somalia, Japan, and Mongolia to express solidarity with the Chilean exile community.[20] Espín stepped to the microphone amid chants of "Cuba! Cuba!" and thunderous applause. "Chile is living in a dark night of fascism," she railed. "Torture, assassinations, unemployment, terror, and desperation con-stitute daily life." She assured her Chilean *compañeros* that "the first free terri-tory of the Americas is with them." Le Thi Xuyen of the Vietnamese Women's Organization told the crowd that the Vietnamese experience showed that im-perialism was not invincible.[21] A Chilean band playing protest songs provided an interlude between speakers, and Communist Party militants from a dozen different countries passed out flyers and publications explaining the state of the struggle in their home communities. The demonstration ended at 2 P.M. with a rousing chorus of "La Internacional."

If the Chile solidarity demonstration was designed to gain pro-Allende allies amid traded accusations of deception and manipulation, it appeared to gain at least one convert. Chicana activist Guadalupe Anguiano, a member of the Chicano political party Raza Unida, told a reporter that everything she had heard about Chile had been false. "We don't know who to believe," she explained, "since all the documents that reach us show Pinochet as a good person who is establishing a democracy in that country."[22] Anguiano, who emerged early on as Raza Unida's most vocal spokesperson at the tribune, had come to Mexico at Echeverría's in-vitation and participated on a panel organized by Jorge Bustamante Fernández, whom Echeverría had drafted to advise the Ministry of Foreign Relations on migration issues and the status of Mexicans living in the United States.[23] An esti-mated seventy students piled into an UNAM auditorium to learn about the Raza Unida, a political party founded in 1970 in Crystal City, Texas, that had quickly developed into a social movement with roots in community organizing and ad-vocacy. By 1975, Raza Unida faced challenges from both within and without and tried to revitalize itself through relationships not only with Mexico but also with Cuba, China, and the PLO.[24] Despite this background, Anguiano expressed as-tonishment at what she heard at the tribune and the demonstration. "Well, I had never seen, I had never heard, nor had I ever really paid attention to the milita-rization of Latin America," she recalled decades later. Listening to testimony of torture and brutality and learning of US involvement in supporting regimes like Pinochet's was "heartbreaking," she remembered. "It was just horrible. I became so disillusioned and so angry."[25]

Underscoring the sense that tribune-goers had to choose between feminism and human rights, the simultaneous scheduling of another demonstration at the same time as the anti-Pinochet protest took place across town in the Casa del Lago, the UNAM-run cultural center in Mexico City's picturesque Bosque de Chapultepec. A group of young leftists from the Women's Liberation Movement, the Socialist League, and the Internationalist Communist Group (a UNAM student organization) had organized a meeting to "protest the character of the IWY conference."[26] Earlier in the week, they had posted flyers all over the engineering school of the National Polytechnic Institute, proclaiming that the IWY conference sought only to obstruct revolutionary movements against capitalist exploitation. Police estimated that roughly 700 young people showed up to demand twenty-four-hour child-care facilities, collective kitchens and laundries, the socialization of housework through a domestic wage, and—above all—free and legal access to abortion.[27] An unidentified US woman described the steps women had taken in the United States to legalize abortion, and a factory worker from an embattled Cuernavaca textile workers' union called for solidarity.[28]

The Mexican press was unsparing in its comparison of these two demonstrations. Chilean exiles criticized reporters for attending too much to "minority groups, such as the one led by Betty Friedan or the movement in favor of lesbians, when there are deep problems, serious situations and profound actions that should reach the public."[29] The coverage of these two protests, however, underscored the respect with which the Mexican press treated Allende supporters and the disdain it showed for feminist issues. In contrast to its reverent article about the anti-Pinochet rally, *El Universal*'s article about the student demonstration stressed only their youth and inexperience, depicting them as children playing revolutionary games. "Beneath a benign sun, girls [*niñas*]—their voices as sharp as their proposals were radical—spoke of the exploitation of women in the capitalist system and the need to unite with the proletarian struggle," the paper reported. The article mocked the students' ratty jeans—"worn with pride because there is no more revolutionary touch than a 'humble' outfit"—as well as their speeches. Describing the protesters as "false-sounding" and "as insipid as they were ill-informed," the *El Universal* reporter sneered, "The youngsters [*jovencitas*], trying to give a grandiose tone to their discourse, with so little originality given their canned and dogmatic repetition and insistence on philosophical concepts that have become linguistic jargon, took a stand for the 'socialization of domestic labor.'" Saying that staging a revolution every Sunday had become a fad at Casa del Lago, the article concluded dismissively that "the representatives of feminist organizations—so few that they seem ghostly" had staged a "festival in which the disoriented nonconformists let loose with their urban hysteria."[30]

Amid this furor over feminists and Chile, the most controversial figure in Mexico City did not have to decide between the two. Betty Friedan had gone to Cuernavaca with a small group of trusted friends to drink margaritas at the quaint Las Mañanitas hotel and then to an afternoon meal at the colonial Casa de Piedra.[31]

Scene 15

¡Domitila a la Tribuna!

On Monday morning, the NGO tribune picked up where it had left off on Friday afternoon. The WIDF, having been excluded from planning the formal programming, claimed the first session of the unscheduled days for a session on applying the UN Declaration on Human Rights, featuring presentations by Hortensia Bussi de Allende of Chile, Ma Thi Chu of the South Vietnamese Women's Union, and the PLO leader Fatima Issam Abdul Hadi. Before Bussi de Allende could speak, an "interminable line of Mexican women lined up to give her flowers and kisses." Describing Latin America as in its second battle for independence, she assailed the US government, the CIA, and transnational corporations for their roles in promoting her husband's overthrow.[1] She called on the UN to launch an investigation of what she dubbed "crimes of the fascist junta." Victoria García, a member of the official Chilean delegation, dismissed Bussi de Allende's descriptions of torture and abuse as fabrications. "The only persons still in jail are criminal or robbers," García insisted. "They robbed our nation of dignity and money."[2]

The renewal of these long-standing disputes over not only human rights but also economic sovereignty and Middle Eastern territorial rights heightened the aspiration that NGOs might offer a way out of these conundrums—that they would bring fresh approaches and new actors who had no desire to revive old scripts. Notably, however, the question of Zionism rarely arose at the tribune.[3] In response to Ojeda Paullada's open dismissals of the NGO tribune, Persinger wrote an open letter to him in the pages of *Xilonen* reiterating the tribune's policy that it would issue no formal statements nor authorize anyone to speak on its behalf, but pointing out that "the draft Plan of Action calls upon the non-governmental sector for its implementation efforts." Such expectations, which Sipilä had reiterated during Friday's visit to the tribune, led NGO members to "see themselves as representatives of the people through whom the Plan can become practice."[4] Patricia Hutar announced at a press briefing that the US embassy had made available 5,000 copies of the United Women's proposals—in both English and Spanish—so that "women around the world will be able to incorporate the ideas with the World Plan of Action."[5]

After Friday's chaotic session, the United Women of the Tribune were determined to show that women could come together behind a core set of concerns, countering all the media representations of women fighting over microphones and exchanging barbs in press conferences. They circulated the newly printed copies of the proposed amendments to the World Plan of Action and scheduled a press conference for what they dubbed a "unity panel" during the early afternoon.[6] Those waiting in the audience might have perused a copy of *Xilonen*, which carried a banner headline, "Will Latin Nations Torpedo World Plan?" and featured a multi-page photo essay documenting the tumult during Friday's lunchtime session that oddly seemed to conflate the conference and the tribune. Women of eight different nationalities took their seats on the presidium in the Medical Center's second auditorium. Betty Friedan watched from the audience as the Mexican feminist Esperanza Brito de Martí stepped to the podium to address the journalists and other tribune participants she imagined would support her calls for unity.

Brito de Martí had grown up among politically engaged intellectuals. Her father had led the conservative Catholic resistance against Mexico's postrevolutionary government and served briefly as rector of the UNAM during an earlier wave of student unrest.[7] Her mother worked as a journalist and was among those who covered the IWY events. She had proclaimed herself a feminist in the pages of *El Universal* in 1966, when the "new wave" of Mexican feminism was still barely a ripple.[8] Brito followed her mother's path, becoming a magazine writer first for women's magazines and then for the dissident but more mainstream *Siempre!* By 1972, she and about two dozen feminists had organized under the ambitious banner of the Movimiento Nacional de Mujeres.

Reports differ about how the conflict started.[9] *El Nacional* reported that a Japanese woman on the presidium demanded an explanation about the proposed amendments being circulated.[10] *Xilonen* recounted that the session was "invaded by a group of Latin American women" who began to disrupt the session almost as it began.[11] McKenna and Friedan both recalled that a group of men showed up—always an ominous sign in their accounts—and choreographed the whole commotion.[12] Estimates vary about how many participated in the protest—"sixty hecklers," according to *Xilonen*, or "200 members of the audience," according to *El Universal*. Regardless of how the mêlée started or how many participated, it quickly consumed the whole session. After shouting down the panelists with cries of "Fascists!" and demands for an explanation of why their views had been excluded from the representation of the tribune, the protesters stood up and walked out. Within a few minutes—amid chants of "Domitila a la tribuna! Domitila a la tribuna!"—the group reentered the auditorium, where

Figure 15.1 Domitila Barrios de Chungara (left) and Esperanza Brito de Martí at the NGO tribune. © Bettye Lane. Courtesy of Schlesinger Library.

Domitila Barrios de Chungara confronted Esperanza Brito de Martí, explaining the impossibility of equality amid so much inequality. María Luisa Correa of the Mexican University Federation dismissed Domitila as the leader of a "subversive group that sabotaged the efforts to unify the opinions of the Latin American women."

Intense arguments erupted on all sides about the tribune's "anti-democratic character" and whether "unity" simply amounted to a gentler term for "imperialism." The confrontation highlighted how blurry the dividing lines had become. Brito, who enjoyed the imprimatur of the Mexican government and had organized the session to showcase Mexicans mediating between the First and Third Worlds, found herself confronting the argument that the Mexican government had advocated throughout the conference.[13] While Ojeda Paullada insisted that no "women's issues" existed apart from "politics," Brito had convened this unity panel precisely to demonstrate that a fundamental set of women's issues might be immune to geopolitics and battles for economic sovereignty.

Other speakers attempted to support Brito's efforts. Greek panelist Helena Doukidou assured the protesters that the US feminists were allies in the struggles against imperialism and fascism, but her efforts were to no avail. Dorothy Height of the National Council for Negro Women tried a different tack. "I want to call upon all my sisters of all colors to work together to eliminate racism, classism, and sexism for all the world," she implored, stressing that African American women understood the pain of discrimination. But she could barely be heard over the continued chanting, and the translators had abandoned their booths.[14] Arguments broke out all over the auditorium, amplified by microphones that had been placed to take questions from the floor, producing what *El Universal* described as a "verbal brawl."[15] After forty-five minutes, Brito threw up her hands in frustration. "Women should be united, no matter if in capitalism, socialism, communism, or any other isms," she told anyone who could hear her over the din. "We will continue our struggle. Thank you very much."

Brito seemed unaware of what inadequate alternatives were available to the dissenters, those they dubbed disruptors or saboteurs. The United Women recognized unity only behind a set of liberal objectives focused on equal educational and work opportunities, which had little relevance for most women, particularly poorer women in poorer areas of the world. "Women were invited to a call to unity among us and to demonstrate that despite differences of ideology, creed, or race, we are all united under the same objectives of equality," Brito told *Xilonen*.[16] Those who disagreed with the United Women's priorities found themselves with little recourse but to challenge the group's legitimacy to represent them.[17] For their part, the women who had labored to put together the United Women's proposals—convening working groups, drafting and redrafting late into the night and through the wee hours of the morning to painstakingly incorporate participants' suggestions—could only see women like Domitila Barrios de Chungara and Marisa de los Andes or the women from CORE and Raza

Figure 15.2 Photo captioned on reverse, "Jacqui Ceballos [NOW] speaking to disruptors"; Domitila Barrios de Chungara appears in left foreground. © Bettye Lane. Courtesy of Schlesinger Library.

Unida as destructive forces seeking to undo everything they had accomplished and offering no concrete alternative proposal that might be incorporated. The United Women's complete refusal to consider anything the group deemed "political" left those who disagreed with no point of entry.

When the commotion died down, Betty Friedan convened an impromptu press conference to tell reporters that the dissenters had confused feminism, which was anti-imperialist and anti-war, with the political repression in their own countries. The tribune meetings, she proclaimed, had demonstrated that the worldwide women's movement was larger, more powerful, and more threatening than anyone had imagined. Asked whether she had attempted to manipulate the tribune meetings, as the protestors had claimed, she laughed, "It's obvious that the tribune is being manipulated, but it is not by the North Americans. It is very strange that in the uproar on Friday, I saw a man pressuring the Latin American women and telling them what they should shout, and I saw that same man in today's set-to. They manipulate [the women] so that they fight against themselves."[18] Unsurprisingly, protesters were miffed by the implication that they were merely puppets of manipulative men, and the Ecuadorian Marisa de los Andes set upon Friedan. Asking why none of the Latin American women's concerns about human rights abuses in Chile, the embargo in Cuba, and the exploitation by transnational corporations appeared in the document produced by US women, de los Andes accused Friedan of being "only concerned with the themes of prostitution and lesbianism."[19] Friedan scrutinized her, turned on her heel, and melted into the crowd.[20]

Friedan's efforts to sway the press were to little avail. "Alongside the powerful current of opinion that holds that true women's liberation is pursued and obtained by seeking the liberation of all those subjugated," editorialized the erstwhile communist Carlos Sánchez Cárdenas in *El Universal*, "the opposite has been expressed, without the force of arguments, by those who take refuge in immediatism, in 'rights,' and in an imprecise demand for 'equality,' and they have tried to prevent the conference from surpassing these impoverished limits."[21] A broader perspective, Sánchez Cárdenas insisted, would prevent "feminists of good faith" from "drowning in resentments, prejudices, and distractions that are stimulated by feminists who try in a calculated manner to contain the movement for women's liberation to serve the interests of capitalism and imperialism." Pointing to Friedan's (*"la señora Friedman"*) complaints that the conference had become too political, he responded, "In the apoliticism of the North American delegate is hidden the politics of opposition to recognizing people's right to liberty."

The only thing the Friedan and de los Andes agreed on was that they were both being pursued by police.[22] Friedan's "Scary Doings in Mexico City" (1976) reads like a Cold War thriller, complete with surveillance, cut phone lines, ominous

Figure 15.3 Security personnel kept a close watch on tribune attendees. © Bettye Lane. Courtesy of Schlesinger Library.

encounters, and "men with guns." They were both mistaken. Although Mexican security police regularly filed reports from the IWY events, they seemed almost entirely preoccupied with what Mexicans said and did: the *campesina* who described the army occupation of Atoyac, Guerrero, and the unexplained disappearances of residents; the Communist Party members who attended a reception at the Cuban embassy; the UNAM professor who told an audience that as soon as the conference ended, everyone who spoke out against the government would be thrown in jail.[23] Marta López Portillo de Tamayo, the president of the WIDF-affiliated Unión Nacional de Mujeres Mexicanas, had been a target of police observation for over a decade; DFS agents watched her closely during the IWY tribune. Those are the types of figures who received more than passing reference in security reports, but the tumultuous events in Mexico City had many participants looking over their shoulders.

Scene 16

The Final Push

If Monday afternoon's abandoned "unity panel" further disintegrated the tribune, the participant-initiated sessions on Tuesday morning would compartmentalize participants even more: four simultaneous sessions took place on IWY objectives and actions, women against imperialism, women and trade unionism, and women in Cuba.[1] Participation continued to fall off as more participants returned to their regular activities—*Excélsior* estimated that only about a quarter of the registrants attended on Tuesday.[2] In a session on "Women Power and the Future," US Congresswoman Bella Abzug tried to counter widespread fatigue with characteristically sardonic cracks dubbing the all-male Senate "stagnation" and joking that becoming a politician had made her fat because she never had time to swim.

When that session let out, the room filled with a group denouncing Latin American detentions, disappearances, and torture and their effects on women and their families. North Vietnamese delegate Nguyen Thi Thao addressed the group in Spanish, commiserating, "If anyone can understand the pain and suffering of oppressed peoples, we can." Domitila Barrios de Chungara again spoke out against conditions in mining communities. A woman from Argentina described the escalating detentions and assassinations carried out by the Argentine Anticommunist Alliance that would bring a military junta to power.[3] Guadalupe Anguiano of the Raza Unida Party sought common cause with Latin American women in proclaiming that Betty Friedan and the US delegation had manipulated the tribune, seeking to secure a World Plan of Action that simply would "substitute maternalism for paternalism, but the oppression would continue." Meanwhile, US and Latin American women met separately to promote dialogue.[4]

Up in Tlatelolco, conference delegates also grew punchy with exhaustion and frustration over objectives left unmet as the end of the conference drew near. Someone passed to Elizabeth Reid a spoof resolution bearing all the apparatus and grammar of an official UN resolution but calling for a *Lysistrata*-style

Figure 16.1 Exhaustion finally got the better of some IWY participants. © Bettye Lane. Courtesy of Schlesinger Library.

"international withholding action" as part of the agenda item to involve women in international peace.[5]

The World Plan of Action did finally escape from the First Committee to be considered and voted upon by the plenary on Monday, with the caveat that the haphazard procedure should not be considered as precedent for future conferences. Instead, amendments, resolutions, and declarations should be submitted several days before the conference to allow sufficient time for delegations to consider and discuss them.[6] The Holy See objected to the language about family planning, and the Chinese delegation abstained because of "differences of principle," but otherwise the committee achieved a precarious consensus on the changes to the introduction and first chapter, on programs for national action. The revised version included what *Xilonen* dismissed as "obligatory references to the New International Economic Order" and "ritual condemnations of apartheid, imperialism, and colonialism" as well as repeated acknowledgments of the different means by which member states might achieve objectives—through the efforts of state agencies, voluntary organizations, or community collectives.[7] The introduction included language about upholding the Charter on the Economic Rights and Duties of States with the disclaimer that states that had opposed CERDS during the General Assembly deliberations continued to do so. Hutar and Jova tried to minimize US differences with CERDS, indicating only small discrepancies over precise language but a general agreement on the

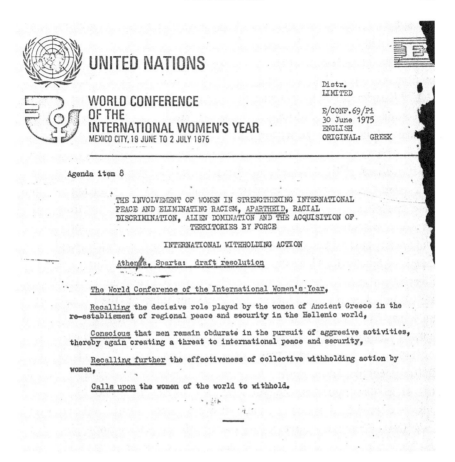

UNITED NATIONS

Distr.
LIMITED

WORLD CONFERENCE
OF THE
INTERNATIONAL WOMEN'S YEAR
MEXICO CITY, 19 JUNE TO 2 JULY 1975

E/CONF.69/P1
30 June 1975
ENGLISH
ORIGINAL: GREEK

Agenda item 8

THE INVOLVEMENT OF WOMEN IN STRENGTHENING INTERNATIONAL
PEACE AND ELIMINATING RACISM, APARTHEID, RACIAL
DISCRIMINATION, ALIEN DOMINATION AND THE ACQUISITION OF
TERRITORIES BY FORCE

INTERNATIONAL WITHHOLDING ACTION

Athena, Sparta: draft resolution

The World Conference of the International Women's Year,

Recalling the decisive role played by the women of Ancient Greece in the
re-establisment of regional peace and security in the Hellenic world,

Conscious that men remain obdurate in the pursuit of aggresive activities,
thereby again creating a threat to international peace and security,

Recalling further the effectiveness of collective withholding action by
women,

Calls upon the women of the world to withhold.

Figure 16.2 This parody bears all the earmarks of a formal proposal to the IWY conference. Courtesy of National Library of Australia.

principle of greater equality.[8] The promising consensus on the World Plan of Action, however, was overshadowed by growing conflict over a G-77 proposal.

The Australian delegation—hoping to succeed in Mexico City where it had not with the consultative committee—had offered a more succinct version of the plan focused on shared concerns rather than a "shopping list" of a few items for each geopolitical bloc. Even its supporters saw the proposal as coming too late for serious consideration, particularly given the crushing number of amendments that already overwhelmed the First Committee. The most pressing concern centered, as ever, on the relationship between improving women's status and the demands for a New International Economic Order. Reid recalled that "a few women who were realistic enough to understand which side had the numbers had attempted to forge tenuous links between these two demands" but that, "although there was an intuitive understanding of the basic importance of the linkage between these two demands, there was still no clear programmatic articulation of it."[9]

Halfway through the conference, the Peruvian delegation had offered an amendment to the Plan's opening paragraph so that, rather than leading with the UN Charter, it would lead with the assertion that the "last vestiges of alien and colonial domination, foreign occupation, racial discrimination, apartheid and neo-colonialism in all its forms are still among the greatest obstacles to the full emancipation and progress of developing countries and of all the peoples concerned."[10] Third World and Warsaw Pact countries lined up in support while a handful of countries, including the United States, United Kingdom, and Chile, challenged the amendment as shifting the plan's focus away from women's issues. Disagreements broke out about procedure—whether amendments would be considered paragraph-by-paragraph, whether the new paragraph overlapped too much with a later one, whether Peru and the UK should confer to try to reach a consensus. The Mexican delegate chimed in to request that CERDS— the "Carta Echeverría"—be included in Peru's amendment. The US delegation challenged the term "neocolonialism" as imprecise and not clearly related to women—to which the Ukrainian delegate responded, "Obviously the U.S. does understand this word," and the Hungarian delegate added, "All countries suffering from neocolonialism know what it means." Again, one delegation after another stated its support for using the term neocolonialism. The committee went back and forth like this, deliberating over every paragraph and, at times, every word. The chair and the secretary tried to move the discussion along, pointing to time constraints; several delegates pleaded that they at least move to discussing the second paragraph.[11]

The First Committee, after considering several strategies for reviewing the 894 submitted amendments, finally acceded to the Sierra Leonean proposal to accept the World Plan of Action as written, altering only the introduction. The amendments about wording would simply be discarded, along with those that the delegates deemed inappropriate. "We must remember that this is not a document binding on Governments," Sierra Leone's Ada Bailor explained, "so the precise wording is not all-important."[12] The committee culled the more substantive amendments into a few "strong resolutions" to be voted on by the conference. Heading into the weekend, two "strong resolutions" emerged: a G-77 resolution on the NIEO and another opposing it.

The proposal that emerged from the closed-door sessions of G-77 countries, dubbed the Declaration of Mexico, not only included language about the "inalienable right of nationalization"—a position that had drawn US and UK opposition for many months—but also listed Zionism among "forms of oppression," such as apartheid and colonialism, that required elimination to achieve women's true emancipation.[13] The first objection, unsurprisingly, came from the Israeli delegation, which insisted that Zionism was "the ideological base of the State of Israel and to demand its elimination is to demand the elimination of the Israeli state." Further, the Israelis asserted, the PLO had no business enjoying representation at the IWY conference, not only because its stated objectives included the destruction of the Israeli state but also because conference deliberations should not include "an organization that deliberately goes out to murder children in school buses and their homes and in markets."[14]

By Tuesday, government delegates grew anxious about how to navigate these conflicts. The plenary convened for ten minutes to receive the draft conference report and promptly adjourned to allow committees to attend to the remaining resolutions. The First Committee, having sent the World Plan of Action to the plenary for consideration, got down to the business of culling the resolutions that would be voted on. The chair moved quickly, pressing some delegates to withdraw redundant resolutions and imploring others to sort out their differences before bringing a consolidated resolution back to the committee.[15]

After deferring some resolutions and dispensing with others, the chair turned to one calling on both national governments and the UN system to allocate sufficient staff and resources to implement the programs set out in the World Plan.[16] The scant, one-page resolution cut to the heart of whether the plan would remain an aspirational set of propositions or would effect significant change in the allocation of resources. As the Filipino delegate put it, "The criticism of the Commission on the Status of Women was that it had no funds and was a paper tool. Are we going on year after year passing resolutions that cannot be implemented?" Margaret Bruce pointed out that only the GA's Fifth Committee—the committee charged with budgetary matters—could make such recommendations but conceded that additional staff could be paid out of the IWY Voluntary Fund. Recognizing the constrained resources, representatives considered whether UN agencies such as the World Health Organization or UNESCO might pursue some of the targets outlined in the World Plan with their funds. The Soviet delegate proposed an amendment such that the UN would meet the demands of the World Plan "within the limits of existing budgets and through a redistribution of existing staff." The committee rejected the Soviet amendment. The Canadian delegate—pointing out that in a recent UN study of how it might expand its role in economic and social development, "among the experts who drew up this report there is not one single woman, nor is there anyone who is interested in the status of women"—proposed adding a fourth paragraph to the resolution calling for the empowerment of the CSW or some other UN body "designed specifically to deal with problems relating to status of women to ensure the implementation of projects set out in WPA and to provide a forum for exchange of views." The amendment passed overwhelmingly. Over objections from several Latin American countries, the Australian delegation shepherded through a resolution on increasing attention to women's health needs, particularly in the area of family planning.

The First Committee then turned its attention to the two controversial declarations, the Declaration of Mexico and another from the United States, the United Kingdom, and West Germany that had been issued in response to it.[17] The two declarations concurred on broad principles about the importance of equal opportunities and incorporating women into political and economic life, about improving the standards of living among the poorest within every community, about sharing responsibilities for family life, and even about some of the international concerns. Like the Declaration of Mexico, the responding declaration included two critical statements: first, that the discrimination against women results in part from the problems of underdevelopment "which exists as a result not only of inadequate internal economic structures but also of a world economic system in need of change" and, second, that the declaration's objectives would only be achieved if international relations were governed by the principles of "the sovereign equality of states, the free self-determination of peoples, the elimination of racial discrimination and of all forms of imperialism, the unacceptability of acquisition of territories by force, territorial integrity, and the non-interference in the domestic affairs of other states, in the manner that relations between human beings should be governed by the supreme principle of absolute equality of men and women." In short, the US- UK-, and West German-sponsored declaration incorporated the main concerns of the Declaration of Mexico, but it pointedly excluded the two most contentious aspects of the latter: the insistence on upholding the Charter of the Economic Rights and Duties of States and the inclusion of Zionism—along with colonialism, neocolonialism, racial discrimination, and apartheid—among those social blights in need of eradication.

The US delegate in the First Committee suggested starting with discussion of its declaration, to which the Soviet delegate promptly responded that the committee should discuss the Declaration of Mexico first. The Filipino, Mexican, and Somalian delegates supported the Soviet proposal; the Ukrainian delegate suggested that both documents might be considered together; and the Canadian and French delegates pointed out that both declarations dealt only obliquely with women and focused mostly on issues that had been discussed in other conferences. The Chilean delegate supported the US-backed proposal, indicating that the Declaration of Mexico mentioned Zionism too frequently. After a brief interlude to discuss a resolution about women's participation in the GA's upcoming special session, the committee returned to the two declarations, and one delegate after another lined up in support of the Declaration of Mexico: the Soviet Union, East Germany, Cuba, Norway, Afghanistan. Belgium—ever the mediator—supported the Canadian statement about the inattention to women and the West German appeal for further negotiations. Algeria moved to close debate; the UK delegate opposed. Yugoslavia backed Algeria; the US delegate opposed. "We have been presented with this declaration on a take-it-or-leave-it basis," the UK delegate protested. "There has been no discussion, and there certainly is no consensus." The chair called a vote on the closure of debate, which passed overwhelmingly, and then a vote on the Declaration of Mexico, which passed with even stronger support. Venezuela requested separate votes on each paragraph where the word Zionism appeared; Venezuela, the United States, and Norway additionally requested separate votes on paragraphs dealing with nationalization and CERDS. These last-ditch efforts all failed. The Declaration of Mexico passed out of the committee with all references to Zionism and economic nationalism still intact on a vote of 89 in favor, 1 (Israel) against, and 14 abstentions. The chair determined that no vote was necessary on the alternative declaration and pronounced the committee's work finished.

Meanwhile, the Second Committee witnessed even more fireworks.[18] When a Cuban resolution demanding that the Chilean military government immediately cease all executions, torture, and persecution passed by unanimous consent, Alicia Romo Román reached the end of her patience, fuming, "I will no longer participate in these meetings. Do what you will, but as a woman I do not want to be complicit nor seen in the future as a puppet of men." Accusing Mexico of hosting the conference only for the opportunity to denigrate Chile, she challenged the UN to send an inspection commission—an offer that would later be withdrawn—and stormed out.[19] Amid heated debates, the committee then approved three other resolutions related to geopolitical conflicts: that the UN would provide aid to assist with the reconstruction of postwar Vietnam; that the Canal Zone be returned to Panama to "eliminate the colonial situation, racism, racial discrimination, and domination and occupation without the consent of the authority which is sovereign in the territory"; and that women proclaim solidarity with Palestinians "in their drive to put an end to the flagrant violations of fundamental human rights committed by Israel in the occupied territories." Although the Vietnam vote enjoyed overwhelming support, the Panama support was considerably more tepid—not least because bilateral negotiations had been under way since the Lyndon Johnson administration.[20] The New Zealand representative Priscilla Williams objected to including a resolution that mentioned women only in a single line that indicated that the colonial situation affected "women as well as men."[21] The vote on the occupied territories drew the most opposition—despite having been sponsored by thirty-four countries—with 71 in favor, 40 abstentions, and 3 votes against. Since the committees intended to operate on a principle of consensus, even three negative votes indicated significant resistance. The Israeli delegate insisted that the resolution rested upon "lies and invented facts" and that he would treat it "with the contempt it deserved," drawing fire from several delegates, including the Jordanian, who described Zionism as "a danger to the world."

The plenary finally reconvened later that afternoon to discuss the rapporteurs' accounts and the draft report of the conference, which still lacked several critical elements.[22] If delegates hoped that these final sessions would resolve their differences, they were badly disappointed. For four hours, the plenary deliberated over the draft report. The Israeli delegation tried in vain to push through a resolution calling for collaboration between Jewish and Arab women to work toward peace. The Cuban delegation succeeded in adding two paragraphs to the report's summary of general debate: one indicating that "many speakers made references to the constant violations of human rights that had taken place in Chile" and another praising the Soviet Union's role in promoting nuclear disarmament.[23] The proposal passed overwhelmingly, precipitating more protests from the Chilean delegation and a reiteration of the empty invitation to send a UN inspection team. Ojeda Paullada finally called a vote on the draft report, which passed handily but with 13 abstentions and 42 other delegations apparently not voting. The delegates then adjourned for dinner.

By the time the plenary reconvened at 10:30 P.M., it had become clear that the debate would not wrap up easily. Some delegates had reluctantly cancelled their return tickets for the next morning and frantically called their home offices to report on developments. Other delegations had simply left a token representative to cast a vote and sent the rest of their contingents home. The evening session opened with geopolitical sparks as the Albanian delegate—a Chinese ally in the Sino-Soviet rivalry that had flared up repeatedly in Mexico City—challenged the Cuban characterization of the Soviet role, accusing the latter of blackmail and tricks.[24] In an effort to expedite matters, the plenary began to adopt draft resolutions from the First Committee without a vote. The first two—on research and training for the advancement of African women and on international cooperation to achieve World Plan of Action objectives—sailed through smoothly. The third resolution condemned apartheid in South Africa, Southern Rhodesia, and Namibia and—most controversially—called for political, economic, social, and military sanctions "with the aim of isolating the minority and racist regimes." The US and UK delegations asked that votes be taken on the remaining resolutions; the Egyptian delegate asked that decisions be taken by a simple majority of representatives present and voting. Calling votes on the remaining resolutions inevitably slowed things down. On the very next vote, on the UN's role in implementing the World Plan, the Soviet Union called for a separate vote on the paragraphs with budgetary implications. Several Latin American nations and the Holy See explained their votes on a resolution about women and health that included language about family planning. Ojeda Paullada finally adjourned the plenary in the wee hours of the morning, having passed only the six resolutions from the First Committee. The plenary would reconvene the next morning to discuss the Declaration of Mexico and the remaining resolutions from the Second Committee.

Scene 17

Unceremonious Closing

The tribune came to a close much as it had begun: with the Margarita Maza de Juárez Women's Movement demonstrating on the esplanade of the Medical Center and a mariachi band performing; a participant from the previous afternoon's session of Latin American women circulating with a petition demanding freedom for political prisoners; and a Spanish woman denouncing the Franco regime.[1] A group of women from the southern Mexican state of Guerrero stood up in the auditorium to express their grievances but were drowned out as Crispin Vázquez's brass band took the stage for the next forty minutes, playing a string of classic mariachi tunes before leading the audience in a melancholy rendition of "Las Golondrinas." Tribunistas danced and sang, snaking through the esplanade in an international conga line while the shyer among them watched from a safe distance.[2] Persinger thanked the Mexican government and all those who expended "their last ounce of effort" to plan and execute the tribune. "We saw here that the Tribune women are not concerned about their own advancement only," Persinger told those remaining. "They are concerned about the advancement of human kind. They are concerned not just about women's rights, but about human rights; not just about the benefits of development for women, but a new economic order for men and women; not for peace at any price, but for peace with justice." Then, giving her audience its marching orders, she declared, "Those who came here are leaders. If the women and men who gathered these past weeks in Mexico do not set a sure course on the tides of change, then the leaders will have ceased to lead."[3] By two o'clock, overall-clad maintenance workers mixed with the lingering participants who hugged, snapped photos, and exchanged addresses. Uniformed police inspected the meeting rooms of the Medical Center, waving their truncheons, as a voice came over the loudspeaker instructing stragglers to vacate the premises. Within minutes, the esplanade was empty.[4]

By the time security guards began brandishing their nightsticks in the Centro Médico, the government delegates in Tlatelolco had just stopped for a lunch break. They had spent the morning discussing the first fourteen of the

Figure 17.1 Cleaning up after IWY, from the *Washington Post*, 2 July 1975. Mike Peters EDTCTN (new) © 1975 King Features Syndicate.

twenty-eight resolutions that came out of the Second Committee's discussions. Many of them were waved through without a vote. No controversy arose on the questions of preventing the exploitation of women and girls and increasing the number of professional women at the UN, for example, despite disagreements over what constituted "exploitation" and concerns that efforts to increase women's representation in the UN system would come at the expense of geographic representation, since so few Third World countries sent women to the UN. A few resolutions that had mentioned family planning or had significant budgetary implications for member states—such as the one on social security and family security for women—required votes and some commentary, but they all passed handily. A few of the resolutions drew modest amendments, such as the Guatemalan delegate proposing the addition of two paragraphs calling for particular attention to integrating indigenous women into the development process. Some of the resolutions that seemed likely to draw controversy cruised through without a vote, such as one calling for the elimination of "tasteless" images of women in the media and another calling for a wholesale reclassification of occupations to eliminate designations of suitability for a particular sex. As the plenary clicked through all the twenty-one resolutions related to the ninth and tenth agenda items—on the integration of women in development and the major obstacles to equality—everything was smooth sailing.

The ride got a bit bumpier when the meeting turned to the remaining seven resolutions, related to the eighth agenda item on the "involvement of women in strengthening international peace and eliminating racism, apartheid, racial discrimination, colonialism, alien domination and acquisition of territories by force." The resolution on the Canal Zone required a vote. The Israeli delegation insisted on a roll-call vote on the resolution on Palestinian and Arab women, which drew only 2 votes against—Israel and the United States—but 36 abstentions. Israel and seven other delegations then made statements explaining their votes. The resolution on Chile passed without a vote but with considerable commentary. Before turning to the Declaration of Mexico, fifteen delegations offered statements about their reservations or concerns about the resolutions.

If consensus seemed frayed by the time the plenary concluded commentary about the resolutions, the discussion and vote on the Declaration of Mexico revealed how little common ground the delegations shared. The Israeli delegation demanded a roll-call vote on all the paragraphs that mentioned Zionism. By a divided vote of 61 in favor to 23 against, with 25 abstentions, the plenary voted to retain the word. The Declaration then passed overwhelmingly with only 2 no votes (once again, the United States and Israel) and 19 abstentions. Thirty-two delegations offered reservations or explanations after the vote, most of them expressing misgivings about the language on Zionism but generally supporting what many saw as a much stronger document than the World Plan of Action itself. Several delegations took the commentary period as an opportunity to re-ignite enmities that had sparked and sometimes flared during the conference. Saying the Soviets favored a "false détente and a false disarmament," the Chinese charged the two superpowers with attacking and then invading small countries and blamed them both for the bloody situation in Chile.[5] The United States, which had remained notably reticent during these final two days of deliberations, declared it "seemed there had been a campaign against the State of Israel."[6]

The conference vote to adopt the language against Zionism marked the first time a UN document would create this equivalence between Zionism and racism—a debate that would roil the General Assembly over the coming years. For the US delegation, the addition of language about Zionism into the Declaration of Mexico arguably offered a fig leaf for opposition that had already been assured with the inclusion of language about the New International Economic Order and the Charter on the Economic Rights and Duties of States. The reference to CERDS in the World Plan of Action carried a carefully worded footnote specifying that it "should not be interpreted as indicating a change in the positions of delegations on the Charter as stated at the twenty-ninth session of the General Assembly."[7] The US State Department had girded itself for a fight over Israel for months. Meeting with Daniel Patrick Moynihan, who would replace John Scali as UN ambassador in the middle of the IWY conference, Ford and Kissinger predicted that Israel would be a flashpoint during his time at the UN.[8] Stressing that the US mission would still seek to build consensus, Moynihan noted, "The only consensus now is screw the United States.

The reputation of the US keeps eroding and that reputation is important to us." UNESCO's expulsion of Israel, he argued, provided an opportunity for the United States to stand firm and demonstrate that it could not be pushed around by the non-aligned countries. "For twenty-five years there have been high politics and low politics in State," Moynihan told Kissinger and Ford. "High politics was security and that was where reputations work. The UN, etc., was low politics; where Mrs. Roosevelt and those who weren't up to the struggle went. If word went out that words matter, we could turn this around."[9] The vote on the Declaration of Mexico—and the UN's decision to list Zionism alongside apartheid, racism, and alien domination—offered the first opportunity during Moynihan's tenure to put the word out that words matter.

Many supporters of the Declaration of Mexico remained ambivalent about listing Zionism among the geopolitical injustices. Still, even the United States, as the Ford Foundation's Adrienne Germain reported later, recognized the Declaration as "one of the best documents of the conference."[10] Rather than the anticipated polemic, it offered a "concise, thoughtful, and substantive statement" stressing that "women of the entire world, whatever differences exist between them, had in common the painful experience of having received unequal treatment." Indeed, people like Elizabeth Reid, ZuZu Tabatabai, and Aída González had collaborated at meetings in New York and Mexico City in hopes of producing a pithier, more inspiring document than the World Plan of Action—a sort of utopian manifesto calibrated to foster a sense of urgency and to galvanize actors to create a new world.[11] The Declaration conjured a world in which the UN had real sway and member states remained true to the UN Charter and the Declaration of Human Rights. Where the World Plan of Action focused on treating symptoms—illiteracy, child marriage, malnutrition—the Declaration tried to excavate underlying causes in colonialism, racism, and economic imperialism.[12] Where the World Plan often positioned women as critical instruments to achieve national and international goals of economic growth and population control, the Declaration inverted that approach—advocating development to relieve women of the "double burden of exploitation" and stressing "child-rearing should not be the cause of inequality and discrimination" but "shared responsibilities among women, men, and society as a whole." Where the World Plan had interim goals (for 1980) and decade-long projects, the Declaration insisted upon the urgency of transformations, calling for "immediate improvement" and demanding that the exploitation of women in developing countries be "rapidly eliminated." Where the World Plan interpellated the Third World cosmopolitan woman—an educated, relatively privileged professional woman who would lead her compatriot sisters into modern liberation—the Declaration asserted that women's universally shared experience of discrimination and marginality rendered them "natural allies in the struggle against any form of oppression" and imbued them with "enormous revolutionary potential for economic and social change in the world today." The World Plan of Action, grumbled New Zealand delegate and ICW leader Miriam Dell, had rendered women as "more effective cogs in a man-made machine."[13] Reid, González, and Tabatabai had hoped that something like the Declaration might supersede the World Plan, leaving the latter as a more pragmatic—if wordy—to-do list, while the punchier Declaration would circulate to everyone from grassroots activists to heads of state. After the consultative committee meetings, Reid had traveled to Mexico City, where she met with González for a "very informal and frank" conversation that Reid opened "by expressing her dissatisfaction with the draft World Plan of Action."[14] González concurred, describing it as "a shallow document and too American-biased" and attributing the problem to US NGOs' "pull within the UN" and "applying pressure in [Margaret] Bruce's office." The two agreed that the draft more closely represented the concerns of developed rather than developing countries and anticipated that the working group established during the consultative committee meetings might continue its work in hopes of achieving a better balance. González had proposed adding a short preamble to the Plan of Action—no more than ten points—to ensure that development concerns got their due.[15] Failure to produce a significant document for the future would be a "disaster," they concurred, and it was critical that there only be one document rather than two.[16] Otherwise, they agreed, the World Plan risked becoming yet another document tossed upon a pile of many others that had made little difference in women's lives. The Declaration in the end incorporated elements of Tabatabai's working paper, Reid's suggestions from the working group, and the Declaration of Caracas that had stressed the importance of CERDS. *El Universal* declared it a triumph of the "Carta Echeverría," although it bore the clear imprint of dedicated and well-situated feminists.[17] It did not become a preamble to the World Plan of Action, but in December the UN would publish the two together as if it were.[18] Only later would the World Plan of Action emerge as the sole document of record.

It was nearly 11 P.M. when Helvi Sipilä delivered her closing remarks to the government conference. After thanking the host country for its hospitality and saluting the bleary-eyed delegates, she offered a series of statements about the conference's novelty—about a UN conference focused on women that dominated the front pages rather than the "women's pages" of major newspapers. If some had bemoaned the conference's political entanglements, Sipilä saw them not as the enduring influence of men at a conference on women's issues but rather as evidence that women had more assertively entered the political realm. Although deliberations over the World Plan of Action and the Declaration of Mexico had highlighted the areas of conflict, they also had demonstrated an increasingly shared set of commitments to eliminating discrimination and economic injustice. "And isn't this what all of us desired out of the Conference: A deep human experience in which the longings of all women all over the world for justice and a better life were palpably experienced on a person-to-person and a nation-to-nation basis?" she asked. "We leave here with a new vision. Now, tired though we are, the real work has just begun."[19]

The departure from Mexico City was less dramatic than the arrival had been. Both tribune-goers and official delegates had left in dribs and drabs for over a week; only a rump group remained, and a few stayed on to travel or to tidy up loose ends. A handful of media fellows from the journalists' encounter stayed on for a two-day workshop sponsored by UNESCO. Three hundred Latin American *campesinas* who had been brought by the Mexican government to attend an agricultural training workshop had their final breakfast with the First Lady and participated in an oratory contest.[20] Those IWY participants who had arrived in Mexico with hopes of reaching consensus around a unified agenda left with an understanding that such an outcome remained impossible. Some had even reached the conclusion that it would be undesirable.

ACT III

LEGACIES

Scene 18

Beyond Mexico City

"We consider the experience in Mexico to be a turning point for the future," wrote the Thai participant Mallica Vajrathon. "5,000 of us from different parts of the world came together, and on top of that, we came from different class structures. The miners were with the daughters of the President and the wives of the VIPs. The men never had anything equivalent!"[1] USIA officer Dorothy Robins-Mowry compared it to Seneca Falls; *Chicago Defender*'s Ethel Payne likened it to Bandung.[2] "It is safe to venture," Payne reported after the conference, "that after Mexico City, the world will not be the same. The rising tide of expectations has gone past evolution to revolution."[3] *The Nation* somewhat begrudgingly dubbed it "historic."[4] The Ghanaian businesswoman Esther Ocloo recalled ten years later, "One had to be in Mexico to believe the level to which the declaration of International Women's Year raised the consciousness and solidarity of women. . . . It seemed as if there was a strong call to all men and women: 'All hands on deck'—to save the world through women."[5]

This sentiment reverberated so many times it almost seemed scripted—and it referred almost invariably not to the formal negotiations at the official conference but to the informal brainstorming sessions of the development workshop or the unpredictable, chaotic encounters at the tribune. Describing the Mexico City conference as an "astonishing experience," Adrienne Germain elaborated, "In Bucharest there had been an NGO forum, but really tightly controlled and more or less attuned to the UN process. The UN—the NGO forum in Mexico City—they had wanted to control, but in fact because so many women came they couldn't really control it to the extent of Bucharest."[6] Helvi Sipilä wrote in a note of appreciation to Mildred Persinger, "I have followed with great interest the developments in the Tribune, and want you to know how many people have expressed to me the thought: 'X shall never be the same again.' . . . For creating the setting for these experiences, all of us at the United Nations and women everywhere will be in your debt forever."[7] Sarah Goddard Power, the chair of the US national commission for UNESCO, described the tribune as "the place where the action was" and applauded Persinger's "quiet, competent stewardship," echoing Sipilä's sentiments, "In my judgment our government and many women are in your debt."[8]

US diplomat Barbara White related to Ambassador Moynihan that, despite what she saw as political distractions of Zionism and CERDS, the "catalytic effect of the conference" would make a significant difference. "In all the UN meetings I have attended over the past two years, I heard more talk during this conference than in any other of what people—both governmental and non-governmental— intend to do when they get home," she reported.[9] But all this promise, warned the French Minister of Women's Affairs, Françoise Giroud, would amount to nothing without dedicated follow-through. "Throughout history," she told reporters, "men have got women to fight their revolutions, but once the fight is terminated, the women return to making coffee. And International Women's Year will have been one more trick if it is subtly deviated toward political goals, national or international, no matter how urgent, respectable or noble."[10]

One thing is certain: women definitely did not go back to making coffee. Many took seriously Sipilä's directive that they return to their communities and make the IWY program their own but found that the geopolitical fracturing that occurred in Mexico City was reproduced writ small around the politics of everyday life—conflicts over land and resources and political office, over family loyalties and religious convictions, over differences of race, ethnicity, and generation. Still, the IWY gatherings galvanized women from a wide range of backgrounds and with diverse objectives and aspirations to take up causes that would define women's activism for decades. Drawing from discussions and experiences in Mexico City, four areas particularly inspired enthusiasm among participants: media, NGO networks, credit, and future conferences to sustain momentum. Each of these areas developed in unexpected ways in subsequent decades and brought more ambiguous results than participants had anticipated, but they served as critical focal points for those returning home from Mexico City to use in translating their energy into action.

Countless publications—some explicitly feminist, others simply directed at women's concerns—started up after the conference. Glen and Mildred Leet's Hotline IWY would, over decades, become a model for conference communication and future activist networking.[11] As much as the organizers and participants hoped to foster a "continuous town meeting of the world," Hotline IWY in practice reiterated and even amplified the voices of the New York–based NGO committee. The Hotline task force in Mexico City consisted entirely of regular members of Esther Hymer's committee as well as a few newcomers such as Fran Hosken, and its postings generally reported on committee members' activities at the tribune and conference.[12] While participants in "focal points" broadened the perspective somewhat beyond New York, Marshall McLuhan's imaginary that "the new electronic interdependence recreates the world in the image of the global village" remained a distant aspiration.[13]

Fran Hosken's WIN News continued until 2003 and published several of Hosken's monographs on female circumcision. In Mexico, the experience of the mass media at the IWY conference—including the impact of *Xilonen* and the Mexican government's own glossy monthly magazine—convinced many feminist leaders that they should concentrate their energies on producing feminist publications analogous to *Ms.* magazine.[14] A group of the Mexican Women's Liberation Movement leadership broke off only months after the IWY events and created the radical collective La Revuelta, which focused solely on producing a magazine of the same name.[15] *La Revuelta* founder Eli Bartra explicitly links the timing to the 1975 IWY conference.[16] Another *La Revuelta* founder, Berta Hiriart, describing herself as a theater type and "not very political," remembers that she had gone with a group of friends to stage some street theater outside the IWY government conference. After that, she recalls, "some of the women from the group were hooked by the feminist movement. We began to go to the meetings, we began to learn a lot of things, we began to read."[17] Several of the remaining Women's Liberation leaders, while continuing other activist endeavors, worked on producing the magazine *fem*, which remained in print until 2005 and most closely resembles *Ms.* "It was the mid-70s," recalls Elena Urrutia about the advent of *fem*, "and a small group of women had already for some years been manifesting our reflections, denunciations, and feminist criticisms through the media within our reach: some in newspapers and magazines, some in radio and eventually television, some in the university. . . . The UN International Women's Year, in 1975 and the consequent International Conference celebrated in Mexico that same year did nothing more than legitimate our concerns and demonstrate to us that our idea of a feminist publication was in effect—as we had thought—a necessity."[18]

The other necessity that participants in Mexico City had identified—particularly in the women and development seminar—was access to credit. In December 1976, the IWY Voluntary Fund became UNIFEM (the UN Development Fund for Women), under the direction of Margaret Snyder, which focused on providing financial and technical assistance.[19] The World Bank created a new position of advisor on women in development, appointing Jamaican economist Gloria Scott to the post. And an idea that arose during the preconference seminar on women and development—of creating ways for women to gain access to credit—grew into Women's World Banking under the leadership of Michaela Walsh of the Rockefeller Brothers Fund.[20] "In advance of the Mexico City conference," recalled Comfort Engmann, a member of the Ghanaian National Council of Women and Development, "we brought women together from all over the country who were operating 'micro-businesses.' We thought that what they needed was education. They pointed out that their daughters who had gone through school were powerless because they didn't have capital, so they couldn't work. They thought that money in the poor person's pocket was the answer. The women made me humble. When I went among them in the markets, they gave me wisdom. I saw that they were right."[21] The bank would give small loans to women who lacked collateral and still serves as a source not only of microfinance but also savings and insurance—an approach that held appeal across a broad ideological spectrum. "This," Esther Hymer's committee noted candidly during its first post-conference meeting, "is a specific answer to the implementation of the New Economic Order."[22]

Hymer's assessment reflected an increasingly influential branch of economic thought at the time. Along with the rise of civil society, the mid-1970s brought what became known as neoliberalism—a growing faith that market forces would resolve all social and political ills. Neoliberalism first became prominent on the world stage during IWY itself, not least in the figure of Milton Friedman, who would win the Nobel Prize in economics the following year. Sara Dowse, the US-born feminist who helped lead the Australian IWY delegation and succeeded Elizabeth Reid as director of Women's Affairs, recalls that 1975 opened with a visit to Australia by Friedman, "doyen of the Chicago school of economics, crusader for monetarism, as it was known at the time."[23] In February 1975, Margaret Thatcher assumed leadership of the UK's Conservative Party, touting the ideas of Friedman and Friedrich von Hayek; she became prime minister in 1979, a year before the like-minded Ronald Reagan would be elected president of the United States.

Many advocates of women's microcredit, however, saw their efforts as countering rather than supporting Thatcherist and Reaganist economic policies. Glen and Mildred Leet, who had run Hotline IWY, founded the Trickle Up Foundation after a visit to the Caribbean island of Dominica spurred them to think in new ways about their shared concern for the world's poorest inhabitants. "Trickle Up was founded in 1979 at a time when 'trickle down' economics was the conventional wisdom," they explain. "The economic philosophy of the time was that if you invest in business at the highest level of society, the benefits would eventually trickle down to the rest of the population. Even foreign aid distribution, for all its good intentions, operated from the same perspective. Yet we watched the poor getting poorer while the rich benefited from this approach."[24] The following year, Women's World Banking—dubbed the "Mexican WWB baby"—was officially incorporated in the Netherlands with an emphasis on supporting small- and medium-scale endeavors.[25]

The UN would convene three subsequent conferences: a 1980 conference in Copenhagen to take stock of progress toward the Decade of Women goals, a 1985 conference in Nairobi to mark the decade's conclusion, and a 1995 conference in Beijing to assess women's status twenty years after IWY. These four gatherings—referred to in short by their locales—have come to periodize the contemporary global women's movement, providing shared points of reference to indicate shifts in strategies and dynamics. Mexico City marked a watershed—abandoning what had been a protocol-bound, institution-centric, Euro-American based movement of women who enjoyed class and educational privileges and opening up an iconoclastic movement of seemingly boundless diversity that experimented with new strategies and created new organizations, many of them based in the Third World and led by the very postcolonial women who had gained prominence during IWY. Reflecting on what made the Mexico City meetings "momentous," Indian economist Devaki Jain explained, "The subject of women was as yet too undefined . . . the era of pure feminism was over."[26] Barely a month after returning home from Mexico City, she and Ela Bhatt, the founder of India's Self-Employed Women's Association (SEWA), had begun to follow up on contacts they had made during the AAAS women and development seminar.[27] "So Mexico, therefore, was a defining moment for me," Jain recalled nearly three decades later. "It was the group that met in Mexico that has still maintained its friendship."[28]

Well before the tumult outside Waldheim's inaugural address, IWY already had given a boost to women's organizing around the world as countries prepared for the Mexico City conference and responded to mandates from within and without to take women more seriously. "Presently, our women are undergoing a transformation which will put them in a better position to develop their traditional values to blend well with the requirements of the new world," Nigerian reporter Laitan Falase explained at the journalists' encounter. "In this respect, a number of organizations are currently championing the cause of women in all spheres, and the declaration of 1975 as International Women's Year has added more drive to the process of change."[29] Thirty years later, Kenyan environmentalist and Nobel laureate Waangari Maathai described the process to an interviewer.[30] "It was around the mid-1970s," Maathai explained, "and many women will remember that was the year when women of the world met in Mexico during the very first United Nations conference on women. It was that conference, by the way, that declared the first women's decade, and we were preparing in Kenya for us to go and participate at that meeting. And it was during that preparation that I listened to the women from the rural areas, and as they articulated their issues, their agendas, their concerns, I noticed that they were talking about the need for fire wood, the need for energy, the need for clean drinking water, the need for food, and the need for income, and all of these connected very closely to the environment. They were complaining because the environment in which they were living could no longer sustain them because it had become degraded, mostly because it had become converted into commercial farms of tea, which were focused on income rather than how to sustain the life in the rural areas."

The process that Maathai described took place in countless communities all over the world around all kinds of concerns, fostering networks and organizations that would endure in one form or another for decades. In Pakistan, the Shirkat Gah—to this day one of the country's most vibrant organizations working for a "gender just society"—started as a collective in 1975 in response to IWY. Its executive director, Farida Shaheed, recalls that Pakistan sent only a small delegation to Mexico City, led by First Lady Nusrat Bhutto, but that the conference "put women on the national agenda" with an emphasis not only on civil and political rights but also on human rights and economic and cultural justice; in 1975, Pakistan passed a declaration on the rights of Pakistani women.[31] "By the end of the [1960s, feminists'] influence had been felt at the United Nations, which responded with a variety of measures, including the series of conferences on women's issues, which began with the 1975 International Women's Year Conference in Mexico City," explains anthropologist Millie Thayer of the transformations of the Brazilian outback. "These events brought together activists—including many Brazilians—from around the world, and spawned a multiplicity of transnational feminist networks, alliances and coalitions."[32]

In places that already had active women's movements, the IWY conference served, according to sociologist Norma Stoltz Chinchilla describing Latin American countries, as an "important catalyst" for women's organizing. "Preparations for and follow-up from the conference stimulated the formation of many official and unofficial groups and conferences," she explains, "conferring on them a degree of legitimacy, protection from political persecution, and, in some cases, access to external funding."[33] Although these endeavors—particularly state-led projects—often focused on educated, professional women or party stalwarts, they created an organizational infrastructure that would support activists from many different corners, from trade unionists to students and even opposition parties.

The energy and excitement generated by the IWY tribune fostered a proliferation of NGOs. In Mexico City, after all, participants and journalists consistently referred to the tribune as "where the action was." For many activists who had found themselves at the margins of official policymaking, NGOs seemed to offer a radical democratic alternative—a means of effecting policy outside the state apparatus. The IWY conference—and, even more, the NGO tribune—had raised awareness among grassroots organizers about a new model of organizing in civil society—one that involved a greater level of collaboration with outside groups and with funding organizations. Grassroots organizations that had operated as collectives on shoestring budgets suddenly found they could access funds from private foundations headquartered in London, Amsterdam, and New York City. In addition, NGO networks offered international contacts, training opportunities, and infrastructural support, granting access to otherwise unimaginable resources.[34] To be sure, many activists were, to say the least, ambivalent about this turn. As Farida Shaheed explains of Pakistani organizations' decision to decline external funding, "We felt that during the resistance movement to the military [in the 1980s] that there were strings attached when you have funding from outside."[35]

Given the experiences in Mexico City, where many activists had felt the sharp divide between the consultative-status NGOs and newer and emergent activist groups, many organizations saw an opportunity to claim state and foundation resources that otherwise remained the exclusive quarry of more establishmentarian organizations.[36] "The conference served to open the UN to many more NGOs," explains participant Devaki Jain. "While earlier it was the bigger, more established NGOs that attended the international conferences, at Mexico City, many smaller, South-based nontraditional NGOs found a meaningful space for themselves that went beyond tokenism."[37] Distinguishing the consultative-status NGOs—"what we called the conservative brand of NGOs"—from what emerged later, Jain told an interviewer, "that was one kind of women's organization. But after Mexico, it changed. There were the newer international networks and international connections."[38] After the exhilaration of the tribune, many activists shared one participant's view that it had "fantastic potential as a fruitful learning-teaching-sharing device and even perhaps as an embryonic 'parliament of the world' both for pressuring progress from stolid governments and for mobilizing a vital international consensus and the political will of affected groups to act."[39]

Soon after she recovered from Mexico City, Mildred Persinger set about establishing the International Women's Tribune Centre (IWTC), which served as a critical resource—particularly in the pre-Internet days—for planning subsequent NGO forums as well as for NGO members who wanted to maintain connections or share experiences.[40] The IWTC started a database of the 6,000 people who registered at the NGO tribune—having no way to track the estimated 1,200 predominantly Mexican participants who walked in once registration was eliminated—that became a resource for those seeking to make connections regionally or on particular issues. The network, like the tribune itself, was open to any NGO that signed up. Having gone through a crash course in tribune planning, Persinger designed the IWTC as a cumulative resource of experiences gained from organizing NGO tribunes. She and others also recognized the growing difficulty of managing the amount of information and documentation produced by UN conferences and their accompanying NGO tribunes and hoped that the IWTC would provide a reliable way to archive all the materials.

Margaret Snyder, the veteran of the Economic Commission on Africa, remembered the period immediately following the Mexico City conference as a golden age of collaboration among NGOs, governments, funding organizations, and international organizations. "But none of them dictated exactly how the money should be spent," she recalled, "so we proposed what should be done, and they agreed. It was an era of new ideas before the turf wars among and within institutions set in. Everybody wanted to join this lively thing that was happening, and there was a very good network of UN civil servants to support that momentum."[41]

If NGO boosters like Esther Hymer and Patricia Hutar imagined a grassroots "private sector," as they described it, in which the drivers of social change resided outside of state apparatuses, the reality was far more ambiguous. The lines between governmental and non-governmental blurred not only in socialist and newly decolonized countries, where state entities played a visible role in women's organizing, but also in places like Australia and the United States, which celebrated an autonomous civil society. Dorothy Height, of the National Council of Negro Women, explained to an interviewer a few months after the conference that USAID funding had underwritten important networking opportunities among women of color across geopolitical divides. Asked whether differences of class and educational backgrounds hindered communication in the group that the NCNW convened, Height explained, "I think you also have to bear in mind that when you're in a group of 6,000, and you come into a group of forty or fifty, and you have a chance to have close contact with people, to talk about problems that you're interested in, to share experiences and learn something, that a lot of those differences of age or whatever" disappear.[42] After the conference, an impressive group of twenty-five mostly African and Caribbean government ministers, lawmakers, and political leaders traveled for two weeks with NCNW women to Mississippi and then Florida.[43] (The visitors received a taste of southern hospitality when two high-level diplomats—the Senegalese vice-president of ECOSOC and the Sierra Leonean representative of the Organization for African Unity—were picked up on a false shoplifting accusation, precipitating a diplomatic kerfuffle.)[44]

Even in this instance—with a well-established NGO collaborating with the agency that many in Mexico City vilified as the Janus-faced emissary of US imperialism—there were limits to how much control the funding entities could exercise. When Daniel Parker had announced the USAID support, he stressed the importance of NCNW's dedication to "self-help development."[45] While Parker understood that emphasis to mean that it would encourage less resource-intensive projects that would rely mainly on the human capital in a community, Height connected it to community organizing and allowing communities to define their own development needs. If Parker thought Height would be an ambassador for US foreign policy among Third World women's organizations, Height saw herself bringing influence in the other direction. She pointed to a principle held by Tanzanian President Julius Nyerere and other G-77 leaders that they not only benefit from development programs but also shape them.[46] When asked what had come out of the IWY conference and tribune, Height explained, "I think it was very significant that people began to get some sense of their differences. There were women there from Communist countries as well as from other socialist countries, as well as capitalist countries. There was a really strong anticapitalism, anti-imperialism thrust that kept swelling."[47]

While participants such as Devaki Jain and Dorothy Height celebrated the diverse, even combative encounters that allowed participants to develop a "sense of their differences," other participants and observers tried to give meaning to Mexico City by imposing some coherence and legibility on the chaos. What had been a partial perspective emerged as the predominant narrative, at least among English speakers. This consolidation began almost immediately, as organizers, journalists, and participants submitted reports and accounts summing up the events.[48] Like the planning of the tribune and conference itself, constraints of resources and logistics meant that those who had most powerfully shaped the IWY narrative continued to do so. When Betty Reardon, a scholar of peace education and a panelist for the session on peace and disarmament, organized a follow-up IWY conference in New York for those who had not made it to Mexico, she invited Mildred Persinger to offer a "global perspective" on the tribune, the *New York Times*'s Judy Klemesrud to present an overview, Margaret Bruce to explain the World Plan of Action, and UN-based Jamaican development economist Gloria Scott to present on the UN's new women in development policies.[49] The first generation of publications about the conference came from US participants, particularly women like Arvonne Fraser and Virginia Allan who had served on the US government delegation.[50]

In these tellings, the United Women of the Tribune and their allies in the Coalition of Latin American Women—those groups that emphasized an equality agenda—consistently appeared as making "constructive" and "helpful" interventions, while critics such as Domitila Barrios de Chungara and Wynta Boynes were dubbed "disruptors," seemingly manipulated by men, who sought only to undermine any attempt at unity. "Underfunded and underpublicized, the IWY Conference in Mexico quickly floundered and sank amidst a multitude of antagonistic groups and general hypocrisy," Miki Sharron wrote in the California-based feminist newspaper *Sister*. Describing what she saw as men's domination of the government conference and the "total disorganization" of the NGO tribune, she observed, "Sadly, many of the groups and discussions had nothing whatsoever to do with women. Many dealt with issues outside of the scope of the IWY conference, the purpose of which was to promote the equality of women."[51] Once again US-based coverage tried to segregate "politics" from "women's issues" and reduced the latter to equality; the notion that the imagined unity simply did not hold together due to IWY's own centrifugal forces seemed inconceivable.

In the end, neither the conference nor the tribune could claim any real consensus. The World Plan of Action and, more emphatically, the Declaration of Mexico had garnered approval but only with a long list of reservations and disclaimers. The English-language *Xilonen* reporter reiterated the idea that an all-women conference would have been more congenial, indicating "male commissars taking the microphone at tricky political moments" to keep "harsh political realities" front and center.[52] Setting aside the intense conflicts among women in the halls of the Centro Médico, the *Washington Post* echoed this notion, reporting vaguely, "Many women stressed that in the corridors, where women talk privately, agreement was easy."[53] The tribune, the *El Universal* columnist Laura Bolaños explained, achieved even higher levels of disorder and dissent as participants "filled the auditoriums to the rafters and overflowed, seizing for themselves the freedom of expression" despite efforts to curtail it. "Never have so many and such things been said before an international audience," she proclaimed, describing the participants as "dominated by progressive, democratic, and anti-imperialist tendencies" of the NGOs. "There were, no doubt," she admitted, "outbursts of every type: sexist, quaint, incoherent, and idiotic to the point of drawing laughter; but the serious and consistent part of the struggle, the deep understanding of the issue and the true objectives, spread throughout the auditorium."[54] Tribune director Marcia-Ximena Bravo, speaking to *Excélsior* after the tribune closed, claimed the clashes as a victory. "Nobody could speak in the name of the Tribune," she explained. "Here the only things that took place were a confrontation of thoughts, an exchange of ideas, a conflict of opinions, and it lent itself to a mosaic of ideologies; nobody can claim a unanimous decision."[55]

Just as in the proposal and planning of the IWY conference, in its aftermath politics was always part of the equation, particularly within the UN itself. Historian Mark Mazower argues that by the mid-1970s the General Assembly had effectively radicalized itself into irrelevance. "Far from becoming a greater check to the ambitions of the world's great powers," he contends, "the General Assembly was increasingly written off as nothing more than a talking shop. Politics at the UN became ever more about symbols and ever less about substance. It was as though decolonization marked not only the UN's triumph but its world-historical culmination."[56] Mazower may overstate the case, since most people experience the UN not through the General Assembly but rather through its many agencies and often indirectly; GA theatrics form only a small part of the picture. Devaki Jain explains, "From 1974 to 2000, in my own life—but I am only an example of others—all of us have been very much more influential in [specialized] agencies than maybe the UN General Assembly or the CSW."[57]

The Declaration of Mexico, unsurprisingly, generated an immediate backlash. Betty Friedan and Helvi Sipilä both received letters from outraged Jewish women about the anti-Zionism statement.[58] Several governments that had supported the Declaration of Mexico tried to distance themselves from the anti-Zionist language.[59] At July's ECOSOC session in Geneva, delegates assiduously avoided reopening the Zionism issue in its discussion of IWY. "Unfortunately, this mood of conciliation was not respected by the Israeli observer," the Australian delegate reported, "who made a brief but impassioned statement at the conclusion of the debate in favour of Zionism, 'the noblest liberation movement of them all.'"[60] Four months later, the General Assembly would cite the Declaration of Mexico in its famous resolution proclaiming "Zionism is a form of racism and racial discrimination," provoking an outcry from Israel and the United States.[61]

The Declaration of Mexico's language about Zionism also had raised awareness about Echeverría's support for Palestine. In August 1975, he made a perfunctory visit to Israel following a trip to the Egyptian port of Alexandria, where he embraced Yasser Arafat and compared him to the nineteenth-century liberal leader Benito Juárez; he returned home to facilitate the opening of a PLO office in Mexico City. During that autumn's GA session, Echeverría actively advocated acceptance of the resolutions equating Zionism with racism, precipitating a tourist boycott by the US Jewish community. When the boycott began to take a toll, Mexican Foreign Minister Emilio Rebasa tried to make amends during a visit to the UN and then to Jerusalem, where he laid a wreath at the grave of Israel's founding father Theodore Herzl and proclaimed Zionism was not, in fact, racism. Rebasa was forced to resign upon his return to Mexico.[62]

Just after Echeverría returned home from his controversial meeting with Arafat, the Australian government held the first of several conferences that followed immediately after Mexico City. Elizabeth Reid had emerged as a feminist rock star during the government conference—a status no doubt strengthened when she registered at the plenary that "sexism" should appear in the World Plan of Action every time the terms "racism, colonialism, and neocolonialism" appeared.[63] She returned to Canberra, to growing anti-feminist sentiment in the media and a teetering Whitlam government. "Instead of giving Reid the welcome she deserved after her performance in Mexico," delegation member Sara Dowse recalled, "both the press and the party excoriated her. The UN conference was represented as a high-priced junket funded by the taxpayer for sex-mad feminists bent on destroying the family."[64]

During the first week of September, Reid ran a conference on "Women and Politics" that reenacted many of the dynamics of the Mexico City tribune—open to "anyone with an interest" and including both the energy and excitement along with the chaos and conflict.[65] "It was the aim of the conference organizers," explained the official report, "to provide a program which was as flexible and as varied as possible."[66] Free child care was available on-site, and the organizers particularly encouraged participation by aboriginal and island women, women from different political parties, and women from more remote parts of the country. Over 700 participants traveled from all over Australia, many with their journeys subsidized by the National Advisory Committee's funds. The list of "overseas guests" seemed designed to generate something closer to the IWY tribune than the conference: British psychoanalyst and feminist theorist Juliet Mitchell, US anti-imperialist lesbian feminist Charlotte Bunch, US lesbian novelist Bertha Harris, and US feminist and sex workers' rights advocate Flo Kennedy, Jamaica-born Canadian politician Rosemary Brown, Fijian development activist Claire Slatter, Meta Van Beek of the Dutch Women's Liberation Movement, and British Women's Liberation member and housekeepers' organizer May Hobbs.[67] Given constraints of language (there would be no simultaneous translation here), availability, and budget, it would be difficult to imagine a lineup better calculated to shake things up.

Shake things up it did. One participant reported to the organizers that the conference had been the "most exciting and fulfilling week of [her] life . . . for many, many reasons, meeting people, conscience stirring, deep, thought-provoking discussions—the lot." Describing talks she had been giving to groups in her small town of Myrtleford, Victoria, to offer a "Christian Woman's Viewpoint" praising the conference, however, she noted that the event had "come under fire" and had "some very unsavoury comments passed about it."[68] Speaking at Brisbane's Women's Action Alliance, which claimed to represent the "silent majority" of women, Queensland's Country Party premier Johannes Bjelke-Petersen reportedly accused "women in high places"—including not only Reid but also First Lady Margaret Whitlam—of promoting pornography, prostitution, easy divorce, and abortion.[69] Reid dismissed Bjelke-Petersen's comments as "absolutely typical insensitive rubbish" dispensed by someone who "just spends his time knocking and trying to destroy the women's movement," then wondered out loud "why he has added pornography to this old list and why he has decided to come out just now."

When conservative politicians brandished the negative press coverage in the prime minister's office, informing him that he could no longer afford to support Reid, he agreed to create some distance by transferring her from his staff to the Department of Prime Minister and Cabinet; she, in turn, resigned. Despite the ambivalence of women's liberationists about Reid's position when it was first created, most expressed dismay at her resignation. A spokeswoman for Sydney's Women's House told reporters Reid had been "crucified"; members of Women's Liberation organized demonstrations.[70] Frieda Brown, the leader of the Christian pro-family organization Festival of Light, celebrated Reid's departure, saying she had represented only radical perspectives and not a cross-section of Australian society.[71] Reid left for New York, where she was scheduled to speak at the UN; barely a month after her resignation, Whitlam was ousted from office in a constitutional crisis.[72] Reid would not return to Australia for a decade but left an indelible feminist mark on Australian politics.[73]

Soon after Reid's resignation, the East Berlin World Congress for IWY took place as planned on October 20–24, holding what the African National Congress's *Voice of Women* described as "undoubtedly the most representative forum ever convened in the history of the international women's movement."[74] If Australia's "Women and Politics" conference seemed designed to reproduce the most dynamic aspects of the Mexico City NGO tribune, the East Berlin conference tried to impose the type of parliamentary order and protocol that more closely resembled the IWY government conference. Erich Honecker, secretary general of Germany's Socialist Unity Party, delivered the opening address stressing the IWY theme of peace and ruefully acknowledging the role of "German imperialism" in undermining it during the twentieth century.[75] Claiming to have "fulfilled the legacy of Clara Zetkin," the German communist and women's rights advocate who famously denounced "bourgeois feminism," Honecker stressed that East German women enjoyed equal access to education and made up half the paid labor force, moving into "all fields of national life and in all trades and professions."[76] Helvi Sipilä spoke at the opening plenary, reiterating the IWY objectives and offering particular commendation to the WIDF.[77] Kurt Waldheim did not attend but sent a message to be read aloud, along with messages from heads of state such as Indira Gandhi, Sirimavo Bandaranaike, Fidel Castro, and Yasser Arafat.[78] Although designated observers and invited guests could attend the conference, only official delegates of NGOs could vote or hold conference offices. Like the Mexico City conference, the Berlin conference had a plenary and committees (complete with presidents, vice-presidents, and rapporteurs); official languages were English, French, Spanish, German, Russian and Arabic; the steering committee consisted of the congress president, WIDF president Freda Brown, and twenty-five elected members "chosen to reflect the composition of the Congress." Committees operated "on the basis of a free exchange of views" and draft reports expressing the consensus as well as any reservations or dissenting opinions.

Frances Doughty, of the New York–based National Gay Task Force, attended out of both a desire to have lesbians represented and a curiosity about East Berlin. "I was naïvely unprepared for almost every aspect of what actually happened," she later wrote. "I had not realized that it would be such a highly structured, formal conference, in which everything, even housing, seating, and individual speakers would reflect national politics and party lines. . . . I also did not know that every effort would be made to discredit feminism, especially within the

United States delegation, by associating it with lesbianism, the middle class, and, most strongly and painfully, with racism. It turned out to be one of the most embattled, exhausting, and educational experiences of my life." Organizers isolated the US delegation in a separate hotel, where they were the only guests and carefully watched by security personnel. Doughty tried to escape the conference's organizational limitations by engaging in what she called "cruising the plenary" to make the sorts of connections that she had found so valuable in the Mexico City tribune, "wandering around the halls and the snack bars looking for women who looked talkable to," but the strictures of the conference made these encounters nearly impossible. She found herself wondering how to make feminism relevant to women whose concerns about racism, imperialism, and poverty dominated discussions in East Berlin.[79]

The final document was voted on at the congress's closing plenary with the same proviso that held at UN conferences, giving it the feel (if not the fact) of an official resolution: "Organizations participating in the Congress shall not be bound by any resolutions adopted by it until they have been ratified by the proper constitutional authorities in accordance with each organization's internal juridical procedures."[80] Hoping that the East Berlin conference might yet assume the same significance as the Mexico City gathering, East German Deputy Minister of Foreign Affairs Peter Florin submitted the final conference report to the UN to be considered alongside the World Plan of Action and the Declaration of Mexico at the GA's thirtieth session.[81]

The United States held an IWY conference in Houston in 1977 that was neither international nor held during IWY and famously became a platform for Phyllis Schlafly's STOP-ERA campaign as well as the setting for Betty Friedan's about-face on the issue of lesbian feminists.[82] New York Representative Bella Abzug, who had advised the US delegation in Mexico City and participated in the NGO tribune, had submitted a bill to Congress calling for a national women's conference as part of the United States' bicentennial celebration. A series of state conferences and a national commission had produced a report, "To Form a More Perfect Union," and the Houston conference was held to deliberate on a twenty-six plank National Plan of Action that, like the World Plan of Action, addressed issues of health care, employment, and disarmament.[83] In addition to Bella Abzug, the conference drew First Ladies Lady Bird Johnson, Betty Ford, and Rosalyn Carter; Barbara Jordan delivered the keynote address. The event also drew cultural and political icons such as writer Maya Angelou, civil rights activist Coretta Scott King, and tennis star Billie Jean King—made famous in part by her 1973 "Battle of the Sexes" victory over Bobby Riggs—as well as feminists Gloria Steinem and Betty Friedan. The Houston conference proved to be as combative as Mexico City, but with the political spectrum shifted toward

Christian conservatives; several state delegations voted against the platform, and the Kansas delegation turned its back and prayed.[84]

At least as important as the formal conferences were the continued personal relationships cultivated in Mexico City. IWY activities had reconnected Devaki Jain with her old friend Gloria Steinem; the two had become close friends and confidantes during Steinem's two years living in Delhi after graduating from Smith College in 1957 but had fallen out of touch. After Mexico City, Jain arranged for Steinem to visit women's groups in Bombay, New Delhi, and Ahmedabad in February 1976, renewing the cross-fertilization of Gandhian and feminist thinking that the two had found so generative nearly two decades earlier. Later that year, Elizabeth Reid joined the Thai UN staffer Mallica Vajrathon, by this point working for the UNFPA after a conference in Amsterdam of the Society for International Development. They traveled to Ireland to join Vajrathon's mother-in-law, renowned feminist and former first lady Ruth Childers, to participate in the historic Women's Peace March where peace activists from Northern Ireland and the Republic of Ireland met on the River Boyne, on the newly constructed Bridge of Peace, demanding an end to the violence. "This," Reid later recalled, "was political dynamite."[85]

During her self-imposed exile from Australia, Reid turned to her UN contacts, who welcomed her enthusiastically. At the General Assembly meeting, she reconnected with Iranian delegation leader Ashraf Pahlavi, who shepherded the IWY documents through the GA. Impressed by Reid's energy and intellect, Pahlavi invited her to Tehran to work on the implementation of several resolutions that had emerged from Mexico City, including the Institute for Research on Women to which Pahlavi had pledged a million dollars. By 1976, Reid was living in Tehran and serving as the first director of the Asian and Pacific Centre for Women and Development.[86] She traveled widely to consult, run workshops, and advise activists and government officials alike, but she found that Tehran had become increasingly inhospitable to foreigners as protests became more frequent and supporters of the Ayatollah Khomeini gained strength. One evening in mid-1978, a group of Islamic faithful—men and women—entered her home and dragged her into an alley behind the house, demanding that she wear a *chador* and shouting at her in Farsi. They insisted she convert to Islam before Muharram, the Shia holiday of remembrance, in November. After several other harrowing encounters—including learning that the driver who carried her between her home and the research center wanted to become a martyr, which he believed he could accomplish by killing three foreigners—Reid took advantage of an invitation from the UNDP to evaluate the Kenyan Women's Bureau and left Tehran for the duration of Muharram. She finally left Iran permanently in February 1979, just ahead of the Islamic revolution.[87]

The Iranian Revolution provided a stark reminder that politics and women's issues were inextricably enmeshed, not only for Iranian women but also for UN-based efforts. The Asian and Pacific Centre for Women and Development that Reid directed was closed after the revolution and relocated to Bangkok; the Institute for Research on Women had not yet opened in Tehran, but it fostered UN-INSTRAW (International Research and Training Institute for the Advancement of Women), which opened in Santo Domingo, Dominican Republic, in 1983. The mid-decade conference slated for Tehran in 1980 to assess progress on IWY goals was promptly relocated to Copenhagen.[88]

If some participants in Mexico City had been caught off guard by the intense conflicts over Zionism and Chile and over how to prioritize efforts to improve women's lives, government delegates and NGO leaders arrived in Copenhagen to more familiar characters, scripts, and repertoire. The Copenhagen conference reiterated the equation of Zionism with racism, this time in the official Programme of Action, prompting the United States, Israel, Canada, and Australia to vote against it. The anti-Zionism language would remain in the official documentation until the 1985 Nairobi conference that concluded the UN Decade for Women. Israeli First Lady Aliza Begin decided to sit out this round, citing her husband's health concerns.[89] When Egyptian First Lady Jehan Sadat rose to speak to the conference plenary in Copenhagen, the Arab delegations walked out in protest against the Camp David accords, led by the PLO militant Leila Khaled, best known for her role in a series of plane hijackings in 1969 and 1970.[90]

The Copenhagen NGO forum also had some fireworks, if less drama than Mexico City. Fran Hosken, the indefatigable founder of WIN News, had by 1980 turned her attention to the issue of female circumcision and chaired one of several panels on the topic in Copenhagen. Although most panels produced only respectful exchange and discussion, according to the Ford Foundation's Elinor Barber, when a group of African women "noisily challenged" Hosken's authority on the subject, Hosken "screamed at them in return."[91] Whatever Domitila Barrios de Chungara's misgivings may have been about the IWY tribune, she agreed to attend the NGO forum for the mid-decade conference. She was in Copenhagen, then, when Bolivia's first and only female president, the left-leaning Lidia Gueiler Tejada, was overthrown in a bloody military coup orchestrated by Gueiler Tejada's cousin. Domitila was joined by Betty Friedan and Bella Abzug, among many others, in a protest march from the NGO tribune to the government conference, where they were met by police. Domitila would remain in exile in Norway and then Sweden until the end of 1983, spending most of her time on a speaking tour of Europe to denounce the Bolivian military regime.[92]

Many participants in both the government conference and the NGO forum left Copenhagen frustrated that so many of the same challenges persisted. "If there is indeed one central concern," wrote Singaporean sociologist Aline Wong after returning home from the NGO forum, "I think it is, What do women want *to be* as women? . . . Women in developing nations feel increasingly ill at ease with their eloquent sisters in the developed world who pose as their intellectual leaders and yet who represent values and ideologies at great variance with their own cultural and religious traditions. In their own ways, women in developing countries have been asking themselves: Do they really understand who we are? Do we want what they want?"[93]

If some of these episodes sparked a sense of déjà vu among those who had attended the Mexico City conference, Copenhagen also signaled a major victory: the presentation of the Convention on the Elimination of Discrimination against Women (CEDAW), a long-negotiated convention—commonly referred to as a bill of rights for women—that the General Assembly had finally approved the previous December. The World Plan of Action stated that a "high priority" should be placed on preparing and adopting a convention to eliminate discrimination against women, and a working group within the CSW immediately set about drafting one. The text of CEDAW drew heavily from the introduction to the World Plan of Action, which explicitly called for an international convention, as well as the Declaration of Mexico—including a call for a New International Economic Order and the eradication of "apartheid, all forms of racism, racial discrimination, colonialism, neo-colonialism, aggression, foreign occupation and domination and interference" but leaving aside any mention of either Zionism or sexism—and followed the model of the Convention of the Elimination of Racial Discrimination. As deliberations in Mexico City had shown, CEDAW advocates recognized that creating an analogy between racism and sexism would be critical to the convention's acceptance and efficacy. The text also reflected tensions between secular and religious conceptions of women's roles and the fact that the women negotiating the convention's initial draft "were proponents of a secular concept of women as individual subjects of rights."[94]

Of course, as a UN convention, CEDAW's provisions would be upheld by signatory national governments and suffered from the weak enforcement mechanisms that plague many UN conventions. The combination of this emphasis on individual rights and on the centrality of states meant that CEDAW would not gain traction among NGO activists for several years, but it began to shape expectations of what women could demand from their governments. CEDAW reporting requirements have remained in subsequent decades a principal mechanism through which women's organizations have pressured their home governments to live up to their promises.

In Copenhagen, the *New York Times* reported, "networking" replaced "consciousness-raising" as the keyword.[95] Elinor Barber judged that Copenhagen "did not generate either as much intellectual stimulation or as much ideological confrontation among the women attending the NGO conference" in Mexico City, not least because participants were prepared for the significant differences among them, but she found the forum did play a critical role in fostering new networks.[96] The seeds for these networks, however, had been sown in Mexico City and fertilized by the conflict and frustration experienced there and in the encounters that followed. Two of the most enduring and influential networks that developed after Copenhagen—both based in the Third World and both still active—grew from strong roots in Mexico City. Importantly, both groups insisted upon labeling themselves as feminist.

A group of Latin American feminists, many of whom had begun their exchanges in Mexico City amid the tussle with the Friedan-led Feminist Caucus, announced in Copenhagen that the first Encuentro Feminista Latinoamericano y del Caribe (Latin American and Caribbean Feminist Encounter) would take place a year later in Bogota for women "engaged in feminist practice" to "exchange experiences and opinions, identify problems and evaluate different practices, as well as plan tasks and projects for the future."[97] While the first encuentro focused largely on relationships of feminist organizations to the male-dominated political left, on the one hand, and the non-feminist women's movement, on the other, subsequent gatherings have ranged widely and contentiously, frequently wrestling with the intractable problem of representation.[98] Much like Mexico City, this first encuentro gathered women with diverse experiences with feminism. As historian Marysa Navarro wrote afterward, "Some had spent time studying or traveling in the United States or Europe and had been in contact with feminists in those countries ever since. Many had left their countries for the first time, had never in their lives attended a feminist meeting, and had never spoken with lesbians."[99] Like the Coalition of Latin American Women who caucused in Mexico City, participants in the first encuentro stressed that Latin American feminism formed part of a broader anti-imperialist struggle. While participants argued about many issues, Navarro explained, "The common denominator among feminists who attended the encuentro is the conviction that Latin American feminism should be committed to profound social change and should direct its activities to women of the most oppressed sectors."

Several years later, another enduring network, Development Alternatives with Women for a New Era (DAWN), formed in preparation for the 1985 decade-ending conference in Nairobi.[100] In August 1984 in Bangalore, India, Devaki Jain convened a group of women, several of whom had first connected in Mexico City and had cultivated those relationships in the interim. In describing DAWN's origins, Jain explains, "We brown/black [women] from the South found that every time we went [to development seminars] we would be in some kind of a position where we were critiquing what was being said by our northern sisters and then huddling together and saying, 'Oh these women, they are neo-colonists.' We were very troubled by racist and intellectual domination type of disturbances. So this I had experienced for three or four years between 1975 and 1980, when the Copenhagen conference was held. Then when we went to the UN conference in Copenhagen, the divide came out very sharply. . . . It be-came very humiliating, because then the people would say, 'These Third World women—these Third World women, they'll come and disrupt this conference. These Third World Women, they are so political.' It was that kind of 'these Third

Figure 18.1 Fijian WYWCA participant Amelia Rokotuivuna, pictured here at a 1 July 1975 tribune session, later became a trustee of DAWN. © Bettye Lane. Courtesy of Schlesinger Library.

World women' like you talk of 'these disturbing punks.' So that was also rather demeaning."[101]

Peggy Antrobus, who had attended the Mexico City conference as the director of the Women's Bureau of the Jamaican Prime Minister, recalls that first gathering in Bangalore as basically a diverse group of friends and colleagues that Jain had acquired over the years. Antrobus had not met Jain in Mexico, since they were split between the government conference and the NGO tribune, but their first meeting demonstrates powerfully the ways that the IWY conference fostered subsequent networks amd informed the development of feminisms around the world. Antrobus had gone to a conference that Elizabeth Reid had organized at the Asian Pacific Centre for Women and Development just prior to the Copenhagen conference. The event was titled "Feminist Ideologies and Structures," but Antrobus had simply told people at home that she was attending a conference on "national machinery"—the bureaucratic structures that had been set up to implement the World Plan of Action. She certainly was not about to tell her colleagues at the University of the West Indies that she was going to a feminist conference. "In Mexico City, all the feminists were white, North American women. . . . When I started working, feminist meant a lesbian," she explained to an interviewer decades later. "I couldn't tell anyone that I was going to a feminist meeting because feminism was a bad word, bad associations, bad connotations; and I did not think of myself as a feminist."[102] But Reid insisted on calling it a feminist conference—as Antrobus noted, the first and only time the UN has sponsored a conference with "feminist" in the title. Years later, she vividly recalled hearing "a woman from North America called Charlotte Bunch" talking about how she discovered her feminism through activism in the US civil rights movement. "So that's when, suddenly, a lightbulb went off in my head, and I thought, this feminism, it has something; it has something to do with power—power relationships between people, whether it is between men and women or black and white or on the basis of class or on the basis of relationships between countries." But Antrobus, much like the feminists who met at the first encuentro in Bogota, felt that Third World women needed a kind of feminism more deeply rooted in their own experiences.

By the time Devaki Jain gathered her friends in Bangalore, discussions at UN conferences and with donor agencies had demonstrated the importance of having their own network. Although the women who would go on to form DAWN fit the description of postcolonial cosmopolitans—most had PhDs and had traveled widely—the founders limited membership to women living in the Third World. "When you are struggling, politically located in your own political fabric, the incentives, the vibes, your priorities, your capacity to do is very different than when you are living in a country with a social security base, where your gas and water supply works, and every morning you read the *Times* of London," Jain argues.[103]

The participants in the Bangalore discussions saw themselves as working on development issues, but Antrobus remembers her surprise when the free-flowing, agendaless conversation yielded diverse understandings of the pressing development issues: women from the Pacific islands talked about nuclear testing, women from south and southeast Asia talked about religious fundamentalism, women from Africa talked about famine, and women from Latin America talked about structural adjustment. For most of the world, the economic theories being tested out in Pinochet's Chile would remain unfamiliar until the 1980s. After the 1982 debt crisis, most Latin American countries were subject to similar policies—promoting market reforms and shrinking social services—under the guise of "structural adjustment programs" required to obtain debt relief. Antrobus first heard the term "structural adjustment programs" only a month before the Bangalore gathering, when a group of Caribbean heads of state announced the implementation of such programs in the region. "Now, I didn't have a clue what it meant," she recalled later, "but from the time that they announced it, it became like a good thing, everybody was talking about it. Nobody was questioning it; it was being adopted totally uncritically. That structural adjustment, whatever it was, was the answer to Caribbean development. Why? Because the head of the Caribbean Development Bank said so and because all the governments had agreed. But when the women from Latin America started talking about what it meant, it just blew my mind."[104]

The group's wide-ranging discussion fostered what would become DAWN's hallmark: holistic, systemic analyses of development questions that understand issues such as militarism, environmental degradation, economic inequality, and gender violence as of a piece. The group produced a platform for the 1985 Nairobi conference and organized several panels for the NGO forum, all of which pointedly included the word "feminism" in their titles. "What was so different about Nairobi," Atrobus recalled, "when you compare it to Mexico City, where feminists were mostly white, even to Copenhagen, where Third World women were beginning to identify themselves as feminists, and Nairobi—it was in Nairobi that the feminists were everywhere, and they were black. . . . It completely changed the way that people thought about the issue of women in development. And I can say that because it changed me, but I also know of a number of women who identified that encounter with black, Third World feminism in Nairobi in 1985 as a turning point in their own politics." The Bangalore group published its platform and realized that they had hit on a critical issue that radically transformed understandings of both feminism and development. The following year, they created DAWN.[105]

Groups like the participants in the Encuentros Feministas and the organizers of DAWN offered a response to those who argued that politics had eclipsed women's issues in Mexico City and Copenhagen. For these activists and intellectuals, women's issues never existed outside of politics and vice versa. DAWN, in particular, concentrated its energies on making women's concerns central at UN conferences about the environment and population. Like many women's NGOs that emerged in the 1980s, DAWN and the Encuentros Feministas remained strongly oriented toward the UN, and their endeavors focused on shaping discussions at the UN women's conferences and other thematic conferences.[106] Their impact at the NGO Forum in Nairobi was evident both because they had arrived better prepared to engage in policy discussions and because they insisted on self-identifying as feminists and sustaining feminist discourses within their communities. In contrast with reactions in Mexico City, women from these organizations strongly supported lesbian participants who held forums, screened films, and circulated materials.[107]

The IWY conference in many ways launched the Women in Development (WID) turn to prominence. Before IWY, as one scholar has noted, less than 1 percent of standard development textbooks considered women at all; after IWY, no discussion of development policies could be complete without attending to women.[108] The International Women's Year also planted the seeds of the critique of WID's instrumentalist approach. Reporting back to the Population Council, Anna Quandt highlighted Elizabeth Reid's objections as particularly noteworthy, stressing that the World Plan of Action "viewed women as instruments toward some other social good—'economic development,' or happy family life. It did not properly emphasize women's rights to health, happiness and status as the rightful social goal in and of itself." The emphasis generated "distortions" in which, for example, health issues that affect all women—such as menopause—are ignored in favor of those related to "population" or "family life." After witnessing how little common understanding existed between First and Third World women at both the conference and tribune, she stressed the importance of devising "a way of including women from the developing world in research, not just in the execution stage, but in the planning and inception of ideas and research leads. This means both that we must go to developing countries to learn from them and that research must be truly collaborative, although I understand how difficult this may be."[109] Jain, who, like Reid, made an enduring impression in Mexico City, stressed afterward, "I was interested particularly in pressing for discussions on the kind of society women would desire, would feel comfortable and content with. For without this vision, choice of measures or policy seemed ad hoc."[110] Ironically, given the hand-wringing in Mexico City over whether "politics" distracted from "women's issues," the response to WID from scholars and practitioners alike had called for a repoliticization of development programs.[111]

In the wake of the UN Decade for Women, WID programs gave way to gender and development (GAD), which sought a more thoroughgoing reimagining of development in a way that challenged—or at least recognized—what were seen as masculine norms.[112] If WID argued that women played an indispensible role in achieving development goals, GAD called for a reconsideration of the goals themselves. It is impossible to know how much of this shift resulted from exchanges in settings such as the UN conferences and how much grew out of the broader political and intellectual shifts in feminism that took place during these years. The question posed by Aline Wong—"What do women want *to be* as women?"—had come to trouble a generation of feminist intellectuals and activists wrestling with the question of what remained of feminism if they rejected not only universalism but also the very idea of a coherent female subject. By 1975, feminism already occupied the liminal space between celebrations of herstory and womanpower and a full-throated challenge to the existence of a universal female subject. The International Women's Year had taken place near the beginning of what historian Daniel Rodgers has aptly termed the "age of fracture," as the apparent certainties of the post–World War II era came apart at the seams.[113] The UN conferences over the course of the Decade for Women both exemplified the fracture and necessitated it. But, as Rodgers points out, "As the age began, very few feminists imagined that the challenge to gendered norms and modes of domination might ultimately destabilize the category of woman itself."[114]

Many of the ideas that would come to dominate feminist debates in the 1980s and '90s resembled concerns activists raised and the NGO forums of the UN women's conferences. In France, deconstructive feminists Julia Kristeva, Luce Irigaray, and Hélène Cixous unsettled the most biologized and naturalized understandings of womanhood with their explorations of semiotics, linguistics, and psychoanalysis.[115] In the Anglophone world, where more essentialized conceptions of womanhood held on a bit longer, Denise Riley's extended essay *"Am I That Name?"* (1988) seemed to echo Aline Wong.[116] Feminist historian Joan Scott offered her first of many provocations to unsettle the meanings of gender (1986), and Judith Butler took up the challenges of French feminism in *Gender Trouble* (1990).[117] "To establish a normative foundation for settling the question of what ought properly to be included in the description of women," Butler argued in a subsequent essay, "would be only and always to produce a new site of political contest. That foundation would settle nothing, but would of necessity founder on its own authoritarian ruse."[118] Had Butler participated in any of the NGO forums she could have dispensed with the conditional tense; every effort to settle the definition of "women" without question foundered amid mutual accusations of authoritarian imposition. While intellectuals like Riley and Butler lack the definitive connection that someone like Ester Boserup (with her interrogation of development programs' effects on women) or feminist economist Marilyn Waring (with her thoroughgoing critique of GDP as a metric) had to the United Nations, their interventions could as easily have reflected the NGO

forum in Copenhagen or a pre-DAWN meeting in Bangalore as university seminar discussions. Indeed, it is easy to imagine that had Judith Butler attended
the IWY conference, she would have sounded much like another philosophy
student, Elizabeth Reid.

As anthropologist Arturo Escobar underscores, the UN Decade for Women
was the "single most important factor in fostering the new visibility of women"
and was "instrumental in creating spaces for Third World women in which to
organize and pursue their agendas, either on their own or through state institutions." All this attention and the WID discourse and programs it generated
were, he hastens to add, "a mixed blessing."[119] The GAD programs that replaced
them—including concepts such as gender budgets, gender mainstreaming,
and gender experts—often came with an imported concept of what gender implied, one that made gender difference seem fixed and dyadic. Some development practitioners expressed concern that the move from WID to GAD had
shifted attention from the concrete—women themselves and their material
conditions—to the abstract. Others, including Jain, who describes herself as
"one of the early ones to do gender differentiation," found that gender moved
quickly from being an analytical tool to simply a way of talking about women.
"So you do gender budgets," she explained in an interview, "the question is, have
you gendered that, have you gendered this—which means that you are looking at the difference between men and women in data or an impact. But it has
sort of become synonymous with women, which is a mistake because women
is an identity based on gender, but it is not gender."[120] While, by intellectual
temperament, Jain is unlikely to offer an understanding as psychoanalytic as
Joan Scott's—that gender is "the attribution of meaning to something that always eludes definition"—she and many others laboring in the development field
share the critique that it cannot be reduced to "the assignment of roles to physically different bodies."[121]

Still, gender discourse began to seep into every corner of the UN system
and through networks of NGOs. At each of the UN women's conferences, the
NGO tribune grew dramatically in both size and diversity, incorporating more
grassroots activists from a wider variety of backgrounds. The estimated participation of roughly 6,000 in Mexico City grew to 12,000 in Nairobi and 30,000 in
Beijing.[122] During this period, the UN women's conferences fostered a dramatic
increase in the number of women's NGOs headquartered in parts of the world
now called the global south.[123] In the meantime, through efforts of organizations
such as DAWN and Charlotte Bunch's Center for Women's Global Leadership
at Rutgers University, concerns around women and gender had gained traction at other UN conferences, most notably the victory of the "Women's Rights
Are Human Rights" campaign at the 1993 UN Human Rights conference in
Vienna.[124]

By the mid-1990s, the setting of a UN conference still offered an important focal point, but it also played a less critical role in most participants' experiences as NGO activists increasingly concentrated their efforts on other vehicles for social change, particularly those less tied to states or to the UN itself. "I think the NGOs have become so alive that they ceased to do what the women were doing pre-1975, [when] the NGOs were taking a lot of time lobbying with their delegations," Jain explains. "Delegates were able to transform the CSW and the General Assembly. Now that route is not the one that we are bothered about because we are so strong outside it. So I think part of the demeaning or downsizing of the UN system is as much the rise of this outside constituency, and therefore the loss of the track necessary to negotiate."[125]

The "rise of this outside constituency" refers to the widely heralded growth in organized civil society—NGOs and new social movements connected not to political parties or labor organizations but rather to more porous, issue-based efforts. Both secular and religious groups tried to circumvent governments in pursuing social change. The considerable growth in NGOs corresponded to a more general turn toward neoliberalism in which private entities took over many of the functions—including governance—that previously pertained to states.[126] More dramatically, when the Berlin Wall came down in 1989 and the Soviet Union dissolved in 1991, the entire geopolitical field was vastly transformed; the difference between the world of the Nairobi conference and the world of the Beijing conference was striking. Indeed, the celebrated unity of the Beijing conference arguably derives less from improved communication among participants from different parts of the world than from the fact that no effective counterweight remained for the Anglo-American agenda that stressed equality, labor-market incorporation, and entrepreneurship—what critics have dubbed free-market feminism.[127] "In Mexico," wrote development economist Bina Agarwal, who did not attend the 1975 conference, "grassroots Southern women, such as the Bolivian worker Domitila Barrios, had to protest persistently against the hijacking of the conference agenda by Northern women and assert: 'Let me speak.' In Huairou [the Beijing NGO forum] the tables had turned. . . . Many Northern women are today finding common ground with Southern women on economic issues, and wanting to be part of collectively defined strategies, including agitating against transnational corporations."[128] Of course, the feminist movement had also become more comfortable working within and through established institutions. "During the sixties, when the new characteristics of the Mexican feminist movement appeared," writes Argentine-born Mexican feminist and health educator Dora Cardaci, "there was a sort of deliberate and conscious rejection of the movement's institutionalization. During [IWY], the Women's Liberation Movement demonstrated radically against its celebration in both the official conference and the parallel forum. Twenty years later, there was practically no opposition, and the Mexican NGOs organized to attend the 1995 Beijing forum."[129]

By the time of the Beijing conference, activists and advocates had grown leery about some ideas that had galvanized participants in Mexico City. Microcredit, while still immensely popular, began to look to some like one more way to force poor women into market models and privatization.[130] NGOs themselves were seen by many more as the handmaidens of neoliberalism rather than as the vehicles for radical grassroots democracy, generating the pejorative term "NGO-ization." Cecilia Olivares, an editor of the Mexican feminist journal *Debate feminista*, explains that one of the journal's hottest-selling issues centered on a roundtable about NGO funding during the lead-up to the Beijing conference, which she describes as "a polemical topic like few others within the [feminist] movement."[131] Scholars have explored the ways that NGO-ization professionalized and privatized grassroots activism, reorienting organizations' objectives away from local concerns and compromising activist leaders through fundraising obligations and opportunities within state and para-state institutions that attenuated their connections with the organizations' bases.[132] These studies highlight the extent to which new-model NGOs have led to the privatization rather than the democratization of policymaking and the ways in which transnational NGOs command fidelity to political and ideological agendas from donor countries.

To be sure, the impact of NGO-ization has been complex. In 1991, in the heyday of the NGO boom, for example, the Mexican publication *La Correa Feminista* was started by the Mexican organization Centro de Investigación y Capacitación de la Mujer (CICAM, Women's Research and Training Center), which was, in turn, funded by a feminist NGO connected with Germany's Green Party (Frauenanstiftung). The magazine was most closely identified with its principal editor, the Bolivian-born, Chilean-raised, Mexico-adopting lesbian feminist Ximena Bedregal, the type of subaltern cosmopolitan who gained prominence through the UN conferences. *La Correa* grew amid critiques of foreign NGOs' growing influence over local and regional feminist organizations; by the 1993 Encuentro Feminista Latinoamericano y del Caribe, *La Correa* had gained regional recognition not least for being one of the most vocal critics of the purportedly deradicalizing effects of NGO-ization.[133]

Until 1998, *La Correa* published trenchant critiques of neoliberalism and capitalist development models, lambasted militarism along with ongoing human rights abuses (including the Mexican government's response to the 1994 Zapatista uprising), and, above all, decried the institutionalization of feminism that blunted its critical impact. Unsurprisingly, by 1998 the editors of *La Correa* found they could no longer sustain these contradictions. The magazine required external financing unavailable to it in Mexico, particularly since its provocations had antagonized many potential supporters. Although the editors insisted that they remained autonomous from *La Correa*'s sponsor, they felt that editorial consistency required them to renounce NGO funding; the magazine promptly was dissolved. Bedregal moved her activism on-line—starting the site Creatividad Feminista—and for six years wrote a regular feminist column for the left-leaning Mexican daily *La Jornada* entitled "Triple Jornada" ("Triple Shift").

In many ways, Bedregal's career captures the legacies of the IWY conference for Mexican feminism as well as feminism more broadly—the prominent role of lesbian activists, ambivalent embrace of NGOs, antipathy toward the state, and efforts to commandeer mass media to feminist ends. But the case of *La Correa Feminista* also demonstrates why scholars have revisited the question of NGO-ization, arguing that transnational NGOs exercised less influence over grassroots organizations than many feared and, in fact, fostered organizations that otherwise would have struggled to survive.[134]

Although the UN operates overwhelmingly by consensus, the UN-sponsored women's conferences have functioned more as incubators of dissent, as spaces of persistent and animating critique. The disagreements, miscommunications, and even traded accusations allowed participants to see more clearly the stakes of their positions and to forge bonds of solidarity with others who shared their priorities. The never-ending challenges over the question of representation point not to the possibility of reaching the perfect constellation of participants who would adequately represent but instead to the importance of recognizing the limits of representation. One of the most important legacies of the Mexico City conference was not a policy development or any single organization but rather the deep and enduring friendships that it forged. If the Betty Friedan-Domitila Barrios de Chungara confrontation was a fantasy—or perhaps simply a metaphor—representing an anticipated conflict, the relationships fostered by the conference were quite real. Some, like that between Elizabeth Reid and Ashraf Pahlavi, took root during the IWY activities; others, like that of Gloria Steinem and Devaki Jain, were renewed and strengthened after Mexico City. For these women and thousands of others like them, IWY had fostered a shared vocabulary and access to shared networks and endeavors that have sustained transnational and increasingly diverse feminisms.

NOTES ON SOURCES, THEORIES, AND METHODS

In researching and writing this book, I became fascinated with the stories and characters that animated IWY and wanted them to occupy center stage. Some of the conceptual and historiographical engagements as well as all of the primary source citations remain in the notes; what follows delves into methodological decisions and theoretical questions that informed my thinking and writing. No historian writing since the Foucauldian turn can dodge the question, "What is your archive?" Although the concern takes on a more literal meaning for historians than it does for literary critics, it still gestures to a generation's worth of reflections on the nature of knowledge production, on why we think we know what we think we know.[1] The multi-scalar and transnational nature of this project set in relief the ways our archives inform our narratives.

As I constructed the archive for this research, I became acutely aware of how strongly material factors shape knowledge production. At every scale, from individuals to global organizations, archival preservation depends upon stability and resources that—like so much else—remain unequally distributed. The fact that Mexico's Ministry of Foreign Relations Archive could identify but never locate the principal files regarding the IWY conference made this less a story about Mexican politics and policy than I had initially intended.[2] The Mexican parts of this story come largely from the secret-police reports (Dirección Federal de Seguridad and Investigaciones Políticas y Sociales, both housed in the Archivo General de la Nación). The United Nations archive contains a bit more documentation, but not nearly to the extent apparently available for the better-funded 1974 Population Conference.[3] The UNESCO archive provides insight into how the sausage gets made, and the US National Archive and Records Administration includes a quite complete set of the US delegation's papers—including UN documents I had been unable to locate elsewhere. Regrettably, the official UN records of this conference (and of most UN activities from this period) are available only in microcard.

As is often the case with women's history, this book benefits tremendously from the personal collections of key individuals who saved and donated their papers and from the institutions that provide the resources to preserve and organize them. I gleaned much of the story about goings-on both within the United Nations and beyond from these collections—particularly the meticulously archived papers of Elizabeth Reid at Australia National University, the uncatalogued papers of Esther Hymer housed in the Church Center across from UN headquarters, and the semi-catalogued papers of Mildred Persinger at Hollins University, as well as several personal collections at the Rubenstein Rare Book and Manuscript Library (Duke University), Tamiment Library/Robert F. Wagner Labor Archives (New York University), and the Arthur and Elizabeth Schlesinger Library on the History of Women (Radcliffe Institute for Advanced Study). The papers for *Xilonen* editor Marjorie Paxson are housed at the Western Historical Manuscript Collection, University of Missouri-Columbia. The documentary evidence on the NGO tribune also draws from the wonderful archives at the Sophia Smith Collection, which holds the papers of the International Women's Tribune Centre as well as several important WINGOs. These archival collections are rich and inspiring, but they clearly over-represent well-educated women from wealthier countries, underscoring the importance of continuing to deepen and expand these collections.

Like many other scholars, I initially turned to oral histories to complement documentary archives. As this project developed into a snapshot of a critical moment in women's activism in many parts of the world, it became clear that oral histories would not form a central part of its method. US- and (to a lesser extent) Mexico-generated sources already constituted too significant a part of the book's evidentiary base, and collecting a global sample of oral histories would require even greater resources than this (quite generously supported) project enjoyed. My early forays into oral history quickly demonstrated that the interviews would yield a fascinating study of how people remember the conference and why people remember it in the ways they do—a question that clearly remains— but they would diverge in important ways from the story that emerged from the documentary evidence. An investigation based largely on oral histories would demand an exploration of the spaces that these divergences create, resulting in a book more about methodology and about developments in subsequent decades than the conference itself.[4]

Journalists played a critical role in shaping narratives of events both at the time and retrospectively.[5] This narrative draws heavily on media accounts, a decision driven partly by necessity and partly by the events themselves. Since the NGO tribune by design took no minutes and issued no final declaration, news reports offer an important balance to participants' accounts. Even for the intergovernmental conference, newspapers provide a useful supplement to the sanitized versions that appeared in the official reports. The newspapers also became characters themselves in this story—as much a part of shaping perceptions and experiences as any of the principal actors. In particular, the English- and Spanish-language coverage differed markedly, creating distinct understandings among their readerships. Most US-based newspapers sent reporters who did not understand Spanish—a reasonable editorial choice for a conference that would offer simultaneous translation of the proceedings and where most participants would speak English but certainly also an indication of the importance most editors ascribed to the event. Those reporters understood what they witnessed through the explanations offered by Anglophone interviewees, resulting in a particular perspective. Most Mexico-based reporters apparently did not understand English.

The starkest example of distinct coverage came in *Xilonen*, which carried articles and essays in Spanish, English, and (occasionally) French. A given issue frequently included Spanish and English versions of the same story; these articles were not direct translations but rather included quite different descriptions, quotations, and information. The heaviest coverage was in the Mexico City dailies—which generally dedicated much of the front page and many inside pages to IWY news for the duration of the conference—followed by a handful of US papers that issued regular reports, albeit frequently in the "women's pages." *El Universal* and *El Nacional* (the ruling party's newspaper) offered the most pro-government coverage, usually parroting the Echeverría administration's line and highlighting its efforts in favor of the G-77.[6] *Excélsior*, under the progressive editorship of Julio Scherer García starting in 1968, had taken advantage of Echeverría's proclaimed "democratic opening" to offer a more critical take; a year after the IWY conference, Echeverría would orchestrate the ouster of Scherer and six other top editors.

The US newspapers also had distinct editorial lines—the *Chicago Defender*, for example, sympathized with non-aligned perspectives; the *New York Times* was reliably pro-Israel. Most of the US newspapers had little patience with Friedan and her allies, depicting feminists as spoiled and solipsistic compared to their Third World sisters, whom they often depicted as an indistinct mass of the downtrodden and abused. Regardless of language abilities and editorial lines, in their efforts to impose legibility on the chaos, news accounts frequently conflated groups of women who saw themselves at odds with one another. Even the most dedicated reporters were hampered by the difficulty of traveling between the two principal sites and the limited facilities available for the overwhelming number of reporters (an estimated 1,500) who showed up.

The media played a key role in the fixation on women's embodiment—which, in this instance, meant rapt attention to an infinite variety in women's bodies, dress, and comportment.[7] In stark contrast to other UN reporting (or any other political reporting), news reports commented constantly on what women wore, how they styled their hair, the proportions of their bodies, and their apparent "femininity." They also commented on women's bodies in other ways—as pregnant, sterilized, or raped; starved or overworked; lesbian or prostitutes' or braless feminist drawing men's notice—that had been absent in the previous year's population and food conferences. In these accounts, as well as numerous background papers and UN reports, women's bodies appear as the necessary sites of modernization, a development that was both welcomed (for finally recognizing women at all) and dreaded (for the policies that inevitably would be inflicted).

Photojournalist Bettye Lane produced fascinating images of the IWY events, bringing the perspective of an activist in the US feminist and gay liberation movements. "To future generations," Gloria Steinem said of Lane, "hers will be the eyes of the movement."[8] Her photographs provide rich illustrations, but it is also interesting to note which figures drew her attention as well as her choices in composition and captioning. She seems to have shared Jacqueline Ceballos's characterization of the "disruptors" but not Nancy Cárdenas's suspicion that the Mexican demonstrators were bought and paid for. She captured not only prominent figures such as Elizabeth Reid and Vilma Espín, and those who gained recognition such as Domitila Barrios de Chungara, Wynta Boynes, and Laurie Bebbington but also anonymous demonstrators, vendors, and mendicants. She shot dramatic hairstyles and amusing bumper stickers as well as the restroom sign at the tribune where "caballeros" had been papered over with a sign for "damas."

This book emerged in part because it became impossible to ignore the number of inaccurate or incomplete accounts of what happened in Mexico City. No book-length study of the IWY conference exists, although there are quite a few shorter, firsthand accounts, including those by journalists and participants.[9] But journalists attended mostly to the spectacular and, with a few exceptions, paid little attention to the day-to-day efforts by thousands of participants. The participants' accounts are necessarily partial, reflecting their own backgrounds, language abilities, moments witnessed, and points when they entered and exited this story. Piecing together a more complete account allows us to see the ways that these narratives diverge from the historical record, to examine collective investments in those narratives, and to explore the ways that the actors themselves constructed narratives—of time and history—and fit themselves into them. The narrative here does not offer a complete and uncontestable truth but rather a new perspective, with the goal of deepening our understanding and appreciation of what was accomplished in Mexico City.

Recent scholarship on "global feminism" has tended to adopt comparative approaches and given little or no attention to the 1975 conference compared to the 1995 Beijing conference.[10] Quite a few studies, however, point to IWY as a critical inflection point for transnational women's organizing.[11] Arguably more telling than references to IWY in the literature on transnational feminisms are the countless references to it in national and regional studies of women's history and women's activism more generally as well as personal accounts of how it created new structures and opportunities. Although there is conspicuously little mention of IWY in the US historiography (which often refers to the 1977 Houston conference), in much of the rest of the world—particularly in areas once imagined as the Third World—histories often point to 1975 or even to the Mexico City events specifically as the moment that launched a women's movement or an important women's organization.[12]

Because most scholars and public intellectuals who write the history of Mexican feminism come from the ranks of those activists who dismissed IWY, there has been only a begrudging recognition that they might have had any impact at all on feminist efforts there. Indeed, the Mexican feminist historiography from the 1980s and '90s barely nods to the events; those interventions that do mention the conference do so only to provide the backdrop for the more radical—and by their lights more authentically feminist—counter-conferences. The elisions are often striking: even the renowned Mexican feminist anthropologist Sylvia Marcos skips the 1975 conference entirely in her review of 1970s Mexican feminism, insisting that Mexican feminists began to discover "the interconnectedness with women's movements the world over" only with the Cairo and Beijing UN conferences in 1994 and 1995, respectively.[13] Some later reflections by such prominent intellectuals as María Luisa Tarrés, Elena Urrutia, and Marta Lamas have acknowledged IWY's importance and the need to understand it better, and a recent MA thesis indicates that perhaps a younger generation of Mexican historians has begun to take up the challenge.[14]

Like many scholars of my generation, I was inspired by the turn toward gender history and particularly the study of feminisms. Historians and development experts have followed similar trajectories of considering women's history (or women in development, WID)—which take women as a given subject—to gender history (or gender and development, GAD)—which understood the meanings of sexual difference to have cultural and ideological rather than biological underpinnings but in many ways still ascribed a fixedness. Gender history explored the processes of meaning-making; GAD specialists argued that gender awareness should inform data collection and resource distribution. In frustration with this apparent stability—of a coherent masculine/feminine reflecting the biologized man/woman—feminist historians have circled back to Denise Riley's formulation of nearly three decades ago.[15] "Instead of veering between deconstruction and transcendence," she suggests, "we could try another train of speculations: that 'women' is indeed an unstable category, that this instability has a historical foundation, and that feminism is the site of the systematic fighting out of that instability—which need not worry us."[16]

Despite Riley's reassurances, of course, the evacuation of the category "women" raises concerns. As historian Joan Scott puts it, "The vertigo that ensues for the historian deprives her of the certainty of her categories of analysis and leaves her searching only for the right questions to ask."[17] More urgently, the consequences of denying the lived experience of sexual differentiation often seem dire—women and girls (identified as such by themselves, or their communities, or their governments) become targets of violence and discrimination, most visibly when they transgress the boundaries of prevailing sex roles. But interrogations of the category of "women" and understandings of gender are critical to challenging the policing of sexual difference. Or, to borrow from the historian Barbara Fields, sex is a fiction, but sexism is a crime against humanity.[18] Understanding the historical production of the "sex" that rationalizes sexist practices remains indispensable to eradicating them.

Like most historians, I turn to theory as a stimulus to ask new questions of the evidence rather than as a prescription (or proscription) for how to make sense of it. What follows here is not a rehearsal of all the conceptual interventions that have informed my thinking but rather a review of those that proved particularly provocative and to which I returned repeatedly as I was researching and writing this book. Some of these thinkers disagree with one another—at times vehemently—either implicitly or explicitly. I will not pretend to resolve those disputes here but simply indicate how my theoretical promiscuity has shaped this narrative.

Piecing together the disparate bits of evidence about the planning, execution, and aftermath of the IWY conference into a narrative entailed imposing legibility and coherence on what would have been experienced as increasingly disjointed and disordered, what for many participants brought not the consolidation of an identity ("woman") but the fraught, anxious experience of its undoing. The process also gave me an opportunity to consider the ways that narrative thinking informs the analysis here, particularly around questions of event, temporality, and performance.[19] IWY participants read (or misread) each other's performances in very different ways: what they understood, quite likely in a common-sensical and unreflective way, as the demeanor that marked one as, for example, feminine or leftist or politically savvy, was entirely historically contingent. Similarly, they understood the time horizons for their interventions in wildly diverse ways. For Domitila Barrios de Chungara or the two women arguing over the microphone in the AP photo, they understood that they might only have this one shot at making themselves heard on a world stage. The CORE activist

Wynta Boynes, on the other hand, could intervene with greater confidence that her organization and movement would not fade from public consciousness any time soon. The government conference brought together those who operated within the deliberative, incremental processes of the United Nations with those engaged in national-liberation struggles.

Given these centrifugal forces, I became intrigued by how the IWY conference emerged as an event in three senses: first, how a set of disparate episodes became linked as a unified, coherent set designated as a single event—in other words, how to describe both its boundaries and its contents; second, how a given event comes to be considered a pivotal historical moment or a conjuncture that changes its surrounding world in a significant way; and, third, how it generated the event of a novel historical subject. It may seem obvious why the IWY conference would be considered an event—it was, after all, created as such. Organizers and journalists alike referred to it as the "world's largest consciousness-raising session," and activists of all stripes produced ephemera that all marked the conference as an event, as a "happening," to borrow the description of one UN staffer. Constant reinscriptions through media coverage, official proclamations, and even dissident critique all form part of what created fidelity to the event: the naming of it that sets it apart from the surrounding historical noise. Otherwise, as Gertrude Stein so pithily put it, there's no there there. Hopefully the preceding narrative has conveyed, however, it was hardly a foregone conclusion that Mexico City would happen at all, much less that it would become the signal event of IWY, a turning point in transnational women's activism, and the launch pad for new forms of feminism.

My thinking on these questions bears the conspicuous influence of two scholars who have theorized extensively about how a given episode emerges as an event out of the muck and chaos of history: philosopher Alain Badiou and historian William Sewell.[20] Badiou examines, in his distinctly mathematical fashion, how human interventions cause a rupture with the everyday happenings and common sense of a moment and through what he terms acts of fidelity; these interventions render a coherent set out of otherwise disparate elements and create a novel historical subject, a singularity out of the infinite possible multiplicities.

If Badiou's conceptualization of the event reflects his grounding in mathematics and ethics, Sewell's notion of "eventful temporality" reflects his engagement with the disciplines of history and sociology, defining events as "that relatively rare subclass of happenings that significantly transforms structures." Sewell asks how high we put the bar to qualify as an "event"—as a historical game changer. "Even the most radical historical ruptures," he concedes, "are interlaced with remarkable continuities."[21] The IWY conference certainly clears this bar, judging by Sewell's criteria for a historical event as "(1) a ramified sequence of occurrences that (2) is recognized as notable by contemporaries, and that (3) results in a durable transformation of structures."[22] Sewell explores the role that historical narrative had played in recasting the storming of the Bastille as an act of popular patriotism and the signal moment of the French Revolution rather than an episode of mob violence. In this narrative, I examine how an event emerged from what would surely have been a non-event of lectures, garden-club meetings, and commemorative stamps.

The critical development that transformed the IWY conference from an interesting historical episode into an event was the decision to open up the NGO tribune to anyone who saw a place for herself there and to actively facilitate diverse perspectives. The fact that consultative-status NGOs played a role in planning a UN conference was in many ways business-as-usual—the everydayness of history that gets ruptured by an event. The rupture was driven by two geopolitical factors: the Cold War and the rise of the Non-Aligned Movement. IWY organizers such as Rosalind Harris and Margaret Bruce clearly perceived an opportunity to gain an upper hand over Eastern bloc countries by appealing to the Third World. The novel historical subject that emerged from IWY, then, was a figure akin to what feminist theorist Niamh Reilly has dubbed the "cosmopolitan feminist," someone like Devaki Jain or Wangari Maathai or Peggy Antrobus.[23] These women were not grassroots activists—although they generally maintained close contact with activists—but rather highly educated professional women who, following IWY, had a hand not only in shaping national and UN policies but also in creating new networks that fostered new generations of cosmopolitan feminists.

Particularly in the decades since IWY, cosmopolitanism has drawn the attention of dozens of scholars, from Anthony Appiah and Homi Bhabha to Pnina Werbner and Slavoj Žižek. Debates have centered on questions of citizenship, ethics, and cultural autonomy, and scholars have attached countless modifiers—such as contested, rooted, subaltern, and vernacular—in an attempt to distance cosmopolitanism from its elite, globe-trotting, rootless origins. The women involved with the UN and with IWY were certainly cosmopolitan by temperament in the most literal sense of understanding themselves as world citizens. Cosmopolitanism, as Werbner describes it, has come to stand for "empathy, tolerance, and respect for or cultures and values . . . living together with difference [and] the urgent need to devise ways of living together in peace in the international community."[24] This matter of "tolerance," however, presumes a hierarchy of legitimacy between the tolerant and the tolerating. "Designated objects of tolerance," explains feminist theorist Wendy Brown, "are invariably marked as undesirable and marginal, as liminal civil subjects or even liminal humans; and those called upon to exercise tolerance are asked to repress or override their hostility or repugnance in the name of civility, peace, or progress. Psychically, the former is the material of abjection and one variety of resentment (that associated with exclusion); the latter is the material of repressed aggression and another variety of resentment (that associated with forsworn strength or domination)."[25] Science studies scholars such as Bruno Latour and Isabelle Stengers stress that embedded within this invocation of tolerance is the presumption of universalism—what the IWY organizers imagined as unity—that might be reached once all petty differences are set aside.[26]

This push for unity gestures toward long-running debates about the nature of hegemony, among which I still find anthropologist William Roseberry's short essay on the "language of contention" to be the most useful to historians.[27] Roseberry proposes using "the concept of hegemony *not* to understand consent but to understand struggle" and to understand that dominant and subaltern groups imply "plurality or diversity; unity is for them a political and cultural problem." Conflicts in the discursive realm—over whether to use words such as sexism, colonialism, and Zionism, or over whether to label protestors as disruptors—illuminate contestations over legitimacy and authority. For Roseberry, who draws heavily on Antonio Gramsci, explosions such as those that occurred at the IWY events offer a window onto the hegemonic process and its limitations.

Another friendly amendment to Gramsci's conception of hegemony comes from Raymond Williams, who also highlights discursive elements in shaping experience. Warning against the reduction of social analysis to fixed terms such as ideology or class perspective, he urges scholars to attend to the "structures of feeling," the "meanings and values as they are actively lived and felt ... affective elements of consciousness and relationships: not feeling against thought, but thought as felt and feeling as thought: practical consciousness of a present kind, in a living and interrelating continuity."[28] While most readers have encountered Domitila Barrios de Chungara through her articulated positions, as they appeared in her co-authored *testimonio* or perhaps one of her pamphlets, the documentation from the IWY tribune offers a glimpse of the structure of feeling that preceded these articulations—the social and material response to encountering alienating ideas and power structures that seemed to disregard the most important aspects of her life and her community.

In an effort to keep these power relations within the frame, many scholars in the past two decades have explored the dynamics of transnational processes (as opposed to global phenomena or state-to-state international interactions.[29] Cultural geographer Cindi Katz offers the thought-provoking metaphor of contour lines that cross the globe creating affinities among people who share similar experiences and perhaps little else, creating a "geographical imagination that cuts through and across received distinctions not only among discrete places, but between such lumpy distinctions as global North and South, East and West, or the First and Third Worlds."[30] While Katz concentrates on those who share material conditions of production and reproduction—what, for example, Domitila Barrios de Chungara may have had in common with miners' wives in West Virginia or Kinshasa—contour lines also followed lines of generation, sexuality, religion, or urbanity, for example. Keeping an eye out for contour lines in materials from IWY allowed me to spot affinities that organizers and the media had not signaled, such as YWCA affiliation or membership in a Unitarian Universalist church or involvement in handicrafts production.

Participants in the IWY events sought something imagined as more organic or more immanent than such affiliations. Many hoped to find solidarity with, as Domitila put it, "people like me."[31] Philosopher Jean-Luc Nancy, particularly with his influential concept of the "inoperative community," helped me to see the ways in which conflicts in Mexico City—what organizers lamented as a failure to achieve unity—were constructive. The aspiration held by some organizers and participants to abandon "politics" in favor of "women's issues" rested upon what Nancy deems a nostalgic and imaginary communion. He stresses, "What this community has 'lost'—the immanence and the intimacy of a communion—is lost only in the sense that such a 'loss' is constitutive of the community itself. It is not a loss: on the contrary, immanence, if it were to come about, would instantly suppress community, or communication as such."[32]

The heterogeneity and entropy that took hold, particularly at the NGO tribune, exemplify the unpredictable encounters that political philosopher Jacques Rancière dubs *dissensus* and what anthropologist Anna Tsing describes as the productive "friction" of global encounters.[33] "Rubbing two sticks together produces heat and light; one stick alone is just a stick," Tsing writes. "As a metaphorical image, friction reminds us that heterogeneous and unequal encounters can lead to new arrangements of culture and power."[34] Rancière's explanation of dissensus as a "difference between sense and sense: a difference within the same, a sameness of the opposite" particularly speaks to the communications and miscommunications at the tribune—to the struggles over microphones, the dueling press conferences, and Domitila's insistence to "let me speak," as her testimonio was titled. "Political dissensus is not a discussion between speaking people who would confront their interests and values," he elaborates. "It is a conflict about who speaks and who does not speak, about what has to be heard as the voice of pain and what has to be heard as an argument on justice."[35]

Although differing with Jean-Luc Nancy and Rancière regarding the stability of a political subject, political theorist Nancy Fraser has applied her critical approach to Jürgen Habermas's concept of the public sphere to consider how such a polyvocal engagement fosters social justice.[36] In particular, she attends to the questions of the public sphere's legitimacy (who gets to participate and under what conditions) and its efficacy (how a consensus developed in the public sphere becomes translated into policy or practice and whether a governing body has the capacity to implement those ideas).[37] In this understanding of a transnational public sphere, the category of citizen—so central to Habermas's original conceptualization—loses its relevance in favor of greater inclusiveness, what Fraser dubs the all-subjected principle that would define inclusion by "joint subjection to a structure of governance that set the ground rules for their interaction."[38] Questions of legitimacy and efficacy arose at the UN itself, of course, as well as the IWY conference, but Fraser's analysis pertains to civil society gathered at the NGO tribune. In particular, it helps to understand the importance of opening up tribune participation beyond consultative-status NGOs as well as the stakes of struggles over which modes of interaction were authorized and which were considered disruptions.

Finally, the interventions of feminist theorist and historiographer Clare Hemmings have raised awareness of the ways that narrations of feminist history often follow patterns of naïve celebrations of purported progress, nostalgia for a lost political engagement, or cautious optimism that scholars might find ways to combine the linguistic turn with attention to materiality. "We may have been convinced by the turn to language, a poststructuralist capacity to deconstruct power and difference, but we know better now," Hemmings ventriloquizes this last group chiding itself. "We know that critique does not alter power relations and indeed that these have endured and strengthened. We know now that postmodern feminism leads to relativism and political incapacity, while women everywhere remain disadvantaged."[39] Hemmings's analysis caught my attention not only because I find myself implicated by it but also because she describes the very debates in play in Mexico City: the relationship between structures and cultures, the role of language, the problems of universalism and relativism, and the extent to which some issues are perceived to trump others.

To adopt Hemmings's language, this history of IWY is arguably a narrative of loss, of melancholic nostalgia for the intensity and dynamism of these encounters and the broad scope of possibilities that seemed to be in play. It is also a reminder that we cannot consider the history of feminisms from any one perspective or in isolation from the geopolitical contexts in which they emerged. Nor, for that matter, can we consider international history apart from the influence of feminist activism and women's organizations. From the first glimmer of the idea of IWY through to its many legacies, every effort to untangle "politics" and "women's issues" only knotted them more tightly together. The resulting conflicts, while often confusing and frustrating to participants on the ground, have fostered dramatic and enduring changes in the policies and practices of international organizations, nation-states, and NGOs.

NOTES

Abbreviations Used in Notes

AGN	Archivo General de la Nación (Mexico City)
DFS	Dirección Federal de Seguridad
EJBP	Journalists' Encounter Background Paper
FFA	Ford Foundation Archive
FRUS	*Foreign Relations of the United States*
ICW	International Council of Women Papers
IWTC	International Women's Tribune Centre Archive
IPS	Investigaciones Políticas y Sociales
MPP	Mildred Persinger Papers
NARA	National Archives and Records Administration (College Park, MD)
NOW-NYC	National Organization for Women, New York City Chapter Records
RAC	Rockefeller Archive Center (Sleepy Hollow, NY)
RG	Record Group
SRE	Secretaría de Relaciones Exteriores, Archivo Histórico "Genaro Estrada" (Mexico City)
UN doc.	Document identified by UN document number and available in UN repositories

Introduction

1. Simpson, "The Washington Press Club Foundation."
2. *El Universal*, 1 July 1975, 1 and 7; *Excélsior*, 1 July 1975, 1.
3. AGN, DFS, 25 June 1975 report on IWY tribune, Exp. 9-342-75, Leg. 7, hojas 83–88; Madonna Gilbert, "Native American Women Denied Voice at International Women's Year Conference," *Akwesasne Notes*, Early Autumn 1975, 33. The question of names has presented a challenge in writing this book. Feminists have pointed out that women are often referred to by their first names and men by their last, making the women seem more familiar and more diminutive.

I generally refer to Domitila Barrios de Chungara by her first name, as that is how she was most widely known. For most other figures, I use last names. Similarly, I have retained the designations First World and Third World because those were the terms used most frequently in the 1970s.

4. Barrios de Chungara and Viezzer, *Let Me Speak!* 204.

5. See, for example, Chinchilla, "Marxism, Feminism, and the Struggle for Democracy in Latin America," note 8; Fuentes, "Entre reivindicaciones sexuales y reclamos de justicia económica"; Lal et al., "Recasting Global Feminisms"; Marchand, "Latin American Women," 59–60; Miller, *Latin American Women*, 200; "Women in the Social, Political, and Economic Transformation of Latin America and the Caribbean," 187; Pratt, "SOFA," 53; "I, Rigoberta Menchú and the 'Culture Wars,'" 48, fn.10; Therborn, *Between Sex and Power*, 103. While I have found many more examples of writers glossing the IWY conference with some version of a Friedan/Barrios de Chungara confrontation, I have found only two instances in which authors express some skepticism about this characterization: Çagatay and Funk, "Comments on Tinker," 778; Waterman, "Hidden from Herstory," 86.

6. Barrios de Chungara and Viezzer, *Let Me Speak!* This *testimonio* was narrated to the Brazilian sociologist Moema Viezzer in part while they were still in Mexico City.

7. Admittedly, specialists on Latin America sometimes substitute Gloria Steinem or, less frequently, Germaine Greer for Betty Friedan, and those without expertise in Latin America rarely can summon the name Domitila Barrios de Chungara. Oddly, the US political scientist Mary Hawkesworth also substitutes Steinem for Friedan (Hawkesworth, *Globalization and Feminist Activism*, 121).

8. On Friedan's work with the United Electrical workers, see Horowitz, *Betty Friedan and the Making of The Feminine Mystique*. On their respective concerns about women and housework, see Friedan, *The Femine Mystique*; Barrios de Chungara and Viezzer, *Let Me Speak*; Barrios de Chungara, *La mujer y la organización*.

9. See, for example, UN Secretariat member Margaret Bruce's remarks to the AAUW-organized seminar at UN headquarters in November 1974 (NARA, RG 220, box 1); CESI press release (UN doc. OPI/CESI Note IWY/17), 15 December 1974; IWY Secretary-General Helvi Sipilä's comments to *World Health*, January 1975, 3; progress report of the Secretary General (UN doc. E/5605), 6 January 1975; US delegation head Patricia Hutar in official press statement on 30 June 1975 (NARA, RG 220, box 22) and interview with *The National Observer*, 19 July 1975; US Representative Mary Ann Krupsak in *Time*, 7 July 1975; Mexican IWY planner Gloria Brasdefer's comments in *Excélsior*, 18 June 1975, 1-B; NGO representative Rita Taubenfeld in her report on 9 July 1975, Elizabeth Reid Papers, folder 88; as well as *New York Times*, 4 June 1975, 45, 19 June 1975, 41, and 3 July 1975, 1; *The Nation*, 19 July 1975, 36; *The Economist*, 5 July 1975, 72; *Newsweek*, 7 July 1975, 28; video "Report from Mexico City" (KVIE, Sacramento, California). An estimated 1,200 journalists attended, along with another 1,200 delegates representing 133 official delegations of member states, observers such as the Holy See and various national liberation organizations, and non-governmental organizations (NGOs) with UN consultative status. Another estimated 6,000 people participated in the NGO tribune.

10. For a recent reconsideration of Bandung and its aftermath, see Lee, *Making a World after Empire*.

11. Prashad, *The Darker Nations*, Chapter One. On the UN as a site for a Third World challenge to colonial powers, see Bosco, *Five to Rule Them All*; Mazower, *No Enchanted Palace; Governing the World*, 275.

12. On the rise in thematic conferences, see Schechter, *United Nations Global Conferences*.

13. On the rise of NGOs in the 1970s, see Iriye, *Global Community*, Chapter Five.

14. For an excellent example, see Davis, *The Making of Our Bodies, Ourselves*.

15. Fomerand, "UN Conferences"; Schechter, *United Nations Global Conferences*.

16. For a helpful discussion of postcolonial cosmopolitanism, see Burton, *The Postcolonial Careers of Santha Rama Rau*.

17. Westad, *The Global Cold War*.

18. On "overrun with North Americans," see Mahnaz Afkhami's comments at "Women and Girls Rising" conference, Ford Foundation, New York City, 11–12 September 2014. Although it is

difficult to measure these interactions, in the formal NGO tribune program, of 109 scheduled speakers, twenty-six were from Latin America and the Caribbean, twenty-one from Africa, and fifteen from Asia (including South and Southeast Asia), four from the Middle East (Lebanon and Iran), and three from Oceania (Fiji and Australia). Of the remaining speakers, eighteen were from Western Europe, six from Eastern Europe, and sixteen from the United States, of whom four were from the underrepresented category of men and five were confined to the role of session chair ("Report: International Women's Year Tribune–1975," November 1975, IWTC, box 3).

19. Barrios de Chungara and Viezzer, *Let Me Speak!* 197. The identification that she sought with "poor people" is as interesting as those she did not name as "people like me"—other Bolivians, indigenous participants, or even Marxists.
20. Friedan, "Scary Doings in Mexico City," 454; Chávez, "Pilgrimage to the Homeland," 173.
21. For a thoughtful consideration of the political desires that lay beneath similar claims to inter-sectionality, see Wiegman, *Object Lessons*.
22. Tinker, "A Feminist View of Copenhagen," 532.
23. Carden, "Feminism in the Mid-1970s."
24. Originally in *University of Washington Daily* and reprinted and distributed by Radical Women; Rosalyn Baxandall, Women's Liberation Research Files, Box 2, Folder 25. US women attending the NGO tribune repeatedly echoed this sentiment (e.g., Rita Taubenfeld to Robert Brown, 9 July 1975, Elizabeth Reid Papers, folder 88; Karen DeCrow report to the National Board, 29 March 1975, NOW-NYC, Box 25, Folder 2 and statement to *Xilonen*, 20 June 1975, 3).
25. Frank, "The Development of Underdevelopment," 19. See also his *Capitalism and Underdevelopment* and *On Capitalist Underdevelopment*.
26. Boserup, *Women in Economic Development*.
27. "Research Study: Politicization of International Technical Organizations," prepared for the CIA, August 1975 (*FRUS*), 1969-76, Vol. E-14, Part I, Doc 80.
28. King, *Roots of Identity*.
29. On decolonial feminism, see Lugones, "Toward a Decolonial Feminism."; "The Coloniality of Gender"; Mohanty, *Feminism without Borders*; Pérez, *The Decolonial Imaginary*. As I explore below, in Mexico City, the anti-imperialist, African American, prostitutes' rights activist Florynce Kennedy might have been the embodiment of decolonial feminism but in the IWY context was held up as an icon of capitalist dissolution. Randolph, *Florynce "Flo" Kennedy*.
30. Snyder, "Unlikely Godmother," 45.
31. *New York Times*, 29 June 1975, 2.
32. Gillingham and Smith, *Dictablanda*, Introduction; Walker, *Waking from the Dream*.
33. For a critical ethnographic take on this concept, see Gutmann, *The Meanings of Macho*.
34. For a more elaborate discussion, see Olcott, "Transnational Feminism."
35. For examples, Friedan, "Scary Doings in Mexico City"; McKenna, *Women in Action*.
36. On ties between the Ford and Rockefeller foundations and the US government (particularly the CIA), see Saunders, *The Cultural Cold War*, 113, ff. On coordination between the State Department and the NGO tribune, see Caroline Ware to Mildred Persinger, 9 June 1975, MPP, box UN World Conference (IWY), folder AA.
37. Mazower, *Governing the World*, 323.

Scene 1: WINGO Politics

1. UN doc. E/CN.6/L.644, 29 February 1972.
2. *Commission on the Status of Women: Report on the Twenty-Fourth Session (14 February–3 March 1972)*, UN doc. E/CN.6/568, 47.
3. Kinnear, *Woman of the World*, 217.
4. On relationships among the early twentieth-century WINGOs see Rupp, *Worlds of Women*.
5. de Haan, "Continuing Cold War Paradigms"; Ghodsee, "Revisiting the United Nations Decade for Women."
6. *New York Times*, 15 January 1948, 8.
7. *New York Times*, 23 October 1949, 44; Committee on Un-American Activities, House of Representatives, "Report on the Congress of American Women," 23 October 1949.

8. Laville, *Cold War Women.*

9. Kinnear, *Woman of the World,* 217; Joo, "Women's International Non-Governmental Organizations," 138.

10. Liang, "The Question of Access to the United Nations Headquarters." See also *New York Times,* 16 April 1953, 3; and 27 March 1954, 1.

11. Consultative status NGOs are accredited to participate in various UN activities, depending on their status. Category I NGOs should have large membership in countries across regions and represent broader social interests; they generally receive accreditation for conferences and the like, while Category II NGOs have "special competence" in one area and a narrower membership base and may be invited only to specialized activities. In 1996, Categories I and II were renamed General and Special. The status categories in principle correspond to an NGO's mission but in practice also reflect prevailing political pressures. In a telling example, IPPF's application for Category B status was rejected in 1953 because of Catholic opposition. It attained Roster status in 1954, was elevated to Category II in 1969, and, on the eve of the UN Population Conference, was promoted to Category I in 1973 (Willetts, *"The Conscience of the World"* 33).

12. Kinnear, *Woman of the World,* 225–30.

13. Kinnear, *Woman of the World,* 217.

14. Iriye, *Global Community*; Connors, "NGOs & Human Rights" in Willets. Although Iriye notes the growth in NGOs related to women's issues, he ignores the Mexico City conference as related to the UN's efforts and the IWY (135).

15. Stephenson, "Women's International Nongovernmental Organizations at the United Nations," 137.

16. ICW statement to ECOSOC, July 1972, ICW, Box 1, Folder 8.

17. Mildred Persinger at roundtable, "Generations of Change: The United Nations International Women's Conferences," Berkshires Conference in Women's History, University of Massachusetts at Amherst, 9–11 June 2011.

18. Elaine Livingstone to Arlie Scott, Betty Friedan, Karen DeCrow, and Jackie Ceballos, 22 March 1975, Betty Friedan Papers, 77-M105; Carton 107, file 1247.

19. The GA had passed a resolution regarding DEDAW five years earlier (UN doc. A/RES/2263 (XXII), 7 November 1967), but many member states had not yet signed, including the United States.

20. UNGA, 27th Session, agenda item 12, "Report of the Economic and Social Council, Report of the Third Committee," 11 December 1972, A/8928.

21. ILO Convention 100 was adopted on 29 June 1951 and came into force on 23 May 1953. Political scientist Sandra Whitworth describes Convention 100 as the most ratified but least implemented of the ILO conventions (Whitworth, "Gender, International Relations and the Case of the ILO," 401).

22. *New York Times,* 4 June 1975, 45; see also *New York Times,* 25 June 1975, 7.

23. Boserup, *Women in Economic Development.* In the foreword to the 1989 edition, Swasti Mitter describes the book as having "inspired the UN Decade for Women" (*Woman's Role in Economic Development,* 1).

24. UNGA Res. 2626 (XXV), 24 October 1970; 2715 & 2716 (XXV), 15 December 1970.

25. Connelly, *Fatal Misconception.*

26. ECOSOC adopted the resolution on 15 June 1972 [UN doc. E/RES/1681 (LII)]. In 1978, the office was renamed the Branch for the Advancement of Women and, in 1993, the Division for the Advancement of Women.

27. Reanda, "Human Rights and Women's Rights: The United Nations Approach," 25. This resembles the US system in which men's benefits are often seen as entitlements while women's are frequently seen as charitable welfare (Nelson, "The Origins of the Two-Channel Welfare State").

28. Tropp memo, 5 June 1973, UNESCO Archive, Sector SHS, Box 165, Folder 1.

29. Shawna Tropp to UNESCO Director, 5 June 1975, UNESCO Archive, Sector SHS, Box 165, folder 1.

30. Dahlitz to Reid, 9 April 1973, Elizabeth Reid Papers, folder 23; *Canberra Times,* 9 April 1973, 1.

31. "The Life of Elizabeth," *ABC* broadcast, 5 August 2005 (http://www.abc.net.au/stateline/act/content/2005/s1432182.htm) and "Landmark Women: Elizabeth Reid," lecture at the National Museum of Australia, 13 October 2013 (http://www.nma.gov.au/audio/transcripts/NMA_Landmark_E_Reid_20131018.html).

32. "The Life of Elizabeth."

33. *Canberra Times*, 26 March 1973, 1.

34. "The Life of Elizabeth."

35. *Canberra Times*, 9 April 1973, 1.

36. Warn, "Ministers and Minders," 152. See also Eisenstein, *Inside Agitators*, Chapter Two.

37. "The Life of Elizabeth."

38. *Canberra Times*, 11 April 1973, 13.

39. *Canberra Times*, 19 May 1973, 2.

40. *Woroni*, 13 April 1973, 4–5.

41. The four NGOs were the Australian affiliates of the ICW (National Council of Women), the WIDF (Union of Australian Women), and the IFBPW (Business and Professional Women's Clubs), and the newcomer, the Women's Electoral Lobby (WEL)—analogous to a cross between the National Organization for Women (NOW) and Women's Equity Action League (WEAL) in the United States. The WEL took a similar drubbing from the press as its US counterparts—the *Canberra Times* referred to the "middle-class trendies of the Women's Electoral Lobby" (2 August 1974, 2).

42. Confidential note for file, 2 October 1974, Elizabeth Reid Papers, folder 23.

43. Reid to JHM Oswin (Secretary, Department of the Media), 28 August 1974, Elizabeth Reid Papers, folder 10.

44. Minutes from 30 May 1973 meeting of the UNAA IWY committee, Elizabeth Reid Papers, folder 23.

45. All correspondence in Elizabeth Reid Papers, folder 23.

46. Restricted memo, UNAA National Committee for International Women's Year, undated [from 26 November 1973 meeting], Elizabeth Reid Papers, folder 23.

47. Australian mission to UN to Prime Minister and Foreign Affairs, 18 March 1974, Elizabeth Reid Papers, folder 21; Reid report to Interdepartmental meeting, 2 May 1974; Elizabeth Reid Papers, folder 20.

48. "Record of Conversation," 8 January 1974, Elizabeth Reid Papers, folder 23.

49. *Canberra Times*, 19 January 1974, 9.

50. "Notes from discussions on International Women's Year in Canada and the US," undated [February/March, 1974], Elizabeth Reid Papers, folder 17. These comments did not appear in her report to government officials (Elizabeth Reid Papers, folder 20).

51. *Canberra Times*, 4 March 1974, 6.

52. Kedgley to Reid, 21 May 1974, Elizabeth Reid Papers, folder 19. Article appeared in *New York Times*, 3 March 1974, 17.

53. Willessee to Whitlam, 24 January 1974 and Whitlam to Willessee, 7 March 1974, Elizabeth Reid Papers, folder 12.

54. Reid to Whitlam, 6 June 1974, Elizabeth Reid Papers, folder 21.

55. Reid to Kedgley, 11 June 1974, Elizabeth Reid Papers, folder 19; Dowse, "The Prime Minister's Women," 392.

56. Correspondence, June–July 1974, Elizabeth Reid Papers, folder 11.

57. Correspondence, February–March 1974, Elizabeth Reid Papers, folder 23.

58. Dahlitz to UNAA IWY committee members, 8 April 1974, Elizabeth Reid Papers, folder 23.

59. Undated clipping [May 1974], Elizabeth Reid Papers, folder 23. The Foreign Affairs Public Information Officer also reported that she had contacted a correspondent at *The Age* (Melbourne).

60. Greenwood to Reid, 16 May 1974, Elizabeth Reid Papers, folder 23.

61. Dahlitz to Reid, 24 September 1974, Elizabeth Reid Papers, folder 23.

62. Unidentified clipping [dateline Ottawa], 10 September 1974, Elizabeth Reid Papers, folder 53. On Sipilä's appointment, see UN doc. SG/A/156, 5 July 1974. Reid enjoyed far greater appreciation in UN circles and abroad than she did at home. She had just faced eviscerating

cuts to her proposed child-care program, and the *Canberra Times* speculated that feminists must by now see her as "more of a supernumerary than a supergirl" (2 August 1974, 2).

63. Confidential note for file, 2 October 1974, Elizabeth Reid Papers, folder 23.

64. Note for file: Discussions with Ms Sipila, 9 October 1974, Elizabeth Reid Papers, folder 17. On Sipilä's visit, see also telegram from UN New York mission to Foreign Affairs, 2 October 1974, Elizabeth Reid Papers, folder 53.

65. *The Australian*, 9 October 1974, Elizabeth Reid Papers, folder 53; for similar clippings, see folders 2 and 5.

Scene 2: Choosing Battles in the Cold War

1. Organizing documents and minutes of both committees are in IWTC, Box 1.

2. Popa, "Translating Equality," 63.

3. "WIDF and the U.N.," *Women of the Whole World*, No. 1 1973 (January): 48–51.

4. Alami to Directeur-général (ILO), 22 May 1973, IWTC, box 1.

5. Alami to Bruce, 27 June 1973; Notes on WINGOs meeting (taken by Alice Paquier of the WYWCA), 7 July 1973; proposals to be submitted to the UN Secretary-General through Mrs. Margaret K. Bruce, 31 July 1973 (all in IWTC, Box 1).

6. Rosalind Harris was certainly aware of the importance of involving people from outside the United States—in a letter to Alice Paquier (WYWCA) about planning the Population Tribune, she asked for suggestions for an executive director. "The office is based in New York because of tying in with UN plans and arrangements—but we want a non-American!" (Harris to Paquier, 27 August 1973; IWTC, box 1).

7. Minutes of Study-Action Group on Integration of Women, 13 March 1973, IWTC Box 1.

8. Alami to Harris, 1 August 1973, IWTC Box 1.

9. Harris to Alami, 9 August 1973, IWTC Box 1.

10. For a US State Department assessment of Soviet peace initiatives at the UN as propaganda, see Airgram A-128, Department of State to All Diplomatic Posts, "Assessment of the 27th UN General Assembly," 5 January 1973, reprinted in *FRUS*, 1969–76, Vol. E-14, Part I, Doc. 1. See also Laville, *Cold War Women*, Chapter Two.

11. Minutes of the Study-Action Group on Integration of Women in Development, 13 March 1973, IWTC papers, box 1.

12. From the original 51 members in 1945, the UN had grown to 99 by 1960 and would reach 144 by 1975. For a year-by-year roster of membership, see https://www.un.org/en/sections/member-states/growth-united-nations-membership-1945-present/index.html.

13. Cited in Mazower, *Governing the World*, 271.

14. Assessment of the 27th UN General Assembly, airgram to all diplomatic posts, 5 January 1973, *FRUS*, 1969–76, Vol. E-14, Part I, Doc 1.

15. Bush to State Department, 17 January 1973, *FRUS*, 1969-76, Vol. E-14, Part I, Doc. 3. On the UN's founding principles and their basis in British imperialism, see Mazower, *No Enchanted Palace*.

16. Conversation between Nixon and Kissinger, 3 February 1973, White House Tapes, *FRUS*, 1969–76, Vol. E-14, Part I, Doc. 4.

17. Memorandum of meeting between Nixon and Scali, 13 February 1973, *FRUS*, 1969–76, Vol. E-14, Part I, Doc. 5.

18. Scali to Secretary of State, 18 May 1973, *FRUS*, 1969–76, Vol. E-14, Part I, Doc 7.

19. Telegram from Secretary of State to all diplomatic posts, 16 August 1973, *FRUS*, 1969–76, Vol. E-14, Part I, Doc. 8.

20. USUN mission to Secretary of State, 21 November 1973, *FRUS*, 1969–76, Vol. E-14, Part I, Doc. 9.

21. Bureau of Intelligence and Research, "The Non-Aligned Group in the UN: Challenge or Obstacle for the US?" 15 January 1974, *FRUS*, 1969–76, Vol. E-14, Part I, Doc. 11.

22. Fulbright to Kissinger, 24 September 1973, and response from Marshall Wright (Asst. Sec. for Congressional Relations), 18 October 1973; 1973, *FRUS*, 1969–76, Vol. E-14, Part I, Doc. 167.

23. Memorandum from Department of State Secretariat Staff to the National Security Council Secretariat, November 9, 1973; *FRUS*, 1969–76, Vol. E-14, Part I, Doc 168. Irene Tinker highlights the importance of personal connections in securing the Percy Amendment. USIA officer Mildred Marcy's husband was the chief of staff for the Senate Foreign Relations Committee, and Representative Donald Fraser, who chaired the House Foreign Affairs Subcommittee on International Organizations and Movements, was married to Arvonne Fraser, the president of Women's Equity Action League (1972–74) who would serve as an advisor to the US IWY delegation. Tinker, "Challenging Women, Changing Policies: The Women in Development Movement," 70–71.

24. Minutes of August 14, 1973 United Nations Economic Committee (UNEC) Meeting on International Women's Year, *FRUS*, 1969–76, Vol. E-14, Part I, Doc. 165; Airgram Department of State to USUN New York, 10 September 1973, *FRUS*, 1969–76, Vol. E-14, Part I, Doc. 166.

25. State to NSC, 9 Nov 1973, *FRUS*, 1969–76, Vol. E-14, Part I, Doc 168. Jean Whittet to Sara-Alyce Wright, 18 November 1974 (MPP, box UN World Conference (IWY), folder I): "Last year a little State Department money was given to Ruth Bacon—a very 'old fashioned' woman whom Mildred Persinger calls 'The Queen of the China Lobby.' She set up a small office in D.C. at Meriden [Meridian] House, but there is virtually no action and no national committee. She has no status with the government."

26. Department of State Memorandum for NSC Secretariat, "Progress Report on International Women's Year," 9 November 1973, *FRUS*, 1969–76, Vol. E-14, Part I, Doc. 168; Memorandum to All UNEC Member from John W. McDonald Jr. (includes quotation from minutes of 2 October 1973 IWY UNEC meeting), 9 November 1973, *FRUS*, 1969–76, Vol. E-14, Part I, Doc. 169.

27. Ambassador Clarence Clyde Ferguson Jr., to State Department, 7 January 1974, Wikileaks (https://wikileaks.org/plusd/cables/1974USUNN00028_b.html). A human rights lawyer, Ferguson had been the US ambassador to UNESCO and one of the principal authors of the 1967 Convention on the Elimination of All Forms of Racial Discrimination. On the United States' continued refusal to support CEDAW, see Baldez, *Defying Convention*.

28. *Women of the Whole World: Journal of the WIDF* No. 2 (Spring 1973), 5.

29. On the State Department response, see Allan, Galey, and Persinger, "World Conference of International Women's Year," 30.

30. Ruth Bacon, "Notes on the 25th Session of the UN Commission on the Status of Women (New York, January 14–February 1, 1974)," IWTC, Box 1. The CSW consisted of representatives from thirty-two member states. ECOSOC elected the states represented, and governments designated the individuals to serve as delegates. Delegates served four-year terms with the possibility for re-election.

31. Paquier's report to the Geneva committee, 22 February 1974, IWTC, box 1.

32. CSW, 25th session, 15 January 1974, UN doc. E/CN.6/L.658.

33. By its 29th session, the GA had passed eleven resolutions regarding the "pattern of conferences" and resolved to establish a committee to study the question (UN doc. A/3351, 18 December 1974).

34. "Draft of edits for ECOSOC resolution," 14 December 1974, IWTC, Box 1. The edits refer to the ECOSOC document E/CN.6/576; the GA resolution is Res 3010 [XXVII]. See also, Joo, "Women's International Non-Governmental Organizations," 179–80.

35. The statement submitted to the CSW (UN doc. E/CN.6/NGO/248, 8 January 1974) was signed by sixteen NGOs, all members of the New York committee.

36. CSW, 25th session, 21 January 1974, UN doc. E/CN.6/L.659.

37. Paquier report to Geneva committee, 22 February 1974, IWTC, box 1. By 1975, the USSR had signed all but one of the eight instruments related to women's status (demurring on the widely unpopular convention defining terms of consent to marry), while the United States had only signed the convention on trafficking (UN doc. E/CONF.66/Add.3).

38. Bacon, "Notes on the 25th Session."

39. "International Women's Year: Report of the Working Group to the Commission on the Status of Women," 30 January 1974, UN doc. E/CN.6/L.588.

40. According to Gallup polls, public confidence in the UN's efficacy reached historic lows in the 1970s, and the political and economic climate in the United States ruled out any substantial support (http://www.gallup.com/poll/116347/united-nations.aspx).
41. Joo, "Women's International Non-Governmental Organizations," 180.
42. CSW, 25th session, 31 January 1974, UN docs. E/CN.6/L.658/Rev.1 & Rev.2. Apart from Kenya and Thailand, all the other signatories were among the sixteen delegations who served on the CSW's IWY working group, which met seven times to discuss the IWY program designed by the Secretary-General in consultation with member states.
43. Bacon, "Notes on the 25th Session"
44. CSW, 25th session, 1 February 1974, UN docs. E/CN.6/L.658, Rev.2; E/CN.6/L.660/Add.15, 31 January 1974.
45. Draft Report of the CSW, Chapter II, 24 January 1974, UN doc. E/CN.6/L.660.
46. Scali to State, 4 February 1974; *FRUS*, 1969–76, Vol. E-14, Part I, Doc 170.
47. Paquier report to Geneva committee, 22 February 1974, IWTC, box 1.
48. Bacon, "Notes on the 25th Session." The sentence appears in all caps as a separate paragraph centered in the page.
49. "Revised International Women's Year Task Force Report," 14 February 1974, Elizabeth Reid Papers, folder 12.
50. Minutes of NGO Committee on IWY, 20 February 1974, IWTC, Box 1.
51. Schuller-McGeachy to Harris, 19 February 1974, IWTC, Box 1.
52. Schuller-McGeachy to Harris, 10 May 1974, IWTC, Box 1; see also, letter from Working Group to Establish a Preparatory Committee for the World Congress of Women, 14 May 1975, and *Bulletin: World Congress for International Women's Year* (Esther Hymer Collection).
53. Niall MacDermot to Waldheim, 6 March 1974; Harris to MacDermot, 4 April 1974; both in IWTC, Box 1.
54. On the connections among the Cold War, the African American civil rights movement, and developments at the UN, see Borstelmann, *The Cold War and the Color Line*; Dudziak, *Cold War Civil Rights*; Plummer, *In Search of Power*.
55. UN docs. A/RES/1904 (20 November 1963) and A/RES/1921 (5 December 1963). On Third World support for the anti-racism declaration, US opposition, and the links between the two resolutions, see Connors, "NGOs and the Human Rights of Women," 155; Hazard, *Postwar Anti-Racism*, 141–43; Lake and Reynolds, *Drawing the Global Colour Line*, 349. On linking DEDAW to the convention against racial discrimination, see Baldez, *Defying Convention*, Chapter Two.
56. Jain, *Women, Development, and the UN*, 46–47.
57. Minutes of meeting, Committee on IWY, 17 April 1974, IWTC, Box 1.
58. Restricted telegram from Australian mission to the UN to the Department of Foreign Affairs, 18 March 1974; Elizabeth Reid Papers, folder 21.
59. For the State Department's account of the special session, see its 5 June 1974 airgram, *FRUS*, 1969–76, Vol. E-14, Part I, Doc. 16.
60. Telegram from State Department to selected diplomatic posts, 13 May 1974, *FRUS*, 1969–76, Vol. E-14, Part I, Doc. 13.
61. Secretary of State to All Diplomatic Posts, 17 May 1974, *FRUS*, 1969–76, Vol. E-14, Part I, Doc. 14.
62. UN doc. E/RES/1851, 16 May 1974.
63. Susan Jane Kedgley to Elizabeth Reid, 21 May 1975, Elizabeth Reid Papers, folder 19.
64. Minutes of meeting, Committee on IWY, 15 May 1974, IWTC, Box 1.
65. Minutes of meeting, Committee on IWY, 29 May 1974, IWTC, Box 1.
66. Esther Hymer to Rosalind Harris, 1 June 1974, IWTC, Box 1.
67. Hymer to Harris, 10 June 1974, IWTC, Box 1.
68. Alami to Margaret Bruce, 27 June 1974; IWTC, Box 1.
69. Minutes of meeting, Committee on IWY, 12 June and 19 June 1974, IWTC, Box 1.
70. Information on the meeting of the representatives of the Working Group to Establish an International Preparatory Committee for the World Congress of Women 1975, held 3 July 1974 in Geneva with Mrs. Sipila, Assistant Secretary General for Social Development and Humanitarian Affairs; MPP, box UN World Conference (IWY), folder L. The document is

unsigned but was likely produced by Alice Paquier and Elizabeth Palmer, who represented the World YWCA.

71. UN press release, 5 July 1974, UN doc. SG/A/156.
72. "Address of Mr. Dwain Epps," 2 July 1974, IWTC, box1.
73. McAtee, *Transformed*, 73.
74. Mazower, *Governing the World*, 286.
75. "World Population Conference Scope Paper," 25 July 1974, *FRUS*, 1969–76, Vol. E-14, Part I, Doc 115; Connelly, *Fatal Misconception*.
76. State Department to All Diplomatic Posts, 22 August 1974, *FRUS*, 1969–76, Vol. E-14, Part I, Doc 17
77. Caspar Weinberger (Secretary of Health, Education, and Welfare; leader of US delegation) to Kissinger, 19 September 1974, *FRUS*, 1969–76, Vol. E-14, Part I, Doc 117.
78. "World Population Conference—Wrap Up," 31 August 1974, *FRUS*, 1969–76, Vol. E-14, Part I, Doc 116.
79. Springsteen to Armstrong, 14 May 1974, *FRUS*, 1969–76, Vol. E-14, Part I, Doc. 171. The *New York Times* described Armstrong as the "best brave front to the public" and the "only one with nerve enough" to make public appearances on behalf of the Nixon administration during the Watergate scandal (*New York Times*, 30 May 1973, 34). In 1976, Patricia Hutar led a campaign to draft Armstrong as the GOP vice-presidential candidate, but instead she was named ambassador to Britain, a position she held from 1976 to 1977 (*Los Angeles Times*, 16 August 1976, B11; *New York Times*, 31 July 2008, B6).
80. NGO Committee on International Women's Year, Minutes of meeting held September 11, 1974, UN Headquarters, New York; IWTC, Box 1.
81. Paquier to Jones, 14 October 1974, cited in Garner, *Shaping a Global Women's Agenda*, 230, n. 24.
82. Of the forty-five NGOs represented at the 30 October meeting, for example, fourteen had clear continuing religious affiliations and another had Methodist roots. Five of these identified as Jewish or Zionist and seven identified as either Catholic or some denomination of Protestant Christian; the other two were Baha'i International and the International Association for Religious Freedom.
83. Harris to Alami, 18 October 1974; Harris to Palmer and Harris to Luisa Giurati, both 21 October 1974; Harris to Alami, 30 October 1974; on "digging out after Bucharest," Harris to Anne Sieve (IPPF), 18 October 1974; all in IWTC, box 1.
84. Harris to Sieve, 18 October 1974, IWTC papers, Box 1.

Scene 3: Getting to Mexico City

1. Secondary accounts have attributed the scuttling of the Bogota plans to upheaval or violence in Colombia, when in fact quite the opposite was the case—this period was among the most non-violent in Colombia's history (e.g., Hawkesworth, *Globalization and Feminist Activism*, 118). The 1974 election rendered Colombia more authentically democratic than it had been in many decades but introduced uncertainty into personnel and budgeting matters. Rosalind Harris attributed Colombia's demurral to political uncertainty (Harris to Anne Sieve (IPPF), 18 October 1974, and Harris to Hymer 21 October 1974, both in IWTC, Box 1), while the *New York Times* simply attributed it to indifference (4 June 1975, 45).
2. Communications regarding the venue change documented in UN Archive, file S-0971-0012-05.
3. UN doc. E/L.1615, 18 November 1974.
4. Philip Agee, in his tell-all book about the CIA, claims Echeverría as a CIA informant (Agee, *Inside the Company*, 525). Historian Christopher Andrew and former KGB agent Vasili Mitrokhin describe efforts to recruit Echeverría, assuring him that breaking with the Pinochet government in Chile and supporting the Movimento Popular de Libertação de Angola (MPLA) in Angola would strengthen his bid to become secretary-general of the UN. Andrew and Mitrokhin, *The World Was Going Our Way*, 102–4.
5. CIA report, "The United Nations: Problems Continue, Potential Erodes," 11 February 1975, *FRUS*, 1969–76, Vol. E-14, Part I, Doc 20.
6. UNGA 29th Session, 3281 (XXIX), Charter on the Economic Rights and Duties of States.

7. General Assembly, "Charter of Economic Rights and Duties of States," 12 December 1974 (UN doc. A/RES/29/3281). The vote was 120 in favor, 6 opposed (Belgium, Denmark, West Germany, Luxembourg, United States, and the United Kingdom), and 10 abstentions (Austria, Canada, France, Ireland, Israel, Italy, Japan, Netherlands, Norway, and Spain).

8. G. to Reid, 6 June 1975, Elizabeth Reid Papers, folder 95.

9. Carey, *Plaza of Sacrifices*; Poniatowska, *La noche de Tlatelolco*.

10. Soto Laveaga, " 'Let's Become Fewer.' "

11. Echeverría submitted the amendment to Congress on 24 September 1974. The passage of a constitutional amendment also reflects Echeverría's UN aspirations, as it brought Mexico in compliance with the 1967 DEDAW.

12. On the impact of this amendment, see Toto Gutiérrez, "El feminismo en México."

13. See, for example, Moya Palencia to Dr. Francisco Guel Jiménez (Governor of Aguascalientes), 26 October 1974, AGN, DFS, Exp. 44-1-74, Leg. 5, hojas 241–42. On coordination with state and local governments, see also AGN, DFS, 22 November 1974 report from Colima, Exp. 100-7-1-74, Leg. 7, hoja 78; AGN, DFS, 10 December 1974 report from Jaliso, Exp. 44-1-74, Leg. 6, hoja 99.

14. Germain to The Files (#L740358), "Conversation with Ros Harris, IWY Tribune, 2/25/75," FFA, Grant no. 75-224.

15. Lili [Hahn] to Doris [Vaughn], Esther [Hymer] and IWY Committee, 27 December 1974, IWTC, Box 3.

16. *México75: Año Internacional de la Mujer* 1, no. 1 (January 1975): 1.

17. AGN, DFS, 10 December 1974, Exp. 44-1-74, Leg. 6, hoja 99.

18. Evans, *Personal Politics*; Gutiérrez Castañeda, *Feminismo en México*; Lau Jaiven, *La nueva ola del feminismo en México*.

19. Lamas, "Mis diez primeros años," 8.

20. These ties sometimes proved fatal —Alaíde Foppa, the leading and most energetic founder of the feminist magazine *fem*, had been born in Barcelona of an Argentine father and Guatemalan mother and had lived in Guatemala during the so-called Guatemalan spring of progressive political leadership. She went into exile in Mexico City after the 1954 coup. When she returned to Guatemala City in 1980 to visit her family, she was detained by military personnel and never heard from again.

21. The citations would be too many to list, but these recollections appear in magazines such as *fem*, *Debate Feminista*, and *La Correa Feminista*.

22. Lamas, "Mis diez primeros años," 9.

23. Cano, "Una ciudadanía igualitaria"; Olcott, *Revolutionary Women in Postrevolutionary Mexico*.

24. Despite generally higher tolerance of dissent, in 1976, Echeverría notoriously sent in military personnel to remove Julio Scherer García as general director of the often-critical *Excélsior* and had also forced the ouster a year earlier of the magazine *Porqué?* See Lawson, *Building the Fourth Estate*. On the limits of the *apertura democrática*, see also Freije, "Journalists, Scandal, and the Unraveling of One-Party Rule."

25. Lamas, "Mis diez primeros años," 8.

26. Lamas, "Mis diez primeros años," 10. Lamas remains Mexico's most prominent feminist and founded the publication *fem*, a close analogue to *Ms.*, as well as the more scholarly but still politically engaged *Debate feminista*.

27. Lau, "El nuevo movimiento feminista," 20–21.

28. Lamas, "Mis diez primeros años," 10.

29. Brito de Martí, "De ingenuas modositas y luchadoras bravías," 17.

30. Report on meeting "Presencia de la mujer mexicana en las filas del Partido Acción Nacional," 18 June 1975, AGN, IPS, Caja 1163-A, Vol. 1, hojas 71–73.

31. Ward, "Mexico City," 36.

32. Ward, "Mexico City," 34–35. The minimum wage at that point was the equivalent of $170 USD per month. These figures presumably exclude the vast informal economy.

33. Walsh, *Founding a Movement*, 9.

34. Hahn to Doris Vaughn, Esther Hymer and the NGO committee, 27 December 1974, IWTC, box 3.

35. For the report, see UN doc. E/56-5, 6 January 1975. For notes on objections, see IWTC, folder "UN World Conf—General Documents, Proposals," Box 1. On the Soviet objection, see NGO Meeting on International Women's Year, Minutes of meeting 22 January 1975, MPP, box UN World Conference (IWY), folder G.

36. Carrillo Flores to Ojeda Paullada, 17 December 1974, IWTC papers, box 3.

37. Notes on call from Marcial Plehn-Mejía, 3 January 1975, IWTC papers, box 3.

38. UN doc. A/C.3/L.2117, 25 October 1974.

39. "Report of the Economic and Social Council: Introductory Statement by Mrs. Margaret K. Bruce at the Third Committee on 23 October 1974," NOW-NYC, Box 23, Folder 11. This formulation was echoed in the UN's press release announcing Mexico City as the new conference site (UN doc. OPI/CESI note IWY/17, 5 December 1974).

40. UN doc. A/C.3/L.2124, 31 October 1974.

41. Doerr to Persinger, 1 November 1974, MPP, box Mexico 1975 (NGO-Forum) box, folder A.

42. Paquier to Persinger and Mildred Jones, 8 November 1974, MPP, Mexico 1975 (NGO-Forum) box, folder A.

43. Paquier to Persinger and Mildred Jones, 8 November 1974, MPP, Mexico 1975 (NGO-Forum) box, folder A; meeting of International, Regional and National Organizations to Establish the International Preparatory Committee for the World Congress for International Women's Year, Tihany, Hungarian People's Republic, 4–5 November 1974, MPP, box UN World Conference (IWY), folder L.

44. Hymer to Harris, 31 December 1974, IWTC, box 1.

45. Harris to Persinger [undated], MPP, box Tribune, Mexico 1975 (NGO-Forum), folder B.

46. Germain, interview by Rebecca Sharpless, June 19–20, 2003; Hartmann, *The Other Feminists*, Chapter Five. On the all-Foundation Women's Task Force that met regularly in 1972–73, see report from Adrienne Germain, "International Programs Related to the Status, Roles, and Opportunities of Women," November 1975, FFA, Doc. 71439.

47. "A Request for Financial Support: IWY Tribune 1975," FFA, grant 75-224.

48. Germain memo to the files (#L74-358), 14 January 1975, FFA, grant no. 75-224.

49. As CONGO president, Rosalind Harris appointed Persinger; she described Persinger later as "my first choice, after considerable consultation," despite the fact that she barely knew her prior to the appointment (Harris to Rosalie Oakes [World Relations Director, YWCA], 14 July 1975, MPP, box Tribune, Mexico 1975 (NGO-Forum), folder A.

50. NGO Committee minutes, IWTC, box 1.

51. As Persinger would remind a student interviewing her in 2006, in the 1960s and '70s the YWCA offered a training ground for activists but later changed "from a movement to a social service organization" (Persinger interview). On the YWCA's important role in transnational women's organizing, see Garner, *Shaping a Global Women's Agenda*.

52. Margaret Mead, "The Emergence of Women into Full Participation in All Parts of Society," lecture delivered to the International Women's Year Task Force, UN Headquarters, New York, 11 September 1974; Elizabeth Reid Papers, folder 53. Persinger's notes in her papers in file "International Women's Year . . . please add to box."

53. MPP, box UN World Conference (IWY), folder T.

54. Persinger to Doerr, undated [mid-November 1974] (MPP, box Mexico 1975 (NGO-Forum) box, folder A).

55. Notes on Meeting of NGO Sub-Committee on the Status of Women, Geneva (by Katherine Strong, WYWCA), 29 January 1975, MPP, box Tribune, Mexico 1975 (NGO-Forum), folder A.

56. Minutes of IWY Organizing Committee (Hymer's), Thursday, March 13, [1975], IWTC, box 2.

57. IWY Tribune Organizing Committee Meeting, 9 January 1975, IWTC, Box 2.

58. See correspondence in IWTC, box 2; NGO Committee on International Women's Year [Hymer's committee], Minutes of meeting February 26, 1975, MPP, box UN World Conference (IWY), folder G.

59. See documentation from FFA grant #PA 750-224; Canadian International Development Agency (CIDA) to Rosalind Harris, 8 May 1975, MPP, Box Tribune Mexico 1975 (NGO-Forum), Folder A.

60. Barber to Committee on Women in ID Programs, 6 February 1975, FFA, grant no. 750-224.

61. Simon to Persinger, 30 May 1975, IWTC, Box 2.

62. On the role of the WYWCA more generally in IWY, see Garner, *Shaping a Global Women's Agenda.* For an example of how these progressive networks operated in Fiji, see George, *Situating Women,* Chapter Two.

63. Persinger to Barber, 18 March 1975, FFA, Grant no. 75-224.

64. Persinger to Organizing Committee, undated [early April], IWTC, box 2.

65. Persinger to Barber, 18 February 1975, FFA, grant no. 75-224.

66. Persinger to Barber, 7 February 1975, FFA, grant no. 75-224.

Scene 4: Follow the Money

1. On South Africa's suspension, see Bailey, "Some Procedural Problems in the UN General Assembly." The United States, Britain, and France voted in the Security Council to veto the decision, but GA President Bouteflika refused to seat the South African delegation.

2. Conference documents available in NARA, RG 220, Records of the U.S. Center for International Women's Year; Subject Files, 1973-1975, A-AS; Box 1 (Box 1, E-1; NC3-220-78-6); folder "AAUW"

3. On Tuckerman's career, see Littlejohns, "Recording UN History," 263–65.

4. *New York Times,* 3 November 1974, 40. Often described as "voluble" or a "colorful maverick," Baroody was made an honorary citizen of New York in 1939 (see his obituary, *New York Times,* 5 March 1979, 29.

5. Unsurprisingly, US feminist newsletters picked up the story, with one describing him as a "representative of the oil-rich desert kingdom where slavery still exists and which is one of five countries of the world where women cannot vote" (*Sister: West Coast Feminist Newspaper,* vol. v, no. 8: 3, December 1974).

6. UN doc. A/C.3/L.2125, 31 October 1974.

7. UN docs. A/C.3/L.2118, 28 October 1974; A/C.3/L.2118/Rev.1, 29 October 1974; A/C.3/L.2118/Rev.2, 1 November 1974.

8. UN doc. A/9887, 27 November 1974.

9. Report on UNGA 29 (Australian delegation), 24 December 1974, Reid papers, folder 94.

10. Walsh, *Founding a Movement,* 8.

11. Report on UNGA 29 (Australian delegation), 24 December 1974, Elizabeth Reid Papers, folder 94.

12. Kedgley to Reid, 7 January 1975, Elizabeth Reid Papers, folder 19.

13. Naghibi, *Rethinking Global Sisterhood.*

14. Betty Friedan, "Coming Out of the Veil," *Ladies' Home Journal,* June 1975, 98–103. Germaine Greer would publish a characteristically caustic account of the visit in "Women's Glib," *Vanity Fair,* June 1988, 32 ff.

15. Letter from Jacqueline Ceballos to NOW-NYC, 3 June 1974, NOW-NYC, Box 3, Folder 12.

16. UN doc. OPI/CESI NOTE IWY/19 December 1974.

17. Allan, Galey, and Persinger, "World Conference of International Women's Year," 32.

18. As of mid-November, Sweden had given $1 million mostly earmarked for development projects, the United States had given $100,000 entirely earmarked for the IWY conference, Norway had given $18,000, and the Philippines had given $5,000 (Elizabeth Reid Papers, folder 5).

19. "International Women's Year: Real Equality Ahead," *Development Forum* 3, no. 1 (January/February 1975): 1 (published by the UN's Centre for Economic and Social Information).

20. "More IWY Activity Next Week," *Delegates World Bulletin* 5, no 4 (24 February 1975): 1022.

21. Inward Telegram, 13 February 1975, Elizabeth Reid Papers, folder 19.

22. Alexander, "Report from Mexico City."

23. Consultation with the Mexican Authorities on the World Conference of the International Women's Year, 17 February 1975, UN archive, document SO 246/3 (1-5-2).

24. Kedgley to Reid, 18 February 1975, Elizabeth Reid Papers, folder 18.

25. Katharine Strong to Mildred Jones and Mildred Persinger, 5 February 1975, MPP, box Tribune, Mexico 1975 (NGO-Forum), folder B.

26. "More IWY Activity Next Week," *Delegates World Bulletin* 5, no 4 (24 February 1975): 1022.
27. Kedgley to Reid, 18 February 1975, Elizabeth Reid Papers, folder 18; UNICEF inter-office memo, Timothy Rothermel to Jack Ling, 21 March 1975, UN Archive, S-0990-0004-07-00001; "Top Women Performers Plan Gala Benefit at U.N.," *New York Times*, 29 January 1975, 23.
28. *London Times*, 19 February 1975, 16.
29. Patricia Tsien to Georg Hennig, 7 March 1975, UN archive, file S-0990-0004-07-00001.
30. Kedgley to Reid, 18 February 1975, Elizabeth Reid Papers, Folder 18. On the march, see "Call for March for International Women's Day" (Betty Friedan Papers, Carton 107, File 1254); "Minutes of the NOW-NY Chapter General Meeting," 20 February 1975 (NOW-NYC, Box 2, Folder 15); and *New York Times*, 9 March 1975, 1.
31. "More IWY Activity Next Week," *Delegates World Bulletin* 5, no. 4 (24 February 1975): 1022. For bios of participants, see Arthur and Elizabeth Schlesinger Library, Betty Friedan Papers, Carton 107, File 1247.
32. *New York Times*, 9 March 1975, 52.
33. Nusenbaum to Friedan, 25 February 1975, Betty Friedan Papers, Carton 107, file 1247.
34. Tropp to Herzog, 18 December 1973, UNESCO Archive, Sector SHS, Box 165, folder 1.
35. Bruce interview, 41.
36. Inwards telegram, undated [c. 10 March 1975], Elizabeth Reid Papers, folder 19.
37. "Draft International Plan of Action," 8 February 1975, UN doc. E/CONF.66/CC/2.
38. Rostow, *The Stages of Economic Growth*. For an excellent analysis of gender in Rostow's classic text, see Saldaña-Portillo, *Revolutionary Imagination in the Americas*.
39. Dunlop to John D. Rockefeller III, 28 February 1975, RAC, Rockefeller Family Papers, Box 46, Folder 281, RG 5: John D. Rockefeller 3rd Papers, Series 3 - Office and Home Files. The memo is available as a UN document: "Working paper submitted by Iran with a view to facilitating discussion of the draft Plan of Action," 3 March 1975, UN doc. E/CONF.66/CC/L.1.
40. In contrast to Rostow, see, for example, Frank, *Capitalism and Underdevelopment*.
41. For a list of the "relevant international instruments," including those of both the UN and its specialized agencies, see UN doc. E/CONF.66/CC/2/Add.1 (25 February 1975).
42. "Statement Made by H.I.H. Princess Ashraf Pahlavi (Iran)," 4 March 1975, UN doc. E/CONF.66/CC/L.2.
43. Inwards telegram, undated [c. 10 March 1975], Elizabeth Reid Papers, folder 19. For a description of the organization of work, see Draft Report of the Consultative Committee, 13 March 1975, UN doc. E/CONF.66/L.3/Add.3. Many observers commented upon Reid's impressive leadership abilities and, in particular, her strength in representing divergent perspectives (e.g., Elaine Livingstone to Arlie Scott, Betty Friedan, Karen DeCrow, and Jackie Ceballos, 22 March 1975, Betty Friedan Papers, 77-M105; Carton 107, file 1247). Elizabeth Reid, personal communication with author, 21 December 2014.
44. Reid, "Women and the New International Economic Order," 138.
45. Elizabeth Reid, personal communication with author, 21 December 2014.
46. Scali to State Department, 19 March 1975; *FRUS*, 1969–76, Vol. E-14, Part I, Doc 176. Lucille Mair would serve as the secretary general on the UN Conference on Women in Copenhagen (1980), Leticia Shahani would assume the same role at the conference in Nairobi (1985).
47. Tropp to Director RMO, 23 April 1975, UNESCO archive, box 166, folder 1. Tropp's characterization echoed in Draft Report of the Consultative Committee, 12 March 1975, E/CONF.66/CC/L.3.
48. "Draft Report of the Chairman of the Working Group of the Consultative Committee for International Women's Year," 14 March 1975, Elizabeth Reid Papers, folder 92.
49. Shawna Tropp to Marie-Pierre Herzog, 11 March 1975, UNESCO Archive, Box 166, Folder 1.
50. Text available in Elizabeth Reid Papers, folder 7.
51. Elizabeth Reid Papers, folder 24.
52. Tropp to Director RMO, 23 April 1975, UNESCO Archive, box 166, folder 1.
53. "Report on United Nations Consultative Committee for International Women's Year," [undated], Elizabeth Reid Papers, folder 18.
54. Scali to State Department, 19 March 1975; *FRUS*, 1969–76, Vol. E-14, Part I, Doc 176.
55. March newsletter from US Center for IWY (Elizabeth Reid Papers, folder 9).

56. Memo from Adrienne Germain to The Files (#L74-358) re Conversation, 3/24/75, R. G. Livingston, 25 March 1975; FFA, Grant no. 75-224. Elizabeth Reid similarly leveraged geopolitical tensions to keep the Foreign Office's attention (Elizabeth Reid Papers, folder 15).

57. WYWCA, "Comments concerning a draft programme of action for International Women's Year," 13 September 1973, MPP, box UN World Conference (IWY), folder Q.

58. "A Beginning Critique of the International Women's Year Plan of Action," Center of Concern, 5 March 1975, NARA, RG 220, Records of the U.S. Center for International Women's Year; Subject Files, 1973-1975; A-AS; Box 1 (Box 1, E-1; NC3-220-78-6); folder "ACTION."

59. John Campbell (Australian mission to the UN) to Reid, 22 April 1975, Elizabeth Reid Papers, folder 92. The plan's length remained a widely shared concern. Adrienne Germain described it to Mildred Marcy as needing "more radical restructuring than I can undertake" but recommended distilling it to a one- or two-page document, using the current version for "general background" (Germain to Marcy, 5 June 1975, NARA, RG220, box 22).

60. Copy of the "Caracas Declaration" available in NARA, RG220, box 22 as well as SRE, VEN-9-1.

61. Telegram from Scali to Kissinger, [21?] May 1975, NARA, RG220, box 22.

62. Telegram from Scali to Kissinger, [21?] May 1975, NARA, RG220, box 22; Secretary of State to All Diplomatic Posts, 28 May 1975, *FRUS*, 1969–76, Vol. E-14, Part I, Doc 178; Secretary of State to US mission to UN, 30 May 1975, *FRUS*, 1969–76, Vol. E-14, Part I, Doc 179.

63. Australian Embassy (Washington) to Foreign Affairs (Canberra), 28 May 1975, Elizabeth Reid Papers, folder 81.

64. Reported by Sara Dowse [Senior Advisor, Department of Prime Minister and Cabinet, and member of the Australian IWY delegation], Australian Prime Minister's office, 28 May 1975, Elizabeth Reid Papers, folder 81.

Scene 5: Opening Acts

1. AGN, DFS, 15 June 1975, Exp. 9-342-75, Leg. 4, hoja 187.

2. Mildred Marcy to Sheila Rabb Weidenfeld (Betty Ford's press secretary), 14 June 1975, NARA, RG 220, Records Relating to the U.N. IWY World Conference, Mexico City, June–July 1974; Subject File A-G; Box 22.

3. *El Universal*, 16 June 1975, 4.

4. Brownmiller, *In Our Time*, 192. Fowler to Morgan, 15 June 1975, Robin Morgan Papers, Box C5.

5. *Hera: A Philadelphia Feminist Publication*, July 1975, 1.

6. Chávez, "Pilgrimage to the Homeland," 171.

7. *El Universal* and *Excélsior*, 16 June 1975, 1; *El Nacional*, 18 June 1975, 3.

8. Sara Dowse, "So What Are Feminists to Do?" speech to Emily's List, 14 August 2014 (in possession of author). Born in the United States, Dowse emigrated to Australia after her parents were called before the House Un-American Activities Committee. She succeeded Elizabeth Reid in the Australian government.

9. The seminar was funded by the AAAS (which, in turn, had received support from USAID), the UN Development Program (UNDP), the UN Institute for Training and Research (UNITAR), and Mexico's National Council on Science and Technology (CONACYT).

10. The Mexico Encounter for Journalists: Summary of Discussions between Aïda González, Hugo Rocha and Snowden T. Herrick, UN Headquarters (New York), 6–7 March 1975; UN Archive (New York), "Items in International Women's Year," Container S-0990-0004; UNESCO, "Working Paper on Education about Development," 28 January 1972 (http://unesdoc.unesco.org/images/0000/000006/000670EB.pdf).

11. AGN, IPS, report for 16 June 1975, Caja 1162-B, Vol. 4, hoja 625; *Excélsior*, 17 June 1975, 5-A.

12. See, for example, Davis, *The Making of Our Bodies, Ourselves*.

13. "Urban Living Group: Highlights of Issues and Recommendations," Working group report from AAAS Women in Development Seminar, NARA, RG 220, box 24. The five working groups focused on health, education, food and small technology, professional organizations, and urban living.

14. *El Universal*, 17 June 1975, 21.

15. *El Universal*, 16 June 1975, 1.
16. *El Universal*, 16 June 1975, 1.
17. As Daniel Rodgers has shown, the idea of "the market" became a particularly powerful ideal in the United States in the 1970s, despite widespread evidence of market imperfections. Rodgers, *Age of Fracture*, Chapter One.
18. Copy available in NARA, RG 220, Box 1.
19. NOW-NYC, box 6, folder 4 and box 15, folder 10.
20. Alexander Szalai, "The Situation of Women in the Light of Contemporary Time-Budget Research," 15 April 1975, UN doc. E/CONF.66/BP/6. Study included surveys in Belgium, Bulgaria, Czechoslovakia, France, East and West Germany, Hungary, Peru, Poland, the Soviet Union, the United States, and Yugoslavia.
21. "The Workshop on Food Production and Small Technology of the AAAS Seminar in Mexico, D.F., June 16–18, 1975," Esther Hymer Collection, Box World Conference on International Women's Year, Folder Development Seminar.
22. "Urban Living Group: Highlights of Issues and Recommendations," Working group report from AAAS Women in Development Seminar, NARA, RG 220, box 24. See also the summary report of the education working group in the same box.
23. "Recommendations of the Working Group on Health, Nutrition, and Family Planning," Working group report from AAAS Women in Development Seminar, NARA, RG 220, box 24.
24. *El Universal*, 18 June 1975, 10.
25. *El Universal*, 19 June 1975, 10.
26. The most widely circulated text on this issue was Dalla Costa and James, *The Power of Women and the Subversion of the Community*.
27. *Universal*, 17 June 1975, secs. 2, 1.
28. *Excélsior*, 17 June 1975, 7-A.
29. *Xilonen*, 20 June 1975, 3.
30. "Report of Group V on Organizations Related to Women in Development," Working group report from AAAS Women in Development Seminar, NARA, RG 220, box 24.
31. "Summary Report of Education Workshop," Working group report from AAAS Women in Development Seminar, NARA, RG 220, box 24.
32. For a more complete discussion, see Olcott, "Empires of Information."
33. Draft Report of the Commission on the Status of Women, 2 March 1972, UN doc. E/CN.6/L.614/Add.9. "Influence of Mass Communication Media on the Formation of a New Attitude Towards the Role of Women in Present-Day Society," 25th sess. of the CSW, 10 January 1974 (UN doc. E/CN.6/581). "Report of the Economic and Social Council, Introductory Statement by Margaret K. Bruce at the Third Committee on 23 December 1974," NOW-NYC, Box 23, Folder 11.
34. For the UNESCO's role in the IWY, see documentation in UNESCO Archive, Central Registry Collection, Sector SHS, boxes 165–71.
35. "Report of the Economic and Social Council, Introductory Statement by Margaret K. Bruce at the Third Committee on 23 December 1974," NOW-NYC, Box 23, Folder 11
36. McPhail, *Electronic Colonialism*, 12. McPhail explores the connections between the NIEO and what was dubbed the New World Information and Communication Order (NWICO). See also Ansah, "The Struggle for Rights and Values in Communication."
37. *El Universal*, 20 June 1975, 10.
38. Videos and transcripts of the shows are available in the Martha Stuart collection at the Schlesinger Library. It seems to have aired in the United States early in 1976 (see *Odessa American* [Texas], 11 January 1976, 75, and *Pasadena Star News* [California] 1 February 1976, 98). Elizabeth Reid recommended using them in Australia as a "consciousness-raising device" (Minutes from National Advisory Council, 7 August 1975, Elizabeth Reid Papers, folder 2). The NGO tribune also aired an episode entitled "Women Speak for Themselves," intended to disabuse viewers of the idea that all US feminists were "radicals" like Betty Friedan and Germaine Greer (*Xilonen*, 1 July 1975, 8; FFA, grant no. 75-224).
39. *IWY Bulletin*, July 1974 and October 1974.
40. *Development Forum* 2, no. 1 (January–February 1975).

41. Marcy to Ingersoll, "Current atmospherics surrounding question of who speaks for the United States at the International Women's Year Conference in Mexico City on June 20," 9 June 1975, NARA, RG 220, Records Relating to the U.N. IWY World Conference, Mexico City, June–July 1974, Subject File A-G, Box 22.

42. NOW-NYC Records, box 15, folder 10; flyer for mass meeting on 23 March 1975, Leslie Cagan Papers, Box 1, Folder 13.6.

43. See papers by Josefina Torres, Margarita García Flores, Martha de la Lama, and Socorro Díaz in Betty Friedan Papers, Carton 107, File 1268,

44. *WIN News* 1 (January 1975): 1. See also, Hosken, "Women and International Communication."

45. Hosken to Waldheim, 10 December 1974, and Anton Prohaska to Hosken, 31 December 1974, both in UN archive, file S-0971-0012-06. The irony of Hosken's appeal would likely have been apparent to them both, since her prominent Viennese Jewish family had fled Austrian in 1938, while he had joined Nazi organizations in his youth and had eventually been assigned to serve in a German army unit in the Balkans, where he was responsible for deporting thousands of Jews to Auschwitz (Meisler, *United Nations*,185–86).

46. Hosken to Harris and Persinger, 14 February 1975, IWTC, Box 2.

47. *WIN News* 1, no. 1 (January 1975).

48. Open letter from Anti-imperialist Women against Population Control, 24 March 1975, Bobbye Ortiz Papers, Box 17, Subject File Latin America 2/4.

49. Documentation on Hotline IWY is available in several places, including Mildred Robbins Leet Additional Papers (2002-M108), Carton 3, Folder Hotline-IWY-Mexico 1975; NARA, RG 220, Box 23, folder "IWY Hotline Mexico City" (including a full dot-matrix printout of the Hotline exchanges); IWTC, box 1; MPP, box Tribune, Mexico 1975 (NGO-Forum), folder J.

50. NARA, RG 220, Box 23, folder "IWY Hotline Mexico City."

51. NGO Committee on International Women's Year, Minutes of meeting, 21 May 1975, MPP, box UN World Conference (IWY), folder G.

52. Background papers are available in several archives, including the Elizabeth Reid Papers (folder 71a) and the Esther Hymer Collection (box International Women's Year Journalists Encounter). Media fellows were selected by the UN Management Committee for Information Projects for IWY (UN archive doc. S-0990-0004-07-00001).

53. Lusangu Naukala, "La Condition de la Femme au Zaïre," 24 June 1975 (EJBP.32).

54. Hannah Kasambala, "The Role of Women in Tanzania," 19 June 1975 (EJBP.11).

55. Drissi Atmani Driss, "La Femme Morocaine," 26 June 1975 (EJBP.30).

56. *Xilonen*, 19 June 1975, 4.

57. "Journalists at IWY—Unedited Transcript," Martha Stuart papers, 87-M126, Carton 2.

58. Francis Wete, "The Status of Cameroonian Women," 15 June 1975 (EJBP.13).

59. Kate Abbam, "The Situation of Women in Ghana," 13 June 1975 (EJBP.1).

60. Fibi Munene, "The Situation of Women in Kenya," 23 June 1975, EJBP.26.

61. Minutes of meeting, Committee on IWY, 6 March 1974, IWTC, Box 1.

62. For a more extended discussion of the conference newspaper, see Olcott, "Empires of Information."

63. Persinger to Elinor Barber, 7 February 1975, FFA, Grant no. 75-224.

64. Germain to Tinka Nobbe (Ford Foundation, Office of Public Broadcasting), 5 March 1975, and memo from Germain to R.G. Livingston, 19 March 1975, both in FFA, Grant no. 75-224; Memo from Germain, 17 March 1975, IWTC, Box 3.

65. Conversation with R. G. Livingston, V.P., German Marshall Fund, 14/3/75–Funding for Daily Newspaper at Mexico IWY Conference, 17 March 1975; Germain to Livingston 19 March 1975; both in FFA, Grant no. 75-224.

66. "Aide Memoire for Discussions in New York: Mexico City Newspaper Project, Some Considerations for IPPF," undated [mid-February], and Dennis to Persinger, 24 March 1975, IWTC, box 3.

67. On Paxson's career, see Voss and Speere, "Marjorie Paxson." See also, "Status Report— IWY Tribune Daily Newspaper," undated [early May 1975], IWTC, box 3.

68. Mary-Jane R. Snyder to Persinger, 13 June 1975, MPP, box Tribune, Mexico 1975 (NGO-Forum), folder E.

69. Letters from Marcia-Ximena Bravo to Eugene Pulliam, publisher of Phoenix *Republic* Helen Copley (publisher of the *San Diego Tribune*); Jean Gannett Hawley (Pres., Portland, Maine, *Press-Herald*); Helene Foellinger (President, Ft. Wayne *Journal-Gazette*), 19 May 1975. The publisher of *Novedades*, which would print and distribute the IWY newspaper, had also suggested contacting Katherine Graham (*Washington Post*) and Miriam Heiskell (*New York Times*), but I have not found any correspondence with them. All documents in IWTC, Box 3.
70. Marjorie Paxson, "Xilonen," *Matrix* (Fall 1975), 26–27.
71. Barber to Germain, 19 June 1975, FFA, grant 75-224A.

Scene 6: Inauguration Day

1. *Xilonen*, 20 June 1975, 5–6.
2. *El Universal*, 16 June 1975, 1 and 19 June 1975, 1.
3. For Waldheim's remarks, see AGN, DFS, Vol. 9-342-75, Exp. 5, hojas 31–32. Mexican newspapers reported endorsements from Venezuela (*El Universal*, 18 June 1975, 12), Peru (*El Universal*, 19 June 1975, 8), France (*Excélsior*, 19 June 1975, 9-A), and Yugoslavia (*El Universal*, 20 June 1975, 11).
4. According to security plans, Echeverría's and Waldheim's wives attended the inauguration but Sipilä's husband did not (AGN, DFS, Vol. 9-342-75, Exp. 5, hojas 54–61).
5. AGN, DFS, Vol. 9-342-75, Exp. 5 and 9.
6. Waldheim to heads of state, 11 February 1975, UN Archive, document S-0990-0004-07-00001.
7. The *Times* continued to run IWY news on the "family food fashions furnishings" page—this article appeared below one about a charity ball at the Waldorf Astoria, "They Arrived at the Party Wrapped in a Flutter of Feathers," 10 May 1974, 43.
8. Memo from Penny Wensley (First Secretary, Australian Embassy in Mexico City) regarding conversation with Aída González Martínez, 28 February 1975, Elizabeth Reid Papers, folder 92.
9. *New York Times*, 19 June 1975, 41; *Newsweek*, 7 July 1975, 28.
10. *Washington Post*, 20 June 1975, A16.
11. Rhodes James to Waldheim, 13 June 1975, UN Archive, file S-0273-0012-03.
12. AGN, DFS, Vol. 9-342-75, Exp. 5.
13. *El Universal*, 20 June 1975, 22.
14. AGN, IPS, 19 June 1975, Caja 1163-A, Vol. 1, hojas 159–65.
15. *Xilonen*, 20 June 1975, 5.
16. Friedan, "Scary Doings," 442. It is possible—both because of the signs the women carried in this incident and later and because the secret police seemed quite suspicious of the group— that they were organized (and perhaps paid) by the Communist Party–affiliated Unión Nacional de Mujeres Mexicanas (UNMM, National Union of Mexican Women; also a WIDF affiliate), whose president, Martha López Portillo de Tamayo, and her husband had a particular fascination with Benito Juárez and his wife Margarita Maza de Juárez.
17. AGN, DFS, 25 June 1975, Exp. 9-342-75, Leg. 7, hojas 83–88.
18. *Excélsior*, 20 June 1975, 1-A, 20-A. See also Greer, "World Conference," 200.
19. Gillingham and Smith, *Dictablanda*.
20. *El Universal*, 21 June 1975, 5.
21. "Conferencia Mundial de la Mujer," 19 June 1975, AGN, DFS, Exp. 9-342-75, Leg. 9, hojas 107–41.
22. *El Universal*, 20 June 1975, 22.
23. Drafts of Waldheim's speech can be found in the UN Archive, folder S-0273-0012-03.
24. Full text available in AGN, Colección Particular de Clementina Batalla de Bassols, Caja 2, Exp. 9, hojas 1–21.
25. *El Universal*, 20 June 1975, 10.
26. *New York Times*, 20 June 1975, 1.
27. *New York Times*, 20 June 1975, 1. Sipilä's address received almost no coverage and only passing mention in the Mexican press.
28. *Xilonen*, 20 June 1975, 2.
29. *El Universal*, 20 June 1975, sec. Cultura y Sociedad, 6.

30. *New York Times*, 19 June 1975, 41.
31. "El Futuro Debe Ser de la Mujer Joven," *Xilonen*, 19 June 1975, 2. (Quotation does not appear in English version of this article.)
32. In UN-speak, this meant that Committee One would consider the World Plan of Action (agenda item 11), and Committee Two would consider agenda items 9 (Current trends and changes in the status and roles of women and men and major obstacles to be overcome in the achievement of equal rights, opportunities, and responsibilities) and 10 (The integration of women in the development process as equal partners with men). Agenda item 8 (The involvement of women in strengthening international peace and eliminating racism and racial discrimination) would be discussed in the plenary sessions. The committees included one representative from each delegation.
33. *Xilonen*, 20 June 1975, 1.
34. For a transcript of the speech, see AGN, Coll. Clementina Batalla Bassols, Vol. 2, Exp. 9, Fs. 1-21.
35. *Washington Post*, 20 June 1975, A-16.
36. *Trinidad and Tobago Newsday*, 14 September 2008; *Virgin Island Daily News*, 7 August 1953, 1; *Washington Afro-American*, 24 November 1953, 11.
37. *Xilonen*, 19 June 1975, 1.
38. Persinger to Dorothy Johnson (Department of Health, Education and Welfare, Chicago), 11 February 1975, IWTC, box 2.
39. AGN, IPS, 19 June 1975, Caja 1163-A, Vol. 1, hoja 159-65; *El Universal*, 20 June 1975, 22.
40. *El Universal*, 20 June 1975, 10.

Scene 7: "Betty Friedan versus the Third World"

1. Baldez, *Defying Convention*, 39, ff.
2. The Feminist Caucus of the International Women's Year [press statement], 18 June 1975, Betty Friedan Papers, Box 37, Folder 1264.
3. *Xilonen*, 19 June 1975, 6.
4. Undated, unsigned handwritten note to Friedan, Betty Friedan Papers, Carton 107, File 1254.
5. *Washington Post*, 22 June 1975, A12; *El Universal*, 21 June 1975, 1; *El Nacional*, 22 June 1975, 6.
6. *Washington Post*, 22 June 1975, A 12.
7. *El Universal*, 22 June 1975, 9.
8. *El Universal*, 22 June 1975, 1.
9. *El Nacional*, 23 June 1975, 5.
10. NGO Committee on International Women's Year, Minutes of meeting held December 4, 1974; IWTC, box 1.
11. Letters from Estilita Grimaldo (23 April 1975, Womantours, Los Angeles) and Rosalyn Chelouche (24 April 1975, The Travel Experience, New York City), IWTC, Box 3.
12. Ad sent from US delegation member Gilda Bojórquez Gjurich to Jill Ruckelshaus, 23 May 1975, NARA, RG 220, Box 22.
13. Nusenbaum to Friedan, 25 February 1975, Betty Friedan Papers, Carton 107, file 1247.
14. Carol Leimas, "International Women's Year: 21 Ways to Make It Come Alive," *AAUW Journal*, April 1975, p. 17.
15. Charlotte Bunch and Frances Doughty, "IWY—feminist strategy for Mexico City," *off our backs* 5, no 5 (30 June 1975): 6.
16. On the Dayton conference, see Wright State University, Department of Special Collections and Archives, Socialist Feminist Conference (MS-141). The Dayton conference overlapped with the IWY conference until the latter was rescheduled to start on 19 June 19 rather than 23 June.
17. Teresa Deni, "Woman Trek—a Journey into IWY," *Hera: A Philadelphia Feminist Publication* 4, no. 1 (Indian Summer, 1975): 1, 3–4.
18. Marlene Schmitz, "International women's year is anti-feminist," *off our backs* 5, no. 3 (31 March 1975): 2.
19. See correspondence between Patricia Burnett (who led NOW's international efforts) and Elayne Snyder (president of NOW-NYC); NOW-NYC, box 3, folder 21; box 6, folder 4; and box 23, folder 11.

20. Patricia Burnett, undated [1974], NOW-NYC, Box 3, Folder 12. Burnett had played an instrumental role in establishing NOW's International Committee, which sought to establish chapters around the world (NOW-NYC, Box 23, Folder 11).

21. Minutes of the NOW-NYC Chapter General Meeting, 20 February 1975, NOW-NYC, Box 2, Folder 15.

22. Karen DeCrow, Report to the National Board, 29 March 1975, NOW-NYC, Box 25, Folder 2.

23. *Washington Post*, 20 June 1975, A26.

24. Charlotte Bunch, "Out Now!" *The Furies* 1, no. 5 (June/July 1972): 12–13.

25. Carol Downer to Robin Morgan, 3 June 1975, Robin Morgan Papers, Box C5.

26. Jova (US Embassy, Mexico) to Secretary of State, 4 April 1975, *FRUS*, 1969–76, Vol. E-14, Part I, Doc 177. This description of Friedan as an exemplar of radical feminism was surprisingly widespread: Ford Foundation officers and consultative-status NGOs described her similarly (memo from Adrienne Germain to Tinke Nobbe, 21 March 1975, FFA, grant no 75-224; International Federation of University Women [Geneva] newsletter, August 1975, MPP, Tribune, Mexico 1975, folder R).

27. Hosken to Friedan, 8 March 1975, and Hosken to Persinger, 10 March 1975, both in IWTC, Box 2. Friedan describes this letter as well in Friedan, "Scary Doings in Mexico City," 448.

28. Friedan to Walker, 19 May 1975, Betty Friedan Papers, Carton 107, File 1248.

29. *New York Times*, 4 June 1975, 45.

30. "Black Woman Heads UN Security Council," *Jet*, 23 November 1972, 18. See also, Jeanne Martin Cissé, "Woman, the First Teacher," *Prospects: Quarterly Review of Education* (UNESCO, Paris) 5, no. 3, 347–51.

31. *Afrika Must Unite* (Vol. 2, no. 14) reprinted in *Pan African Women's Day Newsletter* (online).

32. *Xilonen*, 19 June 1975, 5; *Washington Post*, 25 June 1975, A27. For more on the Redstockings-Steinem dispute, see *Hera: A Philadelphia Feminist Publication* 1, no. 4 (Indian Summer 1975): 16–17; a complete version of the Redstockings' sixteen-page press release (Rosalyn Baxandall Women's Liberation Research Files, Box 1, Folder 30); correspondence between Robin Morgan and Carole Downer, June 1975 (Robin Morgan Papers, Box C5).

33. *Xilonen*, 19 June 1975, 4.

34. E-mail from Gloria Steinem to the author, 20 August 2015.

35. *Xilonen*, 20 June 1975, 4.

36. *Xilonen*, 23 June 1975, 4.

37. "La NOW Verá que la CM no sea Manipulada," *Xilonen*, 20 June 1975, 3.

38. *El Universal*, 21 June 1975, 10.

39. Roberto Blanco Moheno, "Tres Zancudos," *El Universal*, 23 June 1975, 4.

40. Julian Güitron Fuentevilla, "Juicio Crítico: Igualdad Bien Entendida," *El Universal*, 24 June 1975, 5.

41. *El Universal*, 24 June 1975, 19. The countries signing the statement of support included Italy, Indonesia, USSR, Nigeria, Uganda, Greece, German Democratic Republic, People's Republic of China, and France.

42. *New York Times*, 21 June 1975, 3.

43. *El Universal*, 22 June 1975, 6.

44. Report from 20 June 1975, AGN, DFS, Exp. 9-342-75, Leg. 5, hojas 208–16.

45. For the press release with the final draft of Hutar's speech as well as the draft included in the delegates' briefing book, see NARA, RG220, Box 22, IWY-General File.

46. *Excélsior*, 21 June 1975, 1-A.

47. Full text of speech available in Elizabeth Reid Papers, Folder 96.

48. *El Heraldo*, 21 June 1975 (Elizabeth Reid Papers, Folder 87).

49. Report from 20 June 1975, AGN, IPS, Caja 1163-A, Vol. 1, hoja 204–5.

50. Statement attached to minutes of 20 June 1975 Organizing Committee meeting, IWTC, Box 2.

51. *El Universal*, 21 June 1975, 10.

52. *El Nacional*, 21 June 1975, 1 and 8. Notably, *El Nacional*, the PRI newspaper, ran two articles on this panel, both more positive about Friedan than other newspapers.

53. *El Universal*, 21 June 1975, 10.

54. *El Universal*, 21 June 1975, 10.

55. *El Universal*, 21 June 1975, 11.

56. *El Universal,* 21 June 1975, 10.
57. Pacifica Radio Archives, "Betty Friedan vs. the Third World."
58. *El Universal,* 21 June 1975, 1 and 23 June 1975, 3; *El Nacional,* 22 June 1975, 6.
59. *El Universal,* 21 June 1975, 8.
60. *Excélsior,* 21 June 1975, 1-A.
61. See, for example, "Betty (Terrible) Freaman" along with photo captioned "Betty 'La Terrible' Freaman," *El Nacional,* 26 June 1975, 10; *El Universal,* 28 June 1975, 8.
62. AGN, DFS, 20 June 1975, Exp. 9-342-75, Leg. 5, hojas 208–16.
63. Report from 20 June 1975, AGN, DFS, Exp. 9-342-75, Leg. 5, hojas 208–16.
64. Height interview, 197, ff.
65. Height interview, 193–94.

Scene 8: *"This Is an Illegitimate Delegation"*

1. In an indication of the standard choreography of such events in Mexico, the Mexican press reported that the protestors had "staged a surprise invasion" of the embassy or had whistled and shouted outside the embassy, "demanding" entry (*El Universal* and *El Nacional,* 22 June 1975). (The Mexican newspapers most likely had not sent reporters to cover the encounter; these characterizations may have come either from eyewitness accounts or from reporters' own expectations.)
2. Several newspapers estimated the attendance at about 200, Ruth Bacon estimated 200 to 300, and John Jova, the US ambassador, reported to the State Department that between 300 and 400 people had shown up.
3. William Buffum to Kissinger, 7 May 1975, NARA, RG 220, Box 22.
4. Jova to Kissinger, 4 June 1975, *FRUS,* 1969–76, Vol. E-14, Part I, Doc 180.
5. NARA, RG 220, Records Relating to the U.N. IWY World Conference, Mexico City, June–July 1974; Subject File A-G; Box 22.
6. Marcy to Deputy Secretary of State Robert Ingersoll, 9 June 1975, "Current atmospherics surrounding question of who speaks for the United States at the International Women's Year Conference in Mexico City on June 20," NARA, RG 220, Box 22, "IWY 75—General File; WC/IWY Mexico City, June 19-July 2, 1975."
7. *New York Times,* 11 June 1975; NARA, RG 220, Records Relating to the U.N. IWY World Conference, Mexico City, June–July 1974; Subject File A-G; Box 22.
8. *New York Times,* 13 June 1975, 42, and 19 June 1975, 41.
9. William Buffum to Kissinger, 7 May 1975, NARA, RG 220, Box 22.
10. White and Gill, *Suite 3505,* 154.
11. *Los Angeles Times,* 19 June 1975, B1.
12. UN doc., E/Conf.66/2. The rules of procedure initially allowed each delegation to include "one head of delegation and no more than two other accredited representatives and such alternate representatives and advisers as may be required" (5). When delegates voted during the second plenary on the rules governing the IWY conference, they amended the rule to allow for four accredited representatives rather than two.
13. "Mexico City Conference for International Women's Year: Selection of Delegates," undated [after 26 March 1975], NARA, RG 220, Box 22.
14. The delegation consisted almost entirely of people who held positions either in branches of the federal government (e.g., Departments of Justice; State; AID; Labor; or Health, Education and Welfare), high-ranking women in established NGOs (e.g., League of Women Voters, Women's Equity Action League), the directors of the US Center for International Women's Year and the US Commission for the Observance of International Women's Year, and people who had experience working in the UN. The two outliers were Marion Javits (who apparently came only by virtue of her husband's stature as a US senator, raising the ire of Mildred Marcy, who described her as "not a recognized player in this ballpark") and Emily Carssow, an assistant professor of law at the University of Georgia, whom Dean Rusk had nominated.
15. Roberta K. Van Haeften and Douglas D. Caton, "Strategy Paper for Integrating LDC Rural Women into Their National Economies," prepared for the AID Percy Amendment Subcommittee on Agriculture, Nutrition and Rural Development (NARA, RG 220, Records

of the U.S. Center for International Women's Year; Subject Files, 1973–1975; A-AS; Box 1; Folder "AID").

16. Memorandum of Conversation, Department of State, 27 April 1974; *FRUS*, 1969–76, Vol. E-14, Part I, Doc 12.

17. Memorandum of Conversation, Department of State, 31 May 1974; *FRUS*, 1969–76, Vol. E-14, Part I, Doc 15.

18. There are many examples of such articles. See, for example, "Forced Sterilization," *Sister: West Coast Feminist Newspaper*, June 1974, 8. For an excellent review of this policy, see Connelly, *Fatal Misconception*.

19. *New York Times*, 31 January 1992; *Milwaukee Journal*, 13 November 1973, secs. 2, 19; Butterfield, *U.S. Development Aid*, 132–33, 98.

20. On the USAID "public safety" program, see Huggins, *Political Policing*.

21. The most complete recording of this encounter is Pacifica Radio's "Will the Real U.S. Delegation Please Stand Up?" (1975); video footage is included in "Report from Mexico City" (KVIE, Sacramento, California). All direct quotations here come from the Pacifica recording. On Esther Urista, see also Peggy Simpson's AP article, *Yuma Daily Sun*, 24 June 1975, 7.

22. While both the *New York Times* (22 June 1975, 1) and *Xilonen* (23 June 1975, 5) mentioned de Saram's objections, neither mentioned Boynes's initial disruptions. By contrast, the Ford Foundation–sponsored public television coverage focused almost entirely on Boynes, combining several interventions into one long interruption and editing out the considerable ambient noise over which Boynes shouted, making her seem singularly disruptive. Despite Hutar's explanation that Parker would have to leave early, De Saram recounted her intervention in a report to the NOW-NYC executive board, explaining, "As a result, Parker did not speak and left Mexico City very quickly." Someone underlined "as a result" in the minutes and put a question mark in the margin. (Minutes of the NOW-NYC Executive Board Meeting, 14 July 1975, NOW-NYC, Box 1, Folder 8.)

23. A 22 May 1975 Department of State press release stated that the accredited representatives would be Parker; Hutar; Martha Griffiths (the lone Democrat), who had forced the Equal Rights Amendment from committee to the full House; and Jill Ruckelshaus, the president of the National Commission on the Observance of International Women's Year (Buffum to Kissinger, 5 June 1975, NARA, RG 200, Box 22).

24. The White House demonstrated awareness of the racial optics well before this point. In an Oval Office conversation with the newly appointed US ambassador to the UN, John Scali, Nixon had "concurred strongly" with Scali's point that the US delegation lacked racial diversity and "pointed out that since the UN was mostly non-white we should have more blacks on the staff" (Memorandum for the President's Files, 13 February 1973; *FRUS*, 1969–76, Vol. E-14, Part I, Doc 5).

25. On Maymi's background, see Telgen and Kamp, *Notable Hispanic Women*, 265.

26. The speaker cited the endorsement by the Mexican American Women's National Association (MANA) as "among the outstanding women of this country." (MANA testimony before the National Commission on International Women's Year, 15 May 1975; Rosalyn Baxandall Women's Liberation Research Files, Box 3, Folder 13.)

27. Jova to Secretary of State, 21 June 1975, *FRUS*, 1969–76, Vol. E-14, Part I, Doc 181.

28. *Women Today* 5, no. 14 (7 July 1975): 81–86.

29. Jova to Kissinger, 4 June 1975, *FRUS*, 1969–76, Vol. E-14, Part I, Doc 180.

30. *Xilonen*, 23 June 1975, 5.

31. *Los Angeles Herald-Examiner*, 27 July 1975, 2. Joan Dunlop reported to John D. Rockefeller III that the Iranian ZuZu Tabatabai was similarly unimpressed by Hutar, saying that the "leader of the U.S. delegation should have political clout, some vision of the future and some understanding of planning" (Dunlop to Rockefeller, 28 February 1975, Rockefeller Family Papers, Box 46, Folder 281, RG 5: John D. Rockefeller 3rd Papers, Series 3—Office and Home Files). On Hutar's public statements, see also *Los Angeles Times*, 17 January 1974, A22.

32. *Chicago Defender*, 24 June 1975, 5. Payne identified the speaker as Virginia Sitgraves rather than Boynes.

33. *Chicago Defender*, 12 July 1975, 28.

34. Elizabeth Reid Papers, folder 11.
35. Chávez, "Pilgrimage to the Homeland," 176.

Scene 9: "Other Kinds of Problems"

1. Barrios de Chungara and Viezzer, *Let Me Speak!*, 197–98.
2. Barrios de Chungara and Viezzer, *Let Me Speak!*, 194. Domitila's account offers not a transparent recounting of events but rather a quintessential example of *testimonio*—the witness-bearing representations that gained traction amid Latin American counterinsurgency campaigns of the 1970s and '80s and that by the 1990s precipitated anxious debates about subaltern truth-telling. On *testimonio* and its reconsideration, see especially Beverley, "The Real Thing (Our Rigoberta)," 129–39; Nelson, *Reckoning*, Chapter Four.
3. Undated notes, MPP, Box Tribune Mexico, Folder E. For Barrios de Chungara's recollections, see *Let Me Speak*, 194, ff. On inviting people with views diverging from their governments, see Persinger interview. The 1971 documentary about the miners' struggle is *El coraje del pueblo* by Jorge Sanjines.
4. Barrios de Chungara and Viezzer, *Let Me Speak!*, 195.
5. Barrios de Chungara and Viezzer, *Let Me Speak!*, 196.
6. Barrios de Chungara and Viezzer, *Let Me Speak!*, 197–98.
7. Persinger interview.
8. Lagos and Escobar, *Nos hemos forjado así: al rojo vivo y a puro golpe: Historias del Comité de Amas de Casa de Siglo XX*, 68–69.
9. Persinger interview.
10. Recounted in *Let Me Speak!*, 198, ff.
11. *El Universal*, 24 June 1975, 11.
12. *El Nacional*, 27 June 1975, 5.
13. Lenin, *Collected Works*, 429. The characterization was familiar in many Latin American countries where the Marxist canon formed part of the standard university curriculum. It is cited, for example, in the feminist pamphlet by María del Refugio Llamas, Dolores Castro de Peñaloza, and Lilia Flores Porras, "Mujer: la mitad oscura de la vida (Año Internacional de la Mujer 75)" (Mexico: Talleres Rotograficos Zaragoza, 1975).
14. The film screened at the IWY tribune on the evening of Thursday, 26 June (Foster, *This Woman Which is One: Helena Solberg-Ladd's The Double Day*). Solberg-Ladd was the only woman to participate in the social justice–oriented Cinema Novo movement and would go on to write, direct, and produce the groundbreaking feature film *Carmen Miranda: Bananas Is My Business*.
15. *Xilonen*, 25 June 1975, 4.
16. "La mujer en México" (1972), Bobbye Ortiz Papers, Box 18.
17. "Women of the World: Report from Mexico City," *Foreign Affairs*, October 1975, 180.
18. *New York Times*, 24 June 1975, 3, and 25 June 1975, 2.
19. AGN, DFS, 25 June 1975, Exp. 9-342-75, Leg. 7, hojas 83–88.
20. *Excélsior*, 26 June 1975, 1-A. The statement came from the delegations of Venezuela, Honduras, Brazil, Paraguay, and Colombia.
21. Statement by Alfred Neumann, 22 January 1975, UN Archive, file S-0971-0012-06.
22. Height interview, 195.
23. See, for example, *Quicksilver Times*, October 1969, 16–17; *Women's Press* (Eugene, Oregon) 1, no. 2 (January–February 1971), n.p.
24. Carole Lopate, "Letter to the Movement: Women and Pay for Housework," *Liberation*, May/June 1974, 8–11. The principal text for the wages-for-housework movement was Dalla Costa and James, *The Power of Women and the Subversion of the Community*. Although it was unclear where she stood by 1975, in November 1973 Elizabeth Reid had endorsed the idea of wages for housewives in Australia (*The Australian Women's Weekly*, 7 November 1973, 51).
25. *México 75: Año Internacional de la Mujer* 1, no. 1 (January 1975): 6–7.
26. Barrios de Chungara and Viezzer, *Let Me Speak!* 200–201.
27. *New York Times*, 2 July 1975, 40.
28. From when Hong was running for president. *Los Angeles Times*, 27 November 1987.

29. AGN, IPS, 25 June 1975, Caja 1163-A, Exp 1, hojas 444–47.
30. *Chicago Tribune*, 15 July 1974, B7. The NCHE, which had existed in the 1920s had been revived by Dorothy Height and initially funded by the Ford Foundation (Boris and Klein, *Caring for America*, 126–29.)
31. Barrios de Chungara and Viezzer, *Let Me Speak!*, 35.
32. Barrios de Chungara, *La mujer y la organización*, 8.
33. María del Refugio Llamas, Dolores Castro de Peñaloza, and Lilia Flores Porras, "Mujer: la mitad oscura de la vida (Año Internacional de la Mujer 75)" (Mexico: Talleres Rotograficos Zaragoza, 1975), no page numbers.
34. "Statement by Mrs. Maj-Britt Sandlund, Swedish delegate to the Consultative Committee for the World Conference of the International Women's Year at its meeting on March 4, 1975," in (MPP, Box UN World Conference (IWY), Folder E).
35. Margaret Mead, "The Emergence of Women into Full Participation in All Parts of Society," keynote lecture delivered to UN We Believe, UN Headquarters (New York), 11 September 1974. (Copy of speech available in Elizabeth Reid Papers, folder 53.)
36. Report from 24 June 1975, AGN, DFS, Exp. 9-342-75, Leg. 7, hojas 5–15.
37. *México 75: Año Internacional de la Mujer* 1, no. 1 (January 1975): 6–7.
38. *Xilonen*, 26 June 1975, 7; *New York Times*, 19 June 1975, 41 and 2 July 1975, 40. *El Universal* (17 June 1975, 1), by contrast, identified her as having participated in the storied assault on the Moncada Barracks that launched the Cuban revolution. The *Los Angeles Times* (19 June 1975, B1) listed her among the conference celebrities and identified her only as a "Cuban guerrilla fighter."
39. For an account of the congress, see Randall, "'We Need a Government of Men and Women . . . !'". On the Cuban Family Code and its implementation, see King, "Cuba's Attack on Women's Second Shift 1974–1976"; Moya Fábregas, "The Cuban Woman's Revolutionary Experience."
40. *Granma* (Havana), 26 June 1975, 7.
41. Arguelles and Rich, "Homosexuality, Homophobia, and Revolution," 692–94.
42. *El Universal*, 24 June 1975, 19.
43. *El Universal*, 24 June 1975, 1; report from 23 June 1975, AGN, IPS, Caja 1163-A, Vol. 1, hoja 306–8.
44. Jahan and Schwartz, "The International Women's Year Conference and Tribune," 40.
45. On Chileans speaking out, see, for examples, the IPS report on the encounter, AGN, IPS, 17 June 1975, Caja 1162-B, Vol. 4, hojas 702–3; *El Nacional*, 18 June 1975, 6; *El Universal*, 18 June 1975, 12; *Xilonen*, 19 June 1975, 5.
46. "Protection of human rights in Chile," Report of the Economic and Social Council, 17 October 1974, UN doc. A/C.3/L.2114.
47. *El Universal*, 19 June 1975, 1; *Excélsior*, 19 June 1975, 9-A.
48. *El Universal*, 17 June 1975, 21 and 20 June 1975, 10.
49. DFS and IPS reports on Partido Popular Socialista, 12 June 1975, AGN, DFS, Exp. 11-2-75, Leg. 25, hoja 140 and AGN, IPS, Caja 1162-B, Vol. 4, hojas 373–74.
50. *El Universal*, 20 June 1975, 9. I have found no diplomatic correspondence on this matter, but Mexico severed diplomatic relations with Chile after the coup.
51. *El Nacional*, 24 June 1975, 7; *El Universal*, 24 June 1975, 1 and 11.
52. Report on the Misa Panamericana, 22 June 1975, AGN, DFS, Exp. 100-15-4-75, Leg. 2, hojas 116–19.
53. See FFA, Box ID/OVP David Bell, ID Field Office Files.
54. Bobbye Ortiz Papers, Box 13.
55. See, for example, *Sister: West Coast Feminist Newspaper* 4, no. 10 (1973): 10; *What She Wants* (Cleveland) 2, no. 5 (1974): 3; *Peace and Freedom* (WILPF newsletter) 34, no. 2 (1974): 1; NOW-NYC, box 6, folder 4 and box 8, folder 4.
56. *Los Angeles Times*, 24 June 1975, B16.
57. *Washington Post*, 21 June 1974, A3 (UPI story).
58. *El Universal*, 24 June 1975, 19. See also Randolph, *Florynce "Flo" Kennedy*.
59. Elizabeth Reid Papers, folder 90.
60. *El Nacional*, 25 June 1975, 7.

61. Sznajder and Roniger, *The Politics of Exile in Latin America*.
62. "Discurso pronunciado por la Señora Lucía Hiriart de Pinochet," 4 April 1975, UN Archive, File S-0971-0012-06.
63. *El Universal*, 20 June 1975, 22. On women's support for Pinochet, see Power, *Right-Wing Women in Chile: Feminine Power and the Struggle against Allende, 1964–1973*.
64. *El Universal*, 23 June 1975, 1.
65. *El Universal*, 23 June 1975, 1.
66. *El Universal*, 21 June 1975, 9.
67. *El Nacional*, 26 June 1975, 10.
68. *El Universal*, 23 June 1975, 1.
69. *El Universal*, 25 June 1975, 8.

Scene 10: The Politics of Peace

1. AGN, DFS, 24 June 1975, Exp. 9-342-75, Leg. 7, hoja 53.
2. AGN, DFS, 24 June 1975, Exp. 9-342-75, Leg. 7, hojas 5–15; AGN, IPS, Caja 1163-A, Vol. 1, hojas 349, 370–71.
3. *El Universal*, 25 June 1975, 8.
4. *El Nacional*, 25 June 1975, 8.
5. AGN, IPS, 24 June 1975, Caja 1163-A, Exp 1, hojas 370–71.
6. "Plan de Seguridad," no date [June 1975], AGN, DFS, Exp. 9-342-75, Leg. 9, hojas 107–41.
7. For security measures, see AGN, DFS, Vol. 9-342-75, exp. 5, hojas 54–61 and Vol. 9-342-75, exp. 9, hojas 107–41.
8. "¡Vive la Femme!" *El Heraldo*, 21 June 1975 (page unknown, from Elizabeth Reid Papers, folder 87).
9. Medidas de Seguridad que Deberan Adoptarse con Motivo de la Celebración de la Conferencia Mundial del Año Internacional de la Mujer, 11 June 1975, AGN, DFS, Exp. 9-342-75, Leg. 4, hoja 106.
10. For the security account, see the DFS report for 24 June 1975, AGN, DFS, Exp. 9-342-75, Leg. 7, hojas 5–15. For Urquidi's account, see her submission in *Xilonen*, 25 June 1975, 4.
11. *Schenectady Gazette* (AP wire article), 26 June 1975, 12. On Bulengo's feminism, see *The Age* (Melbourne), 22 October 1975, 15.
12. Alexander, "Report from Mexico City."
13. For her work in pediatrics, see Victoria Mojekwu, "Paediatric Education for Nigerian Nurses," *Journal of Tropical Pediatrics* 21 (1975): 72–73.
14. *Milwaukee Journal*, 26 June 1975, section 2, 6 (AP wire article).
15. AGN, IPS, Caja 1163-A, Vol. 1, hojas 406–7.
16. AGN, DFS, 24 June 1975, Exp. 9-342-75, Leg. 7, hojas 5–15.
17. AGN, DFS, 24 June 1975, Exp. 9-342-75, Leg. 7, hojas 5–15.
18. *New York Times*, 25 June 1975, 7.
19. Report from 25 June 1975, AGN, DFS, Exp. 9-342-75, Leg. 7, hojas 83–88.
20. *Excélsior*, 19 June 1975, 9-A.
21. *El Universal*, 21 June 1975, Secc. Cultura y la Sociedad, 1.
22. See, for example, notes from the 15 January 1975 ECOSOC meeting for which the USSR found "agenda not satisfactory, no provision for contribution of women to peaceful relations and racism." The Jamaican delegate had asked at this same meeting why the International Atomic Energy Agency (IAEA) would not be represented at a conference purportedly dedicated to peace. (Handwritten notes on 15 January 1975 ECOSOC meeting, IWTC, Box 1).
23. *Excélsior*, 19 June 1975, 7-A. This language parroted the official position of the Mexican delegation.
24. *El Universal*, 17 June 1975, 21.
25. *El Nacional, El Universal*, and *Excélsior*, all 24 June 1975, 1; *Xilonen*, 1 July 1975, 1.
26. *El Universal*, 2 July 1975, 1.
27. Notably, the issue of "world peace" also arose repeatedly in State Department discussions about population issues — i.e., the idea that a population "bomb" and the attendant resource pressures would pose a threat to world peace. The Soviet centering of the peace theme

appears most clearly in the *note verbale* its UN mission submitted to the Secretary-General (21 February 1975, UN doc. A/10049/Corr.1).

28. See Mexican secret-police reports on the IWY tribune and on Misika Tonaka, 20 and 27 June 1975, AGN, IPS, caja 1163-A, Vol. 1, hojas 219–21, 542–44.

29. On the contemporary geopolitics of human rights, see Burke, *Decolonization and the Evolution of International Human Rights.*

30. UNESCO Archive, Box 165, Folder 1.

31. *The News* (Mexico City), 26 June 1975.

32. WILPF and the WIDF organized a May 1975 Seminar on Peace and Disarmament at UN headquarters (MPP, Box UN World Conference (IWY), Folder G). The Geneva NGO committee and the planned World Congress of Women in East Berlin maintained peace as a principal objective—arguably above those of equality and development (K. Strong, "Notes on Meeting of NGO Sub-Committee on the Status of Women, Geneva," 29 January 1975, MPP, Box Tribune, Mexico 1975 (NGO Forum), Folder A); International Preparatory Committee for the World Congress for International Women's Year, 6 February 1975, Elizabeth Reid Papers, Folder 19).

33. The Secretary-General circulated the draft on 25 April 1973; these figures represent responses received by 31 October 1973. "International Women's Year: Report of the Secretary General," 4 December 1973, UN doc. E/CN.6/L.576.

34. Elizabeth Reid Papers, folder 92.

35. *El Universal*, 17 June 1975, 21.

36. *El Universal*, 22 June 1975, 6.

37. *El Nacional*, 28 June 1975, 7.

38. *The Nation*, 19 July 1975.

39. *El Nacional*, 26 June 1975, 9.

40. *El Universal*, 20 June 1975, 20; AGN, IPS, caja 1163-A, hojas 309–10.

41. Reprinted in *Afrika Must Unite* 2, no. 14.

42. *El Nacional*, 27 June 1975, 7; *El Universal*, 2 July 1975, 15.

43. *El Universal*, 21 June 1975, 10; AGN, IPS, 20 June 1975, Caja 1163-A, Vol. 1, hoja 204–5.

44. *El Universal*, 22 June 1975, 10.

45. *El Universal*, 26 June 1975, 13.

46. The program included 35 official sessions (excluding morning briefings from the intergovernmental conference). The final report on the tribune stated that 192 informal sessions took place—a number that would only include meetings of groups that requested and received a room through the tribune organizers. "Report, International Women's Year Tribune—1975," November 1975, IWTC, Box 3. The informal sessions on peace included a WILPF meeting, two meetings of the International Society of Peace and Religious Freedom, a showing of a film on peace, and, on the penultimate day of the tribune, the Peace Coalition Planning Meeting.

47. AGN, IPS, 27 June 1975, caja 1163-A, Vol. 1, hojas 542–44.

48. Report from 24 June 1975, AGN, DFS, Exp. 9-342-75, Leg. 7, hoja 5–15; *El Nacional*, 28 June 1975, 7; *El Universal*, 28 June 1975, 1.

49. Most accounts see this intervention as critical in framing the Zionism-as-racism argument that made its first UN appearance in Mexico City. See, for example, Kawar, "National mobilization, war conditions, and gender consciousness."

50. "Suspension of Israel from the UN General Assembly," Intelligence Note, Bureau of Intelligence and Research, 3 June 1975, *FRUS*, 1969–76, Vol. E-14, Part I, Doc 73.

51. *El Universal*, 20 June 1975, 1.

52. *El Nacional*, 29 June 1975, 6.

53. *New York Times*, 22 June 1975, 48.

54. *Excélsior*, 18 June 1975, 12-A.

55. *Excélsior*, 18 June 1975, 1-A; *El Universal*, 18 June 1975, 1. Ironically, Prime Minister David Ben-Gurion was reported to have described Meir as the "only man" in his cabinet (see Meir's obituary, *New York Times*, 9 December 1978, 6), repeating almost exactly a remark about Sirimavo Bandaranaike.

56. *Excélsior*, 19 June 1975, 1-A.

57. *Excélsior*, 19 June 1975, 1-A.

58. *El Nacional*, 24 June 1975, 6; *El Universal*, 24 June 1975, 10.

59. *Excélsior*, 18 June 1975, 1-A.

60. *El Universal*, 22 June 1975, 6. Two days later, the paper ran a similarly admiring piece about the Pakistani first lady Nusrat Bhutto. Describing her as a "beautiful woman, more than 1.80 meters tall," the article went on, "She dressed in a silk chiffon sari of bright orange and white, and her well-manicured hands made discreet gestures supporting every phrase that her perfect mouth pronounced" (10).

61. *Xilonen* carried nearly identical stories in English and Spanish, but the English version omitted a statement that appeared in Spanish, "Several months ago, the Israeli parliament claimed the Gaza Strip, the Golan Heights, and the port of Aman El Sheik with its country's borders. This determination was ratified by the Prime Minister, Yitzak Rabin" (24 June 1975, 6).

62. *El Universal*, 21 June 1975, 1.

63. The day before, *El Universal* had run a similarly effusive story about Sadat visiting the trauma center of the Centro Médico and laying a floral offering at Mexico City's independence monument (20 June 1975, 10).

64. *La Prensa*, 21 June 1975, 1.

65. *New York Times*, 22 June 1975, 48.

66. *Washington Post*, 22 June 1975, A12.

67. *Xilonen*, 23 June 1975, 1. The quotation is translated from the Spanish. The English-language version of this article in *Xilonen* is completely different in emphasis and contains only this quotation from the Sadat speech: "We are the natural enemies of war. We are the mothers, the wives and the daughters of those who fight and die. Our very nature is a consecration of the ideas of love and justice. Let us try to be the bearers of those principles of justice and mutual respect which are the only guarantee of progress in our war-torn wilderness" (8). A subsequent article included the first part of the statement but left off the phrase linking Zionism with apartheid (*Xilonen*, 24 June 1975, 6).

68. *Xilonen*, 23 June 1975, 1.

69. *Excélsior*, 19 June 1975, 1-A.

70. *New York Times*, 25 June 1975, 2.

71. *El Universal*, 24 June 1975, 10. Six days later, the official UN roster still listed Sadat as the head of the Egyptian delegation, leaving it unclear whether her early departure had been planned (IWY List of Participants, 30 June 1975, UN doc. E/CONF.66/INF.2, 25).

72. *El Universal*, 26 June 1975, 12.

73. Report from 24 June 1975, AGN, DFS, Exp. 9-342-75, Leg. 7, hoja 5–15; *El Nacional*, 25 June 1975, 7.

74. East to Reid, 24 June 1975, Elizabeth Reid Papers, folder 89. Catherine East, whom Betty Friedan dubbed NOW's "midwife" for her persistence in insisting that women needed an organization analogous to the NAACP, had grown up in the modest middle class in West Virginia and worked her way into civil service. In 1975, she served as the deputy coordinator for the State Department's IWY Secretariat (See obituary, *New York Times*, 20 August 1996). NOW's Karen DeCrow and Jacqueline Ceballos also separately sent notes to Reid as a sympathetic feminist figure in the government conference (Elizabeth Reid Papers, folders 92 and 95).

75. UN doc. E/CONF.66/C.1/L.31.

76. Notes on Committee One discussion, 24 June 1975, Elizabeth Reid Papers, folder 92; NARA, RG 220, box 23, Mary Haselton's file. The US and European delegates voted against the resolution on the grounds that only the Security Council could impose sanctions.

Scene 11: The First Rule of Fight Club

1. Laura Bolaños, "La Tribuna de Organizaciones ¿'no Gubernamentales'?" *El Universal*, 25 June 1975, 5. The Mexican tribune panelists had been handpicked by Ojeda Paullada's commission and included Luisa María Leal (director of the recently created National Population Council), María Lavalle Urbina (high-level PRI politician who had served as first woman to preside over the Mexican Senate and by 1975 ran the Civil Registry), and Rosa Luz Alegría (a physicist and Echeverría's daughter-in-law who directed the newly created Centro para el Estudio de

Medios y Procedimientos Avanzados de la Educación [CEMPAE], which promoted open education programs and created Latin America's first education television station).

2. *El Universal*, 24 June 1975, 1, and 25 June 1975, 5; *Excélsior*, 24 June 1975, 1.
3. Elizabeth Reid Papers, folder 92.
4. On the growing role of NGOs in the 1970s, see Iriye, *Global Community*.
5. NARA, RG 220, Box 23, folder "IWY Hotline Mexico City."
6. Lucile Schuck to Bob [Robert Brown], 4 July 1975, Lucile K. S. Longview Papers, Box 2, Folder 2. Although the metro would have offered a less expensive and often speedier means of transportation than a taxi, none of the official materials from either the Mexican government or the IWY organizers mentioned the metro as an option (Ward, "Mexico City," 46. Only an early scout for the NGO tribune venue observed, "Though the traffic is unbelievable, the Centro Médico is in a direct line with the World Conference site" (NGO Committee on International Women's Year, Minutes of meeting January 8, 1975; MPP, box UN World Conference (IWY), folder G).
7. Greer, "World Conference," 199.
8. Betsy Hauge (Assistant to Pat Whiting) to Persinger, 20 June 1975, MPP, Box Tribune, Mexico 1975 (NGO Forum), Folder C. The same note was delivered to Elizabeth Reid with a handwritten note requesting that she support this position at the conference (Hauge to Reid, 22 June 1975, Elizabeth Reid Papers, folder 87).
9. *El Universal*, 20 June 1975, 3; Report from 20 June 1975, AGN, DFS, Exp. 9-342-75, Leg. 5, hojas 20–16. Briggs, *Reproducing Empire*.
10. Patricia Burnett memo "To the members of the World Feminist Commission," undated [early June 1975?], and handwritten note from Jacqui [Jacqueline Ceballos] to Friedan, undated [probably 23 June 1975], both in Betty Friedan Papers, carton 107, file 1247; travel flyer in NOW-NYC, box 27, folder 17.
11. Report on the "Tribune Speakout," Maxine Hitchcock, 18 July 1975, *FRUS*, 1969–76, Vol. E-14, Part I, Doc 184.
12. *Xilonen*, 25 June 1975, 3.
13. Betty Friedan Papers, Carton 107, file 1254.
14. Matsui, one of six children of Christian ministers, had become interested in feminism while spending time in the United States and Europe as a college student in the 1960s. In 1976, she would found Asian Women in Solidarity against "sex tourism" in Asia (*New York Times* obituary, 5 January 2003). Like Matsui, Hong also attributed her feminist awakening to an encounter with the Women's Liberation Movement during her time in the United States serving as the vice consul in New York and advisor to South Korea's UN mission; she pointed to Gloria Steinem as one of her role models (UPI story about her presidential candidacy, 26 November 1987).
15. *Xilonen*, 26 June, 1.
16. AGN, DFS, 25 June 1975, Exp. 9-342-75, Leg. 7, hoja 74; *Xilonen*, 24 June 1975, 1.
17. AGN, DFS, 26 June 1975, Exp. 9-342-75, Leg. 7, hoja 155.
18. Friedan, "Scary Doings in Mexico City," 454. Friedan was not the only one commenting upon attire that evening; the *El Universal* reporter noted Friedan's "plunging neckline permitted reporters to see part of her figure" (*El Universal*, 28 June 1975, 8).
19. "Extraordinary Meeting of all Women of the Tribune" (flyer), undated [reverse is announcement for Friedan press conference on 25 June], Betty Friedan Papers, Carton 37, File 1264.
20. Rita Taubenfeld to Bob [Robert Brown, International Association for Religious Freedom (IARF)], 9 July 1975, Elizabeth Reid Papers, Folder 88. Taubenfeld relates a litany of complaints about the ways that the more established WINGOs excluded even consultative-status NGOs (like IARF) from important meetings, including the regular morning briefings with the US delegation.
21. AGN, DFS, 25 June 1975, Exp. 9-342-75, Leg. 7, hojas 83–88; for Coalition's statement, see AGN, Colecciones Particulares, Grupo Clementina Batalla de Bassols, Vol. 2, Exp. 9, Fs. 31-32; *El Universal*, 26 June 1975, 1.
22. *El Nacional*, 26 June 1975, 10.
23. AGN, DFS, 25 June 1975, Exp. 9-342-75, Leg. 7, hojas 83–88.
24. AGN, DFS, 25 June 1975, Exp. 9-342-75, Leg. 7, hojas 83–88.

25. Persinger to Pronk, 25 June 1975, MPP, Box Tribune, Mexico 1972 (NGO Forum), Folder K.
26. *Xilonen*, 26 June 1975, 2.
27. Charlotte McEwen to Lucile Schuck, 6 October 1975; clipping of McEwen's article, "6,000 Women at IWY Tribune," published in *Rights and Freedom* (available in Arthur and Elizabeth Schlesinger Library on the History of Women, Lucile Schuck Longview Papers, 2005-M7, Carton 4, folder "Lucile–1975").
28. *Xilonen*, 26 June 1975, 2.
29. Mattelart, "Chile: el golpe de estado en femenino o cuando las mujeres de la burguesía salen a la calle." Mattelart's article was translated into several languages and reprinted in publications throughout the Americas. It first appeared in English as "Chile: The Feminine Side of the Coup or When Bourgeois Women Take to the Streets," *NACLA's Latin America end Empire Report* 9 (September 1975): 14–25.
30. Dorfman and Mattelart, *How to Read Donald Duck: Imperialist Ideology in the Disney Comic* (originally *Para leer el Pato Donald* [Valparaiso, Chile: Ediciones Universitarias de Valparaiso], 1971).
31. *Excélsior*, 26 June 1975, 1-A. On Becerril's advocacy on behalf of Mexican Americans, see Gutiérrez, *The Making of a Chicano Militant*, 239.
32. AGN, IPS, 25 June 1975, Caja 1163-A, Vol. 1, hoja 448. Mexico's two groups of secret police actually offer divergent accounts of this hunger strike (AGN, DFS, 25 June 1975, Exp. 9-342-75, Leg. 7, hojas 83–88). *Excélsior* identified the women as from the United States (26 June 1975, 11-A) and *El Universal* as from the United States, Argentina, Australia, and Canada (26 June 1975, 11).
33. AGN, IPS, 25 June 1975, Caja 1163-A, Exp 1, hoja 54; AGN, DFS, 25 June 1975, Exp. 9-342-75, Leg. 7, hojas 83–88.

Scene 12: Coming Out Party

1. AGN, DFS, 26 June 1975, Exp. 9-342-75, Leg. 7, hojas 155–60.
2. AGN, IPS, 23 June 1975, Caja 1163-A, Vol. 1, hojas 306–8.
3. Barbara Hooks, "Highlighting Women's Achievements," *The Age*, 21 May 1975, 18. In 1974, Warren Farrell, a member of the New York City NOW board, had completed his Ph.D. in political science at NYU and published his first book, *The Liberated Man* (New York: Berkeley Books).
4. Reid to Prime Minister, 26 May 1975, Elizabeth Reid Papers, folder 74.
5. For the speech, see Elizabeth Reid Papers, folder 87. For a description of the response, see *El Nacional*, 24 June 1975, 7; *El Universal*, 24 June 1975, 1.
6. "Liberación Femenina," *Excélsior*, 19 June 1975, 6-A.
7. Laura Teresa, Zepeda, García, "La condición de la mujer en El Salvador," EJBP.3, 13 June 1975 (copy in Elizabeth Reid Papers 71a and Hymer papers). The Mexican press similarly ran several editorials about the threat of Western libertinism and arguing that "The Pill" was an invitation to adultery (e.g., *La Prensa*, 19 June 1975, 8).
8. "La Condition du Femme au Zaïre," EJBP.32, 24 June 1975.
9. *El Heraldo*, 21 June 1975 (from Elizabeth Reid Papers, folder 87); *El Universal*, 21 June 1975, 10; *Novedades*, 24 June 1975, 12. For pre-IWY planning, see Charlotte Bunch and Frances Doughty, "IWY—feminist strategy for Mexico City," *off our backs* 5, no. 5 (30 June 1975): 6.
10. Doughty, "Lesbians and International Women's Year," 145.
11. *El Universal*, 24 June 1975, 1.
12. *El Nacional*, 24 June 1975, 7.
13. AGN, IPS, Caja 1163-A, Vol. 1, hojas 306–8; *Xilonen*, 24 June 1975, 8; *Excélsior* and *El Universal*, 24 June 1975, both p. 1.
14. On the zero-sum game between sexual and economic rights, see Wilson, "The Transnational Geography of Sexual Rights."
15. *El Universal*, 23 June 1975, 4.
16. *Novedades*, 24 June 1975, 12.
17. AGN, DFS, 24 June 1975, Exp. 9-342-75, Leg. 7, hojas 5–15. Documents from Laurie Bebbington and the International Lesbian-Feminist Caucus in Elizabeth Reid Papers, folder 87.

18. *El Universal*, 25 June 1975, 8.
19. *El Nacional*, 25 June 1975, 8.
20. Mogrovejo, *Un amor que se atrevió a decir su nombre*, 67. The "visiting lesbians" most likely included Frances Doughty and Linda Fowler of the US-based National Gay Task Force, which sponsored the forum.
21. Paniagua, "'Francotiradora de la política,'" 45; Mogrovejo, "Sexual Preference," 319–20.
22. Laurie Bebbington sent a copy of the declaration to Elizabeth Reid saying it had been anonymously delivered to Frances Doughty, who distributed it to the press and the tribune (Elizabeth Reid Papers, folder 87). Claudia Hinojosa attributes the unsigned *Declaración de las lesbianas de México* to Cárdenas, insisting that one can recognize the "unmistakable prose of a luminous spokeswoman of Mexican lesbians, the beloved and eternal Nancy Cárdenas" (Hinojosa, "Gritos y susurros," 179).
23. Statement from the International Lesbian Caucus, 27 June 1975; Elizabeth Reid Papers, folder 87.
24. *Xilonen*, 27 June 1975, 4.
25. AGN, DFS, 26 June 1975, Vol. 9-342-75, exp. 7, hojas 155–60; *Xilonen*, 27 June 1975, 6.
26. *El Universal*, 27 June 1975, 8. The US-based *Sister: A West Coast Feminist Newsletter* recounted that Cárdenas introduced herself to the picketer calling for her demise, and the protestor explained that Sánchez Juárez had paid them to demonstrate (August 1975, 3). No other press reported an encounter between Cárdenas and the protestors. Sánchez Juárez, a descendant of the nineteenth-century liberal president Benito Juárez, had attempted to censure Cárdenas's successful adaptation of the play *The Boys in the Band* as an "affront to morality and good customs."
27. Claudia Hinojosa, "El Tour del Corazón," in *Otro mode de ser: mujeres mexicanas en movimiento* (Mexico: Centro de Comunicación Alternativa Alaíde Foppa, 1991) cited in Mogrovejo, *Un amor que se atrevió a decir su nombre*, 67. This dramatic description may have been a bit of exaggeration; one account describes interviewing her afterward in the Centro Médico cafeteria (*El Universal*, 27 June 1975, 8).
28. *Excélsior*, 26 June 1975, 7-A. See also *The Church and the International Women's Year, 1975*, 127.
29. *Excélsior*, 3 July 1975, 7-A. Aviles served as the president of the Unión Católica Latinoamericana de la Prensa in 1969. *El Universal*, 27 June 1975, 1.
30. *Excélsior*, 1 July 1975, 6-A. On Báez-Camargo, see Anderson, *Biographical Dictionary of Christian Missions*, 39.
31. Linda Fowler and Carol Lease (International Lesbian Caucus), "Lesbians Speak Out on IWY," *Xilonen*, 27 June 1975, 4. For brief mentions, see *Xilonen*, 23 June 1975, 1 (although the Spanish version of the article attends more to Doughty's statement than the English, neither one names her).
32. John Jova to Secretary of State, 21 June 1975; *FRUS*, 1969–76, Vol. E-14, Part I, Doc 181.
33. *El Universal*, 26 June 1975, 1.
34. *El Universal*, 25 June 1975, 8.
35. *Diario de México*, 24 June 1975, n.p. (clipping from Elizabeth Reid Papers, folder 87).
36. *Xilonen*, 27 June 1975, 6.
37. *Xilonen*, 27 June 1975, 4.
38. *Excélsior*, 1 July 1975, 6-A.
39. *Excélsior*, 26 June 1975, 7-A.
40. *El Universal*, 24 June 1975, 5. Valerie Solanas's *SCUM Manifesto* was originally self-published in 1967; after her attempt to kill Andy Warhol, it was published commercially and translated into many languages. *El Universal* ran another editorial the following day to condemn the "organization," and the Spanish newspaper *ABC Sevilla* similarly ran a half-page article reporting on a press conference that Solanas and SCUM had held in Mexico City, but I've found no other evidence that Solanas attended (28 June 1975, 28).
41. *El Universal*, 25 June 1975, 4
42. Interview with Howard Smith, *Village Voice*, 25 July 1977, 32.
43. *El Universal*, 27 June 1975, 6.
44. AGN, DFS, 26 June 1975, Exp. 9-342-75, Leg. 7, hojas 155–60.
45. *New York Times*, 27 June 1975, 34.

Scene 13: Chaos in the Tribune

1. *Xilonen*, 27 June 1975, 2. The English- and Spanish-language stories about the meeting with Sipilä differ markedly in emphasis and tone. The Spanish version stresses Friedan's leadership in "subsuming ideological and religious differences under the ideal of feminism" and takes pains to depict the group as geographically representative and procedurally inclusive. The English version does not mention Friedan and highlights the logistical challenges of translating and reproducing the amendments for all delegations to read and the fact that the First Committee would not have time to consider them.
2. *El Universal*, 28 June 1975, 8.
3. *El Universal*, 27 June 1975, 6.
4. *El Universal*, 27 June 1975, 6.
5. *Free-Lance Star* [Fredericksburg, Virginia], 27 June 1975, 9.
6. *Xilonen*, 27 June 1975, 4.
7. *Excélsior*, 28 June 1975, 1-A.
8. *Charleston Daily Mail*, 28 June 1975, 8. *El Universal* (29 June 1975, 1) reported that Friedan had "nearly come to blows" with women from Illinois, including the veteran *Chicago Defender* reporter Ethel Payne. For her part, Payne described a confrontation with Vivian Moore (also named in the *El Universal* article) and a Chicana. Describing Friedan as a "gadfly," Payne reported that she had reiterated her accusation that some African American and Chicana women were "paid agents" (*Chicago Defender*, 12 July 1975, 28). Friedan's accusation may have been off-base, but it had not emerged simply from Friedan's lively imagination: the National Council of Negro Women was funded by USAID, and La Raza Unida had been invited and at least partially funded by the Mexican government (Height interview; author's interview with Guadalupe Anguiano, 6 July 2010, Los Angeles, California; Navarro, *La Raza Unida Party*, 254).
9. Ceballos to Friedan, undated handwritten note, Betty Friedan Papers, box 107, folder 1254.
10. *New York Times*, 23 June 1975, 22; 29 June 1975, 2; *Birmingham Post-Herald*, 23 June 1975, A22. Ingrid to Betty [Friedan] (20 June 1975, Betty Friedan Papers, box 107, folder 1254) describes distributing the release to the international press as well as to the Monday (23 June) meeting of the Feminist Caucus. The Redstockings' press release and Steinem's response to it are available in *off our backs* 5, no. 6 (July 1975): 8–9, 28–33, and *off our backs* 5, no. 8 (September–October 1975): 6, 22–23.
11. *El Universal*, 28 June 1975, 21; AGN, IPS, report from 27 June 1975, Caja 1163-A, Vol. 1, hojas 539–41.
12. AGN, IPS, report from 27 June 1975, Caja 1163-A, Vol. 1, hojas 539–41.
13. *El Universal*, 28 June 1975, 1. Puiggrós lived in exile in Mexico City, where she earned a Ph.D. in education at UNAM, during Argentina's dirty war.
14. *El Nacional*, 28 June 1975, 8.
15. *Xilonen*, 30 June 1975, 1.
16. Simpson, "The Washington Press Club Foundation." For photo, see Introduction, Figure 1.1.
17. *New York Times*, 29 June 1975, 2.
18. *New York Times*, 24 June 1975, 3.
19. *Xilonen*, 30 June 1975, 1.
20. McKenna, *Women in Action*. McKenna was president of Quantum Communications, which the previous year had published her pamphlet, "Cable Television and the Future."
21. McKenna refers twice to a "heavy set Argentinian woman" who wrested control of the microphone from Rascón, which—in addition to being gratuitously catty—seems a description that hardly befits Puiggrós.
22. McKenna, *Women in Action*, viii.
23. McKenna, *Women in Action*, x.
24. Friedan, "Scary Doings in Mexico City," 440; McKenna, *Women in Action*, xi.
25. At least some US feminists understood this dynamic before arriving in Mexico City. Charlotte Bunch and Frances Doughty explained in *off our backs*, "First, there are two quite separate conferences planned. One is for official government delegations and is very closed. . . . Most feminists going to Mexico should know that security at the government's conference will

be tight and efforts to get in are probably useless" (Bunch and Doughty, "IWY—Feminist Strategy for Mexico City").

26. *Xilonen*, 30 June 1975, 1.

27. Report from 27 June 1975, 19:00 hrs., AGN, IPS, Caja 1163-A, Vol. 1, hojas 539–44.

28. *El Nacional*, 28 June 1975, 8.

29. Barrios de Chungara and Viezzer, *Let Me Speak!*, 202–3.

30. Peggy Simpson's article in *The News* (Mexico City), 29 June 1975, 6; Friedan, "Scary Doings in Mexico City," 440.

31. McKenna, *Women in Action*, ii.

32. Persinger's report estimates that roughly 7,000 women attended the NGO tribune, based on sign-in sheets ("Report: International Women's Year Tribune—1975," November 1975, IWTC collection, box 3). *Xilonen*, which had a quite supportive editorial line on the United Women, estimated 2,000 women at the Wednesday meeting (26 June 1975, 1); Maxine Hitchock's report to the US State Department estimates 2,000 as well (*Foreign Relations of the United States (FRUS)*, 1969–76, Vol. E-14, Part I, Doc 184). All of these estimates must be treated as extremely rough and somewhat biased.

33. The text of the amendments proposed by United Women of the Tribune appear in McKenna, *Women in Action*.

34. In the 1970s, Freire was an educational advisor to the INGO the World Council of Churches, based in Geneva. His most influential book, *Pedagogy of the Oppressed*, had first appeared in Portuguese in 1968 and been translated into English in 1970.

35. There are countless examples, but most prominently note the reports to the State Department by Maxine Hitchcock and Ruth Bacon (both of the US Center for IWY) available in *FRUS*, 1969–76, Vol. E-14, Part I, Docs. 184 and 185) See also Friedan, "Scary Doings in Mexico City"; McKenna, *Women in Action*.

36. There is an extensive feminist critique of the ways that direct democracy or participatory democracy generates functional exclusions while offering the appearance of democratic process. See, for examples, Fraser, "Rethinking the Public Sphere"; Freeman, "The Tyranny of Structurelessness"; Phillips, *Engendering Democracy*; "Must Feminists Give Up on Liberal Democracy?"

Scene 14: Counter-congresses

1. Second Committee, 12th meeting, 28 June 1975, NARA, RG 220, box 23, Mary Haselton's file; World Plan of Action, Introduction, paragraph 2.

2. Frances Lee McGillicuddy, "Women's Year Delegates Ask Decade of Development," *The Tablet* (Brooklyn, New York), 12 July 1975 (in MPP, box Tribune Mexico, folder Q). McGillicuddy represented the feminist Catholic organization St. Joan's International Alliance on the New York IWY committee.

3. "National Advisory Committee Weekend Conference," 29 November 1974, Elizabeth Reid Papers, folder 5; Australian National Advisory Committee, International Women's Year, Newsletter No. 5 (May 1975), 12–14 (Elizabeth Reid Papers, folder 8).

4. "Third Plenary Meeting Statement by the Leader of the Australian Delegation, Ms. Elizabeth Reid," 21 June 1975, Elizabeth Reid Papers, folder 96. Full text of speech is also available in a number of other feminist archives, including the Friedan and Persinger papers. The US delegation would later endorse inserting the term "sexism" into the World Plan of Action, but in Hutar's plenary address she pointedly and repeatedly used the more cumbersome "discrimination based on sex."

5. Notes on 11 September 1975 IWY meeting, MPP, from file "IWY-add to box"; "Obstacles to the Attainment of Equality of Women and Men," 7 May 1975, MPP, box UN World Conference (IWY), folder G.

6. *El Universal*, 24 June 1975, 19. For the "sexism" in scare quotes, see the accompanying article on COYOTE as well as the article on "unisex" language (29 June 1975, 1).

7. Josefina Torres, "El sexismo en la comunicación"; Margarita García Flores, "Sexismo y medios de comunicación"; Martha de la Lama, "La mujer en la television"; all in Betty Friedan Papers,

carton 107, file 1268. Lusangu Naukula, "La Condition de la Femme au Zaïre," 24 June 1975, Elizabeth Reid Papers, folder 71a.

8. "NGOs, Liberation Groups, Etc.," Meeting 4, First Committee, 23 June 1975, Elizabeth Reid Papers, folder 92.

9. *New York Times,* 2 July 1975, 40.

10. *El Universal,* 29 June 1975, 1. For the committee's resolution, see Lucile Schuck Longview Papers, 2005-M7, Carton 5, Material for IWY Paper Preparation.

11. *El Universal,* 29 June 1975, 12. Obeng had received her BA at the University of Birmingham and Ph.D. at the University of Liverpool before returning to Ghana. She served as the director of the UNEP Regional Office for Africa from 1974 to 1985.

12. *El Nacional,* 26 June 1975, 9.

13. *Xilonen,* 30 June 1975, 8.

14. *El Nacional,* 28 June 1975, 5. San Martín had lived in Chile until the 1973 coup, when he moved to Paris. He did several stints working for the UN and the World Health Organization and published on, among other topics, the issue of domestic violence. The piece published in *El Nacional* had originally appeared in the UNESCO magazine *El Correo,* no. III (1975).

15. Press statement by Patricia Hutar, 30 June 1975, NARA, RG 220, Records Relating to the U.N. IWY World Conference, Mexico City, June–July 1975; Subject File A-G; Box 22.

16. *Excélsior,* 29 June 1975, 1-A.

17. The characterization of Bussi de Allende as a false widow points to Allende's notorious womanizing and that by 1970 he was living with his personal secretary, although Bussi de Allende remained First Lady.

18. *El Nacional,* 29 June 1975, 6.

19. *El Universal,* 30 June 1975, 9.

20. Report from 29 June 1975, AGN, IPS, Caja 1163-A, Vol. 1, hojas 579–86.

21. *El Nacional,* 30 June 1975, 7.

22. *El Universal,* 30 June 1975, 11.

23. Author's interview with Anguiano, 6 July 2010, Los Angeles, California; AGN, IPS, 26 June 1975, Caja 1163-A, Vol. 1, hojas 511–12. On Bustamante's connection with Echeverría's administration, see Navarro, *La Raza Unida Party,* 254.

24. On Raza Unida's relationship with Echeverría and its development of an "alternative foreign policy" in 1975, see *La Raza Unida Party,* 254–56.

25. Author's interview with Anguiano, 6 July 2010, Los Angeles, California

26. Report on 27 June 1975, AGN, IPS, Caja 1163-A, Vol. 1, hojas 520–21 and 532.

27. Report on 29 June 1975, AGN, IPS, Caja 1163-A, Vol. 1, hojas 587–90.

28. The worker was from the Rivetex cashmere factory, which the year before had broken a strike of mostly women workers and fired the organizers (Suárez López, "Las mujeres de Morelos en las luchas sociales del siglo XX," 373–74.)

29. *El Universal,* 30 June 1975, 9.

30. *El Universal,* 30 June 1975, 10.

31. Handwritten notes, [Helena Fabián], 29 June 1975, Betty Friedan Papers, Carton 107, File 1251.

Scene 15: ¡Domitila a la Tribuna!

1. *Xilonen,* 1 July 1975, 6.

2. *New York Times,* 1 July 1975, 8.

3. Issam Abdul Hadi's intervention is the only documented mention of Zionism I have found at the tribune.

4. *Xilonen,* 1 July 1975, 4; Persinger to Ojeda Paullada, 30 June 1975, MPP, box Tribune, Mexico 1975, folder C.

5. Press briefing by Patricia Hutar, 30 June 1975, NARA, RG 220, Records Relating to the UN IWY World Conference, Mexico City, June–July 1974; Subject File A-G; Box 22,

6. The session was listed in *Xilonen* as a "Global Speak-out: Sexism and Communications" (30 June 1975, 7), but the organizers apparently had dubbed it a "Unity Panel."

7. Kempner and Ordorika, "Contested Values and Disputed Cultural Identity in Mexican Higher Education," 60–62.

8. See "Esperanza Moreno de Brito," *fem* 22, no. 187 (October 1998): 37; www.diariolibertad.org.mx/radio/Agenda_Feminista/Reportajes/Mexico_brito.html (consulted 12 April 2014), and Lau Jaiven, *La nueva ola del feminismo en México.*

9. I was unable to obtain DFS reports for this day; these reports are released at the discretion of the archivist. There appear to have been no IPS reports.

10. *El Nacional*, 1 July 1975, 8.

11. *Xilonen*, 1 July 1975, 1.

12. Friedan, "Scary Doings in Mexico City," 462; McKenna, *Women in Action*, xii.

13. On Mexican feminists initiating the organizing, see Height interview, 194.

14. *Xilonen*, 1 July 1975, 1; *El Universal*, 1 June 1975, 1.

15. *El Universal*, 1 July 1975, 7.

16. *Xilonen*, 1 July 1975, 1.

17. Their own legitimacy was, in turn, questioned. *The News*, the English-language version of the newspaper *Novedades*—which also printed *Xilonen*—referred to the dissenters as "unaccredited Latin American women," which was both moot because the tribune was open to anyone and inaccurate insofar as most of the protestors seemed to have been registered tribune attendants complete with the much-discussed badges.

18. *Excélsior*, 1 July 1975, 1.

19. *El Nacional*, 1 July 1975, 8. The irony would have been lost on de los Andes, but this episode predated Friedan's reversal on what she dubbed the "lavender menace."

20. *Excélsior*, 1 July 1974, 1.

21. *El Universal*, 1 July 1975, 4. On Sánchez Cárdenas, see Bruhn, *Taking on Goliath*, 320. On the Mexican Communist Party's turn to a leftist coalition, see Carr, "Mexican Communism 1968–1981: Eurocommunism in the Americas?"

22. *Excélsior*, 1 July 1975, 1-A. Although Friedan recounted that Mexican security tailed her at all times, I have not found her name in a single DFS or IPS report apart from the one describing her tribune panel, which merely lists her ["Freydan"] as participating; one DFS report mentions that "NAO" (i.e., NOW) held meetings in Hotel Marbella (report from 25 June 1975, AGN, DFS, Exp. 9-342-75, Leg. 7, hoja 74).

23. Reports from 1 July 1975, AGN, IPS, Caja 1163-A, Vol. 1, hojas 672–73 and 677; AGN, DFS, Exp. 9-342-75, Leg. 9, hojas 20–26; report from 2 July 1975, AGN, DFS, Exp. 100-10-1-75, Leg. 53, hoja 269.

Scene 16: The Final Push

1. Oddly, *El Universal* reported that the session on women and trade unions was cancelled amid accusations that the panel consisted of CIA-paid union leaders who "reflected the apolitical syndicalism of George Meaney" (2 July 1975, 15), but *Xilonen* ran a quarter-page article about it (2 July 1975, 3), and DFS agents reported on it, including that fact that the panel showed a film "exalting a US labor leader" (AGN, DFS, Exp. 9-342-75, Leg. 9, hojas 20–26).

2. *Excélsior*, 2 July 1975, 20-A.

3. The literature on Argentina's dirty war (1976–83) and its struggle to reckon with its legacy is too vast to cite here, but of particular interest may be Taylor, *Disappearing Acts.*

4. Report from 1 July 1975, AGN, DFS, Exp. 9-342-75, Leg. 9, hojas 20–26; *Excélsior*, 2 July 1975, 20-A; *El Universal*, 2 July 1975, 15; *Xilonen*, 2 July 1975, 2.

5. Elizabeth Reid Papers, folder 88.

6. "Report of the World Conference of the International Women's Year," UN doc. E/CONF.66/34 (1976), 145; see also *El Nacional*, 1 July 1975, 7.

7. *Xilonen*, 1 July 1975, 1. This was another instance where the English and Spanish coverage diverged noticeably, with the article's Spanish version omitting the dismissive language and instead including issues likely to spark conflict in the upcoming plenary.

8. *El Nacional*, 28 June 1975, 7, and 1 July 1975, 7.

9. Reid, "Women and the New International Economic Order," 138–39.

10. UN doc. E/CONF.66/34.

11. Elizabeth Reid Papers, folder 92.

12. *Xilonen*, 27 June 1975, 1.

13. *El Nacional,* 27 June 1975, 7.
14. *El Universal,* 1 July 1975, 1.
15. Most of this account comes from "Notes on Committee I," 1 July 1975 A.M., Elizabeth Reid Papers, folder 92.
16. World Plan of Action, draft resolution, 26 June 1975, UN doc. E/CONF.66.C.1/L.33.
17. Draft Declaration of Mexico, 28 June 1975, UN doc. E/CONF.66/C.1/L.37 emerged from closed-door deliberations that had taken place during the previous week and over the weekend. The draft declaration from the US, UK, and West German delegations (UN doc. E/CONF.66/C.1/L.22), although dated 25 June 1975, came in response to the G-77 statements.
18. For notes on the Second Committee, see NARA, RG 22, box 23, Mary Haselton's file.
19. Report on 1 July 1975, AGN, DFS, Exp. 9-342-75, Leg. 9, hojas 20–26; *Excélsior,* 2 July 1975, 20-A; *El Universal,* 2 July 1975, 15.
20. Lawrence, "Exception to the Rule? The Johnson Administration and the Panama Canal"; McPherson, *Yankee No! Anti-Americanism in U.S.–Latin American Relations,* Chapter Three.
21. *Xilonen,* 2 July 1975, 1.
22. For the final version, see "Report of the World Conference of the International Women's Year," UN doc. E/CONF.66/34 (New York: United Nations, 1976).
23. Text available in "Report of the World Conference," 137–38.
24. Report on 1 July 1975, AGN, DFS, Exp. 9-342-75, Leg. 9, hojas 20–26. Summaries of the discussions and votes appear in "Report of the World Conference," pp. 151, ff. On Albania's "defection" to the Chinese sphere and Enver Hoxha's resistance to détente, see Hanhimäki, "Détente in Europe, 1962–1975," 205.

Scene 17: Unceremonious Closing

1. Reports on 2 July 1975, AGN, IPS, Caja 1163-A, Vol. 1, hojas 736–38.
2. Report on 2 July 1975, AGN, DFS, Exp. 9-342-75, Leg. 9, hojas 161–67; *Excélsior,* 3 July 1975, 1-A; *El Universal,* 3 July 1975, 1.
3. Press release and handwritten notes on closing remarks, 2 July 1975, MPP, box Tribune, Mexico 1975 (NGO-Forum), folder K.
4. *El Universal,* 3 July 1975, 1.
5. *El Universal,* 3 July 1975, 10.
6. *El Universal,* 3 July 1975, 10.
7. "Report of the World Conference of the International Women's Year," UN doc. E/CONF.66/34 (New York: United Nations, 1976), 12. The US delegation voted against every resolution (including those on women and development and women in rural areas) that included language about CERDS or NIEO (NARA, RG 220, Box 23, Mary Haselton's file).
8. For a laudatory account, see Troy, *Moynihan's Moment.* Troy discusses the importance of IWY, but his account rests entirely on Friedan's writing and papers.
9. Memorandum of conversation, 12 April 1975, *FRUS, 1969–76,* Vol. E-14, Part I, Doc 22.
10. Adrienne Germain to David Bell, 6 August 1975, Ford Foundation Archive, doc 71439; text from Declaration in E/CONF.66/34, p. 124. In addition to the twenty-three delegations who voted against the inclusion of the word and the twenty-five delegations that abstained on the vote, twenty-four others simply did not vote on the question.
11. On the utopian manifesto, see Weeks, "The Critical Manifesto."
12. Elizabeth Reid repeatedly expressed this concern about the World Plan of Action. See, for example, *Xilonen,* 24 June 1975, 1.
13. *New York Times,* 6 July 1975, 130.
14. Two memoranda of conversation (one by the Australian embassy's first secretary Penelope Wensley and the other by González) are available in the Elizabeth Reid Papers, folder 90; Elizabeth Reid, personal communication with author, 21 December 2014.
15. Memo from Penny Wensley (First Secretary, Australian Embassy in Mexico City) regarding conversation with Aída González Martínez, 28 February 1975, Elizabeth Reid Papers, folder 92.
16. "Record of meeting between Ms. Reid, Mr. Galvin and Srta. Aída González Martínez," 21 March 1975, Secretaría de Relaciones Exteriores (Mexico City), Elizabeth Reid Papers, folder 90.

17. *El Universal*, 29 June 1975, 1. Australia also had been a CERDS supporter and participated in the CERDS working group from February 1974 to June 1974. When Prime Minister Whitlam visited Mexico in 1973, he had reaffirmed his support for Echeverría's proposal (telegram from Foreign Office to all posts on United Nations International Economic Issues, 16 May 1975, Elizabeth Reid Papers, folder 81).

18. "World Conference of the International Women's Year, 19 July–2 June, 1975. Declaration of Mexico. Plans of Action."

19. "Statement made by Mrs. Helvi Sipilä, Secretary-General of the World Conference of International Women's Year, at the closing of the conference for IWY," 2 July 1975, UN Archive, file S-0971-0012-05.

20. Reports from 4 July 1975, AGN, IPS, Caja 1163-A, Vol. 2, hojas 98–99; AGN, DFS, Exp. 32-1-75, Leg. 39, hojas 283–84.

Scene 18: Beyond Mexico City

1. MPP, box Tribune, Mexico 1975 (NGO forum), folder T.

2. *USIA World* 9, no. 2 (August 1975), MPP, box UN Conference (IWY), folder AA.

3. *Chicago Defender*, 5 July 1975, 6.

4. *The Nation*, 19 July 1975, 36–37.

5. From Ocloo's 1985 report, "History of Women's World Banking," cited in Walsh, *Founding a Movement*, 8.

6. Sophia Smith Collection, Population and Reproductive Health Oral History Project, Adrienne Germain oral history, 62.

7. MPP box Tribune, Mexico 1975 (NGO forum), folder T.

8. Vajrathon note, undated; Sipilä to Persinger, 2 July 1975; Goddard Power to Persinger, 5 September 1975, MPP, box Tribune, Mexico 1975 (NGO forum), folder T.

9. White to Moynihan, 2 July 1975, *FRUS*, 1969–76, Vol. E-14, Part I, Doc 183. See also White's letter to Karen Keesling (White House Director of Women's Programs), 20 January 1976, *FRUS*, 1969–76, Vol. E-14, Part I, Doc 187. As the only woman with ambassadorial rank in the US mission to the UN, White participated in the General Assembly and Trusteeship Council as well as issue-oriented conferences.

10. *Time*, 7 July 1975, 81. Giroud's quip was popular in the Anglophone press, which frequently included quotations from both Giroud and Elizabeth Reid among those delegates frustrated by the geopolitical disputes at the conference (see also *The Economist*, 5 July 1975, 72; *New York Times*, 2 July 1975, 40; *Los Angeles Herald-Examiner*, 27 July 1975, 2; *Facts on File World News Digest*, 9 August 1975; *Foreign Affairs*, October 1975, 173). Notably, the Mexican press frequently listed them among those who recognized the importance of resolving issues of economic inequality along with sex inequality and understood that these discussions would necessarily take a political turn (*El Universal*, 22 June 1975, 8; 24 June 1975, 19; and 25 June 1975, 8; *El Nacional*, 25 June 1975, 7; *México 75*, No. 8 [August 1975]: 12–13 [interview with Elena Poniatowska]).

11. Friedman, *Interpreting the Internet*; Travers, "Parallel Subaltern Feminist Counterpublics in Cyberspace."

12. Mildred Robbins Leet Papers, carton 3.

13. McPhail, *Electronic Colonialism*, 18; McLuhan, *The Gutenberg Galaxy*, 31. The roster, for example, of participants in the New York "focal point" at UN headquarters closely resembled the roster of organizations represented on Esther Hymer's IWY committee (NARA, RG 220, Box 23, folder "IWY Hotline Mexico City").

14. Olcott, "Empires of Information."

15. Biron, "Feminist Periodicals and Political Crisis in Mexico."

16. Bartra, "El colectivo *La Revuelta* o de cuando las brujas conspiraron," 19.

17. Interview with Berta Hiriart by Mathieu Caulier, February 2007, in possession of author; Caulier, *De la population au genre*, 72; Hiriart, "Reflexión a dos voces," 59–60.

18. Urrutia, "Una publicación feminista," 9.

19. On the transition of the IWY Voluntary Fund to UNIFEM, see UN Archive, folder S-1077-0002-06.

20. Walsh, *Founding a Movement*; Berger, "Giving Women Credit."
21. Walsh, *Founding a Movement*, 12.
22. Minutes of the NGO Committee on International Women's Year, 6 August 1975, MPP, box UN World Conference and IWY, folder G.
23. Dowse, "So What Are Feminists to Do?"
24. *New York Times*, 12 September 1982, 61; http://www.trickleup.org/about/History.cfm.
25. Walsh, *Founding a Movement*, 34–35.
26. *International Women's Year Newsletter* (Department of Social Welfare, India), August 1975, 4 (MPP, box UN Conference (IWY), folder Q.
27. "Dear sister" letter on IWY follow-up, 12 August 1975, Betty Friedan Papers, carton 107, file 1247.
28. Jain interview.
29. Laitan Falese, "Situation of Women in Nigeria," 21 June 1975 (EJBP.24), Esther Hymer Collection.
30. "Wangari Maathai." The Ford Foundation sponsored one such seminar in Nairobi on 21–24 May (FFA, reel 1256, grant no. 755-0404). Maathai would win the 2004 Nobel Peace Prize for founding the Green Belt Movement. In Mexico City, she participated in a session on women and the environment (Report from 26 June 1975, AGN, DFS, Exp. 9-342-75, Leg. 7, hojas 155–60) that took place at the same time as the lesbian forum that drew such attention from protesters and the press.
31. Shaheed, "Tackling History and Culture," 124–25.
32. Thayer, "Transnational Feminism," 248; Thayer, *Making Transnational Feminism*.
33. Chinchilla, "Marxism, Feminism, and the Struggle for Democracy in Latin America," 294.
34. Ferree and Tripp, *Global Feminism*; Friedman, "Gendering the Agenda"; Friedman, Hochstetler, and Clark, *Sovereignty, Democracy, and Global Civil Society*; Keck and Sikkink, *Activists beyond Borders*; Moghadam, *Globalizing Women*.
35. Faria Shaheed presentation to "Women and Girls Rising Conference," New York City, 11 September 2014 (available at http://www.weldd.org/gallery/ farida-shaheeds-video-presentation-women-and-girls-rising).
36. For a catalogue of the ways some NGOs were excluded from meetings and policymaking decisions in Mexico City, see Rita Taubenfeld to Robert Brown [International Association for Religious Freedom], 9 July 1975, Elizabeth Reid Papers, Folder 88.
37. Jain, *Women, Development, and the UN*, 68.
38. Jain interview.
39. Rita Taubenfeld to Robert Brown, 9 July 1975, Elizabeth Reid Papers, folder 88.
40. The papers of the IWTC, directed by Vicki Semler and Anne Walker, are available in the Sophia Smith Collection.
41. Walsh, *Founding a Movement*, 11.
42. Height interview, 202.
43. Ruth Bacon describes this International Seminar in her report to the State Department (NARA, RG 220, Box 22).
44. Height interview, 207–08.
45. The US delegation sponsored a successful resolution calling for "voluntary social promotion programs, such as self-help groups, co-operatives, women's groups and other organizations at all socio-economic levels as an integral part of general local self-help popular projects or programs aimed at national, economic and social development" (White House fact sheet on United Nations World Conference of the International Women's Year, 14 July 1975, NARA, RG 220, Box 22).
46. Height interview, 211.
47. Height interview, 195.
48. "Report: International Women's Year Tribune—1975" (Persinger's report submitted to funding agencies), November 1975, IWTC, box 3; Ruth Bacon's report to Henry Kissinger, 24 July 1975, NARA, RG 220, box 22; Maxine Hitchcock, Report on "The Tribune Speakout," to the July 1975 meeting of the National Commission on the Observance of International Women's Year, Betty Friedan Papers, carton 107, file 1250; Patricia Hutar's report to Kissinger, 3 July 1975, *FRUS*, 1969–76, Vol. E-14, Part I, Doc 182; McKenna, *Women in Action*.

49. Reardon to Persinger, 27 July 1975, MPP, box Tribune, Mexico 1975 (NGO-Forum), folder R.
50. Allan, Galey, and Persinger, "World Conference of International Women's Year"; Fraser, *The UN Decade for Women*; Fraser and Tinker, *Developing Power: How Women Transformed International Development*. For secondary literature that has drawn on these accounts, see Baldez, *Defying Convention*; Garner, *Shaping a Global Women's Agenda*; Hawkesworth, *Globalization and Feminist Activism*; Stienstra, *Women's Movements and International Organizations*; Zinsser, "From Mexico to Copenhagen to Nairobi."
51. *Sister: A West Coast Feminist Newspaper*, August 1975, 2.
52. *Xilonen*, 2 July 1975, 1.
53. *Washington Post*, 3 July 1975, A31.
54. *El Universal*, 2 July 1975, 5.
55. *Excélsior*, 3 July 1975, 1-A.
56. Mazower, *Governing the World*, 272.
57. Jain interview.
58. Correspondence between Sipilä and the International Council of Jewish Women (Buenos Aires, Argentina), UN Archive, file S-0990-0004-07-00001. Phyllis Shire, Rochelle Rose, and Rita Marshall to Friedan, 27 June 1975, and Gloria Goldreich Horowitz to Freidan, 16 July 1975. Friedan misleadingly explained that the tribune had "voted on the World Plan of Action and approved it before the UN conference passed the anti-Zionist resolution" (Friedan to Horowitz, 27 June 1975). All in Betty Friedan Papers, Carton 107, file 1247.
59. US Embassy in Stockholm to Secretary of State, 7 July 1975, NARA, RG 220, box 22; Foreign Affairs (Canberra) to UN Mission in Geneva, 23 July 1975, Elizabeth Reid Papers, folder 81.
60. Report on IWY item at ECOSOC 59, 31 July 1975, Elizabeth Reid Papers, folder 94.
61. UN doc. A/RES/3379 (XXX), 10 November 1975.
62. Schmidt, *The Deterioration of the Mexican Presidency*, 121–29; Magaña Duplancher, "Presiones y decisiones en política exterior"; Olin Muñoz, "'We Speak for Ourselves,'" 61–62; Sharif, "Latin America and the Arab-Israeli Conflict." According to Schmidt, Echeverría quickly reversed his position in response to a tourism boycott by the US Jewish community, leading to a decline of 50–80 percent (depending on whether you credit the *Washington Post* or the *New York Times*) in US tourism in Mexico.
63. "Report of the World Conference of the International Women's Year" (UN doc. E/CONF.66/34), 44.
64. Dowse, "The Prime Minister's Women," 397.
65. For conference brochure, see Elizabeth Reid Papers, folder 7-a. For the National Advisory Committee's account, see National Advisory Committee for International Women's, "International Women's Year: Report of the Australian National Advisory Committee," 146–52.
66. National Advisory Committee for International Women's, "International Women's Year: Report of the Australian National Advisory Committee," 149.
67. For roster, see Elizabeth Reid Papers, folder 5. See also, *The Canberra Times* (identifying Kennedy only as a "political activist and lawyer" who had filed a lawsuit challenging the Catholic Church's tax-exempt privileges), 1 September 1975, 3; Hobbs, *Born to Struggle*; Mitchell, *Psychoanalysis and Feminism*. From the Australian embassy in Washington, Peter Timmins had written to Reid just after the IWY conference to suggest the perennial favorite, Barbara Jordan, as well as the new chair of the National Women's Political Caucus, Audrey Rowe Colom, "a young, black Republican from Washington" (Elizabeth Reid Papers, folder 89).
68. National Advisory Committee for International Women's "International Women's Year: Report of the Australian National Advisory Committee," 151.
69. *Canberra Times*, 1 October 1975, 10. The *Canberra Times* published an odd erratum five months later, under the headline "Apology to Mrs Whitlam," saying Bjelke-Petersen denied making the remarks; the newspaper apologized and withdrew the article without explanation.
70. *Canberra Times*, 4 October 1975, 7; 8 October 1975, 2.
71. *Canberra Times*, 3 October 1975, 1. Frieda Brown clearly is not the same person as the Australian Communist Party member and WIDF leader Freda Brown.

72. Thirty years later, Reid told an interviewer that she warned Whitlam that Governor-General Sir John Kerr—who, according to both Reid's and Whitlam's accounts, had unrequited romantic designs on Reid—was planning to "sack" Whitlam (theage.com, 23 July 2005; Whitlam, *The Truth of the Matter*, 74.).

73. Eisenstein, *Inside Agitators*.

74. *Voice of Women*, No. 1, 4. The *VOW* account was framed as a criticism of the New York planning group, stressing the "impressively wide cooperation [the East Berlin conference] engendered during the preparatory phases and which ensured the successful work of the Congress."

75. "Welcoming Address by Erich Honecker," Berlin, 20 October 1975 (Esther Hymer Collection).

76. Marilyn J. Boxer, "Rethinking the Socialist Construction and International Career of the Concept 'Bourgeois Feminism.'" *American Historical Review* 112, no. 1 (2007): 131–58.

77. UN Archive, file S-0971-0012-06.

78. UN Archive, file S-0990-0004-07-00001.

79. Doughty, "Lesbians and International Women's Year," 146–47.

80. Rules of Procedure, World Congress for International Women's Year 1975, Berlin, GDR, 20–24 October 1975 (MPP, box UN World Conference (IWY), folder L).

81. Letter and documents circulated as UN doc. A/C.3/644 (20 November 1975). For a more complete account of the congress—including the full text of speeches and many full-color photos, see *Women of the Whole World* (Journal of the WIDF), No. 1, 1976.

82. Mansbridge, *Why We Lost the ERA*; Mattingly and Nare, "'A Rainbow of Women'"; Spruill, "Gender and America's Right Turn"; Spruill, *Divided We Stand*.

83. United States National Commission on the Observance of International Women's Year, " . . . *To form a more perfect union* . . ."; *National Plan of Action*.

84. Jo Freeman has a photo of the Kansas delegation (jofreeman.com); see also papers of the anti-ERA and anti-abortion Missouri delegation, International Women's Year, 1977 collection, State Historical Society of Missouri; and Spruill, "The Mississippi 'Takeover.'"

85. Elizabeth Reid, personal communication with the author, 21 December 2014. See also Vajrathon's account (http://www.mallica.com/2010/05/12/rita-childers/) and Stiehm, *Champions for Peace*, 75.

86. The Iranian delegation had first proposed the institute at the consultative committee meetings in March. See also Shawna Tropp to Manuel Jiménez, 13 March 1975, UNESCO archive, box 166; Australian embassy in Tehran to Foreign Affairs, 11 June 1975, Elizabeth Reid Papers, folder 81. On Reid's early experience in Tehran, see *The Australian Women's Weekly*, 31 August 1977, 51–52.

87. Speech by Elizabeth Reid, 18 October 2013, National Museum of Australia (http://www.nma.gov.au/audio/transcripts/NMA_Landmark_E_Reid_20131018.html).

88. Kelly, "Comment on the 1980 International Women's Decade Conference in Iran"; Ghodsee, "Revisiting the United Nations Decade for Women," 6.

89. *New York Times*, 14 July 1980, B12.

90. *The Times* (London), 26 July 1980, 12.

91. Elinor Barber, report from Copenhagen, 23 July 1980, FFA, doc. 008157. As Barber notes, at least one of the panels had been organized by the Association of African Women for Research and Development (AAWORD), another post-Mexico City formation.

92. Barrios de Chungara and Acebey, *Aquí también, Domitila*; Çagatay and Funk, "Comments on Tinker."

93. "Comments on Tinker," 775–76.

94. Zwingel, "From Intergovernmental Negotiations to (Sub)national Change," 404.

95. *New York Times*, 25 July 1980, A12. Political scientists Margaret Keck and Kathryn Sikkink observe of NGOs emerging during this period, "More than any other groups, women's organizations use the terms 'network' and 'networking' to describe their interactions" (Keck and Sikkink, *Activists beyond Borders*, 167).

96. Elinor Barber, report from Copenhagen, 23 July 1980, FFA, doc. 008157. Barber also noted a significantly increased lesbian presence in Copenhagen.

97. Cited in Sternbach et al., "Feminisms in Latin America," 405.

98. Alvarez et al., "Encountering Latin American and Caribbean Feminisms."

99. Navarro, "El primer encuentro feminista de Latinoamérica y el Caribe," 263.

100. Sen and Grown, *Development, Crises, and Alternative Visions*. For DAWN's current work, see Sen and Durano, *The Remaking of Social Contracts*.

101. Jain interview. On the experience of Fijian women at IWY, see George, *Situating Women*, Chapter Two.

102. *A Glimpse at DAWN's History*.

103. Jain interview.

104. *A Glimpse at DAWN's History*.

105. The platform was published as Sen and Grown, *Development, Crises, and Alternative Visions*.

106. Margaret Keck and Kathryn Sikkink note, "The emergence of international women's networks was more intertwined with the UN system" than any of the other international advocacy networks they studied (Keck and Sikkink, *Activists beyond Borders*, 168).

107. Çagatay, Grown, and Santiago, "The Nairobi Women's Conference," 408.

108. Helen Ware cited in Kabeer, *Reversed Realities*, xi.

109. Anna Quandt to Bob Lapham, 17 July 1975, RAC, Population Council, Acc 2, Lapham Files, Box 2, International Women's Year Conference.

110. *International Women's Year Newsletter* (Department of Social Welfare, India), August 1975, 4 (MPP, box UN Conference (IWY), folder Q).

111. This field is extensive, but see, for examples, Benería, *Gender, Development, and Globalization*; Bergeron, *Fragments of Development*; Cornwall, Harrison, and Whitehead, *Feminisms in Development*; Kabeer, *Reversed Realities*; Radcliffe, *Indigenous Women and Postcolonial Development*; Scott, *Gender and Development*.

112. There is some debate about the periodization of shifts in development thinking, but it also centers around the four UN conferences. Rathgeber, "WID, WAD, GAD"; Razavi and Miller, *From WID to GAD*.

113. Rodgers, *Age of Fracture*.

114. Rodgers, *Age of Fracture*, 146.

115. The influential texts are too numerous to cite here but certainly would include canonical texts that quickly made their way into translation: Cixous, "Le rire de la méduse"; Irigaray, *Speculum de l'autre femme*; Irigaray, *Ce sexe qui n'en est pas un*; Kristeva, "Semiotike."

116. Riley, *"Am I That Name?"*

117. Scott, "Gender: A Useful Category of Historical Analysis"; Butler, *Gender Trouble*.

118. Butler, "Contingent Foundations," 16.

119. Escobar, *Encountering Development*, 184.

120. Jain interview.

121. Scott, *The Fantasy of Feminist History*, 6.

122. These are commonly cited numbers and available at unwomen.org; the figures presumably come from IWTC estimates. Whether this increased diversity has significantly expanded the discussions is a topic that surely demands further research. For a skeptical perspective, see Spivak, "'Woman' as Theatre."

123. Stephenson, "Women's International Nongovernmental Organizations at the United Nations," 138.

124. Friedman, "Gendering the Agenda."

125. Jain interview.

126. Mazower indicates that the number of NGOs with ECOSOC consultative status grew from 132 in 1969 to 236 in 1979 to 367 in 1989—nearly tripling in the space of two decades (Mazower, *Governing the World*, 328).

127. Alexander and Mohanty, *Feminist Genealogies*, xxiv; Eisenstein, *Feminism Seduced*.

128. Agarwal, "From Mexico 1975 to Beijing 1995," 88.

129. Cardaci, "Visibilidad y protagonismo," 86.

130. Isserles, "Microcredit."

131. Olivares Mansuy, "Debatiendo sobre el feminismo en México," 77. Refers to issue 12 (1995), titled *Feminismo: movimiento y pensamiento*.

132. Alvarez, "Latin American Feminisms 'Go Global'"; Escobar and Alvarez, *The Making of Social Movements in Latin America*.

133. Biron, "Feminist Periodicals and Political Crisis in Mexico"; Rivera López, "*La Correa Feminista*, red de diffusion del pensamiento feminista autonónomo de las noventa."
134. Alvarez, "Beyond NGO-ization?"; Basu, "Globalization of the Local"; Mayer, Pillsbury, and Mukenge, "T-shirts to Web Links"; Thayer, *Making Transnational Feminism*.

Scene 19

1. Examples of these reflections are extensive and disproportionately dominated by those working in colonial and postcolonial archives. A special issue of the *Radical History Review* 2014, no. 120 (Fall 2014) explores these questions much more extensively. For the most prominent examples, see Arondekar, *For the Record*; Burns, *Into the Archive*; Burton, *Dwelling in the Archive*; Burton, *Archive Stories*; Davis, *Fiction in the Archives*; Derrida, *Archive Fever*; Dirks, *Castes of Mind*; Farge, *Le goût de l'archive*; Foucault, *The Archaeology of Knowledge*; Freeman, *Time Binds*; Guha, "The Prose of Counter-Insurgency"; Steedman, *Dust*; Taylor, *The Archive and the Repertoire*.
2. Archivo de la Secretaría de Relaciones Exteriores (SRE), ONU. EUA Delegación Permanente: ONU 83-1 & ONU 83-2.
3. Connelly, *Fatal Misconception*.
4. For a masterful example of such a study, see James, *Doña María's Story*.
5. For a more extended discussion of the roles of various media, see Olcott, "Empires of Information."
6. Vanessa Freije, who wrote a dissertation on Mexican print media during this period, says that the underfunded *El Nacional* frequently simply reprinted material from *El Universal*—certainly their editorial lines matched up very closely (e-mail communication with author 18 October 2014); Freije, "Journalists, Scandal, and the Unraveling of One-Party Rule."
7. Feminist scholars have given considerable attention to women's peculiar status as embodied subjects. The interventions I have found most useful include Butler, *Bodies that Matter*; Canning, "The Body as Method?"; Grosz, *Space, Time, and Perversion*; Haraway, *Simians, Cyborgs, and Women*.
8. Quoted in materials description at https://www.radcliffe.harvard.edu/news/schlesinger-newsletter/bettye-lane-photographer-womens-movement.
9. Allan, Galey, and Persinger, "World Conference of International Women's Year"; Jain, *Women, Development, and the UN*; Joo, "Women's International Non-Governmental Organizations"; Stienstra, *Women's Movements and International Organizations*; Zinsser, "From Mexico to Copenhagen to Nairobi."
10. Meyer and Prügl, *Gender Politics in Global Governance*; Whitworth, *Feminism and International Relations*; Pietilä and Vickers, *Making Women Matter*; Basu, *The Challenge of Local Feminisms*; Kaplan, Alarcón, and Moallem, *Between Woman and Nation*; Mohanty, Russo, and Torres, *Third World Women*; Smith, *Global Feminisms since 1945*.
11. See, for example, Berkovitch, *From Motherhood to Citizenship: Women's Rights and International Organizations*, 123, 43; Ferree and Tripp, *Global Feminism*, 11; Friedman, "Gendering the Agenda," 318; Jaquette, *Feminist Agendas and Democracy in Latin America*, 7, 14; Stephenson, "Women's Organizations and the United Nations."
12. The list is too extensive to cite here, but see, for examples, Armstrong, *Gender and Neoliberalism*, 44ff. and 196ff; Bhatty, "A Daughter of Awadh," 324; Bolt, *Sisterhood Questioned?* 172, 80; Brand, *Women, the State, and Political Liberalization*, 206; Chinchilla, "Marxism, Feminism, and the Struggle for Democracy in Latin America," 294; Churchill, "Transnational Alliances," 10–11; Franco, *Plotting Women*, 185; Kobayashi, *A Path toward Gender Equality*, 57; Mahmood, *Politics of Piety*, 3; Paidar, *Women and the Political Process in Twentieth-Century Iran*, 159–60; Popa, "Translating Equality"; Thayer, "Transnational Feminism," 248.
13. Marcos, "Twenty-Five Years of Mexican Feminisms." See also Lau, "El nuevo movimiento feminista," 20–21; Hiriart, "Reflexión a dos voces," 59–60; Cardaci, "Visibilidad y protagonismo," 86; Parada-Ampudia, "The Institutionalization of Women's and Gender Studies in Mexico." There is a brief discussion in Lau Jaiven, *La nueva ola del feminismo en México*, 113–15.

14. Tarrés, "Discurso y acción política," 127–23; Lamas, "Fragmentos de una autocrítica"; Fuentes Peralta, "La Conferencia Mundial del Año Internacional de la Mujer y la Tribuna de las Organizaciones No Gubernamentales de 1975. Una aproximación a las discusiones en torno al género"; Fuentes, "Entre reivindicaciones sexuales y reclamos de justicia económica"; Urrutia, "Una publicación feminista." Legal scholar Ricardo Ruiz Carbonell has also recently described 1975 as the *año clave* in Mexican juridical history, not least because of efforts to conform with UN conventions on women's rights (Ruiz Carbonell, "La evolución histórica de la igualdad entre mujeres y hombres en México," 83–84).

15. Most notably, Scott, *The Fantasy of Feminist History*.

16. Riley, *"Am I That Name?"* 5.

17. Scott, *The Fantasy of Feminist History*, 6.

18. "Race belongs to the same family as the evil eye. Racism belongs to the same family as murder and genocide. Which is to say that racism, unlike race, is not a fiction, an illusion, a superstition, or a hoax. It is a crime against humanity" (Fields, "Of Rogues and Geldings," 1400).

19. Olcott, "Transnational Feminism." On questions of performance and ontology I have found particularly useful Butler, *Gender Trouble*; Scott, *The Fantasy of Feminist History*, Chapter Two; Taylor, *The Archive and the Repertoire*. On questions of temporality, I have drawn on Grosz, *Time Travels*; Hoy, *The Time of Our Lives*; Solomon, "Time and Subjectivity in World Politics."

20. Badiou, *Being and Event*; Sewell, *Logics of History*.

21. *Logics of History*, 100, 102.

22. *Logics of History*, 228.

23. Reilly, "Cosmopolitan Feminism and Human Rights." Also helpful for thinking through this concept have been Barlow, *The Question of Women in Chinese Feminism*; Burton, *The Postcolonial Careers of Santha Rama Rau*.

24. Werbner, *Anthropology and the New Cosmopolitanism*, 2.

25. Brown, *Regulating Aversion*, 28.

26. Latour, "Whose Cosmos, Which Cosmopolitics?"; Stengers, *Cosmopolitics*.

27. Roseberry, "Hegemony and the Language of Contention."

28. Williams, *Marxism and Literature*, 132. See also Williams, *Keywords*.

29. For a longer discussion of this literature, see Olcott, "A Happier Marriage?"

30. Katz, "Lost and Found," 8.

31. For a fuller discussion of solidarity around identity, see Olcott, "Globalizing Sisterhood."

32. Nancy, *The Inoperative Community*, 12.

33. Rancière, *Dissensus on Politics and Aesthetics*; Tsing, *Friction*.

34. Tsing, *Friction*, 5.

35. Rancière, "Thinking of Dissensus," 1–2.

36. For a particularly relevant engagement with this debate, see Arditi, "Disagreement without Reconciliation."

37. Fraser, *Scales of Justice*, Chapter Five. For Fraser's classic critique of Habermas, see "Rethinking the Public Sphere."

38. Fraser, *Scales of Justice*, 96 and Chapter Four.

39. Hemmings, *Why Stories Matter*, 4.

BIBLIOGRAPHY

Archives Consulted

AUSTRALIA

Elizabeth Reid Papers, Australian National University (Canberra)

MEXICO

Archivo General de la Nación (AGN, Mexico City)
    Colecciones Particulares, Clementina Batalla de Bassols
    Dirección Federal de Seguridad (DFS)
    Investigaciones Políticas y Sociales (IPS)
Secretaría de Relaciones Exteriores (SRE), Archivo Histórico "Genaro Estrada" (Mexico City)

UNITED STATES

David M. Rubenstein Rare Book and Manuscript Library, Duke University (Durham, NC)
    Bettye Lane Photos
    Bobbye Ortiz Papers
    Robin Morgan Papers
    Victoria Ortiz Papers
    Women's International League for Peace and Freedom (WILPF), Chapel Hill (NC) Branch, Records 1974–2000
Esther Hymer Collection, Ecumenical Women's Resource Center, Church Center of the United Nations (New York City)
Ford Foundation Archive (FFA) (New York City [now relocated to the Rockefeller Archive Center])
Marjorie Paxson Papers, Western Historical Manuscript Collection, University of Missouri-Columbia (Columbia, MO)
Mildred E. Persinger Papers (MPP), Special Collections, Wyndham Robertson Library, Hollins University (Roanoke, VA)
Mudd Library, Princeton University (Princeton, NJ)
    Margaret Snyder Papers
    Women's World Banking Records
National Archives and Records Administration (NARA, College Park, MD) Record Group 220, Records of Temporary Committees, Commissions, and Boards; National Commission on the Observance of International Women's Year (1975), 1973–1978
Rockefeller Archive Center (RAC, Sleepy Hollow, NY)
    Population Council
    Rockefeller Brothers Fund

Rockefeller Family Papers
Rockefeller Foundation Archives
Arthur and Elizabeth Schlesinger Library on the History of Women, Radcliffe Institute for
Advanced Study (Cambridge, MA)
Betty Friedan Papers
Bettye Lane Photographs
Black Women Oral History Project. Interviews, 1976–1981
Catherine East Papers
Clara M. Beyer Papers
Elizabeth Stoffregen May Papers
Florynce Kennedy Papers
Lucile K. S. Longview Papers
Marguerite Rawalt Papers
Mariwyn Somers Papers
Martha Stuart Papers and Videos
Mildred Robbins Leet Papers
Sattareh Farman-Farmaian Papers
Sophia Smith Collection, Smith College (Northampton, MA)
Inter-American Commission of Women Papers
International Council of Women Papers (ICW)
International Women's Tribune Centre Archive (IWTC)
Population and Reproductive Health Oral History Project
Tamiment Library/Robert F. Wagner Labor Archives, New York University (New York City)
Annette T. Rubenstein Papers
Boxed Newspapers Collection
Leslie Cagan Papers
National Organization for Women, New York City Chapter Records (NOW-NYC)
Rosalyn Baxandall, Women's Liberation Research Files

UNITED NATIONS

United Nations Archive (New York City)
UNESCO Archive (Paris)

Works Cited

Agarwal, Bina. "From Mexico 1975 to Beijing 1995." *Indian Journal of Gender Studies* 3, no. 1 (1996): 87–92.
Agee, Philip. *Inside the Company: CIA Diary*. American ed. New York: Stonehill, 1975.
Alexander, Jacqui, and Chandra Talpade Mohanty. *Feminist Genealogies, Colonial Legacies, Democratic Futures*. New York: Routledge, 1997.
Alexander, Shana. "Report from Mexico City." Sacramento, CA, KVIE, 1975.
Allan, Virginia R., Margaret E. Galey, and Mildred E. Persinger. "World Conference of International Women's Year." In *Women, Politics, and the United Nations*, edited by Anne Winslow, 29–44. Westport, CT: Greenwood Press, 1995.
Alvarez, Sonia E, Elisabeth Jay Friedman, Ericka Beckman, Maylei Blackwell, Norma Stoltz Chinchilla, Nathalie Lebon, Marysa Navarro, and Marcela Rıos Tobar. "Encountering Latin American and Caribbean Feminisms." *Signs: Journal of Women in Culture and Society* 28, no. 2 (2002): 537–79.
Alvarez, Sonia E. "Beyond NGO-ization? Reflections from Latin America." *Development* 52, no. 2 (2009): 175–84.
Alvarez, Sonia E. "Latin American Feminisms 'Go Global': Trends of the 1990s and Challenges for the New Millennium." In *Cultures of Politics/Politics of Cultures: Re-visioning Latin American Social Movements*, edited by Sonia E. Alvarez, Evelina Dagnino, and Arturo Escobar. Boulder, CO: Westview Press, 1998.

Anderson, Gerald H. *Biographical Dictionary of Christian Missions*. New York: Macmillan, 1998.

Andrew, Christopher, and Vasili Mitrokhin. *The World Was Going Our Way: The KGB and the Battle for the Third World*. New York: Basic Books, 2005.

Ansah, Paul A. V. "The Struggle for Rights and Values in Communication." In *The Myth of the Information Revolution: Social and Ethical Implications of Communication Technology*, edited by Michael Traber, 64–83. London: Sage, 1986.

Arditi, Benjamin. "Disagreement without Reconciliation: Democracy, Equality and the Public Realm." *Critical Review of International Social and Political Philosophy* 12, no. 2 (2009): 167–81.

Arguelles, Lourdes, and B. Ruby Rich. "Homosexuality, Homophobia, and Revolution: Notes toward an Understanding of the Cuban Lesbian and Gay Male Experience, part I." *Signs* (1984): 683–99.

Armstrong, Elisabeth. *Gender and Neoliberalism: The All India Democratic Women's Association and Globalization Politics*. New York: Routledge, 2014.

Arondekar, Anjali. *For the Record: On Sexuality and the Colonial Archive in India*. Durham, NC: Duke University Press, 2009.

Badiou, Alain. *Being and Event*. London: Continuum, 2005.

Bailey, Sydney D. "Some Procedural Problems in the UN General Assembly." *The World Today* 31, no. 1 (1975): 24–28.

Baldez, Lisa. *Defying Convention: US Resistance to the UN Treaty on Women's Rights*. Cambridge: Cambridge University Press, 2014.

Barlow, Tani E. *The Question of Women in Chinese Feminism*. Durham, NC: Duke University Press, 2004.

Barrios de Chungara, Domitila. *La mujer y la organización*. La Paz, Bolivia: UNITAS, CIDOP, CIPCA, 1980.

Barrios de Chungara, Domitila, and David Acebey. *Aquí también, Domitila!: testimonios*. Mexico City: Siglo Veintiuno Editores, 1985.

Barrios de Chungara, Domitila, and Moema Viezzer. *Let Me Speak!: Testimony of Domitila, a Woman of the Bolivian Mines*. Translated by Victoria Ortiz. New York: Monthly Review Press, 1978.

Bartra, Eli. "El colectivo *La Revuelta* o de cuando las brujas conspiraron." *fem* 20, no. 163 (October 1996): 19–21.

Basu, Amrita. *The Challenge of Local Feminisms: Women's Movements in Global Perspective*. Boulder, CO: Westview Press, 1995.

Basu, Amrita. "Globalization of the Local/Localization of the Global Mapping Transnational Women's Movements." *Meridians* 1, no. 1 (2000): 68–84.

Benería, Lourdes. *Gender, Development, and Globalization: Economics as if All People Mattered*. New York: Routledge, 2003.

Berger, Marguerite. "Giving Women Credit: The Strengths and Limitations of Credit as a Tool for Alleviating Poverty." *World Development* 17, no. 7 (1989): 1017–32.

Bergeron, Suzanne. *Fragments of Development: Nation, Gender, and the Space of Modernity*. Ann Arbor: University of Michigan Press, 2004.

Berkovitch, Nitza. *From Motherhood to Citizenship: Women's Rights and International Organizations*. Baltimore: Johns Hopkins University Press, 1999.

Beverley, John. "The Real Thing (Our Rigoberta)." *Modern Language Quarterly* 57, no. 2 (June 1996): 129–39.

Bhatty, Zarina. "A Daughter of Awadh." *Indian Journal of Gender Studies* 6, no. 2 (1999): 311–25.

Biron, Rebecca E. "Feminist Periodicals and Political Crisis in Mexico: *Fem, Debate Feminista*, and *La Correa Feminista* in the 1990s." *Feminist Studies* 22, no. 1 (1996): 151–69.

Bolt, Christine. *Sisterhood Questioned? Race, Class and Internationalism in the American and British Women's Movements, c. 1880s–1970s*. London: Routledge, 2004.

Boris, Eileen, and Jennifer Klein. *Caring for America: Home Health Workers in the Shadow of the Welfare State*. New York: Oxford University Press, 2012.

Borstelmann, Thomas. *The Cold War and the Color Line: American Race Relations in the Global Arena*. Cambridge, MA: Harvard University Press, 2001.

Bosco, David L. *Five to Rule Them All: The UN Security Council and the Making of the Modern World*. New York: Oxford University Press, 2009.

Boserup, Ester. *Woman's Role in Economic Development*. London: Earthscan, 1989.

Boserup, Ester. *Women in Economic Development*. London: Earthscan, 1970.

Boxer, Marilyn J. "Rethinking the Socialist Construction and International Career of the Concept 'Bourgeois Feminism.'" *American Historical Review* 112, no. 1 (2007): 131–58.

Brand, Laurie A. *Women, the State, and Political Liberalization: Middle Eastern and North African Experiences*. New York: Columbia University Press, 1998.

Briggs, Laura. *Reproducing Empire: Race, Sex, Science, and U.S. Imperialism in Puerto Rico*. Berkeley: University of California Press, 2002.

Brito de Martí, Esperanza. "De ingenuas modositas y luchadoras bravías." *fem* 20 no. 163 (October 1996): 15–18.

Brown, Wendy. *Regulating Aversion: Tolerance in the Age of Identity and Empire*. Princeton, NJ: Princeton University Press, 2006.

Brownmiller, Susan. *In Our Time: Memoir of a Revolution*. New York: Dial Press, 1999.

Bruce, Margaret, interview by Richard Jolly, 23 October 2003. New York: The United Nations Intellectual History Project, 2007. CD-ROM.

Bruhn, Kathleen. *Taking on Goliath: The Emergence of a New Left Party and the Struggle for Democracy in Mexico*. University Park: Pennsylvania State University Press, 1997.

Bunch, Charlotte, and Frances Doughty. "IWY—Feminist Strategy for Mexico City." *Off Our Backs*, 30 June 1975, 6.

Burke, Roland. *Decolonization and the Evolution of International Human Rights*. Philadelphia: University of Pennsylvania Press, 2011.

Burns, Kathryn. *Into the Archive: Writing and Power in Colonial Peru*. Durham, NC: Duke University Press, 2010.

Burton, Antoinette M. *Archive Stories: Facts, Fictions, and the Writing of History*. Durham, NC: Duke University Press, 2005.

Burton, Antoinette M. *Dwelling in the Archive: Women Writing House, Home, and History in Late Colonial India*. New York: Oxford University Press, 2003.

Burton, Antoinette M. *The Postcolonial Careers of Santha Rama Rau*. Durham, NC: Duke University Press, 2007.

Butler, Judith. *Bodies that Matter: On the Discursive Limits of "Sex."* New York: Routledge, 1993.

Butler, Judith. "Contingent Foundations: Feminism and the Question of the 'Postmodern.'" In *Feminists Theorize the Political*, edited by Judith Butler and Joan Scott, 3–21. New York: Routledge, 1992.

Butler, Judith. *Gender Trouble: Feminism and the Subversion of Identity*. New York: Routledge, 1990.

Butterfield, Samuel Hale. *U.S. Development Aid—An Historic First: Achievements and Failures in the Twentieth Century*. Westport, CT: Praeger, 2004.

Çagatay, Nilüfer, and Ursula Funk. "Comments on Tinker's 'A Feminist View of Copenhagen.'" *Signs: The Journal of Women in Culture and Society* 6, no. 4 (Summer 1981): 777–78.

Çagatay, Nilüfer, Caren Grown, and Aida Santiago. "The Nairobi Women's Conference: Toward a Global Feminism?" *Feminist Studies* 12, no. 2 (Summer 1986): 401–12.

Canning, Kathleen. "The Body as Method? Reflections on the Place of the Body in Gender History." *Gender & History* 11, no. 3 (1999): 499–513.

Cano, Gabriela. "Una ciudadanía igualitaria: el presidente Lázaro Cárdenas y el sufragio femenino." *Desdeldiez* (December 1995): 69–116.

Cardaci, Dora. "Visibilidad y protagonismo de las redes y ONG en el campo de salud." In *Feminismo en México: Revisión histórico-crítica del siglo que termina*, edited by Griselda Gutiérrez Castañeda, 83–95. Mexico City: Universidad Nacional Autónoma de México, Programa Universitario de Estudios de Género, 2002.

Carden, Maren Lockwood. "Feminism in the Mid-1970s: The Non-Establishment, the Establishment and the Future." New York: Ford Foundation, 1977.

Carey, Elaine. *Plaza of Sacrifices: Gender, Power, and Terror in 1968 Mexico*. Albuquerque: University of New Mexico Press, 2005.

Carr, Barry. "Mexican Communism 1968–1981: Eurocommunism in the Americas?" *Journal of Latin American Studies* 17, no. 1 (1985): 201–28.

Caulier, Mathieu. *De la population au genre: philanthropie, ONG et biopolitiques dans la globalisation*. Paris: Editions L'Harmattan, 2014.

Chávez, Marisela R. "Pilgrimage to the Homeland: California Chicanas and International Women's Year, Mexico City, 1975." In *Memories and Migrations: Mapping Boricua and Chicana Histories*, edited by Vicki Ruíz and John R. Chávez, 170–95. Urbana: University of Illinois Press, 2008.

Chinchilla, Norma Stoltz. "Marxism, Feminism, and the Struggle for Democracy in Latin America." *Gender & Society* 5, no. 3 (1991): 291–310.

The Church and the International Women's Year, 1975. Vatican City: Pontifical Council for the Laity, 1976.

Churchill, Lindsey. "Transnational Alliances: Radical U.S. Feminist Solidarity and Contention with Latin America, 1970–1989." *Latin American Perspectives* 36, no. 6 (2009): 10–26.

Cixous, Hélène. "Le rire de la méduse." *L'Arc* 61 (1975): 39–54.

Connelly, Matthew. *Fatal Misconception: The Struggle to Control World Population*. Cambridge, MA: Harvard University Press, 2008.

Connors, Jane. "NGOs and the Human Rights of Women at the United Nations." In *"The Conscience of the World": The Influence of Non-Governmental Organisations in the UN System*, edited by Peter Willetts, 147–80. Washington, DC: Brookings Institution, 1996.

Cornwall, Andrea, Elizabeth Harrison, and Ann Whitehead. *Feminisms in Development: Contradictions, Contestations and Challenges*. London: Zed Books, 2007.

Dalla Costa, Mariarosa, and Selma James. *The Power of Women and the Subversion of the Community*. 2d ed. Bristol: Falling Wall Press, 1973.

Davis, Kathy. *The Making of Our Bodies, Ourselves: How Feminism Travels across Borders*. Durham, NC: Duke University Press, 2007.

Davis, Natalie Zemon. *Fiction in the Archives: Pardon Tales and Their Tellers in Sixteenth-Century France*. Stanford, CA: Stanford University Press, 1987.

de Haan, Francisca. "Continuing Cold War Paradigms in Western Historiography of Transnational Women's Organisations: The Case of the Women's International Democratic Federation (WIDF)." *Women's History Review* 19, no. 4 (2010): 547–73.

Derrida, Jacques. *Archive Fever: A Freudian Impression*. Chicago: University of Chicago Press, 1996.

Dirks, Nicholas. *Castes of Mind: Colonialism and the Making of Modern India*. Princeton, NJ: Princeton University Press, 2001.

Dorfman, Ariel, and Armand Mattelart. *How to Read Donald Duck: Imperialist Ideology in the Disney Comic*. New York: International General, 1975.

Doughty, Frances. "Lesbians and International Women's Year: A Report on Three Conferences." In *Our Right to Love: A Lesbian Resource Book*, edited by Ginny Vida, 144–49. Englewood Cliffs, NJ: Prentice-Hall, 1978.

Dowse, Sara. "The Prime Minister's Women." *Australian Feminist Studies* 29, no. 82 (2014): 391–402.

Dowse, Sara. "So What Are Feminists to Do?" *Inside Story* (2014). Published electronically 14 August.

Dudziak, Mary L. *Cold War Civil Rights: Race and the Image of American Democracy*. Princeton, NJ: Princeton University Press, 2002.

Eisenstein, Hester. *Feminism Seduced: How Global Elites Use Women's Labor and Ideas to Exploit the World*. Boulder, CO: Paradigm, 2010.

Eisenstein, Hester. *Inside Agitators: Australian Femocrats and the State*. Philadelphia: Temple University Press, 1996.

Escobar, Arturo. *Encountering Development: The Making and Unmaking of the Third World*. Princeton, NJ: Princeton University Press, 1995.

Escobar, Arturo, and Sonia E. Alvarez, eds. *The Making of Social Movements in Latin America: Identity, Strategy, and Democracy*. Boulder, CO: Westview Press, 1992.

Evans, Sara M. *Personal Politics: The Roots of Women's Liberation in the Civil Rights Movement and the New Left*. New York: Vintage Books, 1980.

Farge, Arlette. *Le goût de l'archive*. Paris: Éditions du Seuil, 2013.

Ferree, Myra Marx, and Aili Mari Tripp. *Global Feminism: Transnational Women's Activism, Organizing, and Human Rights*. New York: New York University Press, 2006.

Fields, Barbara J. "Of Rogues and Geldings." *American Historical Review* 108, no. 5 (2003): 1397–405.

Fomerand, Jacques. "UN Conferences: Media Events or Genuine Diplomacy." *Global Governance* 2, no. 3 (1996): 361–75.

Foster, David William. "This Woman Which Is One: Helena Solberg-Ladd's The Double Day." *Journal of Iberian and Latin American Research* 18, no. 1 (2012): 55–64.

Foucault, Michel. *The Archaeology of Knowledge*. Translated by A. M. Sheridan Smith. New York: Pantheon Books, 1972.

Franco, Jean. *Plotting Women: Gender and Representation in Mexico*. New York: Columbia University Press, 1989.

Frank, Andre Gunder. *Capitalism and Underdevelopment in Latin America*. New York: Monthly Review Press, 1967.

Frank, Andre Gunder. "The Development of Underdevelopment." *Monthly Review* 18, no. 4 (1966): 17–31.

Frank, Andre Gunder. *On Capitalist Underdevelopment*. Bombay: Oxford University Press, 1975.

Fraser, Arvonne S., and Irene Tinker. *Developing Power: How Women Transformed International Development*. New York: Feminist Press at City University of New York, 2004.

Fraser, Arvonne S. *The UN Decade for Women: Documents and Dialogue*. Boulder, CO: Westview Press 1987.

Fraser, Nancy. "Rethinking the Public Sphere: A Contribution to the Critique of Actually Existing Democracy." *Social Text*, no. 25/26 (1990): 56–80.

Fraser, Nancy. *Scales of Justice: Reimagining Political Space in a Globalizing World*. New York: Columbia University Press, 2008.

Freeman, Elizabeth. *Time Binds: Queer Temporalities, Queer Histories*. Durham, NC: Duke University Press, 2010.

Freeman, Jo. "The Tyranny of Structurelessness." *WSQ: Women's Studies Quarterly* 41, no. 3 (2013): 231–46.

Freije, Vanessa. "Journalists, Scandal, and the Unraveling of One-Party Rule in Mexico, 1960–1988." Dissertation, Duke University, 2015.

Friedan, Betty. *The Femine Mystique*. New York: W. W. Norton, 1963.

Friedan, Betty. "Scary Doings in Mexico City." In *"It Changed My Life": Writings on the Women's Movement*, 440–63. Cambridge. MA: Harvard University Press, 1998.

Friedman, Elisabeth J., Kathryn Hochstetler, and Ann Marie Clark. *Sovereignty, Democracy, and Global Civil Society: State-Society Relations at UN World Conferences*. Albany: State University of New York Press, 2005.

Friedman, Elisabeth Jay. "Gendering the Agenda: The Impact of the Transnational Women's Rights Movement at the UN Conferences of the 1990s." *Women's Studies International Forum* 26, no. 4 (2003): 313–31.

Friedman, Elisabeth Jay. *Interpreting the Internet: Feminist and Queer Counterpublics in Latin America*. Berkeley: University of California Press, 2016.

Fuentes, Pamela. "Entre reivindicaciones sexuales y reclamos de justicia económica: divisiones políticas e ideológicas durante la Conferencia Mundial del Años Internacional de la Mujer, México, 1975." *Secuencias* 89 (May–August 2014).

Fuentes Peralta, Pamela Jeniffer. "La Conferencia Mundial del Año Internacional de la Mujer y la Tribuna de las Organizaciones No Gubernamentales de 1975. Una aproximación a las discusiones en torno al género." Universidad Nacional Autónoma de México, 2008.

Garner, Karen. *Shaping a Global Women's Agenda: Women's NGOs and Global Governance, 1925–85*. Manchester: Manchester University Press, 2010.

George, Nicole. *Situating Women: Gender Politics and Circumstance in Fiji*. Canberra: Australian National University Press, 2012.

Germain, Adrienne. "Population and Reproductive Health Oral History Project." Interview by Rebecca Sharpless. Sophia Smith Collection, Smith College, 19–20 June 2003.

Ghodsee, Kristen. "Revisiting the United Nations Decade for Women: Brief Reflections on Feminism, Capitalism and Cold War Politics in the Early Years of the International Women's Movement." *Women's Studies International Forum* 33, no. 1 (2010): 3–12.

Gillingham, Paul, and Benjamin Smith, eds. *Dictablanda: Politics, Work, and Culture in Mexico, 1938–1968*. Durham, NC: Duke University Press, 2014.

A Glimpse at DAWN's History: Interview with Peggy Antrobus. Podcast audio. 2010. http://www.dawnnet.org/feminist-resources/archive/podcasts?page=3.

Greer, Germaine. "World Conference, United Nations' International Women's Year (1975)." In *The Madwoman's Underclothes: Essays and Other Writings*, 198–203. New York: Atlantic Monthly Press, 1986.

Grosz, Elizabeth A. *Space, Time, and Perversion: Essays on the Politics of Bodies*. New York: Routledge, 1995.

Grosz, Elizabeth A. *Time Travels: Feminism, Nature, Power*. Durham, NC: Duke University Press, 2005.

Guha, Ranajit. "The Prose of Counter-Insurgency." In *Culture/Power/History: A Reader in Contemporary Social Theory*, edited by Nicholas B. Dirks and Geoff Eley, 336–71. Princeton, NJ: Princeton University, 1994.

Gutiérrez Castañeda, Griselda, ed. *Feminismo en México: Revisión histórico-crítica del siglo que termina*. Mexico City: Universidad Nacional Autónoma de México, Programa Universitario de Estudios de Género, 2002.

Gutiérrez, José Angel. *The Making of a Chicano Militant: Lessons from Cristal*. Madison: University of Wisconsin Press, 1998.

Gutmann, Matthew C. *The Meanings of Macho: Being a Man in Mexico City*. Berkeley: University of California Press, 1996.

Hanhimäki, Jussi M. "Détente in Europe, 1962–1975." In *The Cambridge History of the Cold War*, Volume II: *Crises and Détente*, edited by Melvyn P. Leffler and Odd Arne Westad. Cambridge: Cambridge University Press, 2010.

Haraway, Donna Jeanne. *Simians, Cyborgs, and Women: The Reinvention of Nature*. New York: Routledge, 1991.

Hartmann, Susan M. *The Other Feminists: Activists in the Liberal Establishment*. New Haven, CT: Yale University Press, 1998.

Hawkesworth, Mary E. *Globalization and Feminist Activism*. New York: Rowman & Littlefield, 2006.

Hazard, Anthony Q. *Postwar Anti-Racism: The United States, UNESCO, and "Race," 1945–1968*. New York: Palgrave Macmillan, 2012.

Height, Dorothy, interview by Polly Cowan, February 11, April 10, May 29, October 6, November 10, 1974; February 2, March 28, May 25, October 5. 1975; February 1, May 31, November 6, 1976, transcript available at Arthur and Elizabeth Schlesinger Library on the History of Women in America, Black Women Oral History Project, and online at http://oasis.lib.harvard.edu/oasis/deliver/~sch01406.

Hemmings, Clare. *Why Stories Matter: The Political Grammar of Feminist Theory*. Durham, NC: Duke University Press, 2011.

Hinojosa, Claudia. "Gritos y susurros: Una historia sobre la presencia pública de las feministas lesbianas." *Desacatos* 6, no. Primavera-Verano (2001): 177–86.

Hiriart, Berta. "Reflexión a dos voces sobre el devenir del feminismo." In *Feminismo en México: Revisión histórico-crítica del siglo que termina*, edited by Griselda Gutiérrez Castañeda, 55–61. Mexico City: Universidad Nacional Autónoma de México, Programa Universitario de Estudios de Género, 2002.

Hobbs, May. *Born to Struggle*. London: Quartet Books, 1973.

Horowitz, Daniel. *Betty Friedan and the Making of The Feminine Mystique: The American Left, the Cold War, and Modern Feminism*. Amherst: University of Massachusetts Press, 1998.

Hosken, Fran. "Women and International Communication: The Story of *WIN News*." In *Women Transforming Communications: Global Intersections*, edited by Donna Allen, Ramona R. Rush, and Susan J. Kaufman, 208–17. London: Sage, 1996.

Hoy, David C. *The Time of Our Lives: A Critical History of Temporality*. Cambridge, MA: MIT Press, 2009.

Huggins, Martha Knisely. *Political Policing: The United States and Latin America*. Durham, NC: Duke University Press, 1998.

Irigaray, Luce. *Ce sexe qui n'en est pas un*. Paris: Éditions de Minuit, 1977.

Irigaray, Luce. *Speculum de l'autre femme*. Paris: Éditions de Minuit, 1974.

Iriye, Akira. *Global Community: The Role of International Organizations in the Making of the Contemporary World*. Berkeley: University of California Press, 2002.

Isserles, Robin G. "Microcredit: The Rhetoric of Empowerment, the Reality of 'Development as Usual.'" *Women's Studies Quarterly* 31, no. 3/4 (2003): 38–57.

Jahan, Rounaq, and P. N. Schwartz. "The International Womens Year Conference and Tribune." *International Development Review* 17, no. 3 (1975): 36–40.

Jain, Devaki, interview by Thomas Weiss, 19 March 2002. New York: The United Nations Intellectual History Project, 2007. CD-ROM.

Jain, Devaki. *Women, Development, and the UN: A Sixty-Year Quest for Equality and Justice*. Bloomington: Indiana University Press, 2005.

James, Daniel. *Doña María's Story: Life History, Memory, and Political Identity*. Durham, NC: Duke University Press, 2000.

Jaquette, Jane S. *Feminist Agendas and Democracy in Latin America*. Durham, NC: Duke University Press, 2009.

Joo, Junhui. "Women's International Non-Governmental Organizations and an International Conference, 1975." MA Thesis, State University of New York, 1984.

Kabeer, Naila. *Reversed Realities: Gender Hierarchies in Development Thought*. London: Verso, 1994.

Kaplan, Caren, Norma Alarcón, and Minoo Moallem. *Between Woman and Nation: Nationalisms, Transnational Feminisms, and the State*. Durham, NC: Duke University Press, 1999.

Katz, Cindi. "Lost and Found: The Imagined Geographies of American Studies." *Prospects* 30 (2006): 1–9.

Kawar, Amal. "National Mobilization, War Conditions, and Gender Consciousness." *Arab Studies Quarterly* 15, no. 2 (1993): 53–67.

Keck, Margaret E., and Kathryn Sikkink. *Activists beyond Borders: Advocacy Networks in International Politics*. Ithaca, NY: Cornell University Press, 1998.

Kelly, Joan. "Comment on the 1980 International Women's Decade Conference in Iran." *Signs* 4, no. 2 (1978): 388–91.

Kempner, Ken, and Imanol Ordorika. "Contested Values and Disputed Cultural Identity in Mexican Higher Education." In *Systems of Education: Theories, Policies, and Implicit Values* edited by Mal Leicester, Celia Modgil and Sohan Modgil, 53–69. London: Falmer Press, 2000.

King, Linda. *Roots of Identity: Language and Literacy in Mexico*. Stanford, CA: Stanford University Press, 1994.

King, Marjorie. "Cuba's Attack on Women's Second Shift 1974–1976." *Latin American Perspectives* 4, no. 1–2 (1977): 106–19.

Kinnear, Mary. *Woman of the World: Mary McGeachy and International Cooperation*. Toronto: University of Toronto Press, 2004.

Kobayashi, Yoshie. *A Path toward Gender Equality: State Feminism in Japan*. New York: Routledge, 2004.

Kristeva, Julia. *Semiotike: Rechereches pour une sémanalyse*. Paris: Seuil, 1969.

Lagos, Maria L., and Emilse Escobar. *Nos hemos forjado así: al rojo vivo y a puro golpe: Historias del Comité de Amas de Casa de Siglo XX*. 1st. ed. La Paz, Bolivia: Asociación Alicia "Por Mujeres Nuevas"; Plural editores, 2006.

Lake, Marilyn, and Henry Reynolds. *Drawing the Global Colour Line: White Men's Countries and the International Challenge of Racial Equality.* Cambridge: Cambridge University Press, 2008.

Lal, Jayati, Kristin McGuire, Abigail J Stewart, Magdalena Zaborowska, and Justine M. Pas. "Recasting Global Feminisms: Toward a Comparative Historical Approach to Women's Activism and Feminist Scholarship." *Feminist Studies* 36, no. 1 (2010): 13–39.

Lamas, Marta. "Fragmentos de una autocrítica." In *Feminismo en México: Revisión histórico-crítica del siglo que termina,* edited by Griselda Gutiérrez Castañeda, 71–79. Mexico City: Universidad Nacional Autónoma de México, Programa Universitario de Estudios de Género, 2002.

Lamas, Marta. "Mis diez primeros años: el MAS y el MLM." *fem,* October 1996, 8–14.

Latour, Bruno. "Whose Cosmos, Which Cosmopolitics? Comments on the Peace Terms of Ulrich Beck." *Common Knowledge* 10, no. 3 (2004): 450–62.

Lau, Ana. "El nuevo movimiento feminista mexicano a fines del milenio." In *Feminismo en México, ayer y hoy,* edited by Eli Bartra, Anna M. Fernández Poncela, and Ana Lau, 13–36. Mexico City: Universidad Autónoma Metropolitana, 2000.

Lau Jaiven, Ana. *La nueva ola del feminismo en México: Conciencia y acción de la lucha de mujeres.* Mexico City: Editorial Planta, 1987.

Laville, Helen. *Cold War Women: The International Activities of American Women's Organisations.* Manchester: Manchester University Press, 2002.

Lawrence, Mark Atwood. "Exception to the Rule? The Johnson Administration and the Panama Canal." In *Looking Back at LBJ: White House Politics in a New Light,* edited by Mitchell B. Lerner, 20–52. Lawrence: University of Kansas Press, 2005.

Lawson, Chappell H. *Building the Fourth Estate: Democratization and the Rise of a Free Press in Mexico.* Berkeley: University of California Press, 2002.

Lee, Christopher J. *Making a World after Empire: The Bandung Moment and Its Political Afterlives.* Athens: Ohio University Press, 2010.

Lenin, Vladimir Il'ich. *Collected Works* (45 vols.) Volume 29. Moscow: Foreign Languages. Publishing House, 1960.

Liang, Yuen-Li. "The Question of Access to the United Nations Headquarters of Representatives of Non-Governmental Organizations in Consultative Status." *American Journal of International Law* 48, no. 3 (July 1954): 434–50.

Littlejohns, Michael. "Recording UN History." In *A Global Affair: An Inside Look at the United Nations,* edited by Amy Janello and Brennon Jones, 258–73. New York: Jones & Janello, 1995.

Lugones, Maria. "The Coloniality of Gender." In *Globalization and the Decolonial Option,* edited by Walter D. Mignolo and Arturo Escobar, 369–90. New York: Routledge, 2010.

Lugones, Maria. "Toward a Decolonial Feminism." *Hypatia* 25, no. 4 (2010): 742–59.

Magaña Duplancher, Arturo. "Presiones y decisiones en política exterior: dos momentos de México ante el conflicto árabe-israelí." *Relaciones Internacionales,* no. 17 (2011): 123–52.

Mahmood, Saba. *Politics of Piety: The Islamic Revival and the Feminist Subject.* Princeton, NJ: Princeton University Press, 2004.

Mansbridge, Jane J. *Why We Lost the ERA.* Chicago: University of Chicago Press, 1986.

Marchand, Marianne H. "Latin American Women Speak on Development: Are We Listening Yet?" *Feminism/Postmodernism/Development,* edited by Marianne H. Marchand and Jane L. Parpart, 56–72. London and New York: Routledge, 1995.

Marcos, Sylvia. "Twenty-Five Years of Mexican Feminisms." *Women's Studies International Forum* 22, no. 4 (8 July 1999): 431–33.

Mattelart, Michèle. "Chile: el golpe de estado en femenino o cuando las mujeres de la burguesía salen a la calle." *Casa de las Américas* 88 (January–February 1975): 75–90.

Mattingly, Doreen J., and Jessica L. Nare. "'A Rainbow of Women': Diversity and Unity at the 1977 US International Women's Year Conference." *Journal of Women's History* 26, no. 2 (2014): 88–112.

Mayer, Doe, Barbara Pillsbury, and Muadi Mukenge. "T-shirts to Web Links: Women Connect! Communications Capacity-building with Women's NGOs." In *Women and Gender Equity in Development Theory and Practice: Institutions, Resources, and Mobilization,* edited by Jane Jaquette and Gale Summerfield, 240–67. Durham, NC: Duke University Press, 2006.

Mazower, Mark. *Governing the World: The History of an Idea*. New York: Penguin, 2012.

Mazower, Mark. *No Enchanted Palace: The End of Empire and the Ideological Origins of the United Nations*. Princeton, NJ: Princeton University Press, 2010.

McAtee, William G. *Transformed: A White Mississippi Pastor's Journey into Civil Rights and Beyond*. Jackson: University Press of Mississippi, 2011.

McKenna, Joan. *Women in Action*. n.p.: Al-Ber Costa Chapter of the United Nations Association, 1976.

McLuhan, Marshall. *The Gutenberg Galaxy: The Making of Typographic Man*. Toronto: University of Toronto Press, 1962.

McPhail, Thomas L. *Electronic Colonialism: The Future of International Broadcasting and Communication*. 2d ed. London: Sage, 1987.

McPherson, Alan L. *Yankee No! Anti-Americanism in U.S.–Latin American Relations*. Cambridge, MA: Harvard University Press, 2003.

Meisler, Stanley. *United Nations: A History*. New York: Grove Press, 2011.

Meyer, Mary K., and Elisabeth Prügl. *Gender Politics in Global Governance*. Lanham, MD: Rowman & Littlefield, 1999.

Miller, Francesca. *Latin American Women and the Search for Social Justice*. Hanover, NH: University Press of New England, 1991.

Miller, Francesca. "Women in the Social, Political, and Economic Transformation of Latin America and the Caribbean." *Capital, Power, and Inequality in Latin America and the Caribbean* edited by Richard L. Harris and Jorge Nef, 174–95. New York: Rowman & Littlefield, 2008.

Mitchell, Juliet. *Psychoanalysis and Feminism*. New York: Pantheon, 1974.

Moghadam, Valentine M. *Globalizing Women: Transnational Feminist Networks*. Baltimore: Johns Hopkins University Press, 2005.

Mogrovejo, Norma. "Sexual Preference, the Ugly Duckling of Feminist Demands: The Lesbian Movement in Mexico." In *Female Desires: Same-Sex Relations and Transgender Practices across Cultures*, edited by Evelyn Blackwood and Saskia Wieringa, 308–36. New York: Columbia University Press, 1999.

Mogrovejo, Norma. *Un amor que se atrevió a decir su nombre: la lucha de las lesbianas y su relación con los movimientos homosexual y feminista en América Latina*. 1a ed. Mexico City: Centro de Documentación y Archivo Histórico Lésbico (CDAHL), 2000.

Mohanty, Chandra Talpade. *Feminism without Borders: Decolonizing Theory, Practicing Solidarity*. Durham, NC: Duke University Press, 2003.

Mohanty, Chandra Talpade, Ann Russo, and Lourdes Torres, eds. *Third World Women and the Politics of Feminism*. Bloomington: Indiana University Press, 1991.

Moya Fábregas, Johanna I. "The Cuban Woman's Revolutionary Experience: Patriarchal Culture and the State's Gender Ideology, 1950–1976." *Journal of Women's History* 22, no. 1 (2010): 61–84.

Naghibi, Nima. *Rethinking Global Sisterhood: Western Feminism and Iran*. Minneapolis: University of Minnesota Press, 2007.

Nancy, Jean-Luc. *The Inoperative Community*. Minneapolis: University of Minnesota Press, 1991.

National Advisory Committee for International Women's Year. "International Women's Year: Report of the Australian National Advisory Committee." Canberra: Government Printer of Australia, 1976.

Navarro, Armando. *La Raza Unida Party: A Chicano Challenge to the U.S. Two-Party Dictatorship*. Philadelphia: Temple University Press, 2000.

Navarro, Marysa. "El primer encuentro feminista de Latinoamérica y el Caribe." In *Sociedad, subordinación y feminismo. Debate sobre la mujer en América Latina y el Caribe: Discusión acerca de la Unidad Producción-Reproducción*, edited by Magdalena León de Leal, Carmen Diana Deere, and Nohra Rey de Marulanda, 261–66. Bogotá: Asociación Colombiana para el Estudio de la Población, 1982.

Nelson, Barbara J. "The Origins of the Two-Channel Welfare State: Workmen's Compensation and Mother's Aid." In *Women, the State, and Welfare*, edited by Linda Gordon, 123–51. Madison: University of Wisconsin, 1990.

Nelson, Diane M. *Reckoning: The Ends of War in Guatemala*. Durham, NC: Duke University Press, 2009.

Olcott, Jocelyn. "Empires of Information: Media Strategies for the 1975 International Women's Year." *Journal of Women's History* 24, no. 4 (2012): 24–48.

Olcott, Jocelyn. "Globalizing Sisterhood: International Women's Year and the Limits of Identity Politics." In *Shock of the Global: The 1970s in Perspective*, edited by Niall Ferguson, Charles Maier, Erez Manela, and Daniel Sargent. Cambridge, MA: Harvard University Press, 2010.

Olcott, Jocelyn. "A Happier Marriage? Feminist History Takes the Transnational Turn." In *Making Women's Histories: Beyond National Perspectives*, edited by Pamela Nadell and Katherine Haulman, 237–58. New York: New York University Press, 2013.

Olcott, Jocelyn. *Revolutionary Women in Postrevolutionary Mexico*. Durham, NC: Duke University Press, 2005.

Olcott, Jocelyn. "Transnational Feminism: Event, Temporality, and Performance at the 1975 International Women's Year Conference." In *Cultures in Motion*, edited by Daniel T. Rodgers, Bhavani Raman, and Helmut Reimitz, 241–66. Princeton, NJ: Princeton University Press, 2013.

Olin Muñoz, María L. "'We Speak for Ourselves': The First National Congress of Indigenous Peoples and the Politics of Indigenismo in Mexico, 1968–1982." Ph.D. Dissertation, University of Arizona, 2009.

Olivares Mansuy, Cecilia. "Debatiendo sobre el feminismo en México." *Revista Estudos Feministas* 12, no. Número especial (September–December 2004): 75–79.

Pacifica Radio Archives. *Betty Friedan vs. the Third World*. North Hollywood, CA: Pacifica Radio Archives, 1975 sound recording, 1 sound disc (48 min.): digital; 4 3/4 in.

Paidar, Parvin. *Women and the Political Process in Twentieth-Century Iran*. Volume 1. Cambridge: Cambridge University Press, 1997.

Paniagua, Lita. "'Francotiradora de la política.'" *Siempre!*, 6 August 1975, 44–45.

Parada-Ampudia, Lorenia. "The Institutionalization of Women's and Gender Studies in Mexico: Achievements and Challenges." In *Women's Studies for the Future: Foundations, Interrogations, Politics*, edited by Elizabeth Lapovksy Kennedy and Agatha Beins, 262–71. New Brunswick, NJ: Rutgers University Press, 2005.

Pérez, Emma. *The Decolonial Imaginary: Writing Chicanas into History*. Bloomington: Indiana University Press, 1999.

Persinger, Mildred, interview by Katherine Ann Lynskey, 21 March 2006, accessed 19 June 2009. http://www1.hollins.edu/classes/anth220s06/lynskeyk/persinger_lynskey_main.htm. (Transcript available from author.)

Phillips, Anne. *Engendering Democracy*. University Park: Pennsylvania State University Press, 1991.

Phillips, Anne. "Must Feminists Give Up on Liberal Democracy?" *Political Studies* 40 (1992): 68–82.

Pietilä, Hilkka, and Jeanne Vickers. *Making Women Matter: The Role of the United Nations*. Updated and expanded ed. London: Zed Books, 1994.

Plummer, Brenda Gayle. *In Search of Power: African Americans in the Era of Decolonization, 1956–1974*. New York: Cambridge University Press, 2012.

Poniatowska, Elena. *La noche de Tlatelolco: Testimonios de historia oral*. Mexico City: Ediciones ERA, 1971.

Popa, Raluca Maria. "Translating Equality between Women and Men across Cold War Divides: Women Activists from Hungary and Romania and the Creation of International Women's Year." In *Gender Politics and Everyday Life in State Socialist Eastern and Central Europe*, edited by Shana Penn and Jill Massino. New York: Palgrave Macmillan, 2009.

Power, Margaret. *Right-Wing Women in Chile: Feminine Power and the Struggle against Allende, 1964–1973*. University Park: Pennsylvania State University Press, 2010.

Prashad, Vijay. *The Darker Nations: A People's History of the Third World*. New York: New Press, 2007.

Pratt, Mary Louise. "I, Rigoberta Menchú and the 'Culture Wars.'" In *The Rigoberta Menchú Controversy*, edited by Arturo Arias, 29–48. Minneapolis: University of Minnesota Press, 2001.

Pratt, Mary Louise. "SOFA: Toward a History of the Future." *Tulsa Studies in Women's Literature* 1, no. 1 (2007): 53–60.

Radcliffe, Sarah. *Indigenous Women and Postcolonial Development: Social Heterogeneity, Rights, and Socionatures.* Durham, NC: Duke University Press, 2015.

Rancière, Jacques. *Dissensus on Politics and Aesthetics.* Translated by Steve Corcoran. London: Continuum, 2010.

Rancière, Jacques. "The Thinking of Dissensus: Politics and Aesthetics." In *Reading Rancière*, edited by Paul Bowman and Richard Stamp, 1–17. London: Continuum, 2011.

Randall, Margaret. "'We Need a Government of Men and Women . . . !' Notes on the Second National Congress of the Federación de Mujeres Cubanos, November 25–29, 1974." *Latin American Perspectives* 2, no. 4 (1975): 111–17.

Randolph, Sherie M. *Florynce "Flo" Kennedy: The Life of a Black Feminist Radical.* Chapel Hill: University of North Carolina Press, 2015.

Rathgeber, Eva M. "WID, WAD, GAD: Trends in Research and Practice." *Journal of Developing Areas* 24, no. 4 (1990): 489–502.

Razavi, Shahrashoub, and Carol Miller. *From WID to GAD: Conceptual Shifts in the Women and Development Discourse.* Volume 1. Geneva: United Nations Research Institute for Social Development, 1995.

Reanda, Laura. "Human Rights and Women's Rights: The United Nations Approach." *Human Rights Quarterly* 3, no. 2 (1981): 11–31.

Reid, Elizabeth Anne. "Women and the New International Economic Order." In *Equality of Opportunity within and among Nations*, edited by Khadija Haq, 137–54. New York: Praeger, 1977.

Reilly, Niamh. "Cosmopolitan Feminism and Human Rights." *Hypatia* 22, no. 4 (Fall 2007): 179–98.

Riley, Denise. *"Am I That Name?" Feminism and the Category of "Women" in History.* Minneapolis: University of Minnesota Press, 1988.

Rivera López, Karen Esmeraldo. "*La Correa Feminista*, red de diffusion del pensamiento feminista autonónomo de las noventa." In *Apróximaciones críticas a las prácticas teórico-políticas del feminismo latinoamericano*, edited by Yuderkys Espinosa Miñoso, 269–82. Buenos Aires: En la Frontera, 2010.

Rodgers, Daniel T. *Age of Fracture.* Cambridge, MA: Harvard University Press, 2011.

Roseberry, William. "Hegemony and the Language of Contention." In *Everyday Forms of State Formation: Revolution and the Negotiation of Rule in Modern Mexico*, edited by Gilbert M. Joseph and Daniel Nugent, 355–66. Durham, NC: Duke University Press, 1994.

Rostow, W. W. *The Stages of Economic Growth: A Non-Communist Manifesto.* Cambridge: Cambridge University Press, 1960.

Ruiz Carbonell, Ricardo. "La evolución histórica de la igualdad entre mujeres y hombres en México." In *Derechos humanos: temas y problemas*, edited by Consuelo Maqueda Abreu and Víctor M. Martínez Bullé Goyri, 69–136. Mexico City: Universidad Nacional Autónoma de México, Instituto de Investigaciones Jurídicas, 2010.

Rupp, Leila J. *Worlds of Women: The Making of an International Women's Movement.* Princeton, NJ: Princeton University Press, 1997.

Saldaña-Portillo, María Josefina. *The Revolutionary Imagination in the Americas and the Age of Development.* Durham, NC: Duke University Press, 2003.

Saunders, Frances Stonor. *The Cultural Cold War: The CIA and the World of Arts and Letters.* New York: New Press, 2013.

Schechter, Michael G. *United Nations Global Conferences.* London: Routledge, 2005.

Schmidt, Samuel. *The Deterioration of the Mexican Presidency: The Years of Luis Echeverría.* Translated by Dan A. Cothran. Tucson: University of Arizona Press, 1991.

Scott, Catherine V. *Gender and Development: Rethinking Modernization and Dependency Theory.* Boulder, CO: L. Rienner, 1995.

Scott, Joan Wallach. *The Fantasy of Feminist History.* Durham, NC: Duke University Press, 2011.

Scott, Joan Wallach. "Gender: A Useful Category of Historical Analysis." *American Historical Review* 91, no. 5 (December 1986): 1053–75.

Sen, Gita, and Marina Durano, eds. *The Remaking of Social Contracts: Feminists in a Fierce New World.* London: Zed Books, 2014.

Sen, Gita, and Caren Grown. *Development, Crises, and Alternative Visions: Third World Women's Perspectives.* New York: Monthly Review Press, 1987.

Sewell, William H. Jr. *Logics of History: Social Theory and Social Transformation.* Chicago: University of Chicago Press, 2005.

Shaheed, Farida. "Tackling History and Culture: Building the Women's Rights Movement and Leveraging Global Conferences for Local Realities in Pakistan." In *Women and Girls Rising: Progress and Resistance around the World,* edited by Ellen Chesler and Terry McGovern, 120–28. New York: Routledge, 2015.

Sharif, Regina. "Latin America and the Arab-Israeli Conflict." *Journal of Palestine Studies* 7, no. 1 (Autumn 1977): 98–122.

Simpson, Peggy A. "The Washington Press Club Foundation's Oral History Project: Getting Women Journalists to Speak of Themselves, for Themselves, for Herstory's Sake." In *Women Transforming Communications: Global Intersections,* edited by Donna Allen, Ramona R. Rush, and Susan J. Kaufman, 290–302. London: Sage, 1996.

Smith, Bonnie G. *Global Feminisms since 1945: A Survey of Issues and Controversies.* London: Routledge, 2000.

Snyder, Margaret. "Unlikely Godmother: The UN and the Global Women's Movement." In *Global Feminism: Transnational Women's Activism, Organizing, and Human Rights,* edited by Myra Marx Ferree and Aili Mari Tripp, 24–50. New York: New York University Press, 2006.

Solomon, Ty. "Time and Subjectivity in World Politics." *International Studies Quarterly,* 5 July 2013.

Soto Laveaga, Gabriela. "'Let's Become Fewer': Soap Operas, Contraception, and Nationalizing the Mexican Family in an Overpopulated World." *Sexuality Research & Social Policy* 4, no. 3 (2007): 19–33.

Spivak, Gayatri Chakravorty. "'Woman' as Theatre: United Nations Conference on Women, Beijing 1995." *Radical Philosophy* January/February 1996.

Spruill, Marjorie J. "Gender and America's Right Turn." In *Rightward Bound: Making America Conservative in the 1970s,* edited by Bruce J. Schulman and Julian E. Zelizer, 71–89. Cambridge, MA: Harvard University Press, 2008.

Spruill, Marjorie J. *Divided We Stand: Women's Rights, Family Values, and the Polarization of American Politics.* New York: Bloomsbury, 2017.

Spruill, Marjorie J. "The Mississippi 'Takeover': Feminists, Anti-Feminists, and the International Women's Year Conference of 1977." In *Mississippi Women: Their Lives, Their Histories,* edited by Martha H. Swain, Elizabeth Anne Payne, and Marjorie Julian Spruill, 287–312. Athens: University of Georgia Press, 2010.

Steedman, Carolyn. *Dust: The Archive and Cultural History.* New Brunswick, NJ: Rutgers University Press, 2002.

Stengers, Isabelle. *Cosmopolitics.* Translated by Robert Bononno. Minneapolis: University of Minnesota Press, 2010.

Stephenson, Carolyn M. "Women's International Nongovernmental Organizations at the United Nations." In *Women, Politics, and the United Nations,* edited by Anne Winslow, 135–53. Westport, CT: Greenwood Press, 1995.

Stephenson, Carolyn M. "Women's Organizations and the United Nations." In *Multilateral Diplomacy and the United Nations Today,* edited by James P. Muldoon Jr., JoAnn Fagot Aviel, Richard Reitano, and Earl Sullivan, 207–28. Cambridge, MA: Westview Press, 2005.

Sternbach, Nancy Saporta, Marysa Navarro-Aranguren, Patricia Chuchryk, and Sonia E. Alvarez. "Feminisms in Latin America: From Bogotá to San Bernardo." *Signs* 17, no. 2 (1992): 393–434.

Stiehm, Judith Hicks. *Champions for Peace: Women Winners of the Nobel Peace Prize*. 2d ed. Lanham, MD: Rowman & Littlefield, 2014.

Stienstra, Deborah. *Women's Movements and International Organizations*. London: St. Martin's Press, 1994.

Suárez López, Rocío. "Las mujeres de Morelos en las luchas sociales del siglo XX." In *Política y sociedad en el Morelos posrevolucionario y contemporáneo*, edited by María Victoria Crespo and Luis Anaya Merchant, 34–81. Cuernavaca: Comisión Especial de Colaboración a los Festejos del Bicentenario de la Independencia de nuestro país y Centenario de la Revolución Mexicana, Congreso del Estado de Morelos-LI Legislatura, Universidad Autónoma del Estado de Morelos, Ayuntamiento de Cuernavaca/ Instituto de Cultura de Morelos, 2010.

Sznajder, Mario, and Luis Roniger. *The Politics of Exile in Latin America*. New York: Cambridge University Press, 2009.

Tarrés, María Luisa. "Discurso y acción política feminista (1970–2000)." In *Miradas feministas sobre las mexicanas del siglo XX*, edited by Marta Lamas, 113–48. Mexico City: Fondo de Cultura Económica; Consejo Nacional para la Cultura y las Artes, 2007.

Taylor, Diana. *The Archive and the Repertoire: Performing Cultural Memory in the Americas*. Durham, NC: Duke University Press, 2003.

Taylor, Diana. *Disappearing Acts: Spectacles of Gender and Nationalism in Argentina's "Dirty War."* Durham, NC: Duke University Press, 1997.

Telgen, Diane, and Jim Kamp, eds. *Notable Hispanic Women*. Detroit: Gale Research, 1993.

Thayer, Millie. *Making Transnational Feminism: Rural Women, NGO Activists, and Northern Donors in Brazil*. New York: Routledge, 2010.

Thayer, Millie. "Transnational Feminism: Reading Joan Scott in the Brazilian *sertão*." *Ethnography* 2, no. 2 (2001): 243–71.

Therborn, Göran. *Between Sex and Power: Family in the World, 1900–2000*. London: Routledge, 2004.

Tinker, Irene. "Challenging Women, Changing Policies: The Women in Development Movement." In *Developing Power: How Women Transformed International Development*, edited by Arvonne S. Fraser and Irene Tinker. New York: Feminist Press at City University of New York, 2004.

Tinker, Irene. "International Notes: A Feminist View of Copenhagen." *Signs: The Journal of Women in Culture and Society* 6, no. 3 (Spring 1981): 531–37.

Toto Gutiérrez, Mireya. "El feminismo en México y su impacto en el discurso jurídico." In *Feminismo en México: Revisión histórico-crítica del siglo que termina*, edited by Griselda Gutiérrez Castañeda, 401–12. Mexico City: Universidad Nacional Autónoma de México, Programa Universitario de Estudios de Género, 2002.

Travers, Ann. "Parallel Subaltern Feminist Counterpublics in Cyberspace." *Sociological Perspectives* 46, no. 2 (2003): 223–37.

Troy, Gil. *Moynihan's Moment: America's Fight against Zionism as Racism*. New York: Oxford University Press, 2013.

Tsing, Anna Lowenhaupt. *Friction: An Ethnography of Global Connection*. Princeton, NJ: Princeton University Press, 2005.

United States National Commission on the Observance of International Women's Year. *National Plan of Action Adopted at National Women's Conference, Nov. 18–21, 1977, Houston, Texas*. Washington, DC: National Commission on the Observance of International Women's Year, 1978.

United States National Commission on the Observance of International Women's Year. " . . . To form a more perfect union . . .": Justice for American Women. Washington, DC: United States Department of State, 1976.

Urrutia, Elena. "Una publicación feminista." *fem* 20 no. 163 (October 1986): 9–11.

Voss, Kimberly Wilmot, and Lance Speere. "Marjorie Paxson: From Women's Editor to Publisher." *Media History Monographs* 10, no. 1 (2008): 1–17.

Walker, Louise. *Waking from the Dream: Mexico's Middle Classes after 1968*. Stanford, CA: Stanford University Press, 2013.

Walsh, Michaela. *Founding a Movement: Women's World Banking, 1975-1990.* New York: Cosimo Books, 2012.

"Wangari Maathai." In *Connection,* edited by Dick Gordon, 00:46:42. WBUR, Boston, 2005.

Ward, Peter M. "Mexico City." In *Problems and Planning in Third World Cities,* edited by Michael Pacione, 28-64. New York: Routledge, 2013 [1981].

Warn, Patti. "Ministers and Minders." In *The House on Capital Hill: Parliament, Politics and Power in the National Capital,* edited by Julian Disney and J. R. Nethercote. Annandale, New South Wales: Federation Press, 1996.

Waterman, Peter. "Hidden from Herstory: Women, Feminism and New Global Solidarity." *Economic and Political Weekly* (1993): 83-100.

Weeks, Kathi. "The Critical Manifesto: Marx and Engels, Haraway, and Utopian Politics." *Utopian Studies* 24, no. 2 (2013): 216-31.

Werbner, Pnina. *Anthropology and the New Cosmopolitanism: Rooted, Feminist and Vernacular Perspectives.* Oxford: Berg, 2008.

Westad, Odd Arne. *The Global Cold War: Third World Interventions and the Making of Our Times.* New York: Cambridge University Press, 2005.

White, F. Clifton, and William J. Gill. *Suite 3505: The Story of the Draft Goldwater Movement.* New Rochelle, NY: Arlington House, 1967.

Whitlam, Gough. *The Truth of the Matter.* Melbourne: Melbourne University Press, 2005.

Whitworth, Sandra. *Feminism and International Relations: Towards a Political Economy of Gender in Interstate and Non-Governmental Institutions.* New York: St. Martin's Press, 1994.

Whitworth, Sandra. "Gender, International Relations and the Case of the ILO." *Review of International Studies* 20, no. 4 (1994): 389-405.

Wiegman, Robyn. *Object Lessons.* Durham, NC: Duke University Press, 2012.

Willetts, Peter. *"The Conscience of the World": The Influence of Non-Governmental Organisations in the UN System.* Washington, DC: Brookings Institution, 1996.

Williams, Raymond. *Keywords.* New York: Oxford University Press, 1976.

Williams, Raymond. *Marxism and Literature.* Oxford: Oxford University Press, 1977.

Wilson, Ara. "The Transnational Geography of Sexual Rights." In *Truth Claims: Representation and Human Rights,* edited by Mark Philip Bradley and Patrice Petro, 251-65. New Brunswick, NJ: Rutgers University Press, 2002.

"World Conference of the International Women's Year, 19 July-2 June, 1975. Declaration of Mexico. Plans of Action." New York: United Nations, 1975.

Zinsser, Judith P. "From Mexico to Copenhagen to Nairobi: The United Nations Decade for Women, 1975-1985." *Journal of World History* 13, no. 1 (2002): 139-68.

Zwingel, Susanne. "From Intergovernmental Negotiations to (Sub)national Change." *International Feminist Journal of Politics* 7, no. 3 (2005): 400-24.

INDEX